Language Change and
Linguistic Diversity

LANGUAGE CHANGE AND LINGUISTIC DIVERSITY

Studies in honour of Lyle Campbell

Edited by Thiago Costa Chacon, Nala H. Lee, and W. D. L. Silva

EDINBURGH
University Press

Edinburgh University Press is one of the leading university presses in the UK. We publish academic books and journals in our selected subject areas across the humanities and social sciences, combining cutting-edge scholarship with high editorial and production values to produce academic works of lasting importance. For more information visit our website: edinburghuniversitypress.com

© editorial matter and organisation Thiago Costa Chacon, Nala H. Lee, and W. D. L Silva, 2022, 2019
© the chapters their several authors, 2022

Edinburgh University Press Ltd
The Tun – Holyrood Road
12(2f) Jackson's Entry
Edinburgh EH8 8PJ

First published in hardback by Edinburgh University Press 2022

Typeset in Ehrhardt MT Pro by
Cheshire Typesetting Ltd, Cuddington, Cheshire
Croydon, CR0 4YY

A CIP record for this book is available from the British Library

ISBN 978 1 4744 8812 9 (hardback)
ISBN 978 1 4744 8813 6 (paperback)
ISBN 978 1 4744 8814 3 (webready PDF)
ISBN 978 1 4744 8815 0 (epub)

The right of Thiago Costa Chacon, Nala H. Lee, and W. D. L. Silva to be identified as the editors of this work has been asserted in accordance with the Copyright, Designs and Patents Act 1988, and the Copyright and Related Rights Regulations 2003 (SI No. 2498).

Contents

List of Figures and Tables		vii
Notes on Contributors		ix
In Memoriam		xiv
List of Abbreviations		xv

1. Language Change and Diversity at the Crossroads of Historical Linguistics, Language Documentation, and Linguistic Typology 1
Thiago Costa Chacon, Nala H. Lee, and W. D. L. Silva

2. Using the Acoustic Correlates of Voice Quality as Explanations for the Changes in the Descriptions of Xinkan Glottalized Consonants 19
Chris Rogers

3. Variation and Change in the Distribution of *-(V)n and *-(V)w in Kaqchikel 47
Raina Heaton

4. Origins of Metathesis in Batsbi, Part II: Intransitive Verbs 72
Alice C. Harris

5. Some Remarks on Etymological Opacity in Austronesian Languages 87
Robert Blust

6. The Relationship between Aquitanian and Basque: Achievements and Challenges of the Comparative Method in a Context of Poor Documentation 105
Joaquín Gorrochategui

7. Evidence, New and Old, Against the Late *k(') > *ch(') Areal Shift Hypothesis 130
David F. Mora-Marín

8. Are All Language Isolates Equal? The Case of Mapudungun 164
Willem F. H. Adelaar and Matthias Pache

9	The Historical Linguistics and Archaeology of Ancient North America: "A Linguistic Look" at the Hopewell *Eve Okura Koller*	187
10	The Lenguas de Bolivia Project: Background and Further Prospects *Mily Crevels and Pieter Muysken*	206
11	The Typology of Grammatical Relations in Tuparian Languages with Special Focus on Akuntsú *Carolina Coelho Aragon and Fabrício Ferraz Gerardi*	224
12	Meskwaki (Algonquian) Evidence against Basic Word Order and Configurational Models of Argument Roles *Ives Goddard and Amy Dahlstrom*	242
13	The Syntax of Alignment: An Emergentist Typology *William O'Grady*	260

Subject and Scholar Index	281
Languages and Linguistic Families Index	285

List of Figures and Tables

Figures

1.1	Interactions and outcomes of HL, LD, and LT	10
2.1	Location of the last speakers of the known Xinkan languages	20
2.2	Spectrogram of [tak'ał] "chest"	28
2.3	Spectrogram of [ṣahaka] "your mouth"	29
2.4	Spectrogram of [it'uł] "flea"	29
2.5	Spectrogram of [wašat'a] "open.ICOMP"	30
2.6	Spectrogram of [paːma] "wing"	30
2.7	Spectrogram of [šam'alika] "your forehead"	31
2.8	Spectrogram of [alij'an] "I show, I teach"	32
2.9	Spectrogram of [mija] "chicken"	33
3.1	Percentage preference for *-on* with agent focus and oblique antipassives of RTVs by Kaqchikel dialect	64
3.2	Percentage preference for *-on* with agent focus and oblique antipassives of RTVs by age	65
4.1	Fusion of *v–oʔ–ar* "come" with *v–ar* "make, do" in present (first change) and loss of final *–o* in third persons and first person inclusive (second change)	76
7.1	Glyphic spellings of proposed non-Mayan loanwords	143
7.2	Early examples of signs with **chV** and **ch'V** values	146
7.3	Detail of incised peccary skull from Copan Tomb 1	152
9.1	The Algonquian language family	192
9.2	Historical locations of Central Algonquian languages superimposed on twenty-first-century states and provinces	193
9.3	Map of Hopewell, Cahokia, and ancient silver mine sites	198
11.1	Map of the location of the Akuntsú in the "Rio Omerê" Indigenous Territory	226
13.1	Two language types	260

Tables

2.1	Proto-Xinkan consonant inventory	21
2.2	CONSONANT TYPE frequencies	34
2.3	CONSONANT SUBTYPE frequencies	34
2.4	Consonant PLACE OF ARTICULATION frequencies	35
2.5	Mean values of statistically significant correlates of CONSONANT TYPE	36
2.6	Mean values of statistically significant correlates of CONSONANT SUBTYPE I	36
2.7	Mean values of statistically significant correlates of CONSONANT SUBTYPE II	36
2.8	Mean values of HNR in two analytical domains	37
3.1	Reflexes of *-(V)w and *-(V)n in absolutive, agent focus, and incorporating constructions	57
3.2	Reconstructions for antipassive-related morphemes	60
3.3	Summary of claims about the shift from -o to -on in Kaqchikel by dialect and source	64
4.1	Person–number–case agreement markers in Batsbi	75
5.1	Comparative evidence for schwa syncope in reflexes of PAN *baqəRu "new"	93
5.2	Evidence for PMP *saŋəlaR "to fry without oil"	95
5.3	Expected and attested POC reflexes of PMP reduplicated monosyllables c.1970	97
5.4	A partial Proto-Oceanic grammatical paradigm relating CP1 and CP2	98
5.5	The reduplication–transitivity correlation in Tok Pisin	100
6.1	Correspondences between Aquitanian and Basque, Gothic and English (Campbell 2011)	116
7.1	Nomenclature and abbreviations used in this chapter	133
7.2	Earliest-dated occurrences of **chV** and **ch'V** signs in Maya Hieroglyphic Database representing examples of *k(') > ch(') shift	148
7.3	Earliest-dated occurrences of **chV** and **ch'V** signs in Maya Hieroglyphic Database not relevant to *k(') > ch(') shift (from pM *ch, *ch', *ty, *ty')	153
8.1	Some Mapudungun–Mochica lookalikes	169
8.2	Some Mapudungun–Cholón lookalikes	171
8.3	Some Mapudungun–Proto-Southern Jê lookalikes	171
8.4	Mapudungun–Chiriguano–Proto-Tupi–Guarani lookalikes	172
8.5	Mapudungun–Jivaroan lookalikes	173
8.6	Mapudungun–Arawakan lookalikes	174
8.7	Mapudungun -ke and its counterpart -ka in Quechua and Aymara	175
8.8	Some forms illustrating the correspondence of Mapudungun ŋ with Aymara r	176
8.9	Some Quechua borrowings in Mapudungun	177
11.1	Set of personal pronouns across Tuparian languages	227
13.1	Case marking in a classic accusative language	264
13.2	Case marking in a classic ergative language	265
13.3	Harmonic word order patterns in accusative languages	266
13.4	Harmonic word order patterns in ergative languages	266

Notes on Contributors

Willem F. H. Adelaar is emeritus professor of Amerindian Languages and Cultures at Leiden University in the Netherlands. He conducted field research on different Quechuan languages and on minor languages of the Andes. He also contributed to the detection of genealogical relations between indigenous languages of the Amazonian region and was involved in international activities addressing the issue of language endangerment. Further areas of his expertise include linguistic reconstruction, language contact, areal linguistics, oral literature and ethno-history of South American and Mesoamerican peoples, as well as the interface of linguistics with archaeological and historical research. His publications include a descriptive grammar and dictionary of Tarma Quechua (1977) and a comprehensive volume on the languages of the Andes (2004), of which he is the main author.

Carolina Coelho Aragon is an adjunct professor at the Federal University of Paraíba. Her work focuses on Brazilian indigenous languages, especially on endangered languages and language maintenance. She received her Ph.D. in Linguistics from the University of Hawai'i at Manoa and her master's from the University of Brasília, both focused on the description of the Akuntsú language. She is one of the editors of TuLaR (Tupían Language Resources) and her research interests involve anthropological linguistics, Tupian ethnohistory, and human rights policies for recently contacted indigenous groups.

Robert Blust is a professor in the Department of Linguistics at the University of Hawai'i. He is a historical linguist with a focus on the Austronesian language family, which contains nearly one-fifth of the world's languages. He has collected field data for ninety-nine Austronesian languages, mainly in Borneo, Papua New Guinea and Taiwan, and has over 270 publications, including a 1,100-page dictionary of Thao, the last surviving member of a primary branch of Austronesian, as well as the first single-authored book to provide a basic typological and historical overview of this entire family. His online open-access Austronesian Comparative Dictionary (www.trussel2.com/acd) is the largest research project ever undertaken on the Austronesian languages, and one of the largest ever undertaken by a single individual in the field of linguistics as a whole. He has also published on several topics in ethnology, most notably why there is a belief in dragons in many parts of the world.

Thiago Costa Chacon is an assistant professor of linguistics at the Universidade de Brasília. He has extensive experience of research among several native groups from South America, especially among the Tukanoan, Arawakan, Yanomami, and Arutani speakers in Northern Amazonia, with particular focus on language documentation, historical linguistics, and different interdisciplinanry topics. He has published in the *Journal of Historical Linguistics*, the *International Journal of American Linguistics*, and the *Journal of Language Relationships*, among others.

Mily Crevels is Senior University Lecturer in Linguistics at Leiden University. Her main research interests are the indigenous languages of South America, especially in the Guaporé-Mamoré and Gran Chaco regions, language dispersal, and linguistic typology. She is the co-founder and editor of the series "Studies in the Indigenous Languages of the Americas" (Brill) and has edited multiple books on the native languages of South America, including the four-volume work *Lenguas de Bolivia* (with Pieter Muysken, Plural 2009–15).

Amy Dahlstrom is an associate professor of linguistics at the University of Chicago. Her work focuses on the morphology, syntax, information structure, and discourse analysis of Algonquian languages, especially Meskwaki and Plains Cree.

Fabrício Ferraz Gerardi graduated in classical languages (Ancient Greek and Latin) and Jewish Studies (with a focus on Ancient Hebrew). He also obtained a master's degree in computational linguistics from the University of Tübingen (Germany), where besides working as a researcher and on his doctoral thesis, he has been, since 2014, teaching courses on syntax (Role and Reference Grammar, RRG), Tupían languages, and linguistic diversity. He is one of the creators and editors of TuLaR (Tupían Language Resources), an online database on various aspects of Tupían languages. He is interested in language structure, language evolution, and anthropological linguistics.

Ives Goddard is Senior Linguist, Emeritus in the Department of Anthropology, National Museum of Natural History, Smithsonian Institution, where he was Associate Curator to Curator (1976–2001) and Senior Scientist (2001–7). He was Linguistic Editor (1970–2007), Managing Editor (1985–8), and Technical Editor (1989–2007) of the *Handbook of North American Indians*. Earlier he was Assistant Professor to Associate Professor of Linguistics at Harvard University (1970–6). He served as the 43rd Hermann and Klara Collitz Professor at the Linguistic Institute of the Linguistic Society of America in 1997. He has worked principally on the languages of the Algonquian family, his major fieldwork being on Munsee, Unami (Delaware), and Meskwaki (Fox).

Joaquín Gorrochategui is Professor of Indo-European Linguistics at the University of the Basque Country at Vitoria-Gasteiz, Spain. He received his Ph.D. from the University of Salamanca in 1982 and continued studies on Celtic linguistics in Bonn. His research activity focuses on the study of pre-Roman languages of Western Europe, especially those spoken in the Iberian Peninsula. He has worked on various aspects, from the interpretation of texts and inscriptions to the study of secondary onomastic material, combining linguistic and historical data in his research. He is the author of a standard monograph on Aquitanian and of papers on ancient Basque, Palaeohispanic languages and epigraphs, historical and comparative linguistics, language contact in antiquity, and Latin epigraphy. He is a corresponding member of Euskaltzaindia (the Royal Academy of the Basque Language) and the Spanish Royal Academy (RAE). He is currently responsible for the Hesperia Data Base for Palaeohispanic Languages and Epigraphs.

Alice C. Harris is a professor of linguistics at the University of Massachusetts Amherst. After receiving her Ph.D. from Harvard University in 1976, she served on the faculty of Vanderbilt University for many years. In 2002 she joined the faculty at Stony Brook, where she served for some years as Graduate Program Director, before leaving for UMass in 2009. She retired in January 2020. In 1974, Harris and a colleague were the first Americans permitted to undertake research in the Republic of Georgia, when it was still part of the USSR. She has continued her work in this region, working principally on Georgian, Laz, Svan, Mingrelian, Udi, and Batsbi. Harris has held major grants or fellowships from the National Science Foundation, the National Endowment for the Humanities, the International Research and Exchanges Board, and the Guggenheim Foundation. She held the Collitz Professorship at the 2011 Linguistics Institute, was elected a Fellow of the Linguistic Society of America in 2012, and served as its president in 2016. In 2020 she was named a Fellow of the British Academy.

Raina Heaton is an assistant professor of Native American Studies and the Assistant Curator for the Native American Languages department at the Sam Noble Museum at the University of Oklahoma. As a linguist she has a decade of ongoing work in language documentation and revitalization in indigenous communities in North America and Central America, most notably with Kaqchikel communities in Guatemala, the Tunica-Biloxi Tribe of Louisiana, and Enenlhet communities in Paraguay. As a curator she works with the Native communities in Oklahoma and beyond to safeguard important language materials and to create digital solutions for responsibly sharing Native language content. She has also worked on global initiatives related to language conservation as a researcher for the Endangered Languages Project and as a mentor for the Language Documentation Training Center.

Eve Okura Koller is an assistant professor at Brigham Young University–Hawai'i in the Department of Anthropology and Department of History, where she teaches courses on language in culture and society, language revitalization, writing systems, and historical linguistics. She holds a Ph.D. in Linguistics from the University of Hawai'i at Mānoa.

Nala H. Lee is an assistant professor of linguistics at the National University of Singapore. She focuses on the extreme poles of multilingualism, particularly on the structural and sociological characteristics of language contact and language endangerment. She specialises in contact languages and is also the co-developer of the Language Endangerment Index, a method of assessing language vitality that was developed for the *Catalogue of Endangered Languages*. She has published in journals such as the *Annual Review of Linguistics*, *Applied Linguistics*, and the *Journal of Language Documentation & Conservation*, among others.

David F. Mora-Marín (BA in Linguistics and Anthropology at KU-Lawrence, 1996; Ph.D. in Anthropology at SUNY-Albany, 2001), has been an associate professor in the Linguistics Department at the University of North Carolina in Chapel Hill since 2004. His research encompasses topics relevant to Mesoamerican language history, addressed primarily through the methods of historical and comparative linguistics, linguistic documentation, historical sociolinguistics, and philology/epigraphy. His publications deal with the nature of orthographic conventions in Mayan hieroglyphic writing, the grammatical structure of Mayan hieroglyphic texts, the origin and development of Mayan inscriptions, the undeciphered Olmec hieroglyphic writing system, the reconstruction of grammatical morphology and morphosyntactic constructions (e.g., indirectives, possession) in earlier stages of the Mayan language family, and the application of the comparative method to test the hypothesis of a common ancestor between the Mayan and Mixe-Zoquean language families. He has also conducted some limited documentation work on Isthmus Mixe (Oaxaca) and Purepecha (Michoacán), with plans for expansion in this area.

Pieter Muysken was Professor of Linguistics at Radboud University Nijmegen and Academy Professor of the Royal Netherlands Academy of Arts and Sciences. His main research interests were Andean languages, Creole languages, and language contact, and in the most recent years, language contact and language history in South America. His numerous books include *Bilingual Speech: A Typology of Code-Mixing* (Cambridge University Press 2000), *The Languages of the Andes* (with Willem Adelaar, Cambridge University Press 2004), *Functional Categories* (Cambridge University Press 2008), and *Language Dispersal, Diversification, and Contact: A Global Perspective* (ed. with Mily Crevels, Oxford University Press 2020).

William O'Grady is a professor in the Department of Linguistics at the University of Hawai'i at Mānoa. He is well known for his writings on syntactic theory and language acquisition, as well as for his work on Korean and Jejueo. A major theme in O'Grady's research is his commitment to emergentism, the idea that language is a complex system whose properties derive from the interaction of more basic factors and forces, especially processing pressures. O'Grady is the author of several books and numerous journal articles. His books include *How Children Learn Language* (Cambridge University Press 2005), *Syntactic Carpentry* (Erlbaum 2005), and *Jejueo: The Language of Korea's Jeju Island* (University of Hawai'i Press 2019). He is the co-editor (with Brian MacWhinney) of *The Handbook of Language Emergence* (Erlbaum 2005) and the co-editor (with John Archibald) of a widely used textbook, *Contemporary Linguistics Analysis* (Pearson Longman 2016), now in its ninth edition.

Matthias Pache is a postdoctoral researcher in linguistics at the University of Tübingen. His research specializations are Native South and Central American languages. He has published various papers on topics in descriptive linguistics, contact linguistics, the historiography of Native American linguistics and typology. Moreover, his research has a major focus on historical linguistics, including the application of the comparative method in the context of Native South and Central American languages.

Chris Rogers is an associate professor of linguistics at Brigham Young University. His research focuses on the description, understanding, and appreciation of linguistic diversity and variation with a particular interest in the indigenous languages of the Americas. He has conducted original fieldwork on six languages from Central and South America, one from Africa, one from India and worked with archived language materials of nine other languages. As a student of Lyle Campbell, he has learned the importance of a holistic approach to linguistic analysis and epistemology.

W. D. L. Silva is an assistant professor of linguistics at the University of Arizona. He is a field linguist specializing in Desano and Siriano, two endangered Eastern Tukanoan languages spoken in the Vaupés region of Brazil and Colombia. He has published in journals such as the *International Journal of American Linguistics* and the *Journal of Language Documentation & Conservation*, among others.

In Memoriam

In memory of Pieter Muysken and Bob Blust, two esteemed mentors and colleagues whom we lost during the production of this book, and whom we will dearly miss.

List of Abbreviations

Chapter 1: Chacon, Lee, and Silva

    HL   historical linguistics
    LD   language documentation
    LT   linguistic typology

Chapter 2: Rogers

    A1   amplitude of first harmonic
    A2   amplitude of second harmonic
    A3   amplitude of third harmonic
    C   any consonant
    COMP   completive
    COPXIG   Consejo del Pueblo Xinka de Guatemala
    COR   coronal consonant
    D   dorsal consonant
    E   ejectives, glottalized obstruents
    G   glottalized consonant
    H1   first harmonic
    H2   second harmonic
    HNR   harmonics-to-noise ratio
    ICOMP   incompletive
    IPA   International Phonetic Alphabet
    L   labial consonant
    O   plain obstruent
    P   plain consonant
    R   glottalized resonants/sonorants
    S   plain sonorant
    SG   singular

	V	any vowel
	VA	following vowel
	VB	preceding vowel

Chapter 3: Heaton

	1	1st person
	2	2nd person
	3	3rd person
	ABS	absolutive
	ANTIP	antipassive
	ASP	aspect
	CAUS	causative
	CLF	classifier
	COMPL	completive
	DEM	demonstrative
	DET	determiner
	DIR	directional
	ENC	enclitic
	ERG	ergative
	EXCL	exclusive
	FOC	focus
	HORT	hortative
	INCOMPL	incompletive
	INTR	intransitive
	NEG	negation
	NMLZ	nominalizer
	NUM	numeral
	OBL	oblique
	PFV	perfective
	PL	plural
	POSS	possessive
	POT	potential
	PREP	preposition
	PRO	pronoun
	PROG	progressive
	PROX	proximal
	PRS	present
	PST	past
	SG	singular
	SUPRL	superlative
	TR	transitive
	TS	thematic suffix
	WH	wh- word

Chapter 4: Harris

ABS	absolutive case
AF	affix
AOR	aorist
AUX	auxiliary
CAUS	causative
CM	class marker
CV	converb
ERG	ergative case
EX(CL)	exclusive
F	female
GEN	genitive
IMPFV	imperfective
IN(CL)	inclusive
INTR	intransitive
OBL	oblique stem formant
PL	plural
PPL	participle
PRS	present
SG	singular
TENS	tense
TRANS	transitive

Chapter 5: Blust

ACD	Austronesian Comparative Dictionary
AN	Austronesian
CP	comparative paradigm
OC	Oceanic
PAN	Proto-Austronesian
PCP	Proto-Central Pacific
PMP	Proto-Malayo-Polynesian
POC	Proto-Oceanic
PPN	Proto-Polynesian
PT	Proto-Tsouic
PWMP	Proto-Western-Malayo-Polynesian

Chapter 6: Gorrochategui

Grammar

dat.	dative
f.	female or feminine
gen.	genitive

m. male or masculine
nom. nominative
pl. plural
sg. singular
suf. suffix

Languages

Aq. Aquitanian
Bq. Basque
E. English
Etr. Etruscan
Gasc. Gascon
Go. Gothic
Ib. Iberian
Lat. Latin
OE. Old English
OIr. Old Irish
PBq. Proto-Basque
PIE. Proto-Indo-European
Rhaet. Rhaetian
Vasc. Vasconic
W. Welsh

Basque dialects

B Bizkaian
G Gipuzkoan
L Labourdin
LN Low Navarrese
Soul. Souletin
Ronc. Roncalese

Chapter 10: Crevels and Muysken

1 first person
2 second person
3 third person
Ø zero morpheme
< > infixation
A transitive subject
AB absential
ADV adverb(ial)
AG agentive
ALL allative

LIST OF ABBREVIATIONS

ART	article
BE	bound element
CLF	classifier
CONT	continuative
DEM	demonstrative
DIST	distal
DISTR	distributive
DR	bivalent direct
DSC	discontinuative
DV	dummy vowel
EVI	evidential
EX	existential (verb)
F	feminine
FUT	future
HORT	hortative
IMP	imperative
INCH	inchoative
IND	indicative
INTL	intentional
INTS	intensive
INV	inverse
M	masculine
MED	medial
MULT	multiple (aspect)
N	neuter
NEUT	neutral (aspect)
NST	non-standing
O	transitive object
OBL	oblique
OBV	obviative
PL.EXCL	plural exclusive
PL	plural
PRC	process verbalisation
PRO	personal pronoun
PROX	proximal, proximate
PST	past
REL	relativiser
REP	repetitive
S	intransitive subject
SG	singular
STAT	stative
SUB	subordinator

Chapter 11: Aragon and Gerardi

AUX	auxiliary
COR	coreferential
DAT	dative
DEM	demonstrative
EFF	effective
EM	emphatic
ESS	essive
EXC	exclusive
FOC	focus
HE	nominalizer of finite embedded clauses
IMPERF	imperfective
INC	inclusive
INS	instrumental-lative
INTERJ	interjection
LOC	locative
NEG	negation
NMLZ	nominalizer
NUC	nuclear case
OBJ	object
PL	plural
PRES	present
PROJ	projective
PROX	proximity
R	relational
RED	reduplication
REL	relative
SG	singular
THV	thematic vowel
TR	transitivizer
UNC	uncertainty
VERBLZR	verbalizer

Chapter 12: Goddard and Dahlstrom

Grammar

0	inanimate verb agreement\n
3	unmarked third person, or third proximate when in opposition to a third obviative
3'	third person (first) obviative
3"	third person second obviative
!	"it was suddenly observed"
>	Subject and object features in verb inflection are separated by ">"

LIST OF ABBREVIATIONS

- (en dash)   separates a preverb or prenoun from its stem.
- ABSENT   absentative demonstrative
- ANIM   animate
- AOR   aorist (proclitic, also suffix marking verbal mode)
- EMPH   emphatic
- FUT   future
- HRSY   hearsay evidential
- IC   initial change (ablaut on vowel of first syllable)
- IMP   imperative
- INAN   inanimate
- IND   independent indicative
- LOC   locative case
- NEG   negative verbal mode
- O   (primary) object
- O2   secondary object
- OBV   obviative
- PART   participle
- PERF   perfective
- PL   plural
- REDUP   reduplication
- SG   singular (animate and proximate if not otherwise specified)
- SUBJ   subjunctive

The glosses of stems requiring an oblique argument indicate the semantic type of oblique in curly brackets. Vowel length is marked with a circumflex over the vowel.

Chapter 13: O'Grady

- 1   1st person
- 3   3rd person
- ABS   Absolutive
- ACC   Accusative
- AF   agent focus
- AGR   agreement
- ANTI   antipassive
- ART   article
- ASP   aspect
- β   base argument
- DEF   definite
- DET   determiner
- ERG   ergative
- F   feminine
- INTR   intransitive
- M   male
- NOM   nominative

OBL	oblique
PERF	perfective
PRED	predicate
PST	past
REL	relative clause marker
SG	singular
TR	transitive

1

Language Change and Diversity at the Crossroads of Historical Linguistics, Language Documentation, and Linguistic Typology

Thiago Costa Chacon, Nala H. Lee, and W. D. L. Silva

1. Introduction

Language change and linguistic diversity are topics that have long traditions in comparative linguistics. One of the earliest seminal works was Conrad Gessner's 1555 book *Mithridate* (Gessner et al. 2009), which presented and analyzed data on more than 100 languages known at that time, using the Lord's Prayer and word lists as samples for cross-linguistic comparisons. Central to Gessner's work was his perception of language change and diversity in time and space. His corpora combined languages from ancient and contemporary times that he assumed would reveal how languages diversified from a common ancestor (Hebrew). Furthermore, Gessner invested in the collection and presentation of data about languages from diverse geographical locations, including the poorly attested, recently documented and "exotic" languages of the *Orbis noui*, that is, the territories of present-day Americas, Oceania, and Eastern Asia, discovered by Portugal and Spain during the fifteenth and early sixteenth centuries (Colombat 2008).

Approaches to language change and linguistic diversity have indeed evolved since then, and they have culminated in the development of specific fields of investigation, especially historical linguistics (HL), language documentation (LD), and linguistic typology (LT). This book continues to explore the topics of language change and linguistic diversity, bringing forth contributions highlighting how research on language change and linguistic diversity relies crucially on the innovations, intersections, and mutual contributions of HL, LD, and LT. In this introductory chapter, we highlight scholarly contributions to the investigation of language change and linguistic diversity at the crossroads of these fields, highlighting how language change, diversity, HL, LD, and LT are symbiotically interrelated as part of a widely developed research program that continues to evolve rapidly in Linguistics.

The volume showcases practical and theoretical case studies dealing with language change and linguistic diversity, bringing a key contribution to the field by its focus on a diverse range of languages which have not often been at the center of traditional language change research, and by exploring the junctures between language change, linguistic diversity, and other related topics that draw on primary linguistic fieldwork. The chapters of this volume cover distinct geographical areas and a wide range of theoretical and methodological issues. The contributions honor the career of the distinguished professor Lyle Campbell—a scholar who has intensively engaged with the investigation of language change and linguistic diversity and who has made seminal contributions to the fields of HL, LD, and LT, and for whom we dedicate this volume as a *Festschrift*.

Campbell's definition of LD combines traditional outcomes of language description with more recent trends concerning language data and language endangerment, as he understands the goals of language documentation as "the creation, annotation, preservation and dissemination of transparent records of a language where that record is understood explicitly to include the production of a grammar and a dictionary, along with a rich corpus of recordings" (Campbell 2016: 251).

Campbell's view on HL emphasizes the centrality of the study of language change, finding out what happened and how and why it happened (Campbell 2020: 1). Campbell views language change as being notably conditioned by present and past social and cultural situations, which brings sociolinguistics into the heart of HL. Therefore, one of the goals is the investigation of historical sociocultural contexts, especially in societies without much, if any, written historical documentation, a situation found where most endangered languages are spoken. Also, for Campbell, HL has a central role in LD and LT, since "a grasp of the ways in which languages can change provides the student with a much better understanding of language in general" as well as an "understanding of universal grammar, language typology and human cognition in general—fundamental to understanding our very humanity" (Campbell 2020: 2).

There has been extensive discussion about the links between LD and LT (see, for instance, Epps 2010 for an overview), as well as a long tradition of research on HL and LT (see Campbell 1996, 1997a, 2020; Luraghi 2017). However, the intersections between LD and HL have been underemphasized, even though there are undisputed links between them. Moreover, there is a practical and urgent need for more work on the intersection of these areas, given the pressure of language endangerment. On the one hand, concerned about language endangerment from the perspective of our ability to understand the world's linguistic diversity, Campbell (2016: 256) highlights the importance of LD for HL by stating that:

> 45% of living languages are threatened …, a quarter (24%) of the linguistic diversity of the world, calculated in terms of distinct language families, is just lost. Those that have been lost to history with inadequate or no documentation leave a huge deficit … we cannot work out their genetic classification, nor can we investigate the many other types of historical evidence that could be gained from linguistic evidence.

On the other hand, and of most significance, Campbell has emphasized the combined role of LD and HL for community-based language revitalization efforts. His view is that historical linguistic investigation of earlier documentation can help recover aspects of grammar, which can be of value for language revival and revitalization programs (Campbell 2016: 268).

Starting from these perspectives of how HL, LD, and LT are intertwined, we set out to explore the patterns by which linguistic research on language change and linguistic diversity integrates all three fields. We start in Section 2 by showing how HL, LD, and LT have been present in Lyle Campbell's views and practices over the fifty years of his academic career. In Section 3, we explicitly lay out the main threads between HL, LD, and LT within the research on language change and linguistic diversity. In Section 4, we summarize the chapters and highlight how they explore the connections between HL, LD, LT and beyond. Section 5 presents our concluding remarks.

2. Historical linguistics, documentation, and typology in Campbell's work

2.1 Background on Campbell's career

Lyle Campbell's career has always been based on the relations between synchronic language documentation, concern about language endangerment, and a broad historical and typological comparative outlook. His lifelong work on American indigenous languages—on many that were mostly undocumented in 1971, when Campbell obtained his Ph.D.—urges an approach where systematic description and comparative investigation were conducted in tandem with language conservation efforts. Partially inherited from the Boasian tradition in linguistics, the kind of research Campbell conducted in his career requires mastering a set of complementary methodological skills and addressing research questions that span multiple subfields of linguistics and go beyond disciplinary boundaries.

Campbell's most celebrated publications exemplify this. Many of his books cover topics on historical linguistics and language change, such as his textbook *Historical Linguistics: An Introduction*, now in its fourth edition (Campbell 2020); his important contribution to the study of diachronic syntax with Alice Harris (Harris and Campbell 1995); the eloquent and thorough account of the history and methods of language classification, with particular focus on long-distance genetic relationships (Campbell and Poser 2008); a glossary of historical linguistics (Campbell and Mixco 2007); and a co-edited volume with a critical assessment on grammaticalization (Campbell and Janda 2001).

In addition to the broader theoretical or technical publications, Campbell also published volumes that were more focused on particular topics. For instance, he has dedicated several of his works to the issue of organizing, cataloguing, and critically assessing the historical information about languages of the Americas, as well as analyzing their genetic, areal, and typological relationships (Campbell and Mithun 1979; Campbell 1997a, 1997b; Campbell and Grondona 2012b), and language isolates (Campbell 2018).

Campbell's primary concern with endangered languages has culminated in several scholarly publications ranging from reference grammars, dictionaries, and practical language materials for the communities (see Campbell 1985; Campbell et al. 2020), to more general approaches to endangered languages, such as the cataloguing and comparison of endangered languages from a local to a global perspective with the development of the *Catalogue of Endangered Language* (ELCat),[1] and a holistic view on the various facets of language endangerment (Campbell and Belew 2018: Rehg and Campbell 2018). The subjects he has covered span a wide range of topics, including LD, HL, language conservation, sociolinguistics, and biocultural diversity.

Indeed, all of these contributions are as a result of Campbell's and other linguists' engagement in a research program structured by concern for descriptive and comparative issues that emerge from bottom-up research, starting with findings in the languages themselves and the needs of their speakers. In this approach to linguistics, this all becomes part of a single enterprise: linguistic fieldwork, language description, typology and universals, the investigation of language change, the sociocultural matters involving the languages investigated, language contact and multilingualism, methods in HL, the interpretation of prehistory, and the relationship between languages, peoples, genes, and cultures.

2.2 On the intersections of HL, LD, and LT in Campbell's work

More than representing a paradigm of a broad research program in Linguistics, Campbell's works are full of specific examples of how HL, LD, and LT have directly interacted with and aided each other. They illustrate how HL, LD, and LT can contribute to the study of language change and linguistic diversity, as well as how they can shed light on interdisciplinary problems and help to assess situations of language endangerment. Ultimately, this can help achieve practical goals in language revitalization.

A seminal case is Campbell's work on language contact between Xinkan and Mayan languages in Mesoamerica. Campbell's analysis revealed that almost all terms for cultivated plants in Xinkan languages are borrowed from Mayan languages. These findings, along with other social and cultural factors, led to the inference that Xinkans were not agriculturalists until their contact with Mayan groups (Campbell 2003). As Campbell (2016: 260) puts it:

> It was the fieldwork documentation of these languages that recorded these words and allowed us to identify them as loanwords. This in turn allowed us to contribute to understanding the history of these languages, and through that to understanding aspects of the prehistory of the Xinkan peoples and of Mesoamerica.

The direct contribution of fieldwork to HL is not the whole story, since the Xinkan case challenges claims of the farming/language dispersal model which emphasizes agriculture as the driving force for language dispersal (Bellwood and Renfrew 2003). As stated by Campbell (2016: 260):

> [Since the] agriculturalist Mayan languages did not spread and wipe out the non-agricultural Xinkan languages ... Xinkans maintained their identity and their language, first as

non-cultivators, then later as cultivators who acquired agriculture through contact with their Mayan neighbors, not by "demic spread" as the [farming/language dispersal] model predicts.

In sum, this case study shows not only how LD aids HL by directly providing the relevant data but also how both fields are necessary to address more general questions in language and cultural history that have broad implications for issues relevant to all humanity, such as what drives language spread across the globe and the role of agriculture in that process.

Campbell's research on the languages of the Chaco region in South America provides concrete examples of how HL and LD are deeply embedded in an overarching approach to language change and linguistic diversity. For instance, the project to document Chorote, Nivaclé, and Wichí (Matacoan) used a combination of LD and sociolinguistics research methods to investigate language change in a context of intense multilingualism involving those three languages in Misión de La Paz, Argentina.[2] In this location, one typically marries someone who speaks a different language, resulting in multilingual households in which a typical interaction consists of the wife using her language and the husband his, a different language. This combination of dual-lingualism and linguistic exogamy in Misión de La Paz, which appears to be unique in the world, is coupled with the avoidance of direct linguistic borrowings, where the names for foreign cultural materials are named by linguistic resources internal to the indigenous languages in Misión La Paz, rather than being borrowed from a foreign language (Campbell and Grondona 2010, 2012a).

Campbell analyzes the localized situation of language contact in the Chaco against its implications for theories of language change. On the one hand, he notices that the three indigenous languages in Misión La Paz have undergone changes that make them structurally more different from one another, rather than structurally more similar as one would expect in such an intense language contact situation. These findings show that linguistic divergence is a possible outcome of intense language contact, not convergence only as typically assumed. This finding is an important contribution to knowledge about language change and linguistic diversification. On the other hand, the way Matacoan languages share traits with non-Matacoan languages inside and outside the Chaco region brings into question the concept of "linguistic areas" as commonly used by linguists. While there is considerable diffusion of structural traits involving languages of the Chaco, these are not cohesive within a geographical area. Instead, they show varying linkages with languages and regions outside the Chaco on all sides, while at the same time often not linking all Chaco languages together. Following up on earlier publications, Campbell suggests that it will be useful to recognize two different kinds of "linguistic areas" (Campbell 2017: 12–13):

> One is the Linguistic Area Sensu Stricto (LASS), a geographical region defined by shared diffused traits mostly contained within and shared across the languages of a clearly delimited geographical area. The other is the Trait-Sprawl Area (TSA), an entity where the individual traits can pattern in disordered ways, some crossing some languages while others cross other languages, with some extending in one direction, others in another, with some overlapping

others in part of their distribution but also not coinciding in other parts of their geographical distribution, some extending also into other linguistic areas. The focus of the TSA is the actual diffused traits themselves rather than their geography ... focusing on actual diffused traits ... rather than on fixing a geographical area to be defined by its shared linguistic traits.

The Chaco region is, then, an excellent example of a Trait-Sprawling Area (TSA), while Mesoamerica, for instance, would stand as a case of a Linguistic Area Sensu Stricto (LASS) (Campbell et al. 1986). Indeed, the notion of investigating the diffusion of linguistic traits by focusing on the traits themselves and answering the question "what happened?" rather than the pure exercise of attempting to impose exact boundaries of a linguistic area, had already appeared in Campbell (2006). This idea moves us away from the traditional "cultural/linguistic areas" approach to a new era of studies that allow for the understanding of language change and linguistic diversity from a broader perspective, treating language traits similar to how biologists look at genetic evolution (Bowern 2015).

In recent years, there has been increasing interest in documenting language variation in the context of endangered languages research (for example, Hildebrandt et al. 2017). These types of work, although sociolinguistic in nature, can benefit from and contribute to the intersections of HL, LD, and LT. For example, Campbell's research has explored topics addressing the ways in which endangered languages change in situations of language attrition, and whether these languages change following universal patterns of language change (Campbell and Muntzel 1989; Palosaari and Campbell 2011). In another instance, Campbell (2016: 258–9) analyzes a case of unnatural sound change in Jumaytepeque (Xinkan), where some semi-speakers unconditionally changed all plain stops to glottalized stops C > C' (see also Chapter 2 by Chris Rogers in this volume). Campbell (1985) also describes cases of sound changes in the Teotepeque variety of Pipil, such as the unconditioned change from *l* > ł or an ongoing sound change from š [ʃ] > ṣ (retroflex [ʃ]) > r:

> š has changed to ṣ ... and now is in free variation with r [alveolar trill]. I believe the later change to /r/ is due to Spanish influence. There is sociolinguistically conditioned variation in local Spanish ... where at least nearby in Guatemala the [š] variant [of Spanish /r/] is stigmatized. I believe that the negative value placed on this variant in Spanish has contributed to the Teotepeque change to /r/, a change in the direction of the prestige variant in Spanish, the dominant language in this setting. (Campbell 1985: 14)

Campbell's analysis of Pipil shows how a perspective on language change can directly impact the synchronic analysis of a language, a case of direct contribution from HL to LD. Also, the Pipil and Xinkan cases support the finding that sound change in endangered languages need not be regular and "does not conform to typological expectations and some linguistic universals ..." since these changes would be impossible in "fully viable languages, where both regularity of sound change and naturalness of changes hold" (Campbell 2016: 268). Here again, as in the Chaco case, LD and the analysis of language contact situations are intertwined in addressing the more general question of how and why languages change.

3. HL, LD, LT, and the investigation of language change and linguistic diversity

As discussed in the previous sections and illustrated by Campbell's work, the investigation of language change and linguistic diversity is fundamentally dependent on the interaction between HL, LD, and LT. In this section, we discuss more specific and general patterns of these interactions. Our goal is to develop a holistic model of how HL, LD, and LT come together in the investigation of language change, linguistic diversity, and beyond. We start with the patterns below to identify the main threads of how HL, LD, and LT relate in the investigation of language change and linguistic diversity.

(1) *Direct contribution*: Each field makes a unique contribution to the understanding of linguistic diversity.
(2) *Indirect contribution*: HL, LD, and LT can precipitate corollaries in the theoretical and practical goals in the other field by providing complementary data, methods, and theoretical frameworks.
(3) *Convergent contributions*: Some fundamental research questions or practical goals—in particular the investigation of language change, language universals, and the theoretical and applied aspects of language revitalization—need to be addressed by relating two or all three fields.

LD clearly makes a fundamental contribution to HL and LT. While LD data and materials derived from it must be as detailed, diverse, and extensive as possible (including in particular the very basics of data and meta-data collection, transcription, and translation), LD is usually part of a more general research framework, guided by approaches to language description, LT, and language conservation efforts, as well as by our knowledge about the social, cultural, and historical contexts of the speakers and the data.

LD and LT are strongly intertwined. Epps (2010) states that there is an interdependent relation between the two fields. On the one hand, LT's commitment to an empirical approach, its goal to test for language universals and the amount of diversity and variability in human languages make it crucially dependent on LD. On the other hand, the activities of LD (what type of data to gather, what methods to use, how to process and represent these data for others) involve the application of cross-linguistically relevant knowledge that makes LD dependent on LT.

LD is also crucial to a comprehensive understanding of language change. Good records and descriptions of synchronic stages of languages are crucial for reconstructing protolanguages, identifying sociolinguistic variation, and language contact phenomena. As suggested by Campbell, linguists doing LD should be aware of and attend to the possible HL contributions their work can make so that information relevant to interpreting the history of the languages involved and to understanding language change is not missed or lost (Campbell 2016: 268).

It is also the case that knowledge about language change and HL can more generally shape or aid LD in many ways (see Himmelman 2012: 188–92 for the use of historical records in language description). Comparative or internal language reconstruction and philological analysis may explain specific patterns in language description, such as morphophonological alternations, suppletion, and the distinctions between homophony and polysemy, among others. Campbell's analysis of Pipil is an illustrative case where considerations about language contact can explain unexpected synchronic morphophonological alternations (see Section 2.2). Also, language reconstruction goals appear in the shaping of LD in the works of Robert Blust (Chapter 5, this volume), who further develops the concept of *comparative paradigms*, which he employs as a useful tool for finding and documenting cognate words across potentially related languages.

Research on complex situations of language contact related to instances of language attrition and endangerment or related to complex patterns of multilingualism (or both) usually requires linguists to innovate their methods and perspectives concerning LD goals. We have seen how Campbell and colleagues molded their project in the Chaco by combining sociolinguistics, HL, and LD, due to the intense and intricate multilingual situation in Misión La Paz (Section 2.2). Similarly, Lüpke (2019) develops clear ideas on how knowledge about language contact shapes our practices and the goals of LD in multilingual settings. According to Lüpke (2019), LD is at the interface of different linguistic disciplines and, as a consequence, LD research should develop a paradigm that privileges neither languages nor repertoires a priori. Instead, it should provide rich and varied data on linguistic practices, offering an empirical foundation for the study of language use, variation and change, in addition to a critical basis for the understanding of concepts such as "speaker," "language," "speech community," or "ethnolinguistic group" (Lüpke 2019: 476).

HL, LD, and LT can also converge to make contributions in the investigation of language change and linguistic diversity. This was seen, for instance, in Campbell and colleagues' research on what is possible in language change, particularly concerning endangered languages (for example, Campbell and Munzel 1989; Palosaari and Campbell 2011). It was also illustrated in the studies on the languages of the Chaco that culminated in the claim that languages can diverge even in—or because of—intense language contact situations (see Campbell and Grondona 2010, 2012a). In addition, HL and LD are both necessary to the study of ongoing processes of language change (Weinreich et al. 1968), in particular in the languages of small and indigenous societies, where LD provides rich data in their sociocultural context, while the comparative framework of HL furnishes understanding of language changes of different social and temporal scopes.

Similarly, typologists often see diachrony as providing the principal explanations for typological diversity and universals of human languages (see Greenberg 1966; Croft 2003). A topic of recent debate is whether there are universal trends of language changes that shape how typological traits correlate with one another, or whether language change is rather specific to certain language families and geographical areas so that correlations involving how typological features interact with each other in a language are mere accidents of the parallel histories of the families and areas looked at (see Blevins 2004; Croft et al. 2011; Dunn et al. 2011).

We end the discussion of convergence with reference to an area that has grown exponentially since the late twentieth century. This is the field of language conservation.

Combined knowledge in HL and LD may help to reverse changes in language ecologies that resulted in some of the modern situations of language endangerment and loss of linguistic diversity. For instance, work on digital and historical archives—by combining skills typical of LD and HL (particularly the philological interpretation of historical documents)—can help by making use of that information to provide a more comprehensive descriptive record of a language that currently lacks fluent speakers. This information is vital for second language learners in revitalization and reclamation activities. As Fitzgerald (2020: 95) points out, "recordings and annotations of texts create a record that plays an essential role for communities seeking to revitalize their language and reverse language shift." Conversely, as they acquire a heritage language, speakers of otherwise dormant languages yield valuable linguistic performances for the understanding of how languages are acquired and how they change in unique sociolinguistic situations and challenge the notion of language extinction (see Leonard 2011).

A case of language reclamation using a combination of HL and LD methods comes from the Pataxó people in eastern Brazil. Pataxó, a Macro-Jê language, went dormant in the mid-1900s, and linguists considered it "extinct" (Urban 1985). Until recently the historical documentation available amounted to no more than 500 words scattered in seven wordlists from several varieties of the language. Since 1998, a group of local Pataxó leaders and school teachers have been reclaiming their heritage language, a process which culminated in the development of an emergent variety called *Patxohã* (Bomfim 2017). This group of scholars and activists established a program that combined the use of the available historical records and the continuous research and documentation of the language among Pataxó rememberers, as well as periods of language immersion among speakers of Maxakali, the genetically most closely related language to Patxohã, spoken by old allies to the Pataxó (Bonfim 2017). LD has been fundamental in that it engaged local researchers in interviewing elders from different villages, registering their idiolects, and providing new and better records of Pataxó language and culture. HL has been crucial to interpretation of the extant documentation and identifying etymologies among the distinct vocabularies that have been recorded throughout history, and to assessing how Maxakali can contribute to the reawakening of Pataxó (Campos 2011; Bomfim 2017). More broadly, this whole process is related to a more extensive packaging where the reawakening of Pataxó is an embodiment of the indigenous reclamation movements from the early 1980s, which fought for the rights of indigenous peoples to control their territory, to have an autonomous indigenous education system, and to have the rights to use and value their heritage language and culture. The Pataxó language reclamation efforts show that the contributions from HL and LD go beyond the realm of language diversity per se and can contribute important input to the study and transformation of human history more broadly.

At a deeper theoretical level, investigation of language change and linguistic diversity is based on the mutual contributions and intersections between HL, LD, and LT. First, linguistic diversity and language change are causally related: on the one hand, understanding of linguistic diversity requires an understanding of how languages and language ecologies can change. Second, linguistic diversity in itself is multidimensional, defined from different perspectives, such as the diversity or uniqueness of typological traits, the number of language families, and their degree of internal divergence

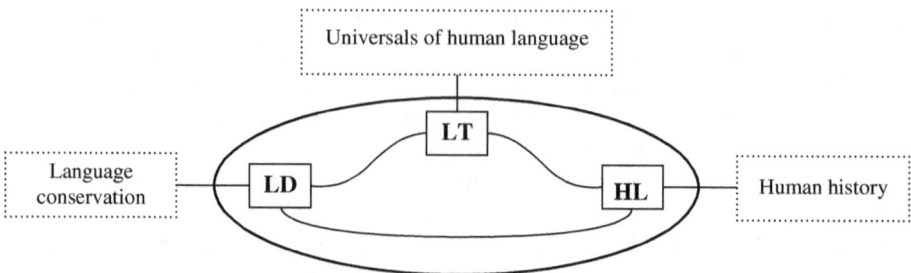

Figure 1.1 Interactions and outcomes of HL, LD, and LT

(Nichols 1992; Nettle 1998), and the complexity of language ecologies and sociocultural interactions reflected in the heterogeneity of speech repertoires of individuals and different social spheres of multilingualism (Mufwene 2001: 4–7; Lüpke 2016). Third, language change and changes in language ecologies are linguistic as well sociocultural, historical processes, which not only make language change complex (Weinreich et al. 1968; Levinson and Gray 2012) but also create the opportunity and means to be followed by, for example, approaches to language revitalization and reclamation. As a result, research on language change and linguistic diversity requires a diverse set of tools and perspectives, calling for some reordering of disciplinary boundaries and goals. Figure 1.1 represents the synthesis involving the different threads and domains integrating HL, LD, and LT with research on language change, linguistic diversity, and beyond.

4. Language change and linguistic diversity: Contributions from this volume

We now turn to the chapters of this volume and to how they deal with research on language change, language documentation, and their intersections. The contributions in these chapters are grounded in studies on an extensive range of languages and language families, from the linguistic isolates Basque and Mapudungun to large language families such as Tupían and Austronesian. They have a broad geographical scope—from the several regions of the Americas to the Pacific, Central Asia, and Europe—and they cover a wide range of issues related to the foci of this volume, from language change to typology and universals, dealing with issues such as etymological opacity in linguistic reconstructions, language contact, onomastics and the study of prehistory, word order, alignment systems, and grammatical relations. In the following sections we introduce each chapter. The discussion is organized around three themes, based on the primary topic of each chapter and how they relate to HL, LD, and LT.

4.1 Language change, documentation, and endangerment

The next three chapters deal specifically with analyses of language change phenomena, showing how the synchronic and sociolinguistically-informed documentation of endangered languages provides crucial data, alongside historical documentation. All three chapters focus on endangered languages and the analysis of variation and ongoing or recent changes. Crucially, they allow for a more comprehensive understanding of synchronic and diachronic changes, and ultimately bridge the LD, HL, and variationist approaches.

We start in Mesoamerica, a region to which Lyle Campbell has dedicated much of his work. In Chapter 2, Chris Rogers gives an overarching account of the diachrony of laryngealized (i.e. glottalized) stops in the endangered Xinkan languages and the indexing role of these stops as markers of ethnolinguistic identity for the last speakers of these languages. He assesses the acoustic properties of these laryngealized stops, their status in modern and pre-modern documentation, and their reconstruction to Proto-Xinkan. He states that diachronic changes correlate with the acoustic measures of the voice quality of glottalized consonants and flanking vowels. This is seen by comparing phonological and morphological properties and descriptions of glottalized consonants in modern and pre-modern resources of the language. He views the diachronic characterization of these consonants as favorable for the language community's current revitalization efforts, where laryngealized consonants are generalized to unexpected phonotactic positions in the speech of rememberers and viewed as a foundational part of the (re)emerging Xinkan cultural-linguistic identity.

Still in Mesoamerica, in Chapter 3 Raina Heaton examines two antipassive-related suffixes in the Mayan language Kaqchikel, comparing their distribution in data from recent fieldwork documentation to their historical distribution in Kaqchikel and several other Mayan languages. Her findings show that in some dialects of Kaqchikel, there is an ongoing merger between two antipassive morphemes that were distinct in Proto-Mayan, a process which is reflected in historical mergers elsewhere in the family. While Heaton offers a comprehensive understanding of ongoing changes from synchronic and diachronic perspectives, her chapter illustrates a heuristic approach to the investigation of language change that is only made possible by combining HL, LD, and LT.

In Chapter 4, set in the Caucasus, Alice Harris analyzes a complex case of metathesis as an ongoing morphophonological change in the verbal paradigms of Batsbi, a language spoken in Georgia. Harris shows clearly the importance of continuous language documentation and the analysis of intergenerational language change in order to elucidate a puzzling morphosyntactic and phonological case both from a synchronic and diachronic perspective. By analyzing historical and reconstructed data with a time span of more than a thousand years of history, Harris analyzes the process that has led to a stage of two alternating forms involving agreement and tense markers (for example, *d-o* vs. *-o-d*, where *-d* is an agreement marker and *-o* indicates present tense). Although these forms appear to be metathesized in the synchronic data, they resulted from a series of phonological and morphological changes that originally had nothing to do with metathesis. Harris argues, however, that native speakers today do interpret this pattern as a regular process of metathesis in verbal paradigms. Indeed, Harris shows that this process spread in the speech of the younger speakers by analogy to other contexts where it did not exist previously.

4.2 Language change, reconstruction, contact, and prehistory

The chapters in this part tackle key issues in the reconstruction of language and culture, the use of the comparative method and investigations of language contact, such as discussion of cases where historical documentation of protolanguages does not match linguists' reconstructions of these same languages, and of how language reconstruction and contact-induced changes can be modeled in layers and networks of shared cultural history among speakers of modern and ancient languages. Several chapters illustrate how key questions in HL require a vast and diversified corpus of linguistic data, highlighting the importance of fieldwork or philology to harvest and analyze new data. As Campbell states, throughout history, comparative and HL work has typically involved both written, well-documented languages and at the same time languages known only from fieldwork documentation (Campbell 2016: 251).

Robert Blust's contribution in Chapter 5 is informed by periods of intensive and extensive fieldwork on about 100 Austronesian languages combined with the analysis of another 700 Austronesian languages in his massive *Austronesian Comparative Dictionary* (Blust and Trussell 2013). The issue for HL that Blust addresses in his chapter is that of etymological opacity, where unique sound correspondences due to intermediate sound change may be recurrent but yet create sound correspondences that are otherwise unattested. Essentially, the identification of intermediate changes can open up possibilities for new *comparative paradigms*, that is, an analytic concept useful for searching and identifying cognates among forms of otherwise opaque cognate forms. Blust's concept of comparative paradigm is also useful for modeling language change, searching for cognates, and greater objectivity in language comparison. It provides a methodological basis for the linguist working with either available documentation or targeted comparative data collected through fieldwork on dialects and genetically related languages. In this context, his paper suggests how HL can benefit not only from data acquired in fieldwork but also can raise questions and provide methods that guide the process of language documentation in the field (see Blust 2018).

Chapters 6 and 7 address the role of philological methods for analyzing ancient written forms in order to expand the language documentation corpora and elucidate questions regarding language change and linguistic reconstruction. In Chapter 6, Joaquín Gorrochategui addresses the relationship between Aquitanian and the Basque language. Gorrochategui applies the comparative method for analysis seeking to extend the Basque linguistic family to cover Aquitanian, a language mentioned by Caesar at the beginning of the Gallic War, documented only by onomastic testimony in Latin. Gorrochategui is primarily concerned with the problems posed by onomastic material, its classification in a multilingual (Aquitanian, Galician, Iberian) tradition, the nature of the cognates, and the relationship between the attested documentation and the picture of Proto-Basque as developed by internal reconstruction.

Chapter 7 extends the philological perspective in historical linguistics to the Mayan family, a group of languages central to Campbell's work. David Mora-Marín addresses the question of the *k(') > *ch(') shift in the Mayan languages, focusing on the problem of its chronology and attestations in Mayan hieroglyphic writing, and the nature of scribal practices and their connection to linguistic ideology. In particular, this chapter provides a detailed evaluation of a proposal that calls for the application of a much later shift than previously anticipated (by circa a millennium), presenting evidence that the shift could have occurred by 100 BC.

In Chapter 8, Willem Adelaar and Matthias Pache extend the language contact focus in HL. They present work on the linguistic isolate Mapudungun, situated in central Chile and parts of Argentina. The chapter uses the vast contemporary and historical documentation of the Mapudungun language (this is one of the rare cases where there has been available documentation since the seventeenth century of a language in South America). Adelaar and Pache present evidence showing that Mapudungun belongs to a type of language isolate that shares linguistic traits more significantly with geographically distant languages, rather than with its neighbors. Adelaar and Pache's analysis of Mapudungun's unique or shared traits reveals layers and networks of contact-induced changes with distinct languages and places in South America. Moreover, the significance of borrowings from Arawakan and Central Andean languages suggests that pre-Mapudungun was probably spoken in the Andean foothills of Western Amazonia.

Chapter 9 addresses the relationship between HL and an understanding of ancient Native American culture. In this chapter, Eve Okura Koller seeks to connect linguistic and archeological evidence for understanding aspects of the linguistic prehistory of North America. Specifically, Koller suggests that the speakers of Central Algonquian languages were one of the groups likely involved in the multilingual Hopewell interaction sphere, which was based in exchange trade networks interconnecting several indigenous groups from North America. Koller uses an analysis of Central Algonquian loanwords in some North American languages as diagnostic of this sphere, as well as archaeological, geographic, and historical evidence in support of this hypothesis.

4.3 Linguistic diversity: Documentation, typology, and change

The final chapters of this volume focus on topics of LD and typology. They address questions about how data and results from LD research may help in HL and LT investigations. In Chapter 10, Mily Crevels and Pieter Muysken present a description of the project aiming to document indigenous languages of Bolivia. Although the focus is primarily on language description and capacity building of local scholars, their research also contributes to a broader understanding of linguistic diversity in South America, particularly in the Amazonian Fringe area. In this context, Crevels and Muysken provide an overview of historical issues in South American language research while highlighting several intriguing typological features that have yet to be investigated (e.g., nominal tense, hierarchical alignment, reference tracking and nominal classification, posture verbs, and deixis). Crevels and Muysken also discuss the successes and shortcomings of almost a decade of LD research on South American languages. The chapter provides valuable insights for scholars undertaking LD research in South America and beyond.

In Chapter 11, Carolina Aragon and Fabrício Gerardi present a comparative investigation of alignment and word order in Akuntsú and related languages Makuráp, Mekéns, Tuparí, and Wayoró, all belonging to the Tuparí branch of the Tupian family and spoken in the state of Rondonia, Brazil. The chapter initially reflects on how the grammatical organization of the Akuntsú language (which Aragon has been documenting for almost two decades in a monolingual fieldwork setting) has changed in tandem with the dramatic social history of its last speakers (the Akuntsú people were victims of a genocide in the 1980s and are now reduced to only one family consisting of five individuals). From a theoretical standpoint, Aragon and Gerardi's findings suggest alignment pattern is not a relevant pattern in the syntax of Akuntsú, since intransitive verbs are expressed through possessive constructions. Word order, nonetheless, plays an important role. While Tuparían languages do not have case marking in nouns and noun phrases to indicate grammatical relations, word order and personal pronominal forms are important for coding grammatical relations. Whereas word order and bound pronominal forms are equally determined by discourse and semantic factors, the former has a greater functional role in determining which argument is the subject or object of a clause.

In Chapter 12, Ives Goddard and Amy Dahlstrom examine argument roles in Meskwaki (Algonquian). Their work is based on an extraordinary corpus of Meskwaki materials written mostly by Meskwaki speakers, and using the Meskwaki syllabary wirtten during 1911–18. The corpus consists of nearly 27,000 pages of narratives and ethnographic information which Goddard and Dahlstrom used for analyzing the discourse conditions that influence the morphosyntax of Meskwaki. According to their analysis, more central (higher ranked) and less central (lower ranked) third persons are distinguished as proximate and obviative, respectively, and one or more preverbal focus positions highlight noun phrases within a sentence. Inflectional marking on nouns and verbs for proximate and obviative specify the syntactic roles of third-person subjects and objects. If the arguments are both obviative they may be distinguished by being ranked according to their linear sequence (as first obviative and second obviative), irrespective of syntactic role. There is no default word order, however, and if the syntactic roles of the two obviatives are obvious on semantic or practical grounds, the order is free. Meskwaki therefore furnishes evidence against claims that syntactic roles can be identified in the abstract sentence structure as a universal property of language. It appears to function best in an analytic model in which functions such as syntactic roles (subject, first object, second object, and oblique) are represented separately from the constituent structure and labeled "*in situ.*" The Goddard and Dahlstrom chapter is an excellent example of how an archive of well-preserved language data becomes an invaluable resource for the study of an endangered language and can contribute to linguistic theory in general.

Finally, in Chapter 13, William O'Grady analyzes syntactic alignment systems using a framework he calls "emergentist typology." Drawing data from a range of different languages, O'Grady addresses complex issues in LT that inadvertently may arise in the process of language documentation and linguistic description. For instance, O'Grady outlines some of the reasons why accusative systems of case marking are more common than ergative systems, and he explains why accusative and ergative cases typically are overtly marked, while nominative and absolutive cases tend to be null. He also discusses the tendency for ergative systems to have more options for verb agreement than nominative–accusative systems. The explanatory strategies

O'Grady employs show high compatibility with the "classic tradition" in typology, which Campbell has largely followed.

5. Conclusions

Lyle Campbell's prolific career, as well as the chapters of this volume, including the discussion presented in this introduction, show the far-reaching possibilities of how HL, LD, and LT can be mutually engaging fields that respond to each other and converge to address more general questions relating to language change and linguistic diversity. In LD research, various types of evidence can be found to support new ways of understanding language change, whether in stable language contact situations or under severe attrition in situations of language endangerment. Likewise, LT and its dimensioning of typological diversity in attempting to explain what is possible (or not) in human languages require both appropriate data from LD and consideration of theories about language change from HL as explanatory causes of typological diversity. The chapters of this volume contribute to HL, LD, LT, and endangered languages. We hope that they demonstrate that the understanding of how languages change goes beyond only HL as conventionally viewed, by contributing to work in LD, to more explanatory descriptions of languages, and also to revitalization programs. Such a detailed and diverse view on the multiple threads that link HL, LD, and LT is timely, given the strides that investigation on language change and linguistic diversity have made in the last couple of decades. By making explicit the possible relations between the scholarly fields primarily related to the investigation of these broad topics, we hope to encourage new perspectives on these intersections, which arguably lie at the foundation of modern Linguistics—as well as in the lifelong work of Professor Lyle Campbell.

Notes

1. Available at <www.endangeredlanguages.com> (last accessed November 20, 2020).
2. 2003–5 Description of Chorote, Nivaclé and Kadiwéu: three of least known and most endangered languages of the Chaco. Endangered Languages Documentation Programme (Rausing Charitable Fund), SOAS [School of Oriental and African Studies, London University] (co-principal investigators Lyle Campbell, Verónica Grondona, and Filomena Sandalo). 2006–9 Wichí. Endangered Languages Documentation Programme (Rausing Charitable Fund), SOAS [School of Oriental and African Studies, London University] (co-principal investigators Verónica Grondona and Lyle Campbell). 2006–9 Wichí: Documentation, Description, and Training (National Endowment for the Humanities, PD-50002-06).

References

Bellwood, Peter, and A. Colin Renfrew. 2003. *Examining the Farming/Language Dispersal Hypothesis*. Cambridge: Oxford: McDonald Institute for Archaeological Research.

Blevins, Juliette. 2004. *Evolutionary phonology: The emergence of sound patterns*. Cambridge: Cambridge University Press.
Blust, Robert. 2018. Historical linguistics in the raw: My life as diachronic fieldworker. In *Studies in Language Companion Series* 194, ed. by Hannah Sarvasy and Diana Forker, 29–43. Amsterdam: John Benjamins Publishing Company.
Blust, Robert, and Stephen Trussel. 2013. The Austronesian Comparative Dictionary: A work in progress. *Oceanic Linguistics* 52.493–523.
Bomfim, Anari Braz. 2017. Patxohã: a retomada da língua do povo Pataxó. *Linguística*, 13.303–27.
Bowern, Claire. 2015. Linguistics: Evolution and language change. *Current Biology* 25.41–3.
Campbell, Lyle. 1985. *The Pipil language of El Salvador*. Berlin: Mouton de Gruyter.
Campbell, Lyle. 1996. Typological and areal issues in reconstruction. In *Linguistic reconstruction and typology*, ed. by Jasek Fisiak, 49–72. Berlin: Mouton de Gruyter.
Campbell, Lyle. 1997a. Genetic classification, typology, areal linguistics, language endangerment, and languages of the north Pacific Rim. In *Languages of the North Pacific Rim*, vol. 2, ed. by Osahito Miyaoka and Minoru Oshima, 179–242. Kyoto: Kyoto University.
Campbell, Lyle. 1997b. *American Indian languages: The historical linguistics of Native America*. Oxford: Oxford University Press.
Campbell, Lyle. 2003. What drives linguistic diversity and language spread? In *Examining the farming/language dispersal hypothesis*, ed. by Peter Bellwood and A. Colin Rerfrew, 49–63. Cambridge: McDonald Institute for Archaeological Research.
Campbell, Lyle. 2006. Areal linguistics: A closer scrutiny. In *Linguistic areas: Convergence in historical and typological perspective*, ed. by Yaron Matras, April McMahon, and Nigel Vincent, 1–31. Hampshire: Palgrave Macmillan.
Campbell, Lyle. 2016. Language documentation and historical linguistics. In *Language contact and change in the Americas: Studies in honor of Professor Marianne Mithun*, ed. by Andrea L. Berez, Diane M. Hintz, and Carmen Jany, 249–71. Amsterdam: John Benjamins.
Campbell, Lyle. 2017. Language contact and language documentation: Whence and whither? In *Proceedings of SALSA 25, Texas Linguistics Forum 60*, ed. by Hannah Foster, Michael Everdell, Katie Bradford, Lorena Orjuela, Frances Cooley, Hammal Al Bulushi, and Ambrocio Gutiérrez Lorenzo. Austin: University of Texas, Austin. <http://salsa.ling.utexas.edu/proceedings/2017/Campbell.pdf> (last accessed August 12, 2021).
Campbell, Lyle. 2018. *Language isolates*. New York: Routledge.
Campbell, Lyle. 2020. *Historical linguistics: An introduction*. 4th edn. Cambridge, MA: MIT Press.
Campbell, Lyle, and Anna Belew (eds) 2018. *Cataloguing of endangered languages*. London: Routledge.
Campbell, Lyle, Luiz Díaz, and Fernando Ángel. 2020. *Nivaclé grammar*. Salt Lake City: The University of Utah Press.

Campbell, Lyle, and Veronica Grondona. 2010 Who speaks what to whom? Multilingualism and language choice in Misión La Paz – a unique case. *Language in Society* 39.1–30.
Campbell, Lyle, and Veronica Grondona. 2012a. Linguistic acculturation in Nivaclé (Chulupí) and Chorote. *International Journal of American Linguistics* 78.335–67.
Campbell, Lyle, and Veronica Grondona (eds) 2012b. *The indigenous languages of South America: A comprehensive guide*. Berlin: Mouton de Gruyter.
Campbell, Lyle, and Richard Janda. 2001. Introduction: Conceptions of grammaticalization and their problems. *Grammaticalization: A Critical Assessment*. Special issue of Language Sciences, Volumes 22–3, 94–112. Oxford: Pergamon Press.
Campbell, Lyle, Terry Kaufman, and T. Smith-Stark. 1986. Mesoamerica as a linguistic area. *Language* 62.530–70.
Campbell, Lyle, and Marianne Mithun. 1979. *The languages of Native America: An historical and comparative assessment*. Austin: University of Texas Press.
Campbell, Lyle, and Mauricio Mixco. 2007. *Glossary of historical linguistics*. Salt Lake City: University of Utah Press.
Campbell, Lyle, and Martha Munzel. 1989. The structural consequences of language death. Investigating obsolescence. In *Studies in language contraction and* death, ed. by Nancy Dorian, 181–96. Cambridge: Cambridge University Press.
Campbell, Lyle, and William J. Poser. 2008. *Language classification: History and method*. Cambridge: Cambridge University Press.
Campos, Carlo Sandro de Oliveira. 2011. Contribuições da língua Maxakalí para a descrição léxico-gramatical da língua Pataxó. Anais do I Congresso Nacional de Estudos Linguísticos, 1–4. Vitória, Espírito-Santo: UFES.
Colombat, Bernard. 2008. L'accès aux langues pérégrines dans le Mithridate de Conr ad Gessner (1555). *Histoire Épistémologie Langage* 30.71–92.
Croft, William. 2003. *Typology and universals*. 2nd edn. Cambridge: Cambridge University Press.
Croft, William, T. Bhattacharya, D. Kleinschmidt, D. E. Smith, and T. F. Jaeger. 2011. Greenbergian universals, diachrony, and statistical analyses. *Linguistic Typology* 15.433–53.
Dunn, Michael, S. J. Greenhill, S. C. Levinson, and R. D. Gray. 2011. Evolved structure of language shows lineage-specific trends in word-order universals. *Nature* 473.79–82.
Epps, Patience. 2010. Linguistic typology and language documentation. In *The Oxford Handbook of Linguistic Typology*, ed. by Jae Jung Song, 634–49. Oxford: Oxford University Press.
Fitzgerald, Colleen M. 2020. Understanding language documentation and revitalization as a Feedback Loop. In *Amazonian Spanish: Language contact and evolution*, ed. by Stephen Fafulas, 81–104. 2020. Amsterdam: John Benjamins.
Gessner, Conrad, Bernard Colombat, and Manfred Peters. 2009. *Mithridate (1555)*. Travaux d'humanisme et Renaissance 452. Genève: Droz.
Greenberg, Joseph H. 1966. Synchronic and diachronic universals in phonology. *Language* 42.508–17.

Harris, Alice, and Lyle Campbell. 1995. *Historical syntax in cross linguistic perspective.* Cambridge: Cambridge University Press.

Hildebrandt, Kristine, Camen Jany, and Wilson Silva (eds) 2017. *Documenting variation in endangered languages.* Language Documentation & Conservation Special Publication 20. University of Hawai'i.

Himmelmann, Nikolaus P. 2012. Linguistic data types and the interface between language documentation and description. *Language Documentation & Conservation* 6.187–207. University of Hawai'i.

Leonard, Wesley Y. 2011. Challenging extinction through modern Miami language practices. *American Indian Culture & Research Journal* 35.135–60.

Levinson, Stephen C., and Russell D. Gray. 2012. Tools from evolutionary biology shed new light on the diversification of languages. *Trends in Cognitive Sciences* 16.167–73.

Lüpke, Friederike. 2019. Language endangerment and language documentation in Africa. In *The Cambridge handbook of African linguistics*, ed. by Ekkehard Wolf, 468–90. Cambridge: Cambridge University Press.

Lüpke, Friederike. 2016. Uncovering small-scale multilingualism. *Critical Multilingualism Studies* 4.35–74.

Luraghi, Silvia. 2017. Typology and historical linguistics. In *The Cambridge handbook of linguistic typology*, ed. by A. Y. Aikhenvald and R. M. W. Dixon, 95–123. Cambridge: Cambridge University Press.

Mufwene, Salikoko S. 2001. *The ecology of language evolution.* Cambridge Approaches to Language Contact. Cambridge: Cambridge University Press.

Nettle, Daniel. 1998. Explaining global patterns of language diversity. *Journal of Anthropological Archaeology* 17.354–74.

Nichols, Johanna. 1992. *Linguistic diversity in space and time.* London/Chicago: University of Chicago Press.

Palosaari, Naomi, and Lyle Campbell. 2011. Structural aspects of language endangerment. In *The Cambridge handbook of endangered languages*, ed. by Peter Austin and Julia Sallabank, 100–19. Cambridge: Cambridge University Press.

Rehg, Kenneth L., and Lyle Campbell (eds) 2018. *The Oxford handbook of endangered languages.* Oxford: Oxford University Press.

Urban, Greg. 1985. On Pataxó and Hãhãhãi. *International Journal of American Linguistics* 51.605–8.

Weinreich, Uriel, William Labov, and Marvin Herzog. 1968. *Empirical foundations for a theory of language change.* Austin: University of Texas Press.

2

Using the Acoustic Correlates of Voice Quality as Explanations for the Changes in the Descriptions of Xinkan Glottalized Consonants

Chris Rogers

1. Introduction

The documentation of endangered languages presents implications for many areas of linguistic research and language community identity.[1] Among these is a link between the documentary resources of a language and its historical reconstruction which in turn informs descriptive standards and revitalization efforts. The purpose of this chapter is to address that link concerning one aspect of Xinkan phonology: the glottalized consonants. The Xinkan language family is a group of at least four extinct languages that were once spoken in southeastern Guatemala: Guazacapán Xinka, Chiquimulilla Xinka, Jumaytepeque Xinka, and Yupiltepeque Xinka (ISO codes: xin, qco, qda, qhq, qsd). These languages have been greatly influenced by the extreme contact in the Mesoamerican Linguistic Area and exhibit borrowings from Mayan, Mixe-Zoquean, Uto-Aztecan, and other languages in the region (see Campbell et al. 1986). The last speakers of the Xinkan languages resided in the departments of Santa Rosa and Jalapa, as shown on the map in Figure 2.1.

Currently, after years of repression, genocide, and marginalization the Xinkan community is engaged in efforts to revitalize their languages and to build a unique cultural identity (see Rogers 2016b, 2020). Due to the lack of speakers, or rememberers, these revitalization efforts are dependent on the available linguistic descriptions of the Xinkan languages. Following from this, both linguists and community members note that discrepancies in these resources are a source of confusion. For example, some grammatical features are not present in all Xinkan records. When a resource is missing features, it opens up discussions about the importance they (might have) had in the languages' grammatical systems. Similarly, general typological linguistic characterizations of other linguistic features do not always match the specific Xinkan elements as recorded in the available documentation. This mismatch makes the descriptions appear to be biased toward some prescriptive standard rather than an objective treatment of

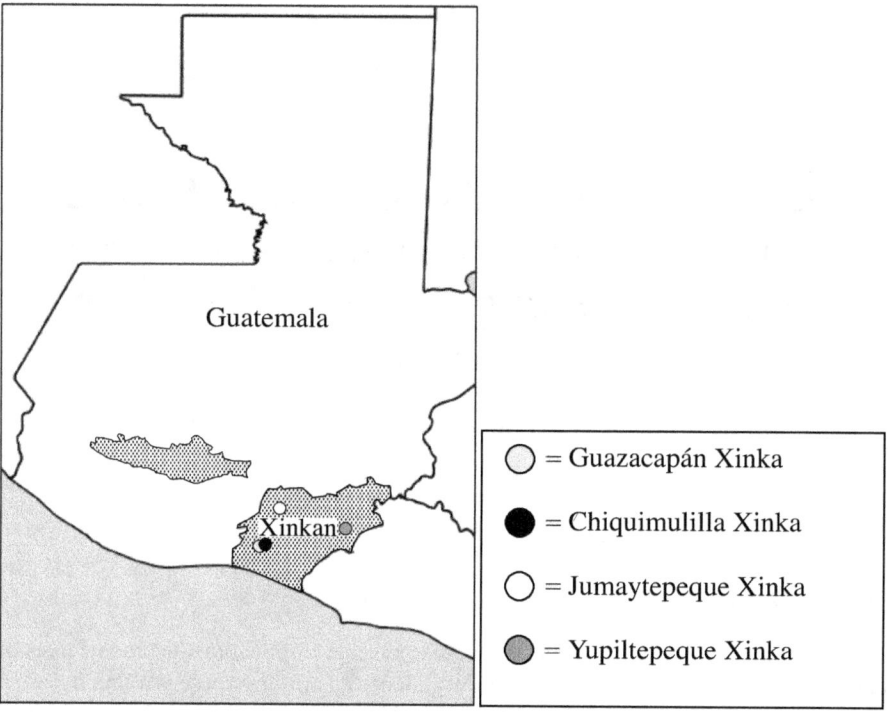

Figure 2.1 Location of the last speakers of the known Xinkan languages

the languages. This chapter focuses on resolving these types of discrepancies related to glottalized consonants and provides a clearer picture of the diachronic properties of these consonants in the Xinkan languages and a better understanding of their value for community revitalization efforts, thus highlighting the link between language documentation and historical linguistic methodologies.[2]

2. Discrepancies about glottalized consonants in Xinkan linguistic descriptions

Among several interesting typological properties, the Xinkan languages have a large number of plain–glottalized consonant pairs (both ejectives and glottalized resonants), which is unusual in the region.[3] These contrasts have been included in most modern descriptions of the Xinkan languages and based on cognate patterns are easily reconstructed in Proto-Xinkan (McQuown 1948; McArthur 1966; Schumann Gálvez 1967; Campbell 1973; COPXIG 2004; Sachse 2010; Rogers 2010, 2016a). The Proto-Xinkan consonant inventory is given in Table 2.1 (based on Rogers 2016a: 193). Each of the individual languages has only minimally diverged from this inventory ([ɬ] has merged with [l] in both Jumaytepeque Xinka and Yupiltepeque Xinka).[4]

As a terminological note, the labels "glottalized" and "glottalic," used elsewhere in the literature, can potentially be used for different though overlapping phenomena.

Table 2.1 Proto-Xinkan consonant inventory

			Labials	Alveolar	Alveopalatal	Palatal	Velar	Glottal
Stop		*voiceless*	p	t			k	
		ejective	p'	t'			k'	ʔ
Fricative		*voiceless*		s				h
		retroflex			š			
Affricate		*voiceless*			tʃ			
		ejective		ts'	tʃ'			
Nasal		*plain*	m	n				
		glottalized	m'	n'				
		plain		l				
	lateral	*glottalized*		l'				
		voiceless		ɬ				
Approximant	*rhotic*	*plain*		r				
		glottalized		r'				
	glide	*plain*	w			j		
		glottalized	w'			j'		

Both have been used to refer to the airstream mechanism characteristic of ejectives and implosives, and both have been used to refer to a secondary articulation on speech sounds (often coinciding with changes of voice quality or phonation—or both). In the latter use, they at least partially overlap with some uses of the term "laryngealized" (see Ladefoged 1971; Laver 1980). To avoid this confusion, I see the terms *glottalized* and *glottalic* as interchangeable and use them as indications of a specific airstream mechanism used for a primary articulation on some consonants (that is, ejectives, implosives, and glottalized resonants). I use the label *laryngealized* for some segments that are secondarily articulated with changes in the larynx. In this sense, the acoustic correlates of these consonants in Guazacapán Xinka, as presented below, indicate that they are acoustically laryngealized.

Despite being reconstructed for the Proto-Xinkan consonant inventory, glottalized consonants are a source of confusion in understanding the recorded history of these languages and for the ongoing language revitalization efforts in the Xinkan community. There are two reasons for this confusion. First, at least half of the earlier resources about the Xinkan languages make little mention of these consonants in the phonology, while more recent resources include all of the contrasts in Table 2.1 (see Maldonado de Matos *c.*1773; Morales 1812; Gavarette and Valdez 1868; Berendt 1875; Brinton 1885; Calderón 1908; Lehmann 1920; Fernández 1938). Second, the last speakers of the languages included glottalized consonants where they were not necessary grammatically (as based on comparisons for all speakers at the time and the grammatical functions of glottalized consonants in Xinkan languages), as a means of partially reinforcing their cultural and linguistic authenticity. Words were often pronounced showing variation in the pronunciation of plain and glottalized consonants without apparent linguistic motivations (Campbell and Muntzel 1989; Rogers 2016b). For example, a single word might be pronounced with either a glottalized consonant or its plain consonant counterpart by the same speaker, *maku* ~ *mak'u* "house" (Rogers 2016a: 43). This phenomenon is further addressed in Section 5 below. Both of these issues create a discrepancy in the value of the consonants to the documentary record of the Xinkan languages. In essence, it is unclear if the authors of the earlier resources omitted them because they were not there, or if they were perceived as something else, and if the hypercorrections by the last speakers represented authentic use of the languages or not. Following from this confusion, at least some community members question the importance of these sounds to their languages (and the representations of them) synchronically and diachronically.

This confusion is complicated by the fact that within the context of colonial linguistic descriptions in Latin America several traditions for representing glottalized consonants existed, but were not used in Xinkan descriptions—making it unclear if these languages, in fact, had glottalized consonants (see Smith-Stark 2005 for an explanation of the possibilities invented for representing these sounds). Moreover, one of these traditions—called the *Parra* letters—was specifically used in colonial Guatemala for adequately representing ejectives in Mayan languages (Carmack 1973: 22; Smith-Stark 2005).[5] However, this tradition of representation was discussed in the earliest Xinkan resource as being inappropriate for the Xinkan languages (Maldonado de Matos *c.*1773). The author of that grammar does recognize that some consonant sounds are different from their plain counterparts but specifically suggests that the difference is about fortition or effort rather than glottalic movement:

> En lugar de aquellos dos quatrillos, usaré de nuestro alphabeto, aunque geminadas...para significar una mui áspera <k> ... así lo tengo que hacer para que viendo el lector dos letras juntas, de la misma pronunciación y naturaleza; venga en conocimiento de que la pronunciación que piden aquellas dos letras juntas es mas doble que la que pide cada una por sí ... porque si la <c> suena como una, y la <k> suena como dos, juntando las dos sonaran como tres o más quia virtus unita fortior. (Maldonado de Matos *c.*1773)[6]

This description suggests that at least some sounds had unique properties in the earliest recorded stages of the Xinkan languages. Furthermore, glottalized consonants (especially ejectives) were identified in languages all over the world since at least the mid-eighteenth century even if descriptions of them were not entirely accurate (Fallon 2002: 4), so it is unusual that by the end of the eighteenth century to not at least recognize them as such if they were indeed present. Resolving this issue has implications for the reconstructions of glottalized consonants in Proto-Xinkan not previously addressed. If they were not present in earlier states of the language, reconstructions and revitalization materials should reflect that. If they were present in earlier states of the language (and exhibited unique properties), the reconstructions and revitalization materials should reflect those properties.

In terms of a comprehensive understanding of glottalized consonants in these languages, the acoustic phonetic features correlated to their articulation have not previously been described for any of the Xinkan languages, leaving a gap in the descriptive resources of the language family. Since the acoustic correlates of glottalized consonants, crosslinguistically, often indicate a continuum of possibilities for the production of this consonant type, the acoustic features of glottalized consonants in Xinkan languages cannot be simply stated without careful empirical investigation (see Kingston 1984; Ingram and Rigsby 1987; Warner 1996). Addressing this descriptive gap is necessary for a better understanding of their synchronic properties and their diachronic development and the value they might have in ongoing Xinkan revitalization efforts, as well as possibly suggesting motivations for the choice of representations across the descriptive resources for the language family. Consequently, the purpose of this chapter is to describe some acoustic correlates of voice quality in the glottalized consonants in Guazacapan Xinka and to suggest some implications for understanding the confusion in the representations of Xinkan languages generally.

In Section 3, the phonological and morphological behaviors of glottalized consonants in Xinkan are compared and contrasted in both modern and pre-modern resources. In Section 4, the acoustic phonetic properties of voice quality for glottalized consonants in Guazacapán Xinka are presented. Lastly, in Section 5, a discussion about the implications of the descriptions in Sections 3 and 4 for resolving the confusions mentioned here (Section 2) as related to reconstruction and the development of revitalization materials is offered.

3. Patterns of glottalized consonants in Xinkan

Collectively, descriptive resources about the Xinkan languages—including wordlists, grammatical descriptions of varying lengths, and information about the speakers of the various languages—provide a good understanding of the grammatical properties of the Xinkan languages. However, the most important source of information comes from the data collected by Terrence Kaufman and Lyle Campbell between 1972 and 1979 and published in Rogers (2010, 2016a). This resource is the most complete and comprehensive description of the grammatical properties of the Xinkan language family available. The information presented there is used in this chapter as a standard of comparison across all of the other Xinkan descriptive resources. Based on this information, the plain–glottalized consonants pairs shown in Table 2.1 above are segmentally contrastive as evidenced by the (near) minimal pairs in (1).[7]

(1) Guazacapán Xinka minimal and near minimal pairs with glottalized consonants
    a. *paki* "wall" *p'ak'a* "key"
    b. *hutu* "tree" *tut'u* "soap"
    c. *naka* "you" *łak'a* "itchy"
    d. *tʃawi* "mud" *tʃ'awi* "hard"
    e. *nama* "painful" *sam'a* "dark"
    f. *naana* "adult female" *haan'ah* "here"
    g. *mali* "ash" *šamaĺ'i* "forehead"
    h. *kara* "heavy" *par'a* "below"
    i. *awa* "moon" *k'aw'a* "in middle of, between"
    j. *šaja* "old person" *šaj'a* "acidic"

Also mentioned in Rogers (2016a: 35), glottalized consonants are phonotactically more restricted than their plain counterparts are. These restrictions on glottalized consonants include that they do not occur word-finally (except for *-n'* and *-j'*), they are rarer after long vowels, they are prohibited as an entire class in consonant clusters, and the subclass of glottalized resonants do not occur in word-initial position. While not overtly exemplified in this chapter, these restrictions motivated many of the philological interpretations of earlier resources and the parameters for the acoustic study.

The contrast between plain and glottalized consonants in Xinkan languages also marks a change in verbal aspect (Rogers 2014, 2016a). Specifically, the contrast between the consonant pairs is neutralized in favor of the glottalized consonant on the rightmost consonant of a verb stem inflected for the incompletive aspect while the default value of this consonant (either plain or glottalized) is present in the completive aspect, as shown in (2).

(2) Chiquimulilla Xinka verb-stem changes reflecting differences in grammatical aspect

	Completive	Incompletive	Gloss
a.	hini	hin'i	"learn, know"
b.	k'ani	k'an'i	"trap"
c.	miimi	miim'i	"sing"
d.	huta	hut'a	"blow"
e.	hapa	hap'a	"pass, wait"
f.	waki	wak'i	"play"
g.	hil'a	hil'a	"to empty"
h.	k'oło	k'ol'o	"peel"

When the consonant undergoing neutralization in this verbal inflection occurs within a consonant cluster, a vowel is inserted between the consonants, in order to avoid having a glottalized consonant in the cluster—a violation of the phonotactic conditions mentioned above. This is shown in (3). The quality of this anaptyctic vowel is harmonically dependent on the vowel before and after it (Rogers 2016a: 45).

(3) Xinkan verb-stem changes reflecting differences in grammatical aspect with consonant clusters

	Completive	Incompletive	Gloss
a.	ełwa	eław'a	"sweep"
b.	tʃarka	tʃarak'a	"open one's mouth"
c.	tintu	tinat'u	"play music"
d.	hirki	hirik'i	"wag"
e.	ohro	ohor'o	"singe"
f.	ɨrsi	ɨrits'i	"bite"
g.	kɨši	kits'i	"roast"

Note that for consonants without a glottalized counterpart in the inventory, a close articulatory approximation is produced in this neutralization, as in (2g–h) and (3f–g);

[h] and [ʔ] never occur in this environment. These contrasts and patterns were first recorded in McQuown (1948) and Schumann (1967). Nevertheless, when compared to the patterns presented above, the older descriptions of Xinkan do show some obvious correspondences. This suggests that their presence in the various languages but not their representations in the descriptions is diachronically valid. Maldonado de Matos (c.1773), likely representing Guazacapán Xinka, inconsistently represents [k'] as <ck> or <ɛ> and occasionally represents [ts'] as <tx> (as mentioned in note 6). The representative correspondences between Maldonado's descriptions and Rogers' (2016a) are shown in (4).

(4) Representation of glottalized consonants in Maldonado de Matos (1772)

	Maldonado de Matos (1772)	Rogers (2016a)	
a.	pula	pula	"to do.COMP"
b.	pula	pul'a	"to do.ICOMP"
c.	mere	mere	"break.COMP"
d.	mere	mer'e	"break.ICOMP"
e.	piri	piri	"see.COMP"
f.	piri	pir'i	"see.ICOMP"
g.	etka	etka	"cover.COMP"
h.	etaka	etak'a	"cover.ICOMP"
i.	matxa	mats'a	"to stick together"
j.	maszi	maši	"fry.COMP"
k.	matxi	mats'i	"fry.ICOMP"
l.	mrys'i	mɨts'a	"bury"
m.	pułi	puułi	"to wash.COMP"
n.	puli	puul'i	"to wash.ICOMP"
o.	ckòmo	k'omo	"knee, elbow"
p.	ɛagui	k'awi	"to pull"

Notice that these data show clear correspondences for segmental contrasts and morphological consonant neutralization.

Morales (1812), representing an unclassified variety of Xinka, does not represent glottalized consonants at all.[8] This is not entirely surprising since the goal of this resource is not a description of a language but has a communicative function, namely an administrative proclamation. Nevertheless, the presence of the anaptyctic vowel breaking consonant clusters with a glottalized consonant in verbs inflected for imperfective aspect can be noted in some words—such as in the word for "open" in (5d).[9]

(5) Representation of glottalized consonants in Morales (1812)

	Morales (1812)	Chiquimulilla Xinka (Rogers 2016a)	
a.	mugpula	mukpul'a	"you did (it).ICOMP"
b.	tumuqui	tum'uki / tumuki	"to finish"
c.	nucay	nuk'ay	"he gave.COMP"
d.	apala	apal'a	"open.ICOMP" (cf. apla "open.COMP")

Similarly, the data presented in Gavarrete and Valdez (1868) are only a short wordlist of an unknown Xinkan variety, and only represent a small subset set of possible glottalized sounds: [j'], [t'], and [n'].[10]

(6) Representation of glottalized consonants in Berendt (1875)
       Berendt (1875)   Rogers (2016a)   Gloss
  a. *ta'yuc* and *tayuk*   *taj'uk*   "hat"
  b. *a'tac>*   *oot'ek*   "bed"
  c. *xi'ñac*   *šin'ak*   "bean"

While neither segmental contrasts nor morphological neutralization is indicated in this resource, the choice of orthographic representation does suggest at least the former was recognized.

The descriptions in Calderón (1908) represent only [ts'] among all of the possible glottalized consonants and only in word-initial position, as shown in (7). Importantly, this sound is not contrasted with its plain counterpart [ts]—which does not exist in Xinkan languages—and neutralization due to changes in verbal aspect is not indicated. However, like other resources, the choice of representation does suggest unique articulations.

(7) Representation of glottalized consonants in Calderón (1908)
       Calderón (1908)   Rogers (2016a)   Gloss
  a. *caman*   *k'aman*   "I hug.COMP"
  b. *tz'ijlijlí*   *ts'iłiłi?*   "smooth"
  c. *tz'imay*   *ts'iimaj*   "Guazacapán"

Finally, Fernández (1938) republished many of the forms first listed in Calderón (1908) and added some additional lexical entries probably of Chiquimulilla Xinka (Sachse 2010: 92). Interestingly, however, Fernández treats the glottalized consonants differently than Calderón did. Sounds corresponding to glottalized resonants in Rogers (2016a) are written as geminates in Fernández's description, and the ejectives are not represented at all (examples are shown in (8)). There is no indication that glottalized consonants are used for changes in verbal aspect, though, again, the unique orthographic representation does suggest a segmental contrast was being noted by the author.

(8) Representation of glottalized consonants in Fernández (1938)
       Fernández (1938)   Rogers (2016a)
  a. *namma*   *nim'a*   eat.ICOMP
  b. *en-nemmá*   *in-nim'a*   1SG.eat.ICOMP

In summary, older descriptions treated what were likely glottalized consonants in two possible ways: (1) as non-glottalized consonants, showing no morphophonological contrast with their plain counterparts; or (2) as restricted to a smaller subset of possibilities when compared to contemporary descriptions (though even those that are indicated are not consistently represented). Both of these observations are in line with the way other languages were being described at the same time, though not of glottalized consonants generally (see Smailus 1989; Smith-Stark 2005). While orthographic conventions (such as in the pre-modern resources) cannot necessarily be relied on as indications of segment articulations or of their acoustic consequences, I suggest these various pre-modern representations reflect differences in what the authors perceived acoustically rather than a change in the number of glottalized consonants in Xinkan languages. This argument means that the consonants had a consistent use throughout the recorded Xinkan history, and at least some of these acoustic properties are reflected in the pre-modern authors' choices for representations. The next section presents some of the acoustic facts of Xinkan glottalized consonants in the speech of the last speakers.

4. Acoustics correlates of glottalized consonants in Guazacapán Xinka

Acoustic phonetic studies of any of the Xinkan languages are non-existent. Moreover, without current speakers of any of the languages, acoustic phonetic studies of Xinkan languages must rely on available audio recordings of previous states of the languages (which are archived in the Archive of the Indigenous Languages of Latin America). This is precisely what has been done below and the recordings used are described and cataloged at length in Rogers (2016a) and briefly discussed below. However, a note of caution is relevant. These Xinkan recordings are digitized copies of reel-to-reel field audio recordings of elicited words, example sentences, and narrative texts recorded by Terrence Kaufman and Lyle Campbell in the 1970s. This means that while they suffer from the same drawbacks that plague most field recordings (that is, there are dogs, children, chickens, and motorcycles that intermittently disrupt the quality of the recording), there is also signal degradation (especially through the introduction of extremely high amounts of white noise) due to the deterioration of the reel-to-reel tapes and further introduced during the digitization process. Furthermore, while there are audio recordings representing speakers of three of the Xinkan languages over a seven-year span (1972–9), not all speakers were recorded performing the same tasks or for the same amount of time. This means that while the recordings are excellent documentation, they were not intended for experimental acoustic analysis of glottalized consonants, and the available information is limited (and potentially presents problems for the validity of the descriptions below). This is not to diminish the value of the recordings and the inspiring work done by both Terry and Lyle in preserving these languages, but only to suggest that full experimental conditions, while ideal, are no longer possible for these languages.

Canonically, glottalized consonants are single consonantal segments articulated with a closure in the oral cavity as well as a closure, or tighter constriction, at the glottis. Ejectives prototypically have vertical movement up of the larynx during production while glottalized resonants do not necessarily include vertical laryngeal movements (Maddieson 2013). However, this differs from what is produced in the Xinkan recordings, where glottalized consonants are impressionistically produced with a lot of intra- and inter-speaker variation. Sometimes they are produced with high levels of creak, others with laryngeal tension, or intensity, and still other times with the expected oral and glottal closures common for ejectives. None of these variations appears to be used consistently by any one speaker for any specific consonantal segment, and often more than one feature is present in the audio recordings for the same consonant. This can be misleading for individuals using the materials who might typically rely on typological descriptions of glottalized consonants generally but do not find evidence of this in the recordings.

For example, [k'] and [ts'] are often produced as canonical ejectives, with full glottal and oral closures along with creak on adjacent vowels. As just one representative example, the [k'] in the word [tak'ał] *tak'alh* "chest" exhibits a longer voice-onset time with multiple stop bursts and lower F0 on flanking vowels (average 180 Hz) than the [k] in the word [ṣahaka] *xahaka* "your mouth" (average F0 of flanking vowels is 206 Hz), represented in Figure 2.2 and Figure 2.3 respectively.[11]

However, [t'], and other ejectives, can be produced with these canonical closures or without them. The spectrogram of [it'uł] *it'ulh* "flea" in Figure 2.4 shows [t'] with two stop bursts (with average F0 of 178 Hz on adjacent vowels) compared to the spectrogram of [waṣat'a] *waxat'a* "open.ICOMP" (with average F0 of 106 Hz on adjacent vowels) which shows only a single stop burst for the same sound, in Figure 2.5.

Turning to some examples of the glottalized resonants, Figure 2.6 shows the spectrogram for the word [paːma] *paama* "wing" where the average F0 of the vowels adjacent to [m] is 208 Hz, while Figure 2.7 shows the spectrogram for the word [ṣam'alika] *xam'alika* "your forehead," where the average F0 of the vowels adjacent to [m'] is 110 Hz.

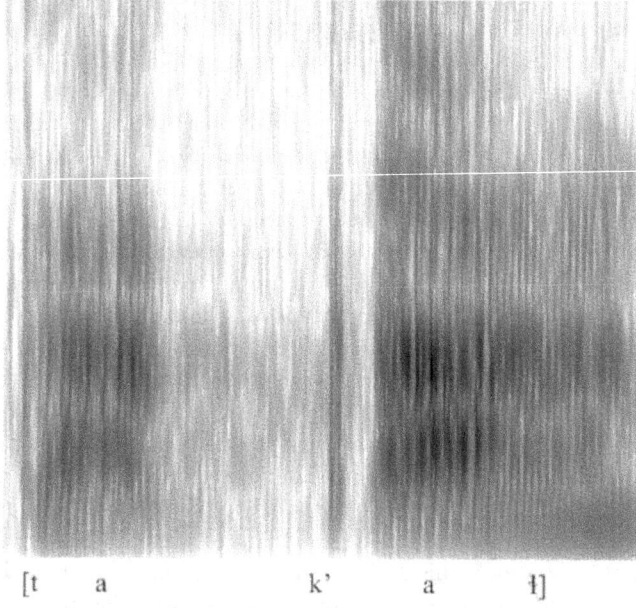

[t   a   k'   a   ł]

Figure 2.2 Spectrogram of [tak'ał] "chest"

CHANGES IN THE DESCRIPTIONS OF XINKAN GLOTTALIZED CONSONANTS

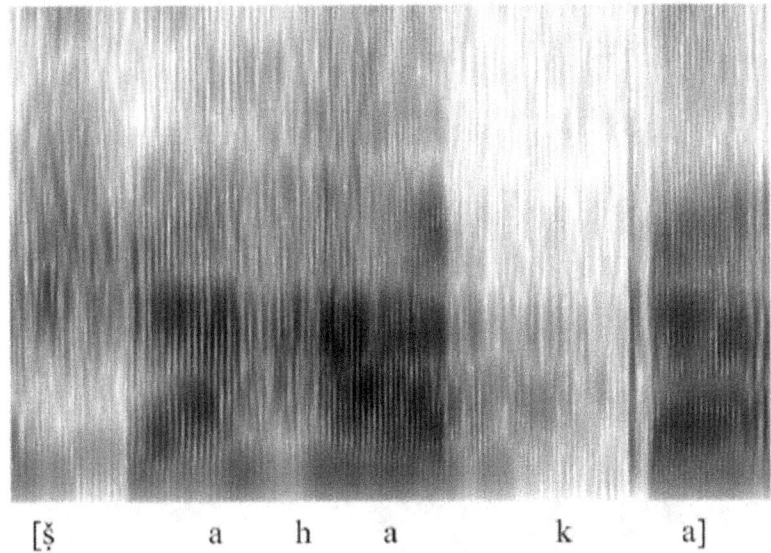

Figure 2.3 Spectrogram of [ṣahaka] "your mouth"

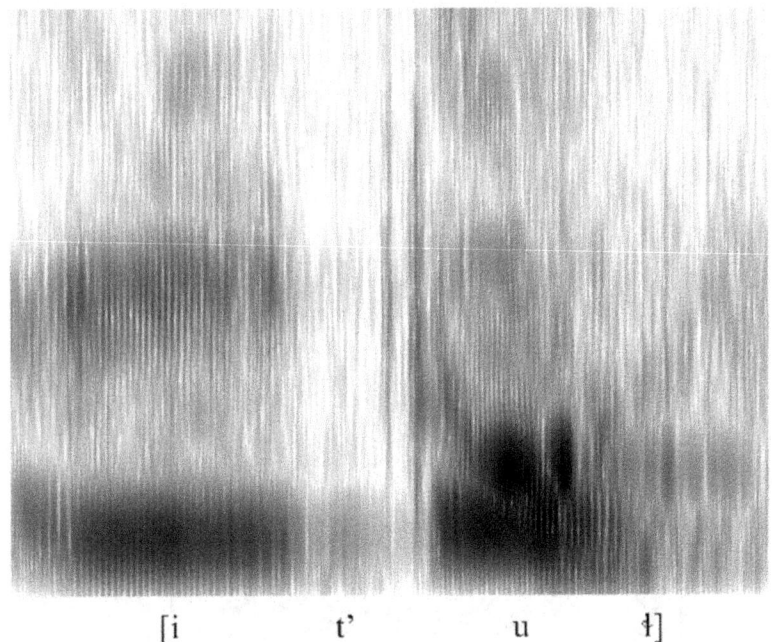

Figure 2.4 Spectrogram of [it'uɫ] "flea"

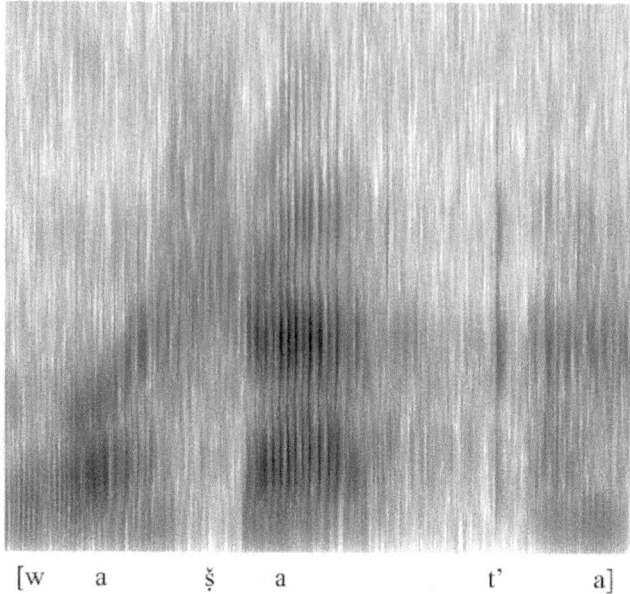

Figure 2.5 Spectrogram of [waṣat'a] "open.ICOMP"

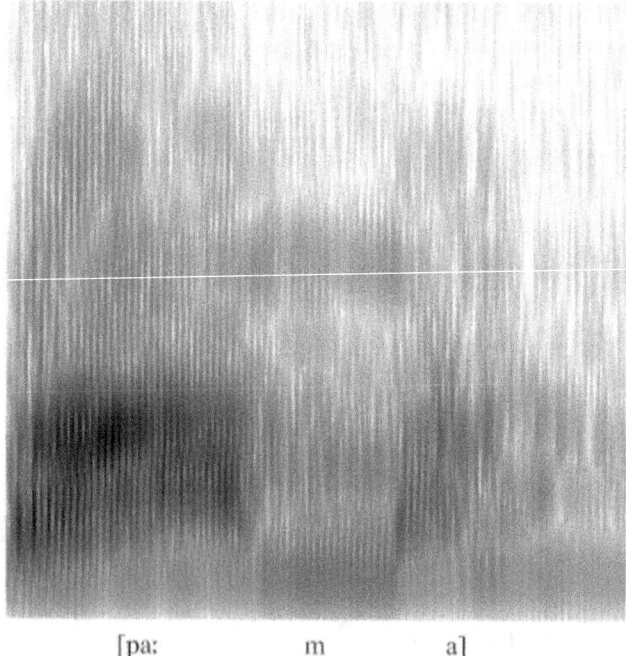

Figure 2.6 Spectrogram of [pa:ma] "wing"

Figure 2.7 Spectrogram of [ṣam'alika] "your forehead"

As expected for sonorants, neither of these spectrograms indicate stop bursts in the respective productions, though voicing does appear to be stronger in the plain [m] compared to the glottalized [m']. Also, glottalized [m'] has noticeably more creak than the plain [m]—further supported by the differences in the fundamental frequencies of the vowels adjacent to the consonants.

However, occasionally glottalized resonants (especially glottalized approximants) are produced without creak and are impressionistically produced with greater tension (unfortunately physiological or aerodynamic tests that might confirm this impression are obviously not possible). This is heard in the contrasts in the words [alij'an] *aliy'an* "I show, I teach" (average F0 of adjacent vowels is 212 Hz) and [mija] *miya* "chicken" (average F0 of adjacent vowels is 220 Hz), as represented in the spectrograms in Figure 2.8 and Figure 2.9, respectively.

This variation in the production of glottalized consonants suggests that a single type of articulation is not used by Xinkan speakers to produce all glottalized consonants and that their canonical typological definition can be misleading if used as a prescriptive basis. However, recent research has shown that glottalized consonants are often marked by changes in some of the acoustic characteristics of vowels and consonants within an utterance. This research suggests that changes in phonation, voice quality, and/or duration can correlate with the difference between plain and glottalized consonants (Ladefoged and Maddieson

Figure 2.8 Spectrogram of [alij'an] "I show, I teach"

1996: 80; Fallon 2002). Accordingly, an investigation of the acoustic patterns was conducted.

In attempting to discover the acoustic correlates of glottalized consonants as a natural class of sounds and of each of the two types of glottalized consonants (ejectives vs glottalized resonants), the audio of a single language was investigated (Guazacapán Xinka) since a larger and more varied sample of audio recordings is available for this language. A pilot investigation (not reported below) of the available recordings in both Chiquimulilla Xinka and Jumaytepeque Xinka show similar results as those reported here. Consequently, the acoustic analysis of glottalized consonants in Guazacapán Xinka is considered representative of the entire family. The Guazacapán Xinka audio recordings include three types: lexical elicitation data, sentence elicitation, and naturalistic speech (mostly monologues) from eight speakers. However, each speaker is not represented equally in the recordings. Some speakers occur in recordings only once or

[m   i   j   a]

Figure 2.9 Spectrogram of [mija] "chicken"

only for one type of recording. Similarly, some recordings are not amenable to acoustic analysis due to the issues discussed at the beginning of this section.

The analyses in the current study were restricted to (relatively) clean audio recordings with minimal signal degradation, interference, and white noise and then further limited to elicitations only. This is because glottalized consonants (and especially glottalized resonants) are often produced like their plain counterparts in natural speech crosslinguistically and the clearest articulations of glottalized consonants were necessary for determining any acoustic correlations (see Maddieson 1984: 115–17; Ladefoged and Maddieson 1996: 77–89, 106–11; Fallon 2002: 120–2; Bird et al. 2008: 493). Recordings of four speakers remained after these limitations: three male (Tomás García [TG], Cipriano Gomez Yermo [CGY], and Lucio Solís Pérez [LSP]) and one female (Teofila Pérez [TP]). These audio recordings were aligned, annotated, and transcribed in ELAN and word tokens containing glottalized consonants in intervocalic contexts, and those containing their plain non-glottalized counterparts were collected for each speaker.

Consonant tokens were studied intervocalically since the phonotactic restrictions mentioned in Section 3 prohibit the entire set of contrasts in all other morphophonological environments. A total of 188 words were collected across the four speakers. More words could be collected from the audio of one speaker (Cipriano Gomez Yermo) but the words collected for the other speakers represent the complete set of glottalized consonants recorded. Consequently, all of the glottalized consonants of Tomás García, Lucio Solís Pérez, and Teofila Pérez are included in the analysis below, but only a limited number of word tokens for Cipriano Gomez Yermo have been included. The limit was a random sampling of five words containing each plain–glottalized consonant pair (that is, 105 word tokens).

Each consonant studied was categorized according to three distinctions: (1) CONSONANT TYPE: plain (P) versus glottalized (G); (2) CONSONANT SUBTYPE: plain obstruents (O), plain sonorants (S), glottalized obstruents (E), and glottalized sonorants (R); and (3) PLACE OF ARTICULATION: labial (L), coronal (COR), and dorsal (D). The frequency statistics of each of these three distinctions are shown in Table 2.2, Table 2.3, and Table 2.4, respectively.

Using a Praat script, the acoustic characteristics of voice quality of each consonant and the adjacent vowels were measured for each word token across the four speakers in four domains. The acoustic measures included, DURATION, MEAN F0, MAXIMUM F0, MINIMUM F0, JITTER, SHIMMER, the HARMONICS-TO-NOISE RATIO (HNR), INTENSITY, SPECTRAL TILT (quantified as the difference between the first and second harmonics, H1-H2), and the difference between the first harmonic and the amplitudes of the first three formants (H1-A1, H1-A2, and H1-A3 respectively). The four domains of analysis included the entire intervocalic envelope meaning adjacent vowels and the

Table 2.2 CONSONANT TYPE frequencies

Type	Speaker			
	TG	TP	CGY	LSP
P	10	15	50	17
G	9	14	55	18
Total	19	29	105	35

Table 2.3 CONSONANT SUBTYPE frequencies

Subtype	Speaker			
	TG	TP	CGY	LSP
O	4	4	20	5
S	6	11	30	12
E	3	5	25	5
R	6	9	30	13
Total	19	29	105	35

Table 2.4 Consonant PLACE OF ARTICULATION frequencies

Place	Speaker			
	TG	TP	CGY	LSP
COR	10	14	65	18
D	2	4	10	5
L	7	11	30	12
Total	19	29	105	35

consonant (VCV), the consonant by itself (C), the preceding vowel by itself (VB), and the following vowel by itself (VA). Of course, not all of these acoustic measures are valid for each of the four domains (for example, obstruent consonants will not necessarily have an indication of F0), and only those analyses which are generally understood to be valid for each domain were considered in the analysis presented below. In all cases, vowel segments were defined as the interval from the offset of the preceding consonant to the onset of the following one (where it was present), and consonant segments were defined by the interval from the start of the oral closure at the end of the preceding vowel to the onset of voicing associated with the following vowel. This results in forty-eight measures for each consonant type, consonant subtype, and consonant place of articulation. Based on these measures, and since the goal was to determine which of the acoustic measures are correlated with consonant type (if any), three tests of logistic regression were performed for each of the three consonantal distinctions used. Statistical significance was measured at the $p < .05$ level for all three tests. The results of each statistical test is reported below.

First, a binomial logistic regression was performed to test the correlation of CONSONANT TYPE (plain vs. glottalized consonants) to the acoustic measures taken. The model was statistically significant, $\chi^2 = 98.9$, df = 51, $p < .001$. The model explained 74.1% (Nagelkerke R^2) of the difference in CONSONANT TYPE. Across the four analytical domains, however, only the DURATION ($p = .04$) and SPECTRAL TILT ($p = .02$) of the preceding vowel and INTENSITY ($p = .03$) of the following vowel were statistically significantly correlated to the type of consonant. As reflected in the mean values of these acoustic measures (in Table 2.5), the preceding vowel is shorter and has less negative tilt and the following vowel has a higher intensity for plain consonants as compared to glottalized consonants.

This can be interpreted to mean that, of the acoustic measures reported here, the consonant itself is not a reliable indicator of glottalization. Rather, the natural class of glottalized consonants, generally, can be distinguished from their plain counterparts in Guazacapán Xinka based on the duration and spectral tilt of the preceding vowel (interpreted here as a change in phonation, such as creak), and the intensity of the following vowel.

Second, a multinomial logistic regression was performed to test the correlation of CONSONANT SUBTYPE to the acoustic measures taken. This model was also statistically significant, $\chi^2 = 277$, df = 153, $p < .001$. The model explained 91.3% (Nagelkerke R^2) of the differences in CONSONANT SUBTYPE. Each of the four consonant subtypes was

Table 2.5 Mean values of statistically significant correlates of CONSONANT TYPE

CONSONANT TYPE	DURATION (VB)	SPECTRAL TILT (VB)	INTENSITY (VA)
P	0.117	−0.857	67.4
G	0.135	−4.79	64.0

correlated to a statistically significant difference in DURATION, JITTER, and SHIMMER in all four analytical domains. As seen in the mean values given in Table 2.6 and Table 2.7, in comparing plain obstruents to plain sonorants, and ejectives to glottalized resonants, obstruents are longer in the VCV and C domains, while the opposite is true for the preceding vowel domain—and the following vowel domain for the ejective/glottalized resonant distinction. Similarly, plain obstruents exhibit greater jitter and shimmer across all four analytic domains compared to plain sonorants. On the other hand, comparing ejectives to glottalized resonants, measures of jitter and shimmer are almost identical in the VCV domain, but ejectives have more jitter but less shimmer in the consonant itself as well as on the preceding vowel. They also exhibit more jitter and more shimmer in the following vowel.

Moreover, the HNR in the VCV and C domains was statistically significant in distinguishing ejectives from glottalized resonants, where glottalized resonants have a higher harmonics-to-noise ratio in both analytical domains than ejectives, as shown in Table 2.8.

SPEAKER was a statistically significant variable in distinguishing plain obstruents from ejectives, and all speakers are shown to have unique voice quality characteristics in distinguishing these consonants. Similarly, only the difference between two of the speakers (Lucio Solís Pérez and Cipriano Gomez Yermo) was statistically significant

Table 2.6 Mean values of statistically significant correlates of CONSONANT SUBTYPE I

CONSONANT SUBTYPE	DURATION (VCV)	JITTER (VCV)	SHIMMER (VCV)	DURATION (C)	JITTER (C)	SHIMMER (C)
O	0.362	0.0239	0.104	0.158	0.0549	0.196
S	0.337	0.0175	0.0882	0.0955	0.0197	0.110
E	0.388	0.0231	0.115	0.152	0.0604	0.187
R	0.359	0.0239	0.113	0.105	0.0399	0.190

Table 2.7 Mean values of statistically significant correlates of CONSONANT SUBTYPE II

CONSONANT SUBTYPE	DURATION (VB)	JITTER (VB)	SHIMMER (VB)	DURATION (VA)	JITTER (VA)	SHIMMER (VA)
O	0.100	0.0205	0.101	0.109	0.0182	0.0963
S	0.126	0.0128	0.0820	0.109	0.0160	0.0946
E	0.128	0.0164	0.0955	0.105	0.0252	0.127
R	0.140	0.0156	0.112	0.117	0.0238	0.120

Table 2.8 Mean values of HNR in two analytical domains

CONSONANT SUBTYPE	HNR (VCV)	HNR (C)
O	9.51	4.10
S	12.7	12.8
E	8.18	1.89
R	8.70	6.28

for ejectives and glottalized resonants. This means that speakers do not show the same acoustic correlations in their productions between plain–glottalized consonant pairs and between ejectives and glottalized resonants, making a single acoustic description of these distinctions unfounded.

A multinomial logistic regression was performed to test the correlation of PLACE OF ARTICULATION with the acoustic measures taken across the four domains. This model was also statistically significant, $\chi^2 = 164$, df = 102, $p < .001$. The model explained 83.1% (Nagelkerke R^2) of the differences correlated with the place of articulation. This means the plain–glottalized consonant pairs were distinguished acoustically but that this distinction was also dependent on the place of articulation. Interestingly, in this model, all acoustic measures were shown to be statistically significant predictors in distinguishing at least some places of articulation, though not all places are predicted by the same acoustic measures. For example, coronals and labials can be distinguished from each other based on many acoustic measures in all four analytic domains. The exceptions include measures of MINIMUM F0, MAXIMUM F0, HNR, SPECTRAL TILT in the VCV domain; HNR, INTENSITY, and SPECTRAL TILT in the C domain; MINIMUM F0, MAXIMUM F0, HNR, H1-A2, H1-A3 in the VB domain; and MEAN F0, MINIMUM F0, MAXIMUM F0, HNR, INTENSITY, and H1-A1 in the VA domain—where these two places of articulation are not statically significantly different in these measures. On the other hand, dorsals versus labials, and dorsals versus coronals are correlated with statistically significant differences for all acoustic measures across all four analytic domains. This is considered to mean that based on the acoustic measures taken, Xinkan speakers (as a group) do not signal changes in place of articulation in a single, consistent manner. Rather consonant place of articulation is signaled in a variety of ways acoustically and that any differences between plain and glottalized consonant are not correlated with any specific place of articulation.

In summary, the acoustic measures of voice quality focused on in this investigation suggest that plain consonants can be distinguished from glottalized consonants as two broad natural classes in Guazacapan Xinka based on the duration and spectral tilt of the preceding vowel, and the intensity of the following vowel. Obstruents can be distinguished from sonorants, generally, based on changes in the duration, jitter, and shimmer of both consonant and vowel segments. Ejectives can be distinguished from glottalized resonants based on the measures of harmonics-to-noise ratio, while speaker variation was also significant for the difference between ejectives, plain obstruents, and glottalized resonants. None of the acoustic measures can be uniquely correlated with changes in place of articulation, and all three places are distinguished from each other through combinations of all the acoustic measures used. Importantly, where the spectral tilt, jitter, and shimmer are indications of the plain–glottalized contrasts, the latter might better be described as "laryngealized" consonants. This term reflects the acoustic analysis above and coincides with the way this term has been used by Laver (1980: 126) and Ladefoged (1971: 126). Whatever descriptive label is used, it is clear that these consonants do not have the behaviors associated with canonical glottalized consonants, as presented in the typological literature (see Maddieson 2013).

Based on the patterns described in Section 3, it is certain that Proto-Xinkan also had glottalized consonants, but with the additional information presented in Section 4, it can be suggested that variation in voice quality on adjacent vowels and the consonant itself signaled this distinction. Similar acoustic changes are also noted above for the differences between plain consonant subtypes, thus suggesting that acoustically and possibly articulatorily glottalized consonants are similar to their plain counterparts in many ways. These findings agree with typological research on the acoustics of glottalized consonants. It has been argued that ejectives can be articulated along a continuum of variables (Kingston 1984; Ingram and Rigsby 1987; Warner 1996) and that ejectives with "weaker" articulations are often perceived as plain consonants in regular (that is, not careful) speech (Fallon 2002: 120–2). Similarly, glottalized resonants (in at least some speech styles) are often perceived and perhaps articulated like their plain counterparts (Maddieson 1984; Ladefoged and Maddieson 1996; Bird et al. 2008). Since a canonical glottalic airstream is perhaps incompatible with sonorants (see Fallon 2002: 310, Ladefoged and Maddieson 1996: 80), the effect is more of a glottal stricture than a glottal closure. This stricture results in laryngealization of the consonant and adjacent vowel(s) that can be lost in regular speech. Similarly, research on the timing of articulatory actions for glottalized resonants suggests they can often be distinguished from the plain counterparts based primarily on duration rather than on other specific articulatory gestures (Howe and Pulleyblank 2001; Esling et al. 2005; Bird et al. 2008).

These general acoustic and articulatory properties of glottalized consonants and their specific characteristics in Xinkan suggest an explanation for the discrepancies in the Xinkan descriptive record mentioned in Section 2. Every linguistic description requires an author to reflect on the nature of language structure and create a conceptual framework for language description, and this is no different for the authors of the pre-modern Xinkan descriptions. While perhaps the pre-modern frameworks were different than the one(s) currently used, the pre-modern representations do reveal interesting characteristics of what was perceived during the production of glottalized consonants. The purpose of the next section is to suggest that pre-modern writers heard the acoustic features described above and represented them individually rather than as a group of features defining a natural class. Similarly, the last speakers of the language overused or hypercorrected their articulations of the glottalized consonants because they understood these features as being aspects of idiosyncratic voice quality rather than indications of segmental contrasts.

5. Discussion of the discrepancies in pre-modern Xinkan resources

As mentioned, glottalized consonants have not been represented consistently throughout the descriptive history of the Xinkan languages. For some uses of these resources, this opens up questions about the validity of the various descriptive resources, the history of the glottalized consonants themselves, and the defining characteristics of glottalized consonants in the Xinkan languages (among other things). The easiest way to resolve these discrepancies is to suggest that the past descriptions of Xinkan languages did not represent glottalized consonants because either they were not comprehensive and thus were missing information, or to esteem the authors of some of the resources as being deficient in their skills or abilities in describing languages, that is, language descriptions are only as good as the data collected and the analytical skills of the linguist. From both of these perspectives, due to recent linguistic advancements, the later descriptions are simply more accurate and have greater value. However, others have remarked on the sophistication of Latin American colonial grammar writers in appreciating the unique sounds they encountered and inventing effective modes of representation for them—including glottalized consonants (Smith-Stark 2005). Consequently, this chapter suggests that in a context where orthography as a reflection of "correct pronunciations" was taken seriously, such dismissals are not fair evaluations. When the phonological and phonetic properties of Xinkan glottalized consonants, as described above, are considered it can be seen that older descriptions of the languages may accurately reflect some of their properties (even if they are not always overtly indicated as important contrasts). Appreciating pre-modern Xinkan resources from this perspective strengthens the importance of glottalized consonants in Proto-Xinkan and throughout the life cycle of these languages.

While there were often no distinct representations for glottalized consonants in the pre-modern Xinkan resources, this is not completely unexpected. Glottalized consonants are unusual when compared to the consonants in more-familiar European languages such as English, Spanish, or German—the native languages of the authors of the Xinkan pre-modern descriptions. The authors of some of the older descriptions might simply have matched the glottalized consonants to the closest representational equivalents in these more familiar languages. This is likely what occurred in scientifically unsophisticated treatments of the languages, such as found in Morales (1812, see Rogers 2020). However, for individuals with a more detailed conceptual framework for the languages they were encountering and who were using this framework for language description (the majority of the pre-modern Xinkan resources), the choice of representations for the glottalized consonants is justified by the acoustic analysis above. This analysis showed that for many of the traditional conceptualizations of consonants, such as voicing, place of articulation, and manner of articulation, glottalized consonants in Xinkan are identical to their plain counterparts. Such similarities make it difficult to perceive a contrast between the two consonant types within traditional descriptive models, and a single orthographic representation for both consonant types seems adequate. Moreover, there is a tendency crosslinguistically for glottalized consonants to occur in an inventory only when their plain counterpart is also present (Greenberg 1970; Maddieson 1984, 2013). By some analyses, this makes plain consonants the unmarked or default value for any specific consonant quality. If the pre-modern authors could not determine which characteristics were essential for defining and then describing glottalized consonants, using representations for their plain counterparts are a reflection of what was understood within their conceptualizations of language.

Nevertheless, as seen in Section 3, not all of the pre-modern authors represented all glottalized consonants as their plain counterparts. Maldonado de Matos (c.1773), the earliest Xinkan description, for example, includes representations for [k'] and [ts'] and no other glottalized consonant. While these representations are not consistently made throughout this work, this reflects a noted typological tendency in the organization of sound inventories that have glottalized consonants. Typologically, ejectives are said to occur more often in the back of the articulatory space (that is, velar and dorsal) where at least one of these sounds occurs, that is, [k'] (Greenberg 1970; Javkin 1977; Fordyce 1980; Maddieson 1984; Henton et al. 1992). A thorough discussion of the motivations for this implication is beyond the scope of the chapter, but the articulatory and acoustic explanations for this tendency are convincing. These explanations focus on the shape of the vocal tract, the process of articulation, and the ease of perception for glottalized consonants as important factors in the preference for ejectives to be produced in the back part of the mouth (Wang 1968; Javkin 1977; Fordyce 1980). That is, glottalized consonants produced further back in the mouth are simply easier to perceive—making [k'] the most prototypical type of ejective, with coronals like [ts'] second. As shown above, moreover, both [k'] and [ts'] in Xinkan occur often (though not always) with the canonical double occlusion characteristics of glottalized consonants (while none of the other glottalized consonants do). Even in repetitions of the same word for the same speaker in the audio corpus, it would seem that sometimes these sounds are ejective and others times they are not. This leads to an obvious descriptive challenge that could be resolved by simply representing each sound the way it was heard. This result is most, if not all, of the glottalized consonants being represented as their plain counterparts and with variations in the representation of [k'] and [ts'] as in Maldonado de Matos (c.1773)—see below for reasons why [ts'] might also have been easier to perceive. In hindsight, without knowing the reasons for this choice, it would appear that the representations are inconsistent and incorrect, but in reality, they are reflections of the articulatory and acoustic properties of these sounds.

Other pre-modern descriptions of Xinkan include other glottalized consonants than those just mentioned, but choose representations that match the acoustic properties discovered above in other ways. For example, the representations in Berendt (1875) only include [j'], [t'], and [n']. As mentioned above, [j'] is often articulated with greater laryngeal tension over other possible characteristics making a contrast between the [j] and [j'] easier to perceive (and Berendt's representation evidence of his descriptive abilities). It is unclear why [t'] and [n'] might be included in this short wordlist, but it is clear the author was perceiving some distinction in these sounds. Similarly, Calderón (1908) only includes [ts'] word-initially. This analytical domain was not included in the study above, but it can be mentioned that in the audio corpus, [ts'] word-initially is only ever articulated and perceived with the canonical double articulation expected of ejectives (the only glottalized consonant that exhibits this consistency). Lastly, Fernández (1938), even though the shortness of this resource explains why not all of the glottalized consonants are not found there, does include consistent representations of some glottalized resonants as geminate consonants. This seems to be an intuitive representation when considered from the perspective of the acoustic descriptions above. There it was shown that one of the key characteristics in distinguishing glottalized resonants from plain sonorants is consonant duration. Representing glottalized resonants as geminate consonants simply focuses on this above other possible characteristics.

Consequently, it is suggested that there is evidence that the glottalized consonants existed throughout the history of the Xinkan languages. And that their representations (while not matching modern conceptualizations) reflect some of the core acoustic properties found in their productions. In fact, as a sort of conclusion, it is possible that the same variation in the production of glottalized consonants noted above was in use during the periods of the pre-modern descriptions and that this variation is reflected in their choice of representations. Thus glottalized consonants have always been a part of the Xinkan languages and that they exhibited similar morphophonological patterns to what is now understood for the language family.

It would be incorrect to assume that because the pre-modern descriptions seem to reflect some of the current acoustic characteristics of Xinkan glottalized consonants and their typological generalizations, we know more about them than we actually do. The correspondence between the collections of acoustic descriptions and the typological generalizations and the pre-modern descriptions seems accurate, but with continued research, these generalizations might need to be reconsidered or restated. All that can be said now is that our current understanding of many of the aspects of glottalized consonants in Xinkan, specifically and typologically more generally, are reflected in the pre-modern representations of Xinkan glottalized consonants.

I want to point out that the acoustic variations studied above can have multiple functions in speech. Phonetic changes like those correlated to the plain–glottalized consonant pairs in Xinkan in Section 4, can affect sound segments individually or take scope over a longer sequence of sounds (what Laver 1980: 2–4 refers to as the distinction between "phonetic segments" and "phonetic settings"). That is, voice quality changes are characteristic of segmental contrasts in some languages and as a non-contrastive voice quality setting in others (in some studies the latter is correlated with age). This creates a potential ambiguity in the perception of the Xinkan consonants, in that, for non-native speakers, it is unclear which of the functions these voice quality changes might have had in the Xinkan languages. That is, without any overt indication (such as practice through regular intergenerational transmission) it would be difficult to perceive the acoustic properties studied above as contrasting phonetic segments or as indicating phonetic characteristics of the voice quality of individual speakers. This is important both for understanding some of the speech patterns of the last speakers and the importance of glottalized consonants in revitalization efforts.

In the speech of some of the last speakers, glottalized consonants became a salient feature even in places not predicted by Xinkan grammatical rules (see Campbell and Muntzel 1989; Sachse 2010; Rogers 2016a). This overuse, or hypercorrection, of glottalized consonants in Xinkan pronunciations has been suggested as being due to imperfect learning or language attrition. However, I would like to take this characterization one step further and suggest that this imperfect learning/attrition included the loss of fundamental competencies which indicate whether the acoustic changes measured above indicating the contrast between plain and glottalized consonants are segmentally contrastive or indications of changes in voice quality. That is, some of the last Xinkan speakers used more glottalized consonants because the segmental contrasts between plain and glottalized consonants—which were signaled by changes in the larynx—were reanalyzed as setting contrasts. Such setting contrasts often spread from a single segment to a larger stretch of speech—such as nasality or lip-rounding (Laver 1980: 2–4). The suggestion, then, is that some speakers were unaware of the boundaries for the laryngeal changes and produced them as a setting rather than a segmental contrast. Perceptually, because of the acoustic correlates of glottalized consonants in Xinkan, this would result in a greater number of glottalized consonants being produced.

Similarly, glottalized consonants have become a salient feature in developing a Xinkan identity in revalorization and revitalization efforts (see Rogers 2016b). These sounds are understood to be unique in the region, and consequently are part of a foundation for a unique cultural-linguistic identity. Parallel to these developing identities, language revitalization efforts that have the goal of helping community members learn about their heritage languages, are driven by second-language learners of Xinkan, who understand the acoustic characteristics of glottalized consonants in the audio recordings to be examples of changes in individual voice quality (for example, due to age or gender) rather than being segmentally contrastive. Since the glottalized consonants do not reflect the canonical descriptions of laryngeal movement on segments, this creates skepticism as to their importance for the use of these languages.

In response to this, it can be stated that the discussion above does suggest that glottalized consonants are important in all resources of the language, even if they are represented in diverse ways. However, in every resource, the presence of glottalized consonants is indicated through the representation of only a subset of some of the acoustic characteristics that they share as a natural class. This means that in revitalization materials they need to be segmentally represented for a complete description of the Xinkan languages, but that their articulation is potentially ambiguous and definitely not to be equated with the canonical descriptions crosslinguistically. They are consonants where changes in the larynx in a variety of ways distinguish them from their plain counterparts, thus underlining the importance of not considering descriptive resources as prescriptive standards, but instead the importance of revitalization as the creation of a new and variable language (rather than adherence to a former state of the language).

While it would be overly ambitious (and perhaps speculative) to suggest that similar conclusions to the ones mentioned here are possible in other languages without a more systematic comparison, two general comments about the practice of language documentation and the valuation of older materials do seem in order. First, when doing salvage linguistics the available language documentation becomes paramount as the only record of a language. When it is no longer possible to create or collect language data, such as the phonetic information missing for the Xinkan languages, the available documentation can usefully be used to suggest how any gaps might be filled. Of course, this will not be applicable to all scenarios, but suggests a viable option for using documented resources to recover "lost" information. The quality and quantity of the available information should never be discounted just because they do not immediately seem to address a specific line of inquiry. Second, the linguist engaged in salvage linguistic work may find useful generalizations about languages "hidden" in the documentary record when those records are considered in light of known cross-linguistic possibilities. This pairing of cross-linguistic generalizations to the available information can potentially increase our understanding of language change, the possibilities for the architectures of (universal and specific) grammar, and a greater appreciation of the languages by the speakers or heritage speakers of language communities.

Notes

1. I would like to thank the editors of this volume for giving us a chance to celebrate Lyle's work. His positive influence on my own thinking and research agenda (and that of many others) cannot be overstated. Specifically related to the content of this chapter, I want to acknowledge the tremendous efforts Lyle and Terry Kaufman have made in documenting the Xinkan languages, without which we would know next to nothing.
2. This work and the dissemination of the Xinkan materials was partially supported by NSF grant 0605368 as described in Rogers (2016a: 13).
3. As a means of comparison, ejectives are estimated to occur in 16–20% of all languages (Ruhlen 1976, 1991; Maddieson 1984, 2013; Catford 1992; Henton et al. 1992; Ladefoged and Maddieson 1996). Glottalized resonants are estimated to occur in 5–6% of the world's languages (Maddieson 2013). These frequency statistics do not represent that for at least some languages with glottalized consonants, there are sometimes two series. Glottalized resonants, for example, are overwhelmingly paired with ejectives in a language's segment inventory, as in the Xinkan languages (Maddieson 1984, 2013).
4. Phonetic transcriptions are given using the International Phonetic Alphabet (IPA), except for [ł] (here meant as a voiceless lateral approximate, not a fricative, but is used for typographical issues) and [š] a voiceless retroflex alveopalatal fricative (for which the IPA does not have a symbol).
5. The Parra letters were invented by Francisco de la Parra, a Franciscan friar in the sixteenth century (c.1500–60). De la Parra used these graphemes in his Vocabulario Trilingue Guatemalateco, which has been lost. However, these letters were hugely influential and all subsequent Guatemalan grammarians employed them in their descriptions of Mayan languages, though not always consistently.
6. "Instead of those two quatrillos [that is, two of the Parra letters], I will use letters from our alphabet, even though geminated, to represent a very rough <k>. This has been done because so seeing a reader two letters with the same pronunciation

and nature next to each other, the [pronunciation] is stronger than either letter on its own because if the [letter] <c> represents one sound, and the [letter] <k> represents two, combining them, together they represent three sounds or better because they are united they are stronger." (translation mine)

7. All data in this chapter are taken from Rogers (2016a) unless otherwise noted.
8. Sachse (2010) suggested that perhaps the data from Morales (1812) might indicate that orthographically [k] was represented variously as <g> or <q> and that [k'] was represented as <c>. However, this is not generally true for the document. Each of the orthographic conventions are used where cognate forms now have both [k] and [k']. Rather the orthographic choices seem to be following Spanish orthographic conventions for representing [k] in use at the time (Rogers 2020).
9. See Rogers (2020) for a complete presentation of this text.
10. This source has been preserved in a manuscript by Carl Harman Berendt (1875) and was also published in Brinton (1885).
11. Audio for these recordings can be heard at <www.languageconservation.org>, Projects > Xinkan (last accessed August 17, 2021).

References

Bird, Sonya, Marion Caldecott, Fiona Campbell, Bryan Gick, and Patricia A. Shaw. 2008. Oral laryngeal timing in glottalised resonants. *Journal of Phonetics* 36.492–507.

Berendt, Carl Herman. 1875. *Vocabularios de la lengua xinca de Sinacatan por D. Juan Gavarrete y de Yupiltepeque y Jalapa por D. Sebastian Valdez, cura de Jutiapa.* Manuscript.

Brinton, Daniel G. 1885. On the language and ethnologic position of the Xinca Indians in Guatemala. *Philosophical Society* 22.89–97.

Calderón, Eustorjio. 1908. *Estudios lingüísticos, vol. 1, Las lenguas (Sinca) de Yupiltepeque y del barrio de norte de Chiquimulilla en Guatemala.* Guatemala: Tipografía Sánchez.

Campbell, Lyle. 1973. On glottalic consonants. *International Journal of American Linguistics* 39.44–6.

Campbell, Lyle, Terrence Kaufman, and Thomas C. Smith-Stark. 1986. Meso-America as a linguistic area. *Language* 62.530–70.

Campbell, Lyle, and Martha Muntzel. 1989. The structural consequence of language death: Investigating obsolescence. In *Studies in language contraction and death*, ed. by Nancy Dorian, 181–96. Cambridge: Cambridge University Press.

Carmack, Robert M. 1973. *Quichean civilization: the ethnohistoric, ethnographic, and archaeological sources.* Berkeley: University of California Press.

Catford, J. C. 1992. Caucasian phonetics and general phonetics. *Caucasologie et mythologie compare: Actes du Colloque international du CNRS* in IVᵉ Colloque de Caucasologie (Sévres, 27–9 juin 1988), ed by Catherin Paris, 193–216. Paris: Peeters.

Consejo del Pueblo Xinka de Guatemala (COPXIG). 2004. *Gramática y diccionario xinka: Una descripción e introducción al idioma.* Chiquimulilla/Santa Rosa, Guatemala: CECI.

Esling, John H., Katherine E. Fraser, and Jimmy G. Harris. 2005. Glottal stop, glottalized resonants, and pharyngeals: A reinterpretaton with evidence from a laryngiscopic study of Nuuchahnulth (Nootka). *Journal of Phonetics* 33.383–410.
Fallon, Paul D. 2002. *The synchronic and diachronic phonology of ejectives*. New York: Routledge.
Fernández, Jesus. 1938. Diccionario del Sinca. *Anales de la Sociedad de Geografía e Historia de Guatemala* 15.84–95, 359–66.
Fordyce, James F. 1980. On the nature of glottalic and laryngealized consonant and vowel systems. *UCLA Working Papers in Phonetics*, 50.150–6.
Gavarette, D. Juan, and Sebastian Valdez. 1868. *Vocabularios de la lengua Xinca de Sinacantan y de Yupiltepeque y Jalapa*. Philadelphia: Berendt Linguistic Library.
Greenberg, Joseph. 1970. Some generalizations concerning glottalic consonants, especially implosives. *International Journal of American Linguistics* 36.123–45.
Henton, Caroline, Peter Ladefoged, and Ian Maddieson. 1992. Stops in the world's languages. *Phonetica* 49.65–101.
Howe, Darin, and Douglas Pulleyblank. 2001. Patterns and timing of glottalization. *Phonology* 18.45–80.
Ingram, J., and B. Rigsby. 1987. Glottalic stops in Gitksan: An acoustic analysis. *Proceedings of the XIth International Conference of Phonetic Sciences* 2.134–7.
Javkin, Hector. 1977. Towards a phonetic explanation for universal preferences in implosives and ejectives. *Annual Meeting of the Berkeley Linguistics Society* 3.559–65.
Kingston, John Clayton. 1984. *The phonetics and phonology of the timing of oral and glottal events*. University of California dissertation.
Ladefoged, Peter. 1971. *Preliminaries to linguistic phonetics*. Chicago: University of Chicago Press.
Ladefoged, Peter, and Ian Maddieson. 1996. *The sounds of the world's languages*. Malden, MA: Blackwell Publishing.
Laver, John. 1980. *The phonetic description of voice quality*. Cambridge Studies in Linguistics 31. Cambridge/New York: Cambridge University Press.
Lehmann, Walter. 1920. *Zentral-Amerika*. Berlin: D. Reimer.
McArthur, Harry. 1966. Xinca. In *Languages of Guatemala*, vol. 23, ed. by M. K. Mayers, 309–12. Berlin/The Hague: Mouton de Gruyter.
McQuown, Norman A. 1948. *Vocabulario Xinca recopilado en Chiquimulilla del 29 al 30 de noviembre (1948) con Mauricio García y Desiderio García González*. Microfilm Collection of Manuscripts on Cultural Anthropology, no. 296, series LVI. Chicago: University of Chicago Library, 1977.
Maddieson, Ian. 1984. *Patterns of sounds*. Cambridge: Cambridge University Press.
Maddieson, Ian. 2013. Glottalized consonants. In *The world atlas of language structure*, ed. by Matthew Haspelmath, S. Dryer, David Gil, and Bernard Comrie, 34–7. Oxford: Oxford University Press.
Maldonado de Matos, Manuel. *c*.1773. *Arte de la lengua Szinca con algunas reflexiones criticas al Arte K'akchiquel*.
Morales, Hermenegildo. 1812. *Proclama traducida del castellano al idioma Zeefe (que se habla en algunas partes del arzobispado de Guatemala) por Dr. Hermenegildo Morales, Presibtero Indio*. Manuscript. Archivo General de Indias, legajo 943. Sevilla.

Rogers, Chris. 2010. *A comparative grammar of Xinkan.* University of Utah Ph.D. dissertation.
Rogers, Chris. 2014. Xinkan verb categorization: Morphosyntactic marking on intransitive verbs. *International Journal of American Linguistics*, 80.371–98.
Rogers, Chris. 2016a. *The use and development of the Xinkan languages.* Austin: University of Texas Press.
Rogers, Chris. 2016b. Indigenous authenticity as a goal of language documentation and revitalization: Addressing the motivations in the Xinkan community. In *Language documentation and revitalization: Latin American contexts*, ed. by Gabriela Pérez Báez, Chris Rogers, and Jorge Emilio Rosés Labrada, 247–72. Berlin: Mouton de Gruyter.
Rogers, Chris. 2020. La traducción en xinka de la "Proclama a los habitantes de Ultramar de 1812." *Tlalocan* XXV.215–86.
Ruhlen, Merrit. 1976. *A guide to the languages of the world.* Stanford: Stanford Language Universals Project.
Ruhlen, Merrit. 1991. *A guides to the world's languages. Vol. 1: Classification with a postscript on recent developments.* Stanford: Stanford University Press.
Sachse, Frauke. 2010. *Reconstructive description of eighteenth-century Xinka grammar.* Utrecht University dissertation.
Schumann Gálvez, Otto. 1967. *Xinca de Guazacapán.* Mexico: Escuela Nacional de Antropología e Historia.
Smailus, Ortwin. 1989. *Vocabulario en lengua castellana y guatemalteca que se llama Cakchiquel Chi: análisis gramatical y lexicológico del Cakchiquel colonial según un antiguo diccionario anónimo.* Hamburg: Wayasbah.
Smith-Stark, Thomas C. 2005. Phonological description in New Spain. In *Missionary linguistics II: Lingüística misionera II: orthography and phonology: selected papers from the Second International Conference on Missionary Linguistics, São Paulo, 10-13 March 2004*, ed. by Otto Zwartjes and Maria Cristina Salles Altman. Amsterdam, Philadelphia: J. Benjamins.
Wang, William S.-Y. 1968. The basis of speech. *Project on Linguistics Analysis, Reports Second Series* (4). Phonology Lab at UC Berkeley.
Warner, Natasha. 1996. Acoustic characteristics of ejectives in Ingush. Paper presented at the *Fourth I I nternational Conference on Spoken Language Processing.* October 5, 1996, Philadelphia.

3

Variation and Change in the Distribution of *-(V)n and *-(V)w in Kaqchikel

Raina Heaton

1. Introduction

The form and function of antipassive and antipassive-like constructions in Mayan languages have been of formal and comparative interest to Mayanists for decades, notably since Thomas Smith-Stark's seminal paper in 1978 on "facts and fictions" about Mayan antipassives. This chapter builds on this tradition on two fronts: first, it revisits the descriptive data on the forms and functions of antipassive-related voice suffixes in Mayan languages to provide a more complete historical picture of how these morphemes evolved within the family. Second, it presents new synchronic data on Kaqchikel which track a merger in progress through a number of Kaqchikel dialects. In the dialects where this merger is taking place, a formerly robust morphological distinction is being neutralized, a process which is reflected in historical mergers elsewhere in the family. In a broader view, this type of investigation furthers our understanding of language change, and highlights some of the contributions that ongoing language documentation can make to historical linguistics.

Section 1 provides background information on the two markers that are the focus of this chapter and the various constructions in which they appear. Section 2 provides details on these markers and constructions in each branch of the Mayan language family, and discusses proposed reconstructions for the two markers in Proto-Mayan. Section 3 presents new data which demonstrate that a merger is taking place in some Kaqchikel dialects, and Section 4 concludes. Data on Kaqchikel are from the author's fieldwork unless otherwise cited, while data on other Mayan languages are assembled from the literature.[1]

1.1 Forms

There are two verbal suffixes that consistently appear as markers of antipassive and antipassive-like constructions in Mayan languages. These have been reconstructed in Smith-Stark (1978: 179) as *-(V)w and *-(V)n, in Dayley (1983: 86–7) as *-w and *-(V)n, and in Kaufman (1986) as *-(o)w and *-(o-)an, which for the sake of convenience will be referred to here as *-(V)w and *-(V)n (see Section 2.8 for comments on these reconstructions). The forms of these two morphemes do not vary greatly among the Mayan languages that have them; as the parentheses imply, sometimes a vowel is present, and that vowel may be short or long (for example, -oon in Tz'utujil vs. -Vn in Sakapultek). *-(V)w cognates often begin with /w/ rather than ending with it, for example -wi or -waj versus -w or -o(w) (see Section 2), although in some cases this is because final -i or -a gets interpreted as an (in)transitive morpheme by some but as part of the *-(V)w morpheme by others (see Craig 1979; Zavala 1997; Mateo Toledo 2008; Coon 2019).

The most important preliminary note with respect to marking is that in many Mayan languages that have them, the distribution of *-(V)w and *-(V)n is reliant in part on transitive verb class. Mayan languages make a distinction between "root" transitive verbs (RTVs) and "derived" transitive verbs (DTVs), which is manifested morphologically in a variety of ways (Dayley 1983; Coon 2016). RTVs—also known as "monosyllabic" transitives since Mayan roots are often CVC syllables—are marked with either *-(V)n or *-(V)w in antipassive-like constructions. "Derived" or "polysyllabic" transitive verbs are morphologically more complex and are often derived from other word classes (for example, Kaqchikel -b'ix-aj "to sing (a song)" from -b'ix "song"). While in some Mayan languages DTVs take the same antipassive voice suffixes as RTVs (for example, -waj in Q'anjob'al (Mateo Toledo 2008: 73)), in about half of the languages they do not. Indeed, DTVs in Ch'orti' take -(y)an in the antipassive, as opposed to -on, -o or -ma with RTVs (Quizar 2020), and almost all K'ichean languages mark DTVs with -n (generally assumed to be a reflex of *-(V)n), regardless of the construction. The difference between RTV and DTV morphological marking is clear for example in Tz'utujil, as shown in (1) versus (2). The syntactic context in both examples is the same, the only difference is the type of verb root involved, which precipitates the use of a different voice suffix (here -ow vs. -n).

Tz'utujil (Dayley 1985: 352)
(1) Root transitive verb with -ow:
Naq x–Ø–sok–**ow**–i
WH   COMPL–3SG.ABS–hurt–***(V)w**–INTR
"Who/what hurt him/her?"

(2) Derived transitive verb with -n:
Naq x–Ø–b'ojte–**n**   eel   ja   wuuj
WH   COMPL–3SG.ABS–carry.roll.of–***(V)n**   away   DET   paper
"Who carried away the roll of paper?"

1.2 Functions

It is difficult to propose a comprehensive functional description for *-(V)n and *-(V)w in Mayan languages other than to say they are associated with antipassive-like functions, namely focusing the agent and/or removing or demoting the patient of a transitive verb. Most Mayan languages have several different constructions which serve these types of functions. Difficulties in functional characterization are related to the fact that (a) not all Mayan languages have all of the constructions which take *-(V)n and *-(V)w in other Mayan languages, (b) which of the two markers appears with a given construction varies by language, and (c) not all Mayan languages have reflexes of both or either *-(V)n or *-(V)w. As such, the functions associated with *-(V)n versus *-(V)w are not uniform across the family, which complicates reconstruction (see Section 2.8).

With that said, there are three antipassive(-like) constructions which are traditionally differentiated in the Mayan literature: the absolutive antipassive, the agent focus construction, and incorporating construction. All three are typically indicated by a reflex of *-(V)n or *-(V)w in the Mayan languages which have them, although some languages have innovated new markers (Huastec, for example), or do not have a morphological marker for the construction (as in agent focus in Yucatec).

Absolutive antipassives are intransitive in that the verb only cross-references the agent and the patient may be completely absent, or in some languages it may be expressed in an oblique phrase. Absolutive antipassives generally have a habitual or durative interpretation common to antipassive constructions in other languages, and tend to appear most frequently with verbs for canonical actions. The following example from Ixil illustrates a typical Mayan absolutive antipassive, where the verb is marked with -on, a reflex of *-(V)n, and the patient can be expressed optionally in an oblique phrase, as shown in (3b).

Ixil (Ayres 1983: 27)
(3) a. Kat a–q'os in (Transitive)
    ASP 2SG.ERG–hit 1SG.ABS
    "You hit me."
  b. Kat q'os–**on** axh (s wi7) (Absolutive)
    ASP hit–***(V)n** 2SG.ABS OBL 1SG
    "You hit me."

Agent focus constructions are antipassive-like in that the verb only cross-references one argument; however, that argument may be either the agent or the patient, depending on the language and/or the context. The agent focus construction exists primarily to circumvent syntactic restrictions on ergative arguments, and therefore it does not appear outside a handful of specific syntactic contexts (see Aissen 2017 for a recent overview). An example of an agent focus clause in Sakapultek is given in (4), where the construction is marked by -iw, a reflex of *-(V)w. Notice that in (4b) the verb cross-references the patient, which is not characteristic of a traditional antipassive (see Janic and Witzlack-Makarevich 2021).

Sakapultek (Du Bois 1981: 172, 248)
(4) a. K–in–a:–č'ay–aŋ (Transitive)
    INCOMPL–1SG.ABS–2SG.ERG–hit–TR
    "You hit me."

b. Ne: wa?   š–in–č'iy–**iw**–ek   (Agent focus)
    WH   DEM   COMPL–1SG.ABS–hit–***(V)w**–INTR
    "Who was it that hit me?"

Finally, the incorporating construction in most Mayan languages is a morphologically intransitive construction where a non-specific patient, unmodified by adjectives, classifiers or other elements, appears immediately following the verb.[2] In some languages its use is required with certain types of patients, while in others its use is largely optional. The following is an example of the incorporating construction in Akatek, which is marked by -*wi* (5b), a reflex of *-(V)w. Additionally, the patient immediately follows the verb and does not take its customary classifier.

Akatek (Zavala 1997: 456)
(5) a. X–Ø–s–nooch–toj   no'   txitam   ixim   aan
         COMPL–3SG.ABS–3SG.ERG–eat.biting–DIR CLF   pig   CLF   corncob
         "The pig ate the corncob."
    b. X–Ø–nooch–**wi**   aan   no'   txitam
         COMPL–3SG.ABS–eat.biting–***(V)w**   corncob CLF   pig
         "The pig was eating the corncob."

These three constructions will be referenced in the following sections to describe the differences in the functional distribution of *-(V)n and *-(V)w across the Mayan language family. A more in-depth discussion of Mayan antipassive(-like) constructions and their relationship to cross-linguistic definitions of antipassives can be found in Heaton (2021).

2. Distribution across Mayan languages

In order to get a sense of the historical development of *-(V)w and *-(V)n, this section explores the distribution of their reflexes across the Mayan language family. The Mayan language family is composed of approximately thirty languages; see Campbell (2016) for a recent classification. K'ichean and Mamean languages make up the eastern branch of the family, while Greater Q'anjob'alan and Cholan-Tseltalan compose the western branch. Yucatecan, Western and Eastern Mayan constitute "core" or Central Mayan, with Huastecan as the other primary branch.

2.1 K'ichean languages

The K'ichean subgroup consists of ten closely related languages. For the six languages that constitute "K'ichean Proper," *-(V)n and *-(V)w have a very similar distribution: all six mark the absolutive antipassive with *-(V)n and agent focus with *-(V)w. For those languages described as having an incorporating construction, that construction is also marked with *-(V)w. Also, although all other K'ichean languages use a reflex of *-(V)n with DTVs, Sipakapense is apparently an outlier in that all agent focus verbs take -*w* (*-(V)w) with both RTVs and DTVs (Barrett 1999: 112).[3]

These languages also have an additional construction which is like agent focus in that it only appears in certain focused agent syntactic contexts, but the patient appears optionally in an oblique phrase. This construction is marked by *-(V)w in all six languages, and is illustrated in (6b) from Kaqchikel where the reflex of *-(V)w is -o.

Kaqchikel
(6) a. X–at–in–ch'äy
    COMPL–2SG.ABS–1SG.ERG–hit
    "I hit you."
 b. Ja rïn x–i–ch'ay–o   aw–ichin
    FOC 1SG COMPL–1SG.ABS–hit–*(V)w   2SG–OBL
    "I hit you."

Although this construction looks similar to an absolutive antipassive as described in Section 1.2 above, this construction differs from the absolutive antipassive in that it takes a reflex of *-(V)w and not *-(V)n, and it cannot be used if the agent is not focused. Compare (6b) with the absolutive antipassive in Kaqchikel in (7), which additionally does not permit the patient to be expressed in an oblique phrase (see Heaton 2017: 324–6).

Kaqchikel
(7) Y–i–ch'ay–on   (rïn)
    INCOMPL–1SG.ABS–hit–*(V)n 1SG
    "I fight (habitually)."

In much of the earlier descriptive literature on K'ichean languages, the construction in (6b) and agent focus are often described as variants of the same construction, either with or without oblique realization of the internal argument (see for example Smith-Stark 1978: 170, Dayley 1983: 17, Stiebels 2006: 529). To avoid conflating this *-(V)w-marked antipassive in K'ichean with either agent focus or the absolutive antipassive, I refer to the structure in (6b) as an "oblique antipassive."

Outside K'ichean Proper, Uspantek follows the same pattern described above for other K'ichean languages where a reflex of *-(V)n appears with absolutive antipassives and a reflex of *-(V)w appears with agent focus and incorporating constructions. In contrast, Poqomam and Poqomchi' both use -w (*-(V)w) for absolutive antipassives, agent focus, and the oblique antipassive pattern illustrated in (6b). It is unclear if Poqomam and Poqomchi' have incorporating constructions. Q'eqchi' likewise has only one of the two suffixes (-o, *-(V)w), which appears with the incorporating construction and the oblique antipassive. Q'eqchi' does not have an absolutive antipassive or agent focus. For an in-depth discussion of the properties of the constructions which take *-(V)n or *-(V)w in K'ichean languages see Heaton (2017: 322–73).

2.2 Mamean languages

The Mamean subgroup includes four languages—Ixil, Mam, Awakatek, and Tektitek (Teko)—and is part of the eastern branch of the Mayan language family. All of these languages only have reflexes of *-(V)n with both RTVs and DTVs, and no evidence of *-(V)w. In Mam and Tektitek, -n is the marker for the absolutive antipassive, which allows the patient to appear in an oblique phrase. This construction can be used in agent-extraction syntactic contexts, although there is no separate agent focus construction. In contrast, Ixil and Awakatek do have agent focus constructions in addition to absolutive antipassives. However, agent focus in both languages is also marked by a reflex of *-(V)n. An example of agent focus in Awakatek is given in (8b), and the construction is marked by -oon.

Awakatek (Larsen 1983: 128–9)
(8) a. Ja   Ø–x–tx'aj   xna7n   b'u7y   jaalu7
       PROX.PST 3SG.ABS–3SG.ERG–wash   woman   rag   now/today
       "The woman washed the rag today."
    b. Xna7n   n–Ø–tx'aj–**oon**   b'u7y   jaalu7
       woman   PROX.PST–3SG.ABS–wash–*(V)n   rag   now/today
       "It was the woman who washed the rag today."

For Mamean languages where data are available, reflexes of *-(V)n also mark incorporating constructions. While Mam has a fairly standard incorporating construction used with a limited set of non-specific patients, Ixil only has something similar to the incorporating construction in the Chajul dialect, where all third person patients of agent focus verbs must be unmodified nouns (Ayres 1983: 37). As such, while Mamean languages have the various syntactic contexts in which antipassive and antipassive-like constructions appear in Mayan languages, all of these constructions are marked by reflexes of *-(V)n.

2.3 Greater Q'anjob'alan languages

The Greater Q'anjob'alan subgroup contains both the core Q'anjob'alan languages as well as Chuj and Tojolabal, for a total of six languages. Greater Q'anjob'alan and Cholan-Tseltalan together make up Western Mayan (Campbell 2017: 44). Q'anjob'al, Akatek, Popti' (Jakaltek), and Chuj all have essentially the same pattern when it comes to the distribution of *-(V)n and *-(V)w across the various antipassive-like constructions. First, all four languages have agent focus constructions marked by a reflex of *-(V)n with both RTVs and DTVs. In most if not all of these languages, this suffix may also appear on verbs in non-finite embedded clauses, a use dubbed the "crazy antipassive" by Kaufman (1990).[4] An example of -on appearing in non-finite contexts in Q'anjob'al is given in (9b).

Q'anjob'al (Coon et al. 2014: 180, 190)
(9) a. Max–ach   y–il–a'   (Transitive)
       ASP–2.ABS 3.ERG–see–TR
       "She saw you."
    b. Chi   uj   [hach   y–il–**on**–i]   ("Crazy antipassive")
       ASP   able   2.ABS   3.ERG–see–*(V)n–INTR
       "She can see you."

All four languages also have incorporating constructions and absolutive antipassives marked by reflexes of (*-(V)w), although Chuj is alone in using -an (*-(V)n) with DTVs in absolutive antipassive constructions. In all four languages, -wi is the marker for the incorporating construction, which is more productive in these languages than in most Eastern Mayan languages. In Chuj -wi can also appear with nouns, positionals, and unaccusative intransitive roots (Coon 2019). The absolutive antipassive in Q'anjob'al and Chuj is marked by -waj, whereas the reflex in Popti' is -wa, and either -wi or -wa in Akatek.

The data available on antipassive-type constructions in Tojolabal are not as rich as they are for other Mayan languages. However, Tojolabal does have an absolutive antipassive which does not allow the patient to be expressed in an oblique phrase. The marker for this construction is -wan with RTVs, which, like the Chuj reflex, can also form intransitive verbs from nominal roots. There is some evidence that suggests that -wan is actually -w-Vn (Furbee Losee 1976: 66), in which case it is possible it is actually a combination of both *-(V)w and *-(V)n. A reflex of *-(V)n also appears with DTVs in absolutive antipassive constructions in Tojolabal.

Mocho' is unlike the other Greater Q'anjob'alan languages in that it appears to only have a reflex of *-(V)n and not *-(V)w. Mocho' only has a single suffix -o:n which serves absolutive antipassive, incorporating, reflexive/reciprocal, and non-finite functions, and additionally derives intransitive verbs from nouns, like in Chuj and Tojolabal. Palosaari (2011) groups these functions together under the label "middle." Mocho' also lacks the use of relational nouns with passives and antipassives, so in some cases an absolutive antipassive-looking verb appears with a juxtaposed, non-oblique patient, as in (10b).

Mocho' (Palosaari 2011: 195, 225)
(10) a. Ka:b–e pa:lach k–lo'o–qe i:xì:m (Transitive)
         two–NUM male.turkey POT–eat–3PL corn
         "Two male turkeys will be eating corn."
     b. Jan lo'–o:n we ù:x (*-(V)n construction with non-oblique patient)
         PRO eat–*(V)n DET meat
         "He ate the meat."

Both Mocho' and Tojolabal lack agent focus constructions.

2.4 Cholan-Tseltalan languages

As the name suggests, the Cholan-Tseltalan branch encompasses both Cholan and Tseltalan languages. There are four Cholan languages, Ch'ol, Chontal, Ch'orti', and the long-unspoken Ch'olti'. While Cholan languages have reflexes of *-(V)w and *-(V)n, they are not typical in that they mostly exist with a limited set of verbs in nominalized or other non-finite contexts. Ch'ol has a suffix -oñ, a reflex of *-(V)n, which has been called the "absolutive antipassive" (Vázquez Álvarez 2011: 306) even though -oñ only appears as part of a nominalized predicate functioning as the object of a light verb. Chontal has a similar set of markers, either -n or -on, which likewise appear primarily in non-finite contexts. However, this suffix does appear as a verbal antipassive with verbs of ingestion in Chontal. Chontal also has an incorporating construction which takes the same marker. The antipassive of the verb "to eat" (ingestion) in Chontal is given in (11b).

Chontal (Osorio May 2016: 107)
(11) a. Kë–k'ux–i–Ø=doko'b   bek'et   (Transitive)
        1.ERG–eat–PFV–3.ABS=PL.EXCL meat
        "We ate meat."
     b. Sam   k'ux–n–Ø–on=doko'b   (Absolutive)
        already eat–**(V)n**–PFV–1.ABS=PL.EXCL
        "We already ate."

Although data from Ch'olti' are sparse, it appears it also has an "absolutive"-type antipassive that appears only in nominalized contexts. However, in Ch'olti' the suffix is -o(h), which is likely a reflex of *-(V)w, and it can involve the suppression of the agent, the patient, or both (Robertson et al. 2010: 187). To complicate the diachronic picture further, Ch'orti' has reflexes of both markers. Unlike Ch'olti' and Ch'ol, Ch'orti' has verbal absolutive antipassives, although the patient cannot be expressed overtly in an oblique phrase. The suffix -o (*-(V)w) is fossilized with only a few verbs, while -on (*-(V)n) is used primarily for habitual actions involving an instrument. The most common absolutive antipassive marker is -ma, which is not cognate, and is rather thought to arise from the agentive suffix -oom (Quizar 2020: 278–9). Since the reflexes of *-(V)n appear in every language except possibly Ch'olti', and the reflexes of *-(V)w which exist in this subgroup are lexicalized, minimally attested and/or occur only in non-finite contexts, it seems likely that there has been a shift in favor of *-(V)n in antipassive-related contexts in most of Cholan.

Cholan languages also have suffixes roughly of the shape -(Vy)a(j) that occur with DTVs in nominalized absolutive and incorporating constructions, and -(y)an suffixes in the same environments in those languages which have verbal antipassives. Example (12) shows a non-finite incorporating construction in Ch'ol with a DTV stem marked with -Vyaj, while a verbal -yan absolutive antipassive with a derived transitive stem in Ch'orti' is given in (13).

Ch'ol (Coon 2013: 152)
(12) Choñkol–oñ   tyi   ts'ujts'–**uyaj**   ñeñe
     PROG–1.ABS   PREP   kiss–ANTIP   baby
     "I'm baby-kissing."

Ch'orti' (Quizar 2020: 257)
(13) E   ixik   a–k'ub'–es–**ya'n**   tama   e   nir–oj
     The   woman   3SG.ABS–believe–CAUS–ANTIP in   the cure–NMLZ
     "The woman believes in curing."

Although Pascual (2007) has claimed that -Vyaj in Ch'ol is cognate with -waj (*-(V)w) in Q'anjob'al, Quizar (2020: 278) contends that the /y/ in Western Cholan was likely epenthetic (see also Vázquez Álvarez 2011: 181 on Ch'ol), and that *-aj* comes from a nominal suffix. However, Quizar does consider *-(y)an* in Ch'orti' to be a reflex of *-*(V)n*, where /y/ has become part of the suffix.

There are two Tseltalan languages, Tseltal and Tsotsil. Both of these languages have absolutive antipassives where the patient cannot be expressed overtly in an oblique phrase. Tseltal marks the construction with *-(a)wan*, Tsotsil with *-van*. Polian (2013: 286) analyzes *-wan* in Tseltal as the nominalizing suffix *-aw* fused with a verbalizing/intransitivizing suffix *-an*, an amalgamation which is more transparent in dialects where the suffix is *-awan*. Since there is evidence elsewhere in the family of both **-(V)w* and **-(V)n* in non-finite and nominalized predicates and verbalized nouns, as well as evidence of the two markers stacking, it is not beyond the realm of possibility that both *-aw* and *-an* are reflexes of **-(V)w* and **-(V)n* respectively. Tseltal also has two unproductive absolutive antipassive suffixes, *-maj* and *-baj*, both of which imply that the patient is inanimate (vs. *-wan* which implies the patient is human) (Polian 2013: 284).[5]

Unlike the other Cholan-Tseltalan languages, Tsotsil has an agent focus construction. Agent focus in Tsotsil is marked by *-on* (**-(V)n*), and is limited to contexts where third persons act on third persons. Agent focus in Tsotsil is also optional, but tends to appear when the patient is more definite, individuated, and animate than the agent (Aissen 1999: 454). An example of an agent focus clause in Tsotsil is given in (14b).

Tsotsil (Aissen 1999: 466)
(14) a. Buch'u i–s–kolta li tzeb–e (Transitive)
        WH   COMPL–3.ERG–help the girl–ENC
        "Who helped the girl?"
     b. Buch'u i–kolta–**on** li tzeb–e (Agent focus)
        WH   COMPL–help–***(V)n** the girl–ENC
        "Who helped the girl?"

2.5 Yucatecan languages

The Yucatecan branch of the Mayan language family is composed of four languages: Yucatec, Lacandón, Mopan, and Itzaj. Like Mamean languages, Yucatecan languages only have reflexes of **-(V)n*. All four languages have an absolutive antipassive construction marked by *-n* which does not permit the patient to be expressed in an oblique phrase. Antipassives with *-n* only appear in completive and dependent contexts, and in Mopan *-n* only exists with a few words (Hofling 2006). Antipassives in Yucatec are also marked by lengthening the root vowel and lowering its pitch in incompletive aspects (Bricker et al. 1998: 349). These antipassives which in Yucatec are marked by tone are marked by a change in vowel quality in Mopan, which has lost phonemic tone. The examples in (15) from Yucatec demonstrate an antipassive in completive aspect which is marked both with *-n* and vowel length/low-tone. Notice that the absolutive antipassive in Yucatec differs from the absolutive antipassive in for example K'ichean languages in that it continues to take transitive status marking.[6]

Yucatec (Bricker 1978: 5)
(15) a. T–a–šok–ah–Ø   (Transitive)
       COMPL–2.ERG–study–COMPL.TR–3SG.ABS
       "You studied it."
    b. Šòok–n–ah–eč   (Absolutive)
       study–**(V)n**–COMPL.TR–2SG.ABS
       "You studied."

Yucatec, Itzaj, and Lacandón also have incorporating constructions which in some contexts is indicated by the same -*n* suffix. Finally, while Yucatec is discussed as having agent focus (Tonhauser 2007, among others), the construction is morphologically unmarked and therefore does not involve a reflex of *-(V)w* or *-(V)n*.

2.6 Huastecan languages

The Huastecan languages are geographically discontinuous with the rest of the family, spoken farther north in Central-Eastern Mexico. While the Huastecan branch of the Mayan family is composed of two languages, very little is known about Chicomulseltec, so I focus here on Huastec. Huastec has both an absolutive antipassive and an incorporating construction. Although there are syntactic restrictions on ergative arguments in Huastec, it lacks an agent focus construction and instead uses the absolutive antipassive in those contexts. Both the absolutive antipassive and the incorporating construction are marked by suffixes unrelated to *-(V)w* and *-(V)n*. Huastec has three markers, *-Vl*, *-Vm*, and *-Vsh*, which are homophonous with markers that derive nominals from transitive verbs (Edmonson 1988: 164)—a likely diachronic source. An example of an absolutive antipassive with an oblique patient in Huastec is provided in (16b), where the verb is marked with *-ux* (*-Vsh*).

Huastec (Kondic 2016)
(16) a. U   txuk–y–al   an   kwaa'txim   (Transitive)
       1.ERG sew–TS–INCOMPL   DET   cloth
       "I sew clothes."
    b. In   txuk–**ux**   ti   kwaa'txim   (Absolutive)
       1.ABS sew–ANTIP   PREP   cloth
       "I sew clothes."

2.7 Data summary

The distribution of the reflexes of *-(V)w* and *-(V)n* across Mayan languages in the three primary constructions in which they appear is summarized in Table 3.1. The table only includes those markers which are clearly related to *-(V)w* and *-(V)n*, and those languages for which there are data (that is, it does not include Chicomulseltec). "N/A" indicates that a language lacks that particular construction, "NC" indicates that there is no cognate marker for that construction/verb type, "UM" indicates that the construction exists in the language but it is not morphologically marked, and

Table 3.1 Reflexes of *-(V)w and *-(V)n in absolutive, agent focus, and incorporating constructions

Subgroup	Language	Absolutive		Agent focus		Incorporating		Main sources
		RTV	DTV	RTV	DTV	RTV	DTV	
K'ichean	K'iche'	-on	-n	-ow	-n	-ow	-n	Mondloch 1981; Davies and Sam-Colop 1990
K'ichean	Achi'	-on	-n	-o(w)	-n			Sis Iboy 2007
K'ichean	Kaqchikel	-on	-n	-o	-n	-o	-n	Author's fieldwork
K'ichean	Tz'utujil	-oon	-(V)n	-o(w)	-n			Dayley 1985
K'ichean	Sakapultek	-Vn	-n	-Vw	-n			Du Bois 1981
K'ichean	Sipakapense	-n	-n	-w	-w			Barrett 1999
K'ichean	Uspantek	-on	-n	-ow	-n	-ow	-n	Can Pixabaj 2007
K'ichean	Poqomam	-w	-in	-w	-in			Smith-Stark 1983
K'ichean	Poqomchi'	-w	-n	-w	-Vn			Brown 1979
K'ichean	Q'eqchi'	N/A	N/A	N/A	N/A	-o	-n	Berinstein 1985
Mamean	Mam	-n	-n	N/A	N/A	-n	-n	England 1983
Mamean	Tektitek	-n	-n	N/A	N/A			Stevenson 1986
Mamean	Awakatek	-oon	-on	-oon	-on			Larsen 1983
Mamean	Ixil	-on	-n	-on	-n	-on	-n	Ayres 1983
Q'anjob'alan	Q'anjob'al	-waj	-waj	-on	-n	-wi	-wi	Mateo Toledo 2008
Q'anjob'alan	Akatek	-w(i)/-wa	-w(i)/-wa	-on	-n	-wi	-wi	Peñalosa 1987; Zavala 1997
Q'anjob'alan	Popti'	-wa	-wa	-n	-n	-wi	—	Craig 1979; Ordóñez 1995
Q'anjob'alan	Mocho'	-o:n	-:n	N/A	N/A	-o:n	-:n	Palosaari 2011
Q'anjob'alan	Chuj	-w-aj	-an	-an	-an	-w-i	N/A	Buenrostro 2013; Coon 2019
Q'anjob'alan	Tojolabal	-w-an	-Vn	N/A	N/A			Furbee Losee 1976; Ramírez del Prado 2017

Table 3.1 Continued

Subgroup	Language	Absolutive		Agent focus		Incorporating		Main sources
		RTV	DTV	RTV	DTV	RTV	DTV	
Cholan	Ch'ol	(-oñ)	(-(Vy)aj)	N/A	N/A	UM	(-Vyaj)	Gutiérrez Sánchez 2004; Vázquez Álvarez 2011; Coon 2013
Cholan	Chontal	-n (/-on)	-(ay)aj	N/A	N/A	(UM)	-(ay)aj)	Knowles 1984; Osorio May 2016
Cholan	Ch'olti'	-o(h) /-ya	(-ya)	N/A	N/A	—	—	Robertson et al. 2010; Becquey 2014
Cholan	Ch'orti'	-on /-o	-(y)an	N/A	N/A	UM[a]	-(y)an	Quizar 2020
Tseltalan	Tseltal	-(a)wan	-(a)wan	N/A	N/A	N/A	N/A	Polian 2013
Tseltalan	Tsotsil	-van	—	-on	-on	—	—	Haviland 1981; Aissen 1987, 1999
Yucatecan	Yucatec	-n	-n	UM	UM	-n	—	Bricker 1978; Sullivan 1984; Lehmann 2015
Yucatecan	Lacandón	-n	-n	UM	UM	-n	—	Hofling 2006, 2014; Bergqvist 2007
Yucatecan	Itzaj	-n	-n	N/A	N/A	-n	—	Hofling 2000
Yucatecan	Mopan	-n	N/A	N/A	N/A		—[b]	Danziger 1996; Hofling 2006, 2011
Huastecan	Huastec	NC	NC	N/A	N/A	NC	NC	Edmonson 1988; Kondic 2016

[a] Lacadena (2000) labels -i as a marker for incorporating constructions with root transitives in Ch'orti'. While this may indeed be the case, -i in many Mayan languages is an intransitive marker, but not a voice marker, so its non-inclusion here indicates uncertainty about this analysis. But regardless, -i is not a reflex of *-(V)n or *-(V)w, and therefore does not have much bearing on the current argument.

[b] Hofling (2011: 20) states that object incorporation is widespread in Mopan and often involves antipassive stems. However, since no examples have been located involving one of the few antipassive stems that is marked with a suffix, I have left this value open.

"—" indicates a lack of information on whether that form exists in that language. Parentheses around an entire suffix indicate that it only appears with non-finite verbs.[7]

To summarize, Huastec has no reflex of either *-(V)w or *-(V)n. Yucatecan and Mamean languages only have reflexes of *-(V)n, which appear with absolutive antipassives and incorporating constructions. While there is evidence of both *-(V)w and *-(V)n in Cholan-Tseltalan languages, they have been combined (as in Tseltalan), or their contexts of use either have been collapsed (as in Ch'orti') or reduced to non-finite contexts in a way that seems to indicate a shift in favor of the use of *-(V)n. Q'anjob'alan languages exhibit a clear pattern where *-(V)w marks absolutive antipassives and incorporating constructions, while *-(V)n is the marker for agent focus, and in some languages appears with DTV stems as well. This is true for all Q'anjob'alan languages with the exception of Mocho', where a broad range of antipassive/middle functions are marked by a reflex of *-(V)n. K'ichean languages follow a different pattern however, where *-(V)w is used with agent focus and the incorporating construction, while *-(V)n marks the absolutive antipassive and appears broadly with DTVs. This true for all K'ichean languages except for Q'eqchi' which lacks an absolutive antipassive (and therefore lacks *-(V)n), and Poqomam and Poqomchi' which use reflexes of *-(V)w for both agent focus and the absolutive antipassive.

2.8 Reconstruction

Several reconstructions have been proposed for the two antipassive-related suffixes in Mayan and their functions. Smith-Stark (1978: 179) proposed reconstructing *-(V)w as an absolutive antipassive marker where the patient can be expressed optionally in an oblique phrase, and *-(V)n as the marker used with focused agents. Smith-Stark additionally reconstructs agent focus in contexts involving a third person argument, and the agent is cross-referenced on the verb. Dayley (1983: 86–7) proposes a similar reconstruction that differs in the details, where *-w allows the patient of a transitive verb to be omitted, *-(V)n is used when extracting ergative arguments, and the patient is cross-referenced on the verb. However, Kaufman (1986) reconstructs the opposite pattern, where *-(o-)an marks a patientless absolutive antipassive which sometimes also has middle-type functions. Kaufman claims *-(o-)w developed later in Central Mayan (eastern and western branches) in agent focus contexts and the verb agreed with the patient. These three hypotheses are summarized in Table 3.2.

Based on the data in Table 3.1, there is little debate that two markers should be reconstructed at some level. First, focusing on Central Mayan: since Mamean and Cholan-Tseltalan languages have experienced a loss of form and/or function such that the synchronic distribution of the two suffixes in these languages likely does not reflect their historical distribution, the question becomes, is a K'ichean-type or Q'anjob'alan-type distribution more conservative, or something in between? Dayley (1983: 86–7) posits that there was a "flip-flop" in K'ichean, based on the observation that "the suffix -(V)n occurs as a marker of the focus antipassive in all Mayan languages, except Yuc[atec]," which partially conflates agent focus and the absolutive antipassive. Smith-Stark (1978: 179–80) proposes that the use of -w for both absolutive and agent focus functions in Poqomam is evidence of an intermediate stage, where

Table 3.2 Reconstructions for antipassive-related morphemes

Source	Absolutive	Agent focus	Incorporating
Smith-Stark 1978	*-(V)w (+/-obl)	*-(V)n (agent)	*-(V)w
Dayley 1981	*-w (-obl)	*-(V)n (patient)	*-w
Kaufman 1986	*-(o-)an (-obl)	*-(o-)w (patient)	—

*-(V)w transitioned from an absolutive antipassive suffix to a marker of agent focus in K'ichean, brought on by a generalization of *-(V)n to derived transitives. In contrast, Kaufman (1986) outlines a theory wherein *-(o-)w developed from the reanalysis of a transitive status marker (which he reconstructs as *-(o-)h/w) in a Yucatec-like agent focus construction. Greater Q'anjob'alan would then have gone through a stage where *-(o-)an and *-(o-)w had roughly the same function (as in Ch'orti') before settling in to be essentially the opposite of the older K'ichean-like functional distribution. Kaufman (1986) also notes that the Q'anjob'alan languages in the Huehuetenango sprachbund tend to be innovative.

There are perhaps no definitive answers in this instance, although it is important to note that subsequent descriptions and additional work on Mayan syntax have helped to further clarify the picture structurally and functionally. The fact that *-(V)n appears in all branches of the family save Huastecan, and that it has an absolutive antipassive function in almost all cases, suggests that it should be reconstructed at least at the level of Proto-Central Mayan with absolutive as at least one of its functions. That would then suggest that *-(V)w had focus/incorporating functions, which would have to be reconstructed at least as far back as the ancestor of the eastern and western branches of the family (it is perhaps more conservative to imagine that Yucatecan and Huastecan languages never had *-(V)w than to assume that they lost it, as in Kaufman's proposal).

In terms of form, given that the vowel in *-(V)w can often be explained as -w plus status marking (see Section 1.1) or phonologically (*chay-w would be an unacceptable sequence in Kaqchikel, for example), it would perhaps be best to simply posit *-w as the reconstructed form, as in Dayley's proposal. As for *-(V)n, reflexes include -o(:)n, -n, and -an, where -an is limited to Tseltalan, Chuj, and Tojolabal. Since /o/ is the most widely distributed vowel, reconstructing *-(o)n might be most appropriate, where the presence of the vowel depends on one's view of Proto-Mayan phonotactics.

3. Synchronic distribution in Kaqchikel

Now that the diachronic history of the relevant antipassive-related suffixes in the Mayan language family has been established, the rest of this chapter will focus on the synchronic distribution of these suffixes in Kaqchikel (K'ichean), where there is evidence of a change in progress. As noted in Table 3.1 and Section 2.1, Kaqchikel has an absolutive antipassive marked with -on, as well as an oblique antipassive, agent focus, and an incorporating construction which are marked with -o with RTVs and -n with DTVs. This is the distribution found in colonial texts, and is still the distribution

THE DISTRIBUTION OF *-(V)n AND *-(V)w IN KAQCHIKEL

for many Kaqchikel speakers today. The examples in (17) are from the *Kaqchikel Chronicles* (Maxwell and Hill 2006), which demonstrate that in colonial Kaqchikel, absolutive (17a), oblique (17b), agent focus (17c), and incorporating (17d) constructions are marked as described above (all examples here are RTVs).

Colonial Kaqchikel (Maxwell and Hill 2006)
(17) a. X–e–suj–**un** chi r–e ajaw doctor Mejía
COMPL–3PL.ABS–accuse–on[8] PREP 3SG–OBL lord doctor Mejía
"They made an accusation before the lord Doctor Mejía."
b. In k–i–ch'ak–**o** k–ichin
1SG HORT–1SG.ABS–win–o 3PL–OBL
"May I defeat them!"
c. Naq mix–Ø–k'am–**o** pe w–ana'
WH PRS–3SG.ABS–bring–o DIR 1SG.POSS–sister
"Who took my sister?"
d. Mani x–Ø–ya'–**o** patan r–onojel juyu'
NEG COMPL–3SG.ABS–give–o tribute 3SG–all hill/territory
"None of the territory paid tribute."

However, in contemporary Kaqchikel one quickly encounters examples which do not conform to these expectations. (18a–c) below provide examples from modern Kaqchikel of an agent focus (18a), an oblique antipassive (18b), and an incorporating construction (18c) all marked with *-on* instead of the expected *-o,* as in (17).

Kaqchikel
(18) a. Rije' x–e–b'an–**on** ri utz–uläj nimaq'ij
3PL COMPL–3PL.ABS–do–on DET good–SUPRL party
"They threw the best party" (author's field notes)
b. Ri lu's ja ri n–i–chap–**on** k–ichin ri ch'oy
DET cat FOC DET INCOMPL–3SG.ABS–grab–on 3PL–OBL DET mouse
"The cat is the one [who] grabs the mice." (Cojtí Marcario et al. 2001: 184)
c. X–Ø–b'an–**on** ch'aj–o'n ri ixöq
COMPL–3SG.ABS–do–on clean–NMLZ DET woman
"The woman did laundry." (author's field notes)

Note that this change does not affect *-on* (*-(V)n*); I have not encountered any examples where the absolutive antipassive can take *-o* instead of *-on.*

It has been noted previously in the Kaqchikel literature that *-o* is gradually falling out of use in favor of *-on.* García Matzar and Rodríguez Guaján (1997) summarize the situation as follows:

> Las variantes de Pa Su'm [Patzún], [Santa Catarina] Palopó y Pa Tz'i' Ya' [Patzicía] y en Iximche' [Tecpán] (ancianos mayores de 70 años) conservan este sistema, otras variantes en cambio antipasivizan así: **-n** con derivados y **-on/un** con radicales. Estas variantes generalizan el uso de la **-n,** lo único que los distingue es la vocal redondeada que le agregan a los radicales.

The varieties of Pa Su'm [Patzún], [Santa Catarina] Palopó, Pa Tz'i' Ya' [Patzicía] and Iximche' [Tecpán] (elders more than 70 years of age) conserve this system [-o/-u for agent focus], while other varieties antipassivize thus: -n with derived [transitives] and -on/un for root [transitives]. These varieties generalize the use of -n, such that the only thing that distinguishes the two is the rounded vowel that is added to root [transitives]. (García Matzar and Rodríguez Guaján 1997: 374; my translation)

Given that the data for García Matzar and Rodríguez Guaján's work were collected over twenty years ago, one might expect *-o* no longer to be in use in any dialect they surveyed since they reported that at the time only speakers over the age of seventy retained *-o*. Majzul et al. (2000) also did a dialect survey and noticed variation in the suffix used with constructions that appear in agent extraction syntactic contexts, but provide a slightly different picture of which dialects use *-on* and which still use *-o*:

En las variantes de Yepocapa, Dueñas, Ayampuc, Parramos, Sumpango, Acatenango, Santiago Sacatepéquez, Balanyá, Tecpán, Santa Apolonia, Patzicía, Itzapa y Santa Catarina Palopó sufijan el antipasivo de enfoque en raíces transitivas con -o/u como también con -on/un. Las variantes de Sumpango, San José Poaquil, San Martín Jilotepeque, San Juan Comalapa, Patzún y Zaragoza marcan específicamente con -on/un y en las otras variantes se utilizan o/u.

The dialects of Yepocapa, Dueñas, Ayampuc, Parramos, Sumpango, Acatenango, Santiago Sacatepéquez, Balanyá, Tecpán, Santa Apolonia, Patzicía, Itzapa y Santa Catarina Palopó suffix the focus antipassive with -o/u as well as -on/un for root transitives. The dialects of Sumpango, San José Poaquil, San Martín Jilotepeque, San Juan Comalapa, Patzún y Zaragoza specifically mark it with -on/un, and the other dialects use -o/u. (Majzul et al. 2000: 172; my translation)

First, Majzul et al. (2000) and García Matzar and Rodríguez Guaján (1997) do not agree on all fronts on which towns are undergoing the shift, and to what extent. Second, neither study provides much detail; communities are described only as having the original pattern, having both markers in play, or as having shifted. The present study seeks to check up on this change in progress, nearly twenty years after the above studies were conducted, as well as provide a more detailed picture of the shift from *-o* to *-on* as it progresses through the Kaqchikel-speaking population.

3.1 The study

A study was conducted by the author in the summer of 2014 to determine the extent of the use of *-on* in constructions which traditionally take *-o*. The study included twenty-seven native speakers from nine different dialects (named for the towns in which they are spoken): San Juan Comalapa, Tecpán, Santa María de Jesús, Santiago Sacatepéquez, Sololá, Patzicía, Patzún, San Andres Itzapa, and San José Poaquil. These Kaqchikel speakers were between the ages of twenty and ~sixty-five (median age thirty-seven) at the time of recording, and were recruited by word of mouth.

Speakers were presented orally with sentences in Kaqchikel modelling contexts where -*o* is expected to appear. They were then asked if they preferred a pronunciation with a final /n/ (-*on/un*), or with a verb ending in a vowel (-*o/u*). All interviews were conducted monolingually in Kaqchikel by the author. The study included seventeen test sentences involving a mix of syntactic contexts (wh-questions, relative clauses, and argument focus/clefts, which are common contexts where agent focus/antipassives appear in Mayan languages), and construction types (agent focus vs. oblique antipassive).[9] The investigation was limited to eliciting examples of agent focus and the oblique antipassive construction, since incorporating constructions are not particularly frequent or entirely productive in contemporary Kaqchikel.[10]

A sample item is given in (19). The parentheses in -*o(n)* indicate that the participant was provided with versions of this sentence with both -*o* and -*on*, and was asked which version they preferred and to repeat the sentence according to how they would say it. The example in (19) also involves an agent focus construction in an argument focus context, where the agent appears preverbally (Kaqchikel is VOS) with the focus particle *ja*.

Kaqchikel
(19) Ja   ri   xtän   x–Ø–chap–o(n)   ri   äk'
      FOC   DET   girl   COMPL–3SG.ABS–grab–o(n) DET   chicken
      "It was the girl [that] grabbed the chicken."

The task also included twelve additional control items. Control items were DTVs, which invariably take -*n*. As expected, all speakers only used -*n* with these items; none used -*o*. A sample derived transitive control item is given in (20).

Kaqchikel
(20) Achike   x–Ø–q'ejelo–n   ri   achin
      WH   COMPL–3SG.ABS–greet–n   DET   man
      "Who greeted the man?"

All sentences were vetted by a native speaker for naturalness and appropriateness. The task took an average of sixteen minutes to complete.

3.2 Results

The percentages for how often speakers reported to prefer -*on* with agent focus and oblique antipassives of RTVs are presented by dialect in Figure 3.1. If the contrast between -*o* and -*on* were currently as robust as it was in the colonial Kaqchikel documentation, all percentages would be zero. The number of speakers interviewed from each dialect is indicated along with the name of each dialect (n = number of speakers). In many cases, speakers found both -*o* and -*on* acceptable, but preferred one over the other. There were thirty responses given where both forms were equally preferred (and speakers claimed to actively use both forms), in which case no preference was recorded.

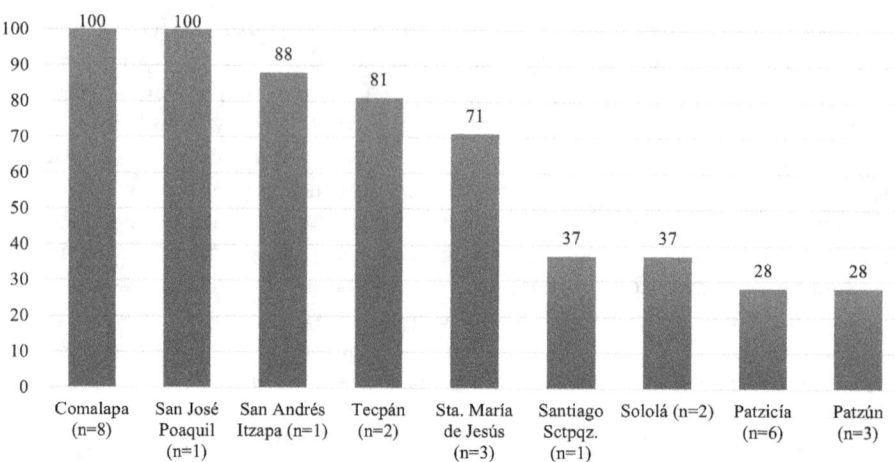

Figure 3.1 Percentage preference for -*on* with agent focus and oblique antipassives of RTVs by Kaqchikel dialect

Surprisingly, of the nine dialects surveyed, none maintains the distinction 100% of the time between -*o* and -*on*. Therefore, at this point in time, all of the dialects of Kaqchikel surveyed here appear to be undergoing a shift from -*o* to -*on*. Not only is -*on* an option in contexts that traditionally only took -*o*, it was preferred more often than -*o* in five of the nine dialects surveyed. Additionally, -*o* has been lost entirely in San Juan Comalapa and likely also in San José Poaquil. Speakers from Patzicía, Patzún, Santiago Sacatepéquez, and Sololá are the most likely to use -*o* most of the time in traditional -*o* contexts, while the other dialects surveyed are more innovative with respect to this feature.

The results of this study are compared with the claims in Majzul et al. (2000) and García Matzar and Rodríguez Guaján (1997) in Table 3.3. A slash indicates that both -*o* and -*on* are present to some extent in a given Kaqchikel dialect. Bolded values for the 2014 survey indicate a point of divergence with at least one of the previous sources.

According to the findings of Majzul et al. (2000), the expectation was that -*on* would be used exclusively in Comalapa, Poaquil, and Patzún, both -*o* and -*on* would be in

Table 3.3 Summary of claims about the shift from -*o* to -*on* in Kaqchikel by dialect and source

Source	Patzún	Patzicía	Palopó	Tecpán	Comalapa	Itzapa	Poaquil	Santiago Sac.
García Matzar and Rodríguez Guaján (1997)	-o	-o	-o	-o/-on (age)	-on	-on	-on	-on
Majzul et al. (2000)	-on	-o/-on	-o/-on	-o/-on	-on	-o/-on	-on	-o/on
2014 survey	**-o/-on**	**-o/-on**	NA	-o/-on	-on	**-o/-on**	-on	**-o/on**

play in Santiago Sacatepéquez, Itzapa, Patzicía, and Tecpán, and -o would still be being used exclusively in Sololá and Santa María de Jesús. Most of these expectations are borne out, although -on is now also an option in Sololá and Santa María de Jesús, and -o actually remains the marker for agent focus and the oblique antipassive construction in the majority of cases in Patzún. The current change regarding -o and -on is actually less far along than projected in García Matzar and Rodríguez Guaján (1997), since several dialects reported to only have -on still use both markers. However, there is also more variability than either source suggested, where dialects that use both markers use/prefer -on versus -o to different extents.

There is also evidence of age-grading, such that younger speakers are more likely to prefer forms with -on over -o (β: -2.73 ± 0.51, p <0.001).[11] The age-grading evidence fits with the idea that this is a change in progress, which has been taking place for more than twenty years (per the documentation in García Matzar and Rodríguez Guaján 1997). The percentage of answers using -on by age group are given in Figure 3.2. Younger speakers (ages twenty–thirty) used -on over -o almost 90% of the time, whereas older speakers used -on in -o contexts 44–53% of the time.

The two speakers from San José Poaquil and San Andrés Itzapa respectively were both twenty years old at the time the data were collected. This leaves open the possibility that the rate of use for -on reported for those dialects is not representative of the dialect as a whole, but rather only of the young adult generation in those places. Given the direction of the age-grading, the overall use of -on in those dialects may be lower (although see also the statements about these dialects from Majzul et al. 2000 corroborating that they are undergoing shift, and the utterance in (18a) said by an elder from Poaquil).

There were a number of other variables which had little or no effect on the distribution. There was no discernible effect for gender of the speaker, and no discernible effect for clause type (wh-questions vs. relativization vs. focus word contexts). There was a small effect for construction type, where -on was used 63% of the time in agent focus constructions versus 55% of the time with oblique antipassives. Given the small effect size (β: 8.98 ± 0.45, p <0.05), it is quite possible the effect would disappear with

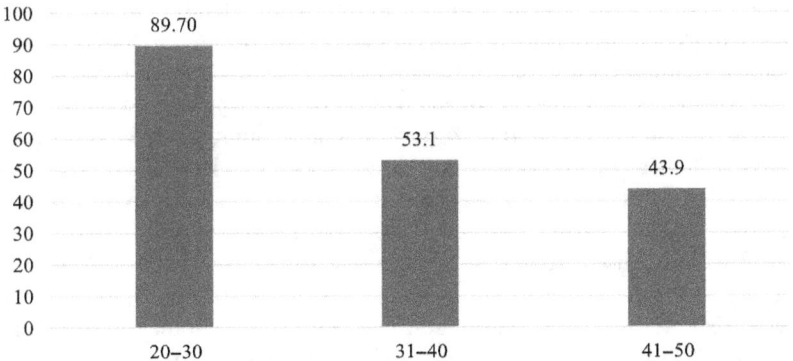

Figure 3.2 Percentage preference for -on with agent focus and oblique antipassives of RTVs by age

a larger number of items. Finally, there was a surprising tendency for *-on* to be preferred with CüC verb roots (so more correctly *-un* rather than *-u*), where it appeared 68% of the time with CüC roots, versus 59% with all other transitive verb roots (which take *-on*). However, only two roots with /u/ regularly appeared in the test items (*-wüx* "to harvest" and *-tzu'* "to see"), so this also could be a lexical effect which would disappear with a broader range of items.

4. Conclusion

This chapter has presented new evidence that Kaqchikel is undergoing a change, where the suffix *-on* is appearing with constructions in contexts which formerly only permitted *-o*. All dialects surveyed allow at least some use of *-on* in contexts where we would otherwise expect *-o*. Some dialects, like San Juan Comalapa, have completely lost *-o* in favor of *-on* in all contexts and for all ages. Age-grading suggests that even in dialects where *-o* is still the predominant marker, Kaqchikel will likely continue to shift towards *-on*.

This merger of *-o* and *-on* in favor of *-on* has happened elsewhere in the Mayan language family. A comparison of these two markers and their functions across the family show that Mamean languages and Mocho' (and perhaps Yucatecan) underwent a similar merger where *-(V)w* was lost entirely in favor of *-(V)n*, even if the syntactic contexts and in some cases also the constructions (for example, agent focus in Ixil) maintained the same characteristics otherwise. Cholan-Tseltalan went through a similar process, although the functions that *-(V)w/*-(V)n*-marked constructions served have largely disappeared. Fossilized traces of both markers can be found in Cholan languages, although *-on* appears to be more common, and is likely the only reflex in Ch'ol and Chontal. It therefore seems that a loss of *-(V)w* in favor of *-(V)n* is a common occurrence in the family, and Kaqchikel is following this same trajectory. For Kaqchikel, I would hypothesize that the merger is being driven by analogy to the plethora of *-n*-marked DTVs with all constructions in all contexts (similar to Dayley's (1983) hypothesis for the functional "flip-flop" in K'ichean).

These data provide a more nuanced view of how the shift from *-(V)w* to *-(V)n* continues to progress in Kaqchikel, and how modern patterns relate to historical patterns within the Mayan language family. This type of investigation of language change provides a more comprehensive understanding of synchronic as well as diachronic variation, and combines goals and approaches from documentary, historical, and variationist traditions. In the case of Mayan languages, the type of study described here serves as follow-up documentation to track new developments. New documentation and analyses allow us to see the types of changes described here in a modern context, as processes in progress, rather than static endpoints represented by the moment the language was first described. Additionally, preparation of datasets like that compiled in Table 3.1 highlights the descriptive holes that still exist, which for Mayan largely lies in a lack of detailed information on incorporating constructions, even in what are otherwise fairly well-described languages. I hope that this chapter encourages further work on the diachrony of different constructions and affixes in Mayan.

Notes

1. The orthography used in the examples matches the original source. As such, the same sounds may be written in different ways. For example, /š/ appears as both š and x (as in Mayan orthographies), and glottal stop can be represented by ', ?, or 7.
2. Yucatec is the only language where the incorporated patient physically appears within the verb complex.
3. While some examples in Barrett (1999) gloss an -*n* as an agent focus marker (exs. 94, 313, 355, 486), in all cases it seems possible these could be absolutive antipassives.
4. See Coon et al. (2014) for a possible explanation which unifies these two contexts.
5. Polian (2013: 288) claims that -*maj* comes from the nominalizer -*om* plus the intransitiviser -*aj*. The origin of -*baj* is less clear, but it may have come from a nominalizer -*Vb* plus the same -*aj* suffix.
6. 'Status' in Mayan linguistics refers to sets of suffixes which appear on verbs and indicate transitivity, clause type, and/or aspect. The extent to which languages make use of these suffixes varies within the family.
7. Similar versions of this chart appear in several publications, namely Smith-Stark (1978: 177–9), Lacadena (2000: 172, 176), Yasugi (2005: 80), and Stiebels (2006: 552). Note, however, that often the labeling for the three antipassive-like constructions are not comparable across sources, and this table also benefits from descriptive work that was not available to earlier authors.
8. In Kaqchikel and other K'ichean languages, the form of this suffix is -*on*, unless the vowel of the root is /u/, in which case it harmonises to -*un*.
9. There were an additional three items in the original design, for a total of twenty target items. However, these involved the verb -*ajo'* "to want, like," which has an irregular marking pattern where it commonly surfaces either as -*ajowan* or -*ajo'n*, which is invariant. Therefore, these items were excluded from the final results.
10. The incorporating construction is used mostly with highly regularised activities (for example, *yipono wäy* "I make tortillas"), and is often considered strange or unacceptable with less common verb–patient combinations.
11. All beta values, standard errors, and p-values reported in this chapter were calculated using a generalised linear regression model that was fit to the presence or absence of -*on*, with dialect, age, gender, clause type, and construction type as predictors.

References

Aissen, Judith. 1987. *Tzotzil clause structure*. Dordrecht: D. Reidel.
Aissen, Judith. 1999. Agent focus and inverse in Tzotzil. *Language* 75.451–85.
Aissen, Judith. 2017. Correlates of ergativity in Mayan. In *The Oxford handbook of ergativity*, ed. by Jessica Coon, Diane Massam, and Lisa Travis, 737–58. Oxford: Oxford University Press.
Ayres, Glenn. 1983. The antipassive "voice" in Ixil. *International Journal of American Linguistics* 49.20–45.

Barrett, Rusty. 1999. *A grammar of Sipakapense Maya*. University of Texas at Austin dissertation.
Becquey, Cédric. 2014. *Diasystème, diachronie: Etudes comparées dans les langues cholanes*. Vrije Universiteit Amsterdam dissertation.
Bergqvist, Henrik. 2007. Agent focus in Yukatek and Lakandon Maya. In *Proceedings of the 33rd Berkeley Linguistics Society*, ed. by Zhenya Antić, Charles Chang, Clare Sandy, and Maziar Toosarvandani, 28–39. Berkeley: The Berkeley Linguistics Society and the Linguistic Society of America.
Berinstein, Ava. 1985. *Evidence for multiattachment in K'ekchi Mayan*. University of California dissertation.
Bricker, Victoria. 1978. Antipassive constructions in Yucatec Maya. In *Papers in Mayan linguistics*, ed. by Nora C. England, 3–24. Columbia, MO: University of Missouri.
Bricker, Victoria, Eleuterio Po'ot Yah, and Ofelia Dzul de Po'ot. 1998. *Dictionary of the Maya language as spoken in Hocabá, Yucatan*. Salt Lake City: University of Utah Press.
Brown, Linda Kay. 1979. *Word formation in Pocomchi (Mayan)*. Stanford University dissertation.
Buenrostro, Cristina. 2013. *La voz en Chuj de San Mateo Ixtatán*. El Colegio de México Centro de Estudios Lingüísticos y Literarios dissertation.
Campbell, Lyle. 2017. Mayan history and comparison. In *The Mayan languages*, ed. by Judith Aissen, Nora C. England, and Roberto Zavala Maldonado, 43–61. London: Routledge
Can Pixabaj, Telma Angelina. 2007. *Gramática uspanteka [Jkemiik yoloj li uspanteko]*. Guatemala: Cholsamaj. Oxlajuuj Keej Maya' Ajtz'iib'.
Cojtí Marcario, Narciso, Martín Chacach Cutzal, and Marcos Armando Cali. 2001. *Diccionario Kaqchikel*. Proyecto Lingüístico Francisco Marroquín. Guatemala: Editorial Cholsamaj.
Coon, Jessica. 2013. *Aspects of split ergativity*. Oxford Studies in Comparative Syntax. Oxford: Oxford University Press.
Coon, Jessica. 2016. Mayan morphosyntax. *Language and Linguistic Compass*, Special issue: Mayan Linguistics 10.515–50.
Coon, Jessica. 2019. Building verbs in Chuj: Consequences for the nature of roots. *Journal of Linguistics* 55.35–81.
Coon, Jessica, Pedro Mateo Pedro, and Omer Preminger. 2014. The role of case in A-bar extraction: Evidence from Mayan. *Linguistic Variation* 14.179–242.
Craig, Colette Grinevald. 1979. The antipassive and Jacaltec. In *Papers in Mayan Linguistics*, ed. by Laura Martin, 139–64. Columbia, MO: Lucas Brothers.
Danziger, Eve. 1996. Split intransitivity and active inactive patterning in Mopan Maya. *International Journal of American Linguistics* 62.379–414.
Davies, William D., and Luis Enrique Sam-Colop. 1990. K'iche' and the structure of antipassive. *Language* 66.522–49.
Dayley, Jon. 1983. *Voice and ergativity in Mayan languages. Studies in Mesoamerican Linguistics, Survey Report 4*, 3–119. Survey of California and Other Indian Languages, UC Berkeley Department of Linguistics.

Dayley, Jon P. 1985. *Tzutujil grammar.* University of California Press.
Du Bois, John W. 1981. *The Sacapultec language.* University of California dissertation.
Edmonson, Barbara Wedemeyer. 1988. *A descriptive grammar of Huastec (Potosino Dialect).* Tulane University dissertation.
England, Nora C. 1983. *A grammar of Mam, a Mayan language.* Austin: University of Texas Press.
Furbee Losee, Louanna. 1976. *The correct language: Tojolabal: A grammar with ethnographic notes.* New York: Garland Publishing.
García Matzar, Pedro (Lolmay), and José Obispo Rodríguez Guaján (Pakal B'alam). 1997. *Rukemik Kaqchikel Chi' = Gramática Kaqchikel.* Guatemala: Editorial Chojsamaj.
Gutiérrez Sánchez, Pedro. 2004. *Las clases de verbos intransitivos y el alineamiento agentivo en el Chol de Tila, Chiapas.* Centro de Investigaciones Superiores en Antropología Social MA thesis.
Haviland, John. 1981. *Skop Sotz'leb: El Tzotzil de San Lorenzo Zinacantan.* Mexico City: Universidad Nacional Autónoma de México.
Heaton, Raina. 2017. *A typology of antipassives, with special reference to Mayan.* University of Hawai'i dissertation.
Heaton, Raina. 2021. Antipassive and antipassive-like constructions in Mayan languages. In *Antipassive: Typology, diachrony, and related constructions*, ed. by Katarzyna Janic and Alena Witzlack-Makarevich, 549–78. Amsterdam: John Benjamins.
Hofling, Charles Andrew. 2000. *Itzaj Maya grammar.* Salt Lake City: University of Utah Press.
Hofling, Charles Andrew. 2006. A sketch of the history of the verbal complex in Yukatekan Mayan languages. *International Journal of American Linguistics* 72.367–96.
Hofling, Charles Andrew. 2011. *Mopan Maya-Spanish-English dictionary/Diccionario Maya Mopan-Español-Inges.* Salt Lake City: University of Utah Press.
Hofling, Charles Andrew. 2014. *Lacandon Maya-Spanish-English dictionary/Diccionario Maya Lacandón-Español-Inges.* Salt Lake City: University of Utah Press.
Janic, Katarzyna, and Alena Witzlack-Makarevich. 2021. The multifaceted nature of the antipassive construction. In *Antipassive: Typology, diachrony, and related constructions*, ed. by Katarzyna Janic and Alena Witzlack-Makarevich, 1–39. Amsterdam: John Benjamins.
Kaufman, Terrence. 1986. Outline of comparative Mayan grammar I: Morphology and particles. Manuscript.
Kaufman, Terrence. 1990. Algunos rasgos estructurales de los idiomas Mayances con referencia especial al K'iche'. In *Lecturas sobre la lingüística Maya*, ed. by Nora England and Stephen Elliott, 59–114. Antigua, Guatemala: CIRMA.
Knowles, Susan Marie. 1984. *A descriptive grammar of Chontal Maya (San Carlos dialect).* Tulane University dissertation.
Kondic, Ana. 2016. Antipassive in South Eastern Huastec (Maya, Mexico). Paper presented at the 49th annual meeting of the Societas Linguistica Europaea (SLE), Naples, Italy.

Lacadena, Alfonso. 2000. Antipassive constructions in the Maya glyphic texts. *Written Language and Literacy* 3.155–80.
Larsen, Thomas. 1983. Aguacatec syntax from a functional perspective. In *Survey report no. 4*, ed. by Alice Schlichter, Wallace L. Chafe, and Leanne Hinton, 120–219. Survey of California and Other Indian Languages.
Lehmann, Christian. 2015. Valency classes in Yucatec Maya. In *Valency classes in the world's languages*, ed. by Andrej Malchukov and Bernard Comrie, 1427–80. Volume 2: Case studies from Austronesia and the Pacific, the Americas, and theoretical outlook. Comparative Handbooks of Linguistics. Berlin: Mouton de Gruyter.
Majzul, Filiberto Patal, Pedro Oscar García Matzar, and Carmelina Espantzay Serech. 2000. *Rujunumaxik ri Kaqchikel chi': Variacíon dialectal en Kaqchikel*. Ciudad de Guatemala, Guatemala: Cholsamaj.
Mateo Toledo, B'alam Eladio. 2008. *The family of complex predicates in Q'anjob'al (Maya); their syntax and meaning*. University of Texas dissertation.
Maxwell, Judith M., and Robert Hill. 2006. *The Kaqchikel chronicles: The definitive edition*. Austin: University of Texas Press.
Mondloch, James L. 1981. *Voice in Quiche-Maya*. SUNY Albany dissertation.
Ordóñez, Francisco. 1995. The antipassive in Jacaltec: A last resort strategy. *Catalan Working Papers in Linguistics* 4.329–43.
Osorio May, José del Carmen. 2016. *Temas de la sintaxis del yokot'an "chontal" de Tecoluta, Nacajuca, Tabasco*. Centro de Investigaciones y Estudios Superiores en Antropología Social dissertation.
Palosaari, Naomi Elizabeth. 2011. *Topics in Mocho' phonology and morphology*. University of Utah dissertation.
Pascual, Adán. 2007. *Transitividad y dependencia sintáctica y discursiva en Q'anjob'al*. Centro de Investigaciones y Estudios Superiores en Antropología Social MA thesis.
Peñalosa, Fernando. 1987. Major syntactic structures of Acatec (dialect of San Miguel Acatán). *International Journal of American Linguistics* 53.281–310.
Polian, Gilles. 2013. *Gramática del tseltal de Oxchuc*. México: Centro de Investigaciones y Estudios Superiores en Antropología Social.
Quizar, Robin. 2020. Tracing the Ch'orti' antipassive system: A comparative/historical view. *International Journal of American Linguistics* 86.237–83.
Ramírez del Prado, Alejandro Curiel. 2017. Tojolabal. In *The Mayan languages*, ed. by Judith Aissen and Nora C. England, 570–609. London: Routledge.
Robertson, John S., Danny Law, and Robbie A. Haertel. 2010. *Colonial Ch'olti': The seventeenth-century Morán manuscript*. Norman: University of Oklahoma Press.
Sis Iboy, Nikte' María Juliana. 2007. *Ri utuxiik tzij pa Achi/Derivación de palabras en Achi*. Oxlajuuj Keej Maya' Ajtz'iib' (OKMA). Cholsamaj.
Smith-Stark, Thomas. 1978. The Mayan antipassive: Some facts and fictions. In *Papers in Mayan linguistics*, ed. by Nora England, 169–87. Columbia: University of Missouri Press.
Smith-Stark, Thomas. 1983. *Jilotepequeño Pocomam phonology and morphology*. University of Chicago dissertation.

Stevenson, Paul Spencer. 1986. *A preliminary grammar of the Tectitec (Mayan) language*. University of Texas at Arlington MA thesis.
Stiebels, Barbara. 2006. Agent focus in Mayan languages. *Natural Language & Linguistic Theory* 24.501–70.
Sullivan, Paul R. 1984. Noun incorporation in Yucatec Maya. *Anthropological Linguistics* 26.138–60.
Tonhauser, Judith. 2007. Agent focus and voice in Yucatec Maya. *Proceedings of the 39th Meeting of the Chicago Linguistic Society*, 540–58. Chicago: Chicago Linguistic Society.
Vázquez Álvarez, Juan Jesús. 2011. *A grammar of Chol, a Mayan language*. University of Texas at Austin dissertation.
Yasugi, Yoshiho. 2005. Fronting of nondirect arguments and adverbial focus marking on the verb in classical Yucatec. *International Journal of American Linguistics* 71.56–86.
Zavala, Roberto. 1997. Functional analysis of Akatek voice constructions. *International Journal of American Linguistics* 63.429–74.

4

Origins of Metathesis in Batsbi, Part II: Intransitive Verbs

Alice C. Harris

1. Introduction

In Harris (2013), I showed how one kind of metathesis in Batsbi originates in derived transitive verbs.[1] Metathesis is a phonological process by which two segments change order, for example XYZ becomes ZYX (where Y may be null). The goal of the present chapter is to show that in the speech of younger speakers the process I previously described has spread to intransitive verbs derived with the intransitivizing suffix -*al*.

In this chapter, I describe relevant aspects of the structure of verbs in Batsbi and briefly review the origins of metathesis in derived transitive verbs (Sections 2 and 3). I present in Section 4 a variety of morphological types of verbs, showing that metathesis does not occur in these. In Section 5, I present the facts of metathesis in derived intransitives, and in Section 6, I argue that metathesis spread from transitives to intransitives. Section 7 contains a brief conclusion.

2. Basic verb morphology in Batsbi

Batsbi is a native name for the language that the Georgians call Tsova Tush. It is spoken in a single village and is severely endangered, with the youngest speakers now around sixty, with a handful of exceptions.

For the purposes of this chapter we need morphological information primarily about the verb. Verbs may take a lexically governed gender–number prefix, illustrated in the left-hand column of (1). In the examples, *d*- is the default gender–number marker and stands in for the others. Not all verbs with gender–number prefixes occur in doublets of the kind in (1), but such examples are effective in showing that these prefixes are lexically governed. (In these examples, -*ar* forms the masdar, a declinable deverbal noun.)

(1) d–ahar "to take; bring; castrate" ahar "to steal; grind"
 d–eblar "to place; lay; put down in" eblar "to thread; put"

d–ebc'ar	"to tie"		ebc'ar	"to push; weigh; milk"
d–ot:ar	"to pour into"		ot:ar	"to stand, stay"
d–ot'ar	"to go; go over"		ot'ar	"to spread"

Gender–number affixes are glossed as "CM," as they are traditionally known in the Caucasus as class markers. These markers indicate the gender and number of the subject of an intransitive (in the absolutive or ergative case, see below) or the direct object of a transitive.

The types of verbs from a derivational point of view are listed in (2) and further described below in this section.

(2) Batsbi verb types from a derivational point of view
  a. derived transitive verbs, with the suffixes –CM–i/Ø
  b. derived intransitives, with the suffixes –CM–al
  c. derived intransitives, with the suffixes –CM–is
  d. causatives, formed with the suffix –it
  e. basic transitives (which lack derivational suffixes)
  f. basic intransitives (which lack derivational suffixes)

Transitive verbs can be derived with the suffix -i, which is most often unrealized, indicated below with a zero for ease of recognition. This suffix is always preceded by a gender–number marker, as illustrated in (3). These suffixes are used both with verbs that happen to require a gender–number prefix, as in the left-hand column of (3), and with ones that do not, as in the right-hand column.

(3)
d–uc'–d–Ø–ar	"to fill"		k'ac'k'ar–d–Ø–ar	"to shrink"
d–aq–d–Ø–ar	"to nurse"		q'et':–d–Ø–ar	"to open"
d–ol–d–Ø–ar	"to begin, start"		tag–d–Ø–ar	"to build, make"

Intransitive verbs can be derived with the suffix -al, which also is preceded by a gender–number marker, as illustrated in (4).

(4)
d–ag–d–al–ar	"to show o.s., be seen"		tag–d–al–ar	"to be done, made"
d–opx–d–al–ar	"to heat up; dress"		teps–d–al–ar	"to fall (down)"
d–arž–d–al–ar	"to unfurl" (e.g., flower)		xerc–d–al–ar	"to change"

Although it does not appear to be productive, the suffix -is, also always preceded by a gender–number marker, could at one time derive intransitives. Some examples are given in (5).

(5)
layt:–d–is–ar	"to fall"		qayc'–d–is–ar	"to grip, grasp"
heyč'–d–is–ar	"to stare at"		uyl:–d–is–ar	"to ferment, leaven"
toh–d–is–ar	"to fall asleep"		quyl:–d–is–ar	"to be put, placed"

The causative suffix -it also derives verbs, as illustrated in (6).

(6) d–eq'–it–ar "to cause to divide, share" tet'–it–ar "to cause to cut"
    d–ax–it–ar "to let out" xat:–it–ar "to cause to read"

Finite forms of basic transitives, (7), and basic intransitives, (8), have no derivational suffix.

(7) d–al–ar "to bring (anim. object)" ebc'–ar "to weigh (TRANS, IMPFV)"
    d–ah–ar "to bring (inanim. object)" meł–ar "to drink"
    d–ał–ar "to give" ał–ar "to say"

(8) d–aɣ–ar "to come here" labc'–ar "to play"
    d–ot'–ar "to go" ʕam–ar "to become accustomed to"
    d–a:x–ar "to live" qerł–ar "to be afraid"

Having or not having a gender–number prefix is not relevant to the derivational type of the verb.

Every verb form must have at least one suffix indicating a tense or a non-finite form. We are most concerned in this chapter with the present and future tenses, since that is where CV metathesis occurs. Transitive verbs indicate the present and future tenses with the suffix -o, while intransitives may use any vowel.[2] The infinitive is marked with -an, while the masdar is marked with -ar, illustrated in (3–8).

Case marking in Batsbi is basically ergative–absolutive. The example in (9) illustrates an ergative subject and an absolutive direct object in a transitive sentence.

(9) nana–s meždar kħek–o–b
    mother–ERG cornbread(b/).ABS prepare–PRS–CM[3]
    "Mother prepares cornbread."

In Batsbi, first and second person singular, first person plural exclusive, and second person plural subjects of intransitives may be absolutive or ergative under certain circumstances (see Holisky 1987 for details).

(10) a. as txabus zoreš y–ex–n–as
        I–ERG yesterday very CM–get.drunk–AOR–1SG.ERG
        "Yesterday I got very drunk (on purpose)."
    b. so txabus zoreš y–ax–i^n–s^w
        I–ABS yesterday very CM–get.drunk–AOR–1SG.ABS
        "Yesterday I got very drunk (by accident)."

(When the /i/ of the aorist suffix -in is lost by a regular process in (10a), it causes the /a/ of the stem to become /e/.)

First and second person singular, first person plural exclusive, and second person plural subjects or direct objects condition agreement with those arguments, but only one argument is marked for person–number–case in a given verb form. Third person singular and plural and first person plural inclusive do not condition

Table 4.1 Person–number–case agreement markers in Batsbi

Person	Ergative	Absolutive
1SG	$-as$	$-s^w$
2SG	$-aħ$	$-ħ^w$
1EXCL	$-atx$	$-tx^w$
2PL	$-eš, -aiš$	$-iš^w$

person–number–case agreement. Table 4.1 presents the agreement markers; (10) above illustrates this.

Morpheme-initial vowels in agreement suffixes in Table 4.1 are affected by certain preceding vowels. In particular, /a/ is lost from the ergative person–number–case markers when it would immediately follow the -o marking present and future tenses in transitives.

In polysyllabic words, front vowels are lost in word-final position. Under the same circumstances, round vowels may be lost or reduced to lip rounding on the preceding consonant. In word-final position, /h/ is optionally lost. Syncope deletes vowels after the first in a word if they are followed by a CV sequence; for example, sak'er "neck. ABS" ~ sak'r-ev "neck.INST," where /e/ in the stem is followed by the CV sequence r-e (Mikelaʒe 1977).

3. Metathesis I: CV metathesis through reanalysis

Notice that in (11), in the first person singular and plural exclusive and in the second person, morphemes occur in the order -CM-o-; in this example the CM is -v-. CM-TNS- is the order found among CMs and markers of other tenses (and markers of various non-finite forms), as illustrated in (12). In (12), an aorist paradigm, the aorist marker, here -(e)n, always follows the CM, here -y (and the transitivizer -i).

(11) v–oʔ–v–o–s   [CM–bring–CM–PRS–1SG.ERG]   "I will bring him."
    v–oʔ–v–o–(h)   [CM–bring–CM–PRS–2SG.ERG]   "You will bring him."
    v–oʔ–o–v   [CM–bring–PRS–CM]   "S/he will bring him."
    v–oʔ–v–o–tx   [CM–bring–CM–PRS–1EXCL.ERG]   "We (EXCL) will bring him."
    v–oʔ–v–w–iš   [CM–bring–CM–PRS–2PL.ERG]   "Y'all will bring him."
    v–oʔ–o–v   [CM–bring–PRS–CM]   "They will bring him."

(12) y–oʔ–y–i–n–as   [CM–bring–CM–TR–AOR–1SG.ERG]   "I brought her."
    y–oʔ–y–i–n–a(h)   [CM–bring–CM–TR–AOR–2SG.ERG]   "You brought her."
    y–oʔ–y–i–e^n [CM–bring–CM–TR–AOR]   "S/he brought her."
    y–oʔ–y–i–n–atx   [CM–bring–CM–TR–AOR–1EXCL.ERG]   "We (EXCL) brought her."
    y–oʔ–y–i–n–eš   [CM–bring–CM–TR–AOR–2PL.ERG]   "Y'all brought her."
    y–oʔ–y–i–e^n [CM–bring–CM–TR–AOR]   "They brought her."

In contrast, in the third persons (and in the first person inclusive, illustrated in (13)), the order is instead -*o*-CM. That is, there is metathesis.

(13) ve   mil–o–d
     we (INCL)   cold–PRS–CM
     "We (F, INCL) are cold."

In derived transitives and other verbs that behave like them, such as the verb in (13), it is only CMs that metathesize. No other consonants participate in this metathesis (Harris 2013).

In first and second person forms, except first person inclusive, the sequence of morphemes for derived transitives is as in (14).

(14) (CM) + stem + CM + TR + TNS + Person–number–case

In most tenses, third person forms have the same structure, except that person–number–case is not marked. In verbs of other types, a similar sequence is found. However, in the third person and first person inclusive of the present and future of derived transitives, the final sequence is changed to +TNS+CM, with the transitive marker (-*i*/Ø) not showing up in these tenses. This is metathesis.

In the Nakh languages, the CM and -*i*/Ø illustrated in (3) originated as follows. The auxiliary corresponding to modern Batsbi *dar* (*d-Ø-ar*) "make, do" grammaticalized to become the suffix that derives transitives from intransitives. It brought with it a prefixal CM. This can be represented as the first change in Figure 4.1.

AF1-	Core	-AF2	-AF3	AF4-	Periphery	-AF5
v-	oʔ	-o	?	v-	-i/Ø	-o
CM	STEM	PRS	PPL/CV	CM	AUX	PRS

↘

AF1-	Core	-AF2	-AF3	-AF4	-Periphery	-AF5
v-	oʔ	-o		v-		-o
CM	stem	PRS		CM	TRANS	PRS

↘

AF1-	Core	-AF2	-AF3	-AF4	-Periphery	-AF5
v-	oʔ	-o		v-		
CM	stem	PRS		CM	TRANS	PRS

Figure 4.1 Fusion of *v–oʔ–ar* "come" with *v–ar* "make, do" in present (first change) and loss of final –*o* in third persons and first person inclusive (second change)

In most tenses, the tense marker of the original main verb, affixes 2 and 3 (if present), were lost. In the present and future, it is likely that participles or converb forms were used with the auxiliary *dar* "make, do" in pre-Batsbi. This seems likely because these forms are used in comparable constructions with auxiliaries in the modern language (for this and other details, see Harris 2013). Today, present and future participles are formed with the *-o* suffix (AF2), followed by the participial formant *-ni*, realized today as -n^y or -*n* (AF3) (Holisky and Gagua 1994). The present–future converb is formed by adding -*š* (AF3) to the present–future *o* (AF2). While in most tenses AF2 and AF3, if present, were both lost, Batsbi retained the present–future marker, -*o* (AF2), of transitive verbs; this "trapped" *o* is documented in the Batsbi Dictionary (Kadagiʒe and Kadagiʒe 1984), reflecting a rather older version of Batsbi than that spoken in 1984.[4]

(15) ʕurdʕurde^n nana–s   šari^n bader   d–e:px–o–d–^{w}
      every.morning   mother–ERG   self's   child(d/d).ABS   CM–dress–PRS–CM–PRS
      "Every morning the mother dresses her child." (Dict 202b)

(16) gigo–s   c'ipel   xen–e^n c'en–buy   teg–o–d–^{w}
      Gigo–ERG   beech   tree–GEN   house(d/d).OBL–PL.ABS make–PRS–CM–PRS
      "Gigo builds houses of beech." (Dict 275b)

In (15–16), the trapped *o* is AF2 in the middle stage of Figure 4.1. The final -^{w} is AF5, /-o/; it undergoes the regular reduction of round vowels described at the end of Section 2.

CV metathesis in the present and future tenses of derived transitive verbs developed through retention of the -*o* from the present or future tense marking of the main verb, together with the productive reduction, then loss of word-final vowels, as schematized in the second change in Figure 4.1 and in (17).

(17) Stages of change in third person forms[5]
      Pre-Nakh: *teg–o–š   d–o
                       STEM–PRS–CV   CM–PRS
      Pre-Batsbi: *teg–o–d–o
                       STEM–PRS–CM–PRS
      Early Batsbi, with vowel reduction: teg–o–d–^{w} (cf. (16))
                                                  STEM–PRS–CM–PRS
      Early Batsbi, with optional vowel loss: teg–o–d
                                                  STEM–PRS–CM
      Later Batsbi: teg–o–d   "S/he builds/makes it."
                       STEM–PRS–CM

Person–number–case agreement was added in pre-Batsbi, perhaps in the nineteenth century. Recall that person–number–case agreement does not apply in third person forms or in first person inclusive. A similar summary of changes in first and second person forms is provided in (18), using the first person singular as an example.

(18) Stages of change in first and second person forms (example: 1 SINGULAR)

Pre-Nakh:	*teg–o–š	d–o
	STEM–PRS–CV	CM–PRS
Pre-Batsbi:	*teg–o–d–o	*teg–o–d–o–as (parallel forms)
	STEM–PRS–CM–PRS	STEM–PRS–CM–PRS–1SG.ERG
Early Batsbi, with vowel reduction:	*teg–o–d–o–s	(*a > Ø / o + __)
	STEM–PRS–CM–1SG.ERG	
Early Batsbi, with further vowel loss:	teg–d–o–s	(*o > Ø / __CV)
	STEM–CM–1SG.ERG	
Later Batsbi:	teg–d–o–s	"I build/make it."
	STEM–CM–1SG.ERG	

The order of changes may have been different from that represented here. What is important is that each of the changes is regular and productive. The *-a* in the final suffix of *teg-o-d-o-as* deletes regularly in hiatus with *-o*, though this has not been described in detail in the literature (but see Holisky and Gagua 1994: 158). The syncope that eliminates the left-most present tense marker, *-o*, from *teg-o-d-o-s* applies regularly to suffixal vowels followed by a CV sequence (Mikelaʒe 1977). On the other hand, its loss could have been morphological (see Harris and Faarlund (2006) for losses of this type).

Given that the "trapped" present tense marker is eliminated regularly by syncope from first and second person forms, that the right-most present tense marker is eliminated regularly by word-final vowel reduction in third person forms, and that the resulting forms show an alternation of the orders *-o-d* and *-d-o-*, as in (11), it is perhaps not surprising that this alternation was reinterpreted as metathesis. The proof that it is indeed treated as metathesis by native speakers comes in part from the evidence provided here in Section 5.

4. Which verbs show metathesis?

Thus far I have limited the discussion to derived transitives with the suffixes -CM-*i*/Ø. We have identified five other morphological types of verbs in Batsbi. The list in (19) is repeated from (2).

(19) Batsbi verb types from a derivational point of view
   a. derived transitive verbs, with the suffixes –CM–*i*/Ø
   b. derived intransitives, with the suffixes –CM–*al*
   c. derived intransitives, with the suffixes –CM–*is*
   d. causatives, formed with the suffix –*it*
   e. basic transitives (which lack derivational suffixes)
   f. basic intransitives (which lack derivational suffixes)

In Section 2, examples of each type are given; in Section 3 and in Harris (2013), type (19a) is examined. In the remainder of this section, I discuss types (19c–f), showing that there is no metathesis in intransitives derived with -CM-*is*, causatives, basic transitives, or basic intransitives. In Section 5 we turn to type (19b). It is the morphology that determines the conjugation class and the presence or absence of metathesis, and consequently there are a few exceptions in the correlations between conjugation class and the description I have provided in (19). The verb "be cold," (13), is one such exception, since it is syntactically intransitive but has the form of a derived transitive and is conjugated as one.

We examine the issue of whether metathesis occurs in other verb types in the order (19d) causatives, (19c) derived intransitives with the suffixes -CM-*is*, (19e) basic transitives, and (19f) basic intransitives. The goal of this section is to show that metathesis applies only in types (19a–b), derived transitives (with -CM-*i*/Ø) and intransitives (those formed with -CM-*al*). At the same time, I show that the consonants that metathesize are limited to those in morphological functions, the gender–number markers *v*, *y*, *b*, *d*, and derivational *l*, and does not include *v*, *y*, *b*, *d*, *l* when they are parts of lexical morphemes.

Causatives are, of course, transitive, and like all other transitives, they use -*o* to form the present and future tenses. The forms of causatives in the present and future tenses are parallel to those of derived transitives (see (14)).

(20) Present tense paradigm of causative verb
    ʕam–d–it–o–s   [become.accustomed–CM–CAUS–PRS–1SG.ERG]   "I teach."
    ʕam–d–it–o–(h)   [become.accustomed–CM–CAUS–PRS–2SG.ERG]   "You teach."
    ʕam–d–it-ʷ   [become.accustomed–CM–CAUS–PRS]   "S/he teaches."
    ʕam–d–it–o–tx   [become.accustomed–CM–CAUS–PRS–1EXCL.ERG]   "We (EXCL) teach."

    ʕam–d–it–u–iš   [become.accustomed–CM–CAUS–PRS–2PL.ERG]   "Y'all teach."
    ʕam–d–it-ʷ   [become.accustomed–CM–CAUS–PRS]   "They teach."

Notice that in the third person, -*o* here is reduced to -ʷ by the rule that regularly reduces word-final vowels in polysyllabic words (see end of Section 2). In the causative, metathesis did not develop as part of grammaticalization, as it did in derived transitives (Section 3), and metathesis did not spread to the causative in any person–number combination. Forms elicited from younger speakers, such as *ak'-y-it-*ʷ "s/he causes to fall down (of nuts in a tree)," *ix-it-*ʷ "s/he lets her in," and *tet'-it-*ʷ "s/he causes to cut" are parallel to forms in the Dictionary, such as *xat:-it-*ʷ "causes him to read," *ak'-y-it-*ʷ "they cause to fall down (of nuts in a tree)" (Kadagiʒe and Kadagiʒe 1984: 801b, 33b). No forms show CV metathesis.

The suffix sequence -CM-*is* is apparently not productive, but a few examples will serve to show that forms of the type (19c) have no metathesis. Elicited forms such as *toh-v-is-*ʷ "he falls asleep" or *heč'-d-is-*ʷ "he stares at" parallel examples such as *qayc'-d-is-*ʷ "he grips, grasps" from the Dictionary (Kadagiʒe and Kadagiʒe 1984: 823a).

Basic transitives are those lacking any derivational suffix. Sample conjugations are given in (21–23).

(21) Present tense paradigms of basic transitives
    xi mełּ–o–s   "I drink water."   (xi "water")
    xi mełּ–o–(h)   "You drink water."

xi mel–ʷ   "S/he drinks water."
xi mel–o–tx   "We (EXCL) drink water."
ve xi mel–ʷ   "We (INCL) drink water."   (ve "we–INCL")
xi mel–w–iš   "Y'all drink water."
xi mel–ʷ   "They drink water."

(22) ebc'–o–s   "I weigh." (TR)
     ebc'–o–(h) "You weigh." (TR)
     ebc'–ʷ   "S/he weighs." (TR)

(23) meq tet'–o–s "I cut bread."   (meq "bread")
     meq tet'–o–h "You cut bread."
     meq tet'–ʷ   "S/he cuts bread."

As we see in all of these paradigms of basic transitives, *-o* or its reduced form, *-ʷ*, consistently follows the verb stem and fails to metathesize with the preceding consonant, whether this is preceded by a vowel, as in (21) and (23), or is part of a cluster, as in (22). Thus, we do not get forms such as **eboc'* "s/he weighs (TR)"; basic transitives do not have CV metathesis.

Basic intransitives may form the present and future with *-o*, *-e*, *-u*, or *-i*, as illustrated in the partial paradigms below. Recall that round vowels in word-final position are reduced to *-ʷ* or lost altogether, while unround vowels are lost in this position.

Present tense paradigms of basic intransitive verbs of various subtypes:

(24) y–aγ–o–s   "I (F) come."
     y–aγ–o–h   "You (F) come."
     y–aγ–ʷ   "She comes."

(25) y–ax–e–s   "I (F) live."
     y–ax–e–h   "You (F) live."
     y–ax   "She lives."

(In (24–25) feminine singular is indicated by the prefix *y-*.) Once again we find no metathesis in basic intransitives in *-o*, (24), or *-e*, (25).

Historically "go" formed the present with *-u*, and "play" with *-i*, but typically both vowels are lost word-finally (*u* may be retained as lip rounding on the preceding consonant, written here as *-ʷ*). However, in the imperfects *yot'ur* "she was going" and *labc'ir* "s/he was playing," the vowel is retained before /–ra/, which is added to the present stem to form the imperfect. The stem *-ot'-* becomes *-uit'-*, and *labc'-* becomes *lebc-* as part of regular processes following loss of *-u* and *-i* (Mikelaʒe 1977). The ergative person markers (*-as*, *-ah*, etc.) are ordinarily used with both "go" and "play" (see Section 2 above and Holisky 1987 on the use of ergative and absolutive markers with intransitive verbs).

(26) y–uit'–as   CM–ot'–u–1SG.ERG   "I (F) go."
     y–uit'–ah   CM–ot'–u–2SG.ERG   "You (F) go."
     y–uit'   CM–ot'–u   "She goes."

(27) lebc'–as   labc'–i–1SG.ERG   "I play."
     lebc'–ah   labc'–i–2SG.ERG   "You play."
     lebc'   labc'–i   "S/he plays."

The partial-paradigms in (26–27) are more complex than those in (24–25); the loss of high vowels regularly conditions change in the vowel of the preceding syllable (Mikelaʒe 1977). This may be considered metathesis, but it is not the kind of CV metathesis that we are looking at in this chapter. CV metathesis in (27) would give the ungrammatical output *labic'. In the Dictionary we find forms parallel to those in (24–25), even with consonant clusters, for example, tepx^w "hits" (not *tepox) and dayt:^{w} "pours (INTR), runs" (not *dayot:) (Kadagiʒe and Kadagiʒe 1984: 281a, 29a). Elicited forms show the same regularity, for example qebl^w "s/he covers, closes" (not *qebol), tebl^w "call, name" (not *tebol). Thus, we do not find CV metathesis with basic intransitives.

We have seen that there is no metathesis of vowels with preceding consonants in (20–27), but we might consider whether the vowels metathesize when the stem happens to end in one of the consonants that also serves as a CM (-v, -y, -b, -d). There is also no metathesis in these situations, as shown by (28a–d).

(28) a. /tiv–o/   tiv^w "S/he rests."
     b. No examples with y at the end of the stem.
     c. /ab–o/   ab^w "S/he sews."
     d. /a^{n}hd–o/   a^{n}hdo   "S/he moans."

Reduction, not metathesis, occurs whenever o would be word-final immediately following a stem, including a stem ending in the consonant l, as shown in (29). This is significant because l is the consonant o metathesizes with in other environments, as shown in Section 5.

(29) y–al–o–s,   v–al–o–s   [CM–bring.IMPFV–PRS–1SG.ERG]   "I bring her/him."
     y–al–o–h,   v–al–o–h   [CM–bring.IMPFV–PRS–2SG.ERG]   "You bring her/him."
     y–al–^{w},   v–al–^{w} [CM–bring.IMPFV–PRS]   "S/he brings her/him."

Consider present and future tense forms of verbs with stems ending in Cl; does l metathesize with the following vowel? As shown in these forms from the Dictionary, for older speakers it does not: y-ebl-^{w} "it lays [an egg]," tebl-^{w} "is named," qebl-^{w} "wears a head covering" (Kadagiʒe and Kadagiʒe 1984: 220b, 275a, 833b). Younger speakers use the same forms: y-ebl-^{w} "it lays [an egg]," tebl-^{w} "is named," qebl-^{w} "wears a head covering." It appears that /l/ in clusters does not metathesize with the following vowel for either group of speakers.

In summary, among the verb types listed in (2), and repeated in (19), only transitives derived with –CM-i/Ø have been shown to have metathesis. In the third person and first person inclusive forms of other verbs, the word-final vowel that marks the present and future tenses either reduces or deletes. In particular, apart from CMs, we have seen no metathesis of present–future *–o* with any consonant, whether root or suffixal, without respect to the place or manner of articulation of the consonant. In Section 5 we take up the final type, derived intransitives, (19b).

5. Intransitives derived with the suffix -*al*

The productive type of derived intransitives is formed with the suffix -*al*, which must be preceded by a CM. An example showing the regularity of this in the aorist is given in (30).

(30) y–aq–y–al–i^n–s^w CM–grow–CM–INTR–AOR–1SG.AB   "I (F) grew."
     y–aq–y–al–i^n–h^w CM–grow–CM–INTR–AOR–2SG.ABS   "You (F) grew."
     y–aq–y–al–i^n CM–grow–CM–INTR–AOR   "She grew."
     d–aq–d–al–i^n–tx^w CM–grow–CM–INTR–AOR–1EX.ABS   "We (F, EXCL) grew."
     d–aq–d–al–i^n–š^w CM–grow–CM–INTR–AOR–2PL.ABS   "Y'all (F) grew."
     d–aq–d–al–i^n CM–grow–CM–INTR–AOR   "They (F) grew."

Other tenses are regular in the same way.

All derived intransitives formed with -CM-*al* are irregular in the present and future. In first and second person singular and in first person exclusive and second person plural, the CM is lost, and the derivational suffix plus the present–future tense formant show up as -*l*-*a* in the present and in tense–aspect–mood categories based on it, such as the imperfect. So, where we expect the sequence -CM-*al*-V, where the V might be any vowel, which would serve as the present and future tense marker for that verb, we actually find the sequence -*l*-*a*. In the speech of older speakers, the sequence -*l*-*a* remains in the third person singular and plural and in the inclusive. In the speech of younger speakers of Batsbi, the sequence -*l*-*a* is replaced in those person–number combinations by -*o*-*l*, as in the examples below.

(31) Older   Younger   Gloss   Translation
      y–aq–l–a–s^w =   CM–grow–INTR–PRS–1SG.ABS   "I (F) grow."
      y–aq–l–a–h^w =   CM–grow–INTR–PRS–2SG.ABS   "You (F) grow."
      y–aq–l–a   yaqol   CM–grow–INTR–PRS   "She grows."
      d–aq–l–a–tx^w =   CM–grow–INTR–PRS–1EX.ABS   "We (F, EXCL) grow."
      d–aq–l–e–š   =   CM–grow–INTR–PRS–2PL.ABS   "Y'all (F) grow."
      d–aq–l–a   daqol   CM–grow–INTR–PRS   "They (F) grow."

(The equal sign here means "the same as in the column to the left.") The Dictionary provides copious examples of the third person form used by older speakers; a few are given in (32).

(32) Additional examples from the dictionary (older speech)   Expected
      aɬ–l–a   (36a)   "is said"   /aɬ–CM–al–V/
      ax–l–a   (56a)   "is misled, errs"   /ax–CM–al–V/

ep'c'qep'c'–l–a (222b) "to stretch (oneself)" /ebc'qebc'–CM–al–V/
d–et:–l–a (223b) "to flutter INTR" /d–et:–CM–al–V/

The present tense (which also serves as future for these verbs) of derived intransitives is "irregular" in the sense that it is unlike the present tense forms of other verbs, which simply add *o* or another vowel to the imperfective stem to form the present.[6] On the other hand, it is "regular" (consistent) in the sense that all intransitives derived with -*al* form the present in the same way. This consistency is illustrated in (33), with data from younger speakers only. Paradigms (34–36) provide examples of this type of verb in the present tense.

(33) Additional examples from younger speech

First person		Third person	
ebc'las	"I weigh."	ebc'ol	"S/he weighs. (INTR)"
yepxlas	"I (F) dress."	yepxol	"She dresses."
leč'q'las	"I hide."	leč'q'ol	"S/he hides."
kot:las	"I grieve."	kot:ol	"S/he grieves."
axlas	"I deceive."	axol	"S/he deceives."
		yeblol[7]	"It begins."
		tet'ol	"It cuts."

(34)
Attested	Expected	Gloss	Translation
ebc'–l–a–sʷ	ebc'–CM–al–a–sʷ	weigh–CM–INTR–PRS–1SG.ABS	"I weigh. (INTR)"
ebc'–l–a–hʷ	ebc'–CM–al–a–hʷ	weigh–CM–INTR–PRS–2SG.ABS	"You weigh. (INTR)"
ebc'–o–l	ebc'–CM–al–a	weigh–CM–INTR–PRS	"S/he weighs. (INTR)"
ebc'–l–a–txʷ	ebc'–CM–al–a–txʷ	weigh–CM–INTR–PRS–1EX.ABS	"We (EX) weigh. (INTR)"
ebc'–l–e–šʷ	ebc'–CM–al–a–išʷ	weigh–CM–INTR–PRS–2PL.ABS	"Y'all weigh. (INTR)"
ebc'–o–l	ebc'–CM–al–a	weigh–CM–INTR–PRS	"They weigh. (INTR)"

(35)
Attested	Expected	Gloss	Translation
mal–l–a–sʷ	mal–CM–al–a–sʷ	tire–CM–INTR–PRS–1SG.ABS	"I get tired."
mal–l–a–hʷ	mal–CM–al–a–hʷ	tire–CM–INTR–PRS–2SG.ABS	"You get tired."
mal–o–l	mal–CM–al–a	tire–CM–INTR–PRS	"S/he/it gets tired."
mal–l–a–txʷ	mal–CM–al–a–txʷ	tire–CM–INTR–PRS–1PL.ABS	"We (EXCL) get tired."
mal–l–e–šʷ	mal–CM–al–a–išʷ	tire–CM–INTR–PRS–2PL.ABS	"Y'all get tired."
mal–o–l	mal–CM–al–a	tire–CM–INTR–PRS	"They get tired."

(36)	Attested	Expected	Gloss	Translation
	y–epx–l–a–s	CM–epx–CM–al–a–as	CM–epx–CM–INTR–PRS–1SG.ERG	"I (F) dress."
	y–epx–l–a–h	CM–epx–CM–al–a–ah	CM–epx–CM–INTR–PRS–2SG.ERG	"You (F) dress."
	y–epx–o–l	CM–epx–CM–al–a	CM–epx–CM–INTR–PRS	"She dresses."

The third person and inclusive forms undergo metathesis.

6. Discussion

The occurrence of *-o-l* in the third person does not necessarily indicate that metathesis has occurred. In principle, the speaker/learner could go from the input *y-aq-l-a* from older speakers (see (31)) to the output *yaqol* in some other way. The *-o* itself must have been generalized from the paradigm of derived transitives. Let us examine two hypotheses: (a) The ending *-l-a* metathesized, with the *a* being replaced by *o*. (b) The ending *-o-*C, with no metathesis involved, was generalized from derived transitives, such as those in (11). But what is the C on Hypothesis (b)? Only the gender–number markers—*v*, *y*, *b*, and *d*—undergo CV metathesis. Thus Hypothesis (b) makes the prediction that the C in derived intransitives would be one of the consonants used to represent CMs—*v*, *y*, *d*, or *b*. Examples (31) and (33–36) show that this does not occur. Transitive verbs provide a model for the development of *-ol* only to the extent that the *o* comes from transitives, and metathesis is involved. The ending *-ol* could not have been extended by analogy from derived transitives without explicit metathesis within the derived intransitives. On this basis I conclude that Hypothesis (a) is correct, and the process that produces forms like the third person in (31) and (34–36) is metathesis.

Generalizing the metathesis found in derived transitive verbs and in derived intransitive verbs, we can state the conditions on metathesis in younger speakers as in (37).

(37) CV > VC metathesis occurs if
- a vowel would otherwise be final in the phonological word, and
- metathesis would not put the vowel inside another morpheme.

The second condition is difficult to state, because *l* is not itself a morpheme, but what is left of a morpheme after it is reduced. We can state the metathesis as in (38).

(38) C + o → oC / + __ #

It has often been noted (see for example Hume 2001) that stating metathesis formally is always a problem, in that we must put two elements to the left of the arrow. In this case, we must actually put three symbols to the left of the arrow. The "+" to the left of the arrow is necessary to prevent the application of metathesis in monosyllabic words such as *so* "I." In the environment of the rule, the "+" prevents metathesis from occurring incorrectly in the third person forms in (29) and following. The "#" is necessary to prevent metathesis from applying in the first and second person forms in all of the paradigms above.

7. Conclusion

From the fact that metathesis spreads to a new set of verbs, where trapped -*o*- had not been retained, we can see that the process illustrated for derived transitive verbs has been interpreted by speakers as "real" phonological metathesis, even though it did not have a phonetic origin and is not particularly expected from a phonetic point of view.

Notes

1. I am grateful to my consultants, especially Naira Tsiskarishvili. I appreciate research support from the University of Massachusetts Amherst.
2. Present and future both use the same vowel, but for many verbs they are distinguished by the fact that the present is based on the imperfective stem, and the future on the perfective. For example, present tense *let'-d-o-s* "I add it" is based on the imperfective stem –*let'*-, while the future *lat'-d-o-s* "I will add it" is based on the perfective stem –*lat'*-. Some verbs do not distinguish between perfective and imperfective stems. These verbs have a single tense, which serves as both present and future.
3. The gender–number markers required by some verbs are given in parentheses after the meaning of the noun root, with the singular form before the slash, and the plural after.
4. The authors of the Dictionary (abbreviated "Dict" here) were a father and son, born in 1861 and 1895, respectively. The work was published in 1984, eight years after the death of the son and forty-seven years after that of the father.
5. Here it is assumed that the main verb was represented in the form of a converb, marked by -*š*. This assumption is not crucial to the analysis, and the main verb may have appeared instead as a present–future participle or as a finite verb in the present tense.
6. It may appear that the present tense forms of intransitives derived with -CM-*al* as "irregular" could have arisen in an entirely regular way. The vowel that designates present tense, apparently –*a*, might have conditioned syncope, an entirely productive rule. This would, in principle, delete the *a* of –*al*, juxtaposing the *l* with the CM and the consonant that precedes it. This cluster could, in principle, have simplified by removing the CM, not a regular process. But this scenario is unlikely, because the simple verb *d-al-ar* "die," which was grammaticalized, becoming the intransitivizer, has the same irregularity (*la* "dies"), yet does not fit the structural description for syncope. We can rule out later analogical reshaping of "die," since Ingush and Chechen have essentially the same irregularity: *le* "dies" (Nichols 2004: 58a, Nichols and Vagapov 2004: 90a). Thus the irregularity in the derived intransitives comes from the irregularity in the etymon.
7. For the verb *debldalar* "begin," Kadagiӡe and Kadagiӡe (1984: 220b) list the forms used by both older and younger speakers, *deblla* and *deblol*, respectively. This could

have been the first verb into which metathesis was extended because it otherwise has juxtaposed *l*'s. Other verbs I know of with stems ending in *l* (see Section 4) do not correspond to derived intransitives, thus avoiding possible juxtaposition of two *l*'s.

References

Harris, Alice C. 2013. Origins of metathesis in Batsbi. In *In search of universal grammar: From Old Norse to Zoque*, ed. by Terje Lohdahl, 221–37. Amsterdam: John Benjamins.

Harris, Alice C. and Jan Terje Faarlund. 2006. Trapped morphology. *Journal of Linguistics* 42. 289–315.

Holisky, Dee Ann. 1987. The case of the intransitive subject in Tsova-Tush (Batsbi). *Lingua* 71.103–32.

Holisky, Dee Ann, and Rusudan Gagua. 1994. Tsova-Tush (Batsbi). In *The indigenous languages of the Caucasus, 4: North East Caucasian, Part 2*, ed. by Rieks Smeets, 147–212. Delmar, NY: Caravan Press.

Hume, Elizabeth. 2001. Metathesis: Formal and functional considerations. In *Surface syllable structure and segment sequencing*, ed. by Elizabeth Hume, Norval Smith, and Jeroen van de Weijer, 1–25. Leiden: HIL Occasional Papers.

Kadagiʒe, Davit, and Nik'o Kadagiʒe. 1984. *C'ova-tušur-kartul-rusuli leksik'oni* [Tsova-Tush-Georgian-Russian dictionary]. Tbilisi: Mecniereba.

Mikelaʒe, M. 1977. Xmovanta redukcia bacbur enaši [Reduction of vowels in the Batsbi language]. *Macne* 3.118–27.

Nichols, Johanna. 2004. *Ingush-English and English-Ingush dictionary*. London: RoutledgeCurzon.

Nichols, Johanna, and Arbi Vagapov. 2004. *Chechen-English and English-Chechen dictionary*. London: RoutledgeCurzon.

5

Some Remarks on Etymological Opacity in Austronesian Languages

Robert Blust

1. Introduction

Every historical linguist is aware that extreme sound change can conceal the cognation of linguistic forms.[1] Favorite examples in Indo-European often include Armenian, as with Latin *trēs*, Armenian *erek* "three." With over 1,200 languages and many more dialects (Simons and Fennig 2020) the Austronesian (AN) language family offers many comparisons that are as well-disguised as those cited by Indo-Europeanists for Armenian. One of many possible examples that can be chosen from the Austronesian Comparative Dictionary, or ACD (Blust and Trussel ongoing) is Tsou (south-central Taiwan) *cronə*, Rennellese (Polynesian outlier, Solomon Islands) *aga* "path, way, road," which can be shown to be cognate, but only after much work. The stages in demonstrating this relationship can be laid out as follows:

Comparison 1: Tsou cronə: Rennellese aga "path, way, road"
I. Proto-Austronesian (PAN) to Tsou

PAN *zalan > (1, 2) Proto-Tsouic (PT) *calánə > (3) *clánə > (4) *cránə > (5) Tsou *cronə* "path, way, road" (Tsuchida 1976: 223).

(1) PAN *d (voiced alveolar stop) and *z (voiced palatal affricate) merged as PT *c: PAN *dapaN > PT cápalə > Tsou *caphə* "sole of the foot," *q<um>uzaN > PT *m-ucáNə > Tsou *machə* "to rain."
(2) Echo vowels were added after final consonants in Proto-Tsouic, but the echo vowel for *-aC is schwa: PAN *bəRas > PT *vərasə > Tsou *fərsə* "husked rice," *qayam > PT *ʔažámə > Tsou *zomə* "bird."
(3) Unstressed penultimate vowels were lost in Tsou: PAN *bulaN > PT *vuláłə > Tsou *frohə* "moon, month," PAN *daNum > PT *całúmu > Tsou *chumu* "water."
(4) PAN *l became Tsou /r/: PAN *paliSi > PT *palíSi > Tsou *prisi-a* "taboo," PAN *saləŋ > PT *salə́ŋə > Tsou *sroŋə* "pine tree."

(5) Stressed *a became Tsou /o/: PAN *Cau > PT *cau > Tsou *cou* "person, human being," PAN *qayam > PT *ʔayámə > *zomə* "bird."

II. PAN to Rennellese

PAN *zalan > (1) Proto-Oceanic (POC) *salan > (2) Proto-Central Pacific (PCP) *sala* > (3) Proto-Polynesian (PPN) *hala > (4,5) Rennellese *aga* "path, way, road."

(1) PAN *z > POC *s: PAN *zaRum > POC *saRum "needle," PAN *quzaN > POC *qusan "rain."
(2) PAN *-C > PCP zero: PAN *laŋiC > PCP *laŋi "sky," PAN *ənəm > PCP *ono "six."
(3) POC *s > PPN *h: POC *soŋe > PPN *hoŋe "famine," POC *masakit > PPN *mahaki "sick, painful."
(4) PPN *h > Rennellese zero: PPN *hau > Rennellese *au* "needle; tattooing needle," PPN *huhu > Rennellese *uu* "female breast," PPN *ʔahu > Rennellese *ʔau* "gall, bile."
(5) PPN *l > Rennellese /g/ ([ŋg]): PPN *lima > Rennellese *gima* "five," PPN *loli > Rennellese *gogi* "sea slug," PPN *fale > Rennellese *hage* "house."

Since both Tsou *cronə* and Rennellese *aga* derive from PAN *zalan through sound changes that are clearly recurrent in each language, there is no basis for calling an etymology such as this "opaque," regardless of how well-concealed the relationship may be due to diverging paths of accumulated sound change. Opaque etymologies, on the other hand, involve unique sound correspondences, and are therefore initially indistinguishable from chance resemblances. What distinguishes etymological opacity from chance resemblance is the operation of an intermediate sound change which itself is recurrent, but that creates a sound correspondence that may otherwise be unattested.

2. Opaque etymologies in Austronesian

The purpose of this chapter is to show that some etymologies which may not be as phonetically obscure as Tsou *cronə*, Rennellese *aga* are more challenging to the comparative method, since a priori they violate established rules of sound correspondence, yet are demonstrably cognate. Following its use in synchronic phonology I will use the term "opacity" to describe the relationships involved. As used by Kiparsky (1973), phonological rules are "opaque" if the relationship between underlying form and surface representation is obscured by application of an intermediate rule.[2] In the comparative examples considered here cognation is obscured by medial vowel syncope and cluster reduction in original trisyllables that end up as non-matching disyllables in the modern languages.

It will be well to start with a case that differs from most others in that the rule of medial vowel syncope is sporadic rather than regular, and applies to only one of the two reflexes compared.

2.1 Case 1: PAN *paŋudaN > Palauan oŋór, Hawaiian hala "pandanus"

At first look even experienced comparativists might not be prepared to consider Palauan *oŋór*: Hawaiian *hala* "pandanus" as related forms, but careful comparative work shows that they are. The stages in demonstrating this relationship can be laid out as follows, where PMP is Proto-Malayo-Polynesian (the immediate ancestor of the non-Formosan AN languages), the Formosan languages cited here represent three primary branches of the family, and the non-Formosan languages are assigned to a fourth primary branch, "Malayo-Polynesian":

Comparison 2: Palauan oŋór: Hawaiian hala "pandanus"

PAN *paŋudaN "pandanus"

Formosan:
Kavalan *payzan* "pandanus"
Rukai (Tona) *paŋudal* "pineapple"[3]
Paiwan *paŋudaL* "pineapple; *Pandanus odoratissimus*, var. sinensis"

PMP *paŋdan/paŋədan "pandanus"

Philippines:
Ilokano *paydán* "the screw pine, *Pandanus tectorius* Sol."
Cebuano *páydan* "any of the plants of the genus *Pandanus*, esp. *tectorius*"

Western Indonesia:
Malay *pandan* "Generic for all such *Pandanaceae* as are used for fine matwork or plaitwork"

Madagascar:
Malagasy *fandrana* "*Pandanus* sp."

Western Pacific:
Leipon *padr* "pandanus sp., probably *Pandanus tectorius*"
Wuvulu *paxa* "pandanus"
Mussau *arana* "littoral pandanus: *Pandanus tectorius*"
Woleaian *fash(a)* "pandanus, pineapple"

Central Pacific:
Fijian *vadra* "the pandanus tree: *Pandanus odoratissimus*"
Tongan *fā* "kind of pandanus which sends down shoots from the branches to the ground"
Samoan *fala* "name given to a number of tree-like plants of the genus *Pandanus*; mat"

Given just these limited data it is fairly easy to see how PAN *paŋudaN became Hawaiian *hala*:

(1) There was medial vowel syncope (irregular in this form, although as will be seen, medial schwa syncope in the environment VC__CV is shared by many AN languages, and the PMP form may have been *paŋədan rather than *paŋdan).
(2) PAN *N merged with *n everywhere outside Taiwan. This gave rise to forms like those in Ilokano or Cebuano, although as noted above, these are ambiguous for *paŋdan or *paŋədan.
(3) The preconsonantal nasal in *paŋdan underwent place assimilation to the following stop, producing forms like Malay *pandan*.
(4) The cluster *nd became *dr, a prenasalized alveolar trill in Proto-Oceanic (ancestral to about 460 languages in Melanesia, Micronesia, and Polynesia). This produced POC *padran.
(5) Final consonants were lost in most Oceanic languages, yielding *padra.
(6) POC *p became Proto-Polynesian *f.
(7) POC *dr became Proto-Polynesian *r, yielding PPN *fara "pandanus."
(8) Proto-Polynesian *r merged with *l in Nuclear Polynesian (all but Tongan and Niue), giving *fala.
(9) Proto-Polynesian *f became Hawaiian *h*, producing the attested *hala*.

As the reader might already have anticipated, the greater challenge lies in deriving Palauan *oŋór*.

Here are the steps:

(1) First, PAN *paŋudaN reduced to PMP *paŋdan, or *paŋədan, as shown above; whichever of these forms was found in PMP produced pre-Palauan *paŋə́dan.
(2) *p became Palauan *w*, hence *paŋə́dan > *waŋə́dan: *p > w: *pitu > e-*wíd* "seven," *puki > *wuk* "vagina," *pukət > *wúkəð* "casting net."
(3) *wa-* from *pa-* contracted to *o*, hence *waŋə́dan > *oŋə́dan: *pa/wa- > o-: *pa-muket > *o-múkəð* "catch fish by casting net," *paniki > *olík* "flying fox, fruit bat," *paka-təlu > *okə-ðéy* "thirty," *pa-zalan "make something go or move" > *o-r-ráyl* "to lead (as animal), to drive (as car)," *waqay-ña > *oʔí-l* "his/its leg."

This gets us from *paŋudaN to pre-Palauan *oŋə́dan. As can be seen from the preceding examples, stress in pre-Palauan was penultimate, and in the modern language it maintains its position on the erstwhile penultimate syllable in words that have lost the final vowel.

(4) Stressed schwa became *e* or *o* without stateable conditions: PMP *təkən > *ðekəl* "punting pole," *ləñab > *yelab* "flood," *Rəbək > *s<u>ebək* "to fly"; PMP *təRas > *ðort* "ironwood tree: *Intsia bijuga*," PMP *tuqəlan "bone" > *ðaʔóyl* "spine, backbone," PMP *ənəm > *e-l-óləm* "six," PMP *la(m)baq > *yóbaʔ* "ravine, valley," PMP *bəRsay > *bəsós* "canoe paddle" (note that here a schwa was inserted within the consonant cluster in penultimate position, and then *-ay, which contracted to –*e* disappeared like other final vowels; *R became *r* before dentals, but otherwise became *s*, and *s normally became *t*, but a derived sequence of sVs evidently did not change).

This gets us from *oŋə́dan to *oŋódan.

(5) PMP *d became Palauan r: PMP *tiŋadaq > ðəŋárəʔ "look upward," PMP *tuduq > ðúrəʔ "to leak (as a roof)," PMP *danum > ralm "fresh water," PMP *daqan > ráʔəl "branch."

This gets us from *oŋódan to *oŋóran.

(6) PMP unstressed vowels preceding a final consonant reduced to schwa or dropped entirely (for the former cf. reflexes of *tiŋadaq, *tuduq or *daqan immediately above; for the latter cf. reflexes of *pa-zalan or *danum above).

This gets us from *oŋóran to *oŋórn.

(7) PMP *n became Palauan l: PMP *ba-b<in>ahi (pre-Palauan *ba-bínay) > Palauan babíl "female, woman," PMP *bulan > Palauan búyl "moon, month," PMP *nanaq > laləʔ "pus," PMP *niuR > Palauan líus "coconut."

This gets us from *oŋórn to *oŋórl.

(8) The treatment of derived final consonant clusters is not entirely clear. In PMP *quzan > ʔull "rain," expected -rl became -ll ([ʔúləl]). In other cases the second member of a final consonant cluster was dropped, as with PMP *bituqən > btuʔ (expected **btuʔl) "star," *qumun > ʔum (expected **ʔuml) "earth oven," or *qumaŋ "hermit crab" > ʔum (expected **ʔumŋ) "type of snail." Given its closeness to the attested form we can only assume that the expected *oŋórl underwent final cluster reduction like the words for "star," "earth oven," and "type of snail."

What makes this comparison opaque is that, although Palauan reflects the medial vowel of the original trisyllable, Hawaiian does not. Following standard assumptions of sound change in the latter we would expect PMP *paŋədan to yield Hawaiian **hanola rather than hala. The obscuring fact that Palauan has a velar nasal that appears to correspond irregularly to Hawaiian l is due to medial schwa syncope in the ancestry of Hawaiian (and many other languages), giving rise to *-ŋd-, then *-nd-, then *-dr- ([ndr]), then *-r-, and finally *-l-, while the two consonants were kept apart in Palauan, either by retention of PMP *ə, or by subsequent insertion of schwa, which then acquired regular penultimate stress.

2.2 Case 2: PMP *timəRaq > Tagalog tiŋgáʔ, Malay timah "tin, lead"

In a three-volume work that laid the foundations for a comparative phonology of the Austronesian languages, the German medical doctor and linguist Otto Dempwolff (1934–8) began volume 1 with an "inductive" reconstruction of what he called "Urindonesisch," based on just three languages, Tagalog, Toba Batak, and Javanese. As Dempwolff was careful to point out (but some others misunderstood), following the idealist philosophy of the "As if" formulated by Hans Vaihinger in 1911 (Vaihinger 1968), these three languages were chosen to represent the range of phonological correspondences that he had already examined in some 150–200 languages spanning much of the geographical range of the Austronesian family. Rather than basing his comparison on just three languages, then, his position was that these languages were *representatives* of a much larger set. In volume 2 his reconstructed "Urindonesisch" was tested deductively against eight languages, including three in insular Southeast Asia (Malay, Ngaju Dayak, and Malagasy), two in Melanesia (Fijian and Sa'a), and three in Polynesia (Tongan, Futunan, and Samoan). This led him to rename the reconstruction he proposed "Uraustronesisch," a language that linguists today would call Proto-Malayo-Polynesian rather than Proto-Austronesian (which cannot be reconstructed without data from Formosan languages). The third volume was a set of a little over 2,200 reconstructions together with supporting evidence.

Dempwolff's work is dated today, but one enduring feature of his method that stands out is his dogged insistence on the regularity of sound change (he called himself a "Neogrammarian"), and his thoroughness in finding cognates where these existed. Given these scholarly traits it would be surprising to discover that he had overlooked fairly straightforward cognates found in the comparison of such languages as Tagalog and Malay, yet he did. To choose a prominent example of Dempwolff's failure to recognize cognation where it was opaque, comparison 3 was completely overlooked:

Comparison 3: Tagalog tiŋgá? : Malay timah "tin, lead"

Tagalog	tiŋgá?	lead (the metal)
Malay	timah	tin; also a generic term covering zinc or spelter (*t. sari* = "floral tin"), lead (*t. hitam* = "black tin"), and tinned iron (*t. puteh* = "white tin")

The first thing to note is that these forms are native, not loans. Some of the most important tin deposits in the world are found in the Malay peninsula, where small nuggets are present in surface layers, and a word for tin can be reconstructed to at least a language ancestral to those of the Philippines and western Indonesia. Dempwolff's reconstruction recognized lexical bases of two types: CVCVC, where all consonants are optional, and CVCCVC, with two subtypes: CVNCVC, where N is a homorganic nasal that may or may not be present in every reflex, as in *tumbuq "to grow" (but reflexes of *tubuq in many languages), or $C_1V_1C_2C_1V_1C_2$, where the base was a reduplicated monosyllable that was monomorphemic in PAN, as with *tuktuk "knock, pound, beat." Given this established template the Tagalog form *tiŋgá?* could only reflect an etymon with *-ŋg-, and if that was the case Malay should have the same nasal-stop sequence. The comparison Tagalog *tiŋgá?* : Malay *timah* was therefore impossible, since *g* : *m* is not a sound correspondence: Tagalog *g* reflects PMP *g or *R (probably an alveolar trill that was backed in many daughter languages), and Malay *m* reflects only *m. The possibility that the sound correspondences in this comparison might be misaligned as a result of templatic change (as change from a trisyllabic protoform to disyllabic comparata in the daughter languages), and that the two nasals might therefore be the proper locus of correspondence was not considered, perhaps because ŋ : m is also not a recurrent sound correspondence between these languages.

The chance that Dempwolff may have overlooked a valid cognate set that is of some interest, both phonologically and culturally, becomes clear when we expand the comparison to Bikol, a near-relative of Tagalog, where we find two pronunciations of the related form: *timgá? ~ tiŋgá?* "lead (the metal)." Given this information it immediately becomes apparent what has happened. Since heterorganic clusters are reconstructed only in reduplicated monosyllables, the medial cluster in Bikol *timgá?* must be a product of vowel syncope, and the pronunciation *tiŋgá?*, which is all that survives in Tagalog, must be due to nasal place assimilation.

It is well-established that PAN and PMP had a four-vowel system *i, *u, *a, *ə (conventionally written *e), and that the schwa was shorter than other vowels. One consequence of the shorter duration of schwa is that it was much more prone to deletion in certain environments. The most notable of these is VC__CV, an environment in which schwa syncope is particularly common across much of the Austronesian language family, as shown in Table 5.1, where reflexes above the dotted line show schwa syncope and those below the dotted line do not.

Schwa syncope is so common in this and various other words that it is tempting to reconstruct PAN *baqRu, with no medial vowel. However, this would violate an otherwise well-established canonical template, and would also fail to explain the agreement of Moken, Malay, Nias, Sundanese, Palauan, and all Oceanic witnesses in pointing to a schwa between *q and *R.

Table 5.1 Comparative evidence for schwa syncope in reflexes of PAN *baqəRu "new"

		PAN	*baqəRu	new
F		Bunun	baqlu	new
		Amis	fa?loh	new
WMP		Itbayaten	va?yo	new; fresh; modern; recent
		Bikol	ba?gó	new
		Hanunóo	bág?u (< met.)	new
		Agutaynen	ba?lo	new
		Kalamian Tagbanwa	baklu?	new
		Chamorro	pa?go	now, today
		Moken	kəloi (< *bakəloi)	new
		Malay	baharu ~ baru	new; fresh; now at last
		Nias	bohou	new
		Sundanese	bahayu	new; fresh; now at last
		Palauan	bə?ós	new; clean
OC		Bali (Uneapa)	vaghoru	new
		Mono-Alu	haolu	new
		Arosi	haoru	new, recent; youthful, vigorous
		Tongan	fo?ou	new, fresh; strange, unfamiliar

Note: F = Formosan, WMP = Western Malayo-Polynesian, OC = Oceanic.

A residue of schwa syncope in the environment VC__CV is, in fact, a synchronic process in Tagalog, where the schwa has become *i unless conditioned by an adjacent rounded vowel, as in *qatəp > *atíp* "roof thatch," but *apt-án* "to thatch a roof," *datəŋ > *datíŋ* "arrival," but *datn-án* "to visit, come upon," or *Sajək > *halík* "a kiss," but *halk-án ~ hagk-án* "to kiss someone." With only this much information, then, it appears safe to conclude that Tagalog *tiŋgá?* reflects *timəgaq or *timəRaq, and that Malay reduced derived heterorganic consonant clusters to single segments.

Having reasoned our way to this position the next step is to search for languages that might provide direct confirmation of a trisyllable, and the following languages do just that:

- Western Bukidnon Manobo (Mindanao, southern Philippines) *timəya?* "the metal, lead"
- Kelabit (northern Sarawak, Malaysian Borneo) *səməra?* "lead (metal)"
- Gorontalo (northern Sulawesi) *timohe* "tin, lead."

Each of these words can be traced to *timəRaq, giving us the final, disambiguated form of the reconstruction (Kelabit shows regular *t > s/__i, followed by neutralization of all prepenultimate vowels as schwa, as in *timun > *simun* "cucumber," *tinaqi > *sina?ih ~ səna?ih* "intestines," or *gaRami > *gəramih* "rice stubble").

Perhaps the most significant conclusion from establishing this single etymology is that Malay and other languages of western Indonesia that now limit medial consonant clusters to homorganic nasal-stop sequences, may once have permitted a wider variety of medial clusters, much like those found in modern Philippine languages, a point to which I return below.

2.3 Case 3: PMP *saŋəlaR > Bikol *saŋlág* "frying of grains or peanuts," Malay *səlar* "branding; to brand"

A second example of an opaque comparison is one that Dempwolff cannot be faulted for overlooking, since Tagalog lacks a form related to Malay *səlar*, although one appears in its close relative, Bikol.

Comparison 4: Bikol mag-saŋlág "to fry (without oil)": Malay səlar "branding; to brand"

Once again, we are confronted with sound correspondences that are a priori impossible, since only obstruents allow medial prenasalization. To demonstrate that these forms are cognate we need to add other languages to the comparison, which shows that, like reflexes of *timəRaq, these conventionally non-corresponding cognates in Bikol and Malay reflect an original trisyllable with medial schwa, as shown in Table 5.2.

In some ways this comparison is more transparent than that supporting PMP *timeRaq, since the Bikol medial cluster and Malay /l/ share an element in common.

Table 5.2 Evidence for PMP *saŋəlaR "to fry without oil"

PMP		*saŋəlaR	to roast, fry without oil
WMP	Isneg	saŋlāg	prepare coconut oil by cooking the milk
	Ifugaw (Batad)	haŋlag	roasting spatula used to roast grains in a vat
	Bikol	mag-saŋlág	to fry grains such as rice or corn; to fry peanuts
	Cebuano	saŋlág	to roast something in a pan without oil
	Mansaka	sallag	to roast, cook without water or lard
	Iban	səlar	(of fire) lick, touch, singe, burn
	Malay	səlar	branding
	Minangkabau	saŋlar ~ salar	broiling
CMP	Kambera	hoɲu	to bake, roast (as maize, coffee beans)
	Tetun	sona	to roast; to fry

Note: CMP = Central-Malayo-Polynesian, including most of the languages of the Lesser Sunda and Moluccan islands of eastern Indonesia.

In other ways, however, it is less transparent, since no known daughter language retains a trisyllabic shape.

There is no need to enter into details about the historical development of these forms in each language, but it should be noted that Malay again shows evidence of having reduced earlier heterorganic consonant clusters in medial position. This is made particularly clear by the longer variant in its close relative, Minangkabau (sometimes called "Minangkabau Malay") of west-central Sumatra. The other feature of this comparison that is obscured by the reduction of an original trisyllable to disyllables in all known daughter languages is the correspondence of the penultimate vowels. Malay penultimate schwa can regularly correspond to /a/ in Isneg or Bikol, but not in Ifugaw, Cebuano, or Mansaka, so this sound correspondence is irregular if we assume that the proto-form was disyllabic. However, Malay regularly neutralized the contrast of *a and schwa in prepenultimate syllables, as in PMP *qapəju > həmpədu "gall, gall bladder," *kamuniŋ > kemuniŋ "a tree: *Murraya* sp.," or *taliŋa > taliŋa "ear." The derivation of Malay səlar from a trisyllabic etymon is thus fully supported by recurrent sound correspondences: *saŋəlaR > saŋəlar > səŋəlar > səŋlar > səlar. Note that the deleted consonant in this comparison is the first member of the derived cluster (*-ŋl- > -l-), while in *timah* it was the last member of the derived cluster (*-mr- > -m-), a point to which I return below.

Although it is a truism in historical linguistics that cognation is not dependent on phonetic similarity, scholars in sister disciplines (such as social anthropology) often harbor the misconception that phonetic similarity is the basis for recognizing related linguistic forms. This can, of course be true, where both or all languages compared have fairly simple historical phonologies and the forms compared have consequently not diverged widely from their ancestral prototype. But any attempt to seek an equivalence of phonetic similarity and cognation is bound to fail where sound change has been extensive, for here real cognates may show little or no phonetic similarity, just as phonetically similar forms that do not show recurrent sound correspondences can be mistaken for real cognates when in fact they are products of convergence.

Of the comparisons considered so far, the first, which is not a product of opaque change, and the second, which is only partly a product of opaque change, show the least phonetic similarity, since none of the segments in Tsou *cronə*, Rennellese *aga*, or in Palauan *oŋór*, Hawaiian *hala* are identical. By contrast, the only mismatch in Tagalog *tiŋgáʔ* : Malay *timah* "tin" is *-ŋg-* : *-m-*, which is not a sound correspondence, and no doubt was the reason Dempwolff (1934–8: Volume 3) passed over this comparison in silence. Similarly, Bikol *saŋlág*: Malay *səlar* would be straightforward under standard comparative assumptions, except for the velar nasal.

3. Comparative paradigms

Each of the three preceding cases of etymological opacity illustrates the role of comparative paradigms (CPs) in historical linguistics: certain etymologies were "invisible" under standard assumptions about cognate searching, but were shown to be products of recurrent sound change once medial vowel syncope in trisyllables was recognized. In effect, the validity of these comparisons only became evident after the guiding principles for cognate identification were modified.

Blust (1977) defined a comparative paradigm as a set of assumptions guiding research with particular reference to the search for cognate forms. This term can easily be misunderstood, given the common use of "paradigm" in linguistics to designate a set of grammatically related forms. In the present context "paradigm" is used rather in the sense that the historian of science Thomas Kuhn intended, namely as a set of guiding principles for the conduct of scientific research (Kuhn 1962). In Kuhn's conception, "normal science" consists of puzzle solving: the basic parameters of a field of study are agreed upon, and the task of daily research is to follow these universally adopted parameters in solving what are essentially puzzles in the data that are studied. In any field anomalies accumulate over time, and once these reach a critical mass the entire structure of the field is overthrown by a revolutionary conception of how to proceed with the investigation of data. Linguists should have no trouble recognizing this process in the history of their field: first the Neogrammarians, then Saussure, and then Chomsky led scientific revolutions in linguistics: the way that research was conducted before and after these pivotal figures changed fundamentally, as the very notion of what constitutes an interesting question was transformed by adopting a new paradigm.

3.1 CP1 and CP2

What has been generally overlooked is that the transformation of a scientific paradigm need not affect the entire structure of a field of study: paradigm shifts are also possible in more restricted domains, such as the guiding principles for cognate identification in historical linguistics. In Blust (1977) this was demonstrated for cognate searching in Oceanic languages. The major comparative paradigm used to find Oceanic cognates of forms in the Austronesian languages of insular Southeast Asia (there called CP1) essentially looked for (1) phonological mergers, and (2) loss of final consonants, since the latter is a feature of perhaps 90% of all Oceanic languages. Formally, CP1 was thus stated as follows:

CP1:   PMP   *CV(C)CVC
       POC   *CVCVC
       most OC languages CVCV

Comparisons such as Malay *taŋis*, Hawaiian *kani* "weep; mourn," Malay *laŋit*, Hawaiian *lani* "sky," or Malay *tumbuh* : Hawaiian *kupu* "grow" followed in a straightforward manner from this set of assumptions, and permitted the identification of many related morphemes. However, several attractive comparisons that stood outside CP1 suggested that perhaps CP1 was putting theoretical "blinders" on the search for Oceanic cognates. In particular, the POC finder list of Grace (1969) and other publications of the same period contained half a dozen forms that looked like reflexes of PMP reduplicated monosyllables, but departed from them in ways that were not previously seen as systematic, as shown in Table 5.3.

Table 5.3 Expected and attested POC reflexes of PMP reduplicated monosyllables c.1970

PMP	POC (expected)	POC (proposed)	Gloss
*butbut	*puput	*puti	to pluck, uproot
*gasgas	*kakas	*kasi	to scrape off
*karkar	*kakar	*kari	to scratch up
*ñamñam	*ñañam	*ñami	to taste
*təktək	*totok	*toki	to hack off
*tuktuk	*tutuk	*tuki	to knock, pound, beat

The first question that these data raised was whether the PMP reconstructions were actually related to those proposed for POC, since a mechanical procedure for cognate identification (namely, the use of CP1) shows a lack of correspondence. However, by insisting on using CP1 we would miss a recurrent pattern: in each case the POC form that was then accepted corresponds to the last syllable of the expected POC form, with an extra vowel *-i. It was therefore concluded that we might reasonably hypothesize that the attested POC forms contain a fossilized suffix.

In fact, Pawley (1972) posited POC *-i "close transitive," one of two pivotal transitive suffixes in the grammar of POC. Given these observations I proposed a second comparative paradigm, CP2, as follows:

CP2:   PMP $*C_1V_1(C_2)C_1V_1C_2$
       most OC languages CVCi (in verbs)

Once this novel method of cognate searching was adopted some thirty-seven plausible comparisons were uncovered, most of which had previously been overlooked (Blust 1977: 27–8). But this was only the beginning of the harvest to be reaped. If forms such as PMP *butbut would, by CP1 produce POC *puput, but were shown by CP2 to produce *puti "pluck, uproot," it seemed clear that both forms could be derived from a *grammatical paradigm* in which transitive verbs were derived from simple bases by suffixation with *-i. In other words, intransitive bases lacked morphology, while transitive bases carried it, as shown in Table 5.4.

Table 5.4 A partial Proto-Oceanic grammatical paradigm relating CP1 and CP2

Intransitive	Transitive	
*puput	*puput-i	to pluck, pull out
*kakas	*kakas-i	to scrape
*kakar	*kakar-i	to scratch up
*ñañam	*ñañam-i	to taste
*totok	*totok-i	to hack off
*tutuk	*tutuk-i	to knock, pound, beat

Further cognate searching confirmed this reconstruction, and suggested that, for reflexes of PMP reduplicated monosyllables, a POC grammatical paradigm had become fragmented, and the parts disassociated in many daughter languages, as seen in Lau (Solomon Islands) *fufu* "pick fruit" (< *puput), and *fusi* "pluck" (< *puput-i), or Samoan *tutu* "beat mulberry bark on a special anvil" (< *tutuk), and *tuʔi* "knock, hit, strike" (< *tutuk-i), each of which is listed as a separate lexical entry in dictionaries of these languages (Milner 1966; Fox 1974). Moreover, the full trisyllabic forms have been retained in some languages, as Sa'a *huhu-si* "to pluck, pick off" (given as a transitive verb) versus *huhu* "to pluck, pick off" (given as an intransitive verb), or Tongan *tutuki* "to knock or nail," given as a monomorphemic dictionary entry.

3.2 The reduplication–transitivity correlation in Oceanic languages

The insight that a POC grammatical paradigm of the form *puput (intr.): *puput-i (trans.) could have undergone widespread reduction to *puput (intr.): *put-i (trans.) takes us back to the disyllabic canonical target that is pervasive in Austronesian languages. A grammatical paradigm with intransitive verb base and transitive counterpart suffixed with *-i had already been established by Pawley (1972), and now all that was needed with reduplicated monosyllables was to recognize that a common mechanism in linguistic change had reduced forms like $*C_1V_1C_1V_1C_2\text{-}i$ first to *CVC-i, and then to *CVCi in many Oceanic languages, once the cohesion of an original grammatical paradigm was broken. That mechanism, of course, is haplology.

It was known since the beginning of the twentieth century that many Austronesian languages favor a disyllabic canonical target, using devices such as epenthesis, reduplication, canonical reduction (as by irregular loss of glottal stop or /h/ between like vowels, which then coalesce), or loss of a morpheme boundary to restore a disyllabic form that has been reduced by regular sound change, or extended by morphology (Brandstetter 1916; Blust 2007). Finally, it was already well-known in the mid-1970s that many Oceanic languages show a correlation between reduplication and transitivity such that reduplicated verb stems are used intransitively, and non-reduplicated verb stems are used transitively. Examples of mechanisms used to satisfy the disyllabic canonical target in Austronesian languages are:

(a) epenthesis

PMP	pre-Tiruray	Tiruray	
*buhək	buk	əbuk	head hair
*nahik	nik	ənik	climb
*tau	taw	ətəw	person
*tuhud	tud	ətur	knee

(b) restorative reduplication

PMP	Old Javanese	Modern Javanese	
*zuRuq	duh	duduh	juice, sauce
*duha	ro/roro	loro	two
*tuRut	tut/tuut	tutut	to follow
*baRah	wa/waa	wawa	ember

(c) canonical reduction

Tagalog *laʔás* "cracked, split (wood)" : *laslás* "ripped, torn"

Tagalog *tahán* "act of ceasing or stopping" : *tantán* "cessation, stoppage"

Tagalog *súhol* "bribe" : *sulsól* "instigation to do evil or some improper act"

(d) loss of a morpheme boundary

PMP	Old Javanese	Modern Javanese	
*bəReqat	bwat, a-bwat	abot	heavy
*zauq	doh, a-doh	adoh	far, distant
*təRas	twas, a-twas	atos	hard (material)

In the last of these categories the Old Javanese bases (recorded on ninth- to fifteenth century palm leaf manuscripts) were nominal (*bwat* "weight," *doh* "distance," *twas* "hardness"), and the prefixed forms were stative verbs (*a-bwat* "heavy," *a-doh* "far, distant," *a-twas* "hard"). However, in modern Javanese the stative morpheme boundary has been lost just in bases that became monosyllabic through regular sound change, producing new dictionary entries that begin with fossilized *a-*, a prefix that is otherwise still productive in the language.

Given this variety of mechanisms conspiring to restore a lost disyllabism in content morphemes, it is clear that haplology would provide yet another way to satisfy this constraint, and this is exactly what would be needed to get from POC *tutuk : *tutuk-i to intermediate *tutuk : *tuk-i, and then to Samoan *tutu : tuʔi* and the like in modern Oceanic languages.

Examples of the reduplication–transitivity correlation in Tok Pisin (New Guinea Pidgin English), which show a relexified structure found in many Oceanic languages, are given in Table 5.5.

Table 5.5 The reduplication–transitivity correlation in Tok Pisin

Transitive form		Intransitive form	
wasim	to wash s.t.	waswas	to bathe, wash oneself
tingim	to remember, think of something	tingting	to think, ponder
lukim	to see s.t.	lukluk	to look
tokim	to say s.t., speak	toktok	to talk

In terms of general linguistic typology there is no particular reason why intransitive verbs should be reduplicated, while their transitive counterparts are not. But if POC paradigm mates of the type *tutuk: *tutuk-i had reduced to *tutuk: *tuk-i and then to *tutu : tuki*, as is the case in many attested Oceanic languages, a template would have existed for associating intransitive verbs with reduplication and transitive verbs with unreduplicated bases plus -i. A template could only have been extended if a sufficiently large number of examples existed for the pattern to be prominent in the centuries immediately following the breakup of POC, and the data discovered to date suggest that this was very likely the case

Once this correlation was established, it could be applied to unreduplicated bases, as in the following derivation for Mokilese of eastern Micronesia, based on the contrast of what Harrison (1973: 428ff) calls "telic transitive verbs" and their intransitive counterparts:

*qunap-i	*qunap	"to pluck; to scale"
unap-i	unap	*q > Ø
una-pi	una	-C > Ø, shift of morpheme boundary
———	unauna	reduplication
una-p	unaun	-V > Ø
una	———	*p > Ø
wina]$_t$	winaun]$_i$	breaking

In short, the decision to adopt CP2 uncovered a historical basis for the ubiquitous reduplication–transitivity correlation in Oceanic languages, and showed that, appearances notwithstanding, it was not found in Proto-Oceanic, since it can be fully explained as a phonologically driven syntactic drift, or more exactly, as a syntactic drift powered by canonical constraints.

4. A new comparative paradigm for Philippine–Malay etymologies

The preceding discussion of CP2 may appear to have been a digression, but it was a digression with a purpose, namely to focus attention on comparisons (c) and (d) as evidence that many more Philippine–Malay etymologies may be uncovered once it is recognized that opaque etymologies such as Tagalog *tiŋgáʔ* : Malay *timah* "tin, lead," or Bikol *mag-saŋlág* : Malay *səlar* "fry without oil" point to the need for a new comparative paradigm to recover trisyllabic etyma that are reflected with medial consonant clusters in Philippine languages corresponding to single consonants in languages of western Indonesia, represented here by Malay, since this is lexically the most conservative of all Austronesian languages (Blust 2000: 329, Blust and Trussel ongoing). In other words, once it is recognized that a single intervocalic consonant in Malay can correspond to a variety of medial consonant clusters in Philippine languages the way is suddenly open to recognizing many new comparisons that had previously been passed over because they were "invisible" to the standard comparative paradigm used to identify cognates. This was, in fact, done in Blust (1982), and continues to be done today. Some of these are well-known etymologies that would have been recognized in any case (and were by Dempwolff 1934–8: Volume 3), because the reduction of consonant clusters in languages of western Indonesia had a minimal effect on the shape of the form, as with PMP *tuqəlaŋ "bone," or PAN *binəSiq "seed rice":[4]

PMP	*tuqəlaŋ	bone
Itbayaten	toʔxaŋ	bone
Itneg	tulʔáŋ (< met.)	bone
Bikol	tuʔláŋ	bone
Old Javanese	tahulaŋ	bone
Chamorro	toʔlaŋ	bone
Malay	tulaŋ	bone
PAN	*binəSiq	seed rice
Thao	finshiq	seed rice
Tagalog	binhíʔ	seed (chosen for the nursery)
Malay	bəneh	seed; plant seed

However, others are better-disguised, and it will be well to mention a few of them to drive home the point that opaque etymologies in Austronesian languages are not rare, and to show that Tagalog *tiŋgáʔ* : Malay *timah* "tin" is not the only Tagalog : Malay comparison that Dempwolff failed to see. Rather, opaque etymologies in Austronesian languages are as common as original trisyllables that contained a medial schwa, since this was the environment for syncope, and it was schwa syncope that gave rise to historically secondary medial consonant clusters, nearly all of which simplified to single consonants in Malay and other languages of western Indonesia:

PWMP	*bakəlad	fish corral
Tagalog	baklád	fish corral
Iban	bəlat	cane fishing screen or net
Malay	bəlat	screen trap for fish
PWMP	*cidərit	squirt out in a stream
Cebuano	sídlit	squirt out in a stream
Malay	ceret	looseness of the bowels, diarrhea
Minangkabau	cirit	looseness of the bowels, diarrhea

PWMP	*lagətub	blistered
Cebuano	lagtúb	inflamed, blistered (as s.t. cooked crisp)
Malay	lətup	blister on skin
PWMP	*patəlaŋ	interval, alternating (as bands of color)
Tagalog	patláŋ	interval; space between
Malay	pəlaŋ	striped, banded (in coloring)
PWMP	*rabənut	yank or jerk s.t. away from s.o.
Tagalog	labnót	plucked out
Cebuano	lábnut	pull s.t. with a jerk
Malay	rəbut	snatching, tearing at
PWMP	*sapələd	tart or harsh taste
Cebuano	sáplud	slightly bitterish in taste
Malay (Java)	səpat	harsh, acid, tart, of taste
PWMP	*taŋəpi	edge, riverbank
Cebuano	táŋpi ~ támpi	bank of a body of water, edge of surface
Malay	təpi	edge, brink
PWMP	*tupəlak	push away
Cebuano	túplak	push s.o. or s.t. away
Malay	tolak	pushing away or pushing off
PWMP	*utəŋaq	shake loose, come off
Cebuano	útŋaʔ	let go of s.t. attached firmly
Malay	uŋah	be shaking loose (as a tooth)

It cannot be entirely predicted which consonant in a medial cluster drops in Malay, although a fuller set of comparisons than that given here suggests that *l* was weak as the first member of a cluster, and strong as the second member, with some notable exceptions (as *sapələd > səpat).

In any case, few of these comparisons were recognized before Blust (1982), for the simple reason that, starting with the Malay member one would look for disyllables with a single medial consonant in Philippine languages, as Dempwolff evidently did, and in using this comparative paradigm a Tagalog cognate of Malay *bəlat* "screen trap for fish" should be **bilát or **bilád rather than the attested *baklád*, and so forth with most other comparisons of this type. Needless to say, in form-based searches (which is the way that cognate searching usually is done) this would lead to numerous oversights.

5. Conclusions

Although it is often straightforward, cognate searching can be challenging, both because sound changes may be extreme even when completely predictable from established precedents, and because the operation of some sound changes may effectively change the rules that normally apply to cognate identification, creating unique sound correspondences that are nonetheless clearly not products of chance. As I hope I have shown with the examples in this chapter, it is comparisons of the latter type that would appear to exemplify a kind of opacity comparable to that described in synchronic phonologies. Finally, given the reduction of *a to schwa in Malay reflexes of (C)aCəCV(C), it is clear that these bases remained trisyllabic until the neutralization of prepenultimate *a and schwa, and this means that forms like Malay *səlar* must have passed through stages *saŋəlaR > *səŋəlaR > *səŋlaR > *səlar*, from which it follows that the development of medial consonant clusters as a result of schwa syncope was independent in languages of the Philippines and western Indonesia.

Notes

1. It is my pleasure to dedicate this paper to Lyle Campbell, who became a colleague at the University of Hawai'i late in his career (2010). Few scholars who I have known in my forty-three years as an academic have such a range of interests, knowledge, and talents, and I feel fortunate to have had him close at hand during the past seven years for a variety of stimulating conversations, many of which I couldn't have had with anyone else. I am grateful to Victoria Chen for comments which led to improvements in an earlier version of this chapter. Any remaining errors are my own.
2. Kiparsky was specifically concerned with ordered rules in a synchronic phonology, and in particular with how the prior application of one rule could render the conditions for application of a subsequent rule "opaque," meaning that the environment for a later rule to apply could not be stated in terms of surface segments. As an example, he noted the raising of the diphthongal nucleus ay to əy before /t/ in some dialects of English, even where a flapping rule had already weakened intervocalic /t/ to a flap (as in "writing"), making it impossible to state the condition for raising in terms of surface phonetic properties.
3. Due to its similarity in shape to the pandanus fruit, and its greater economic importance in the modern world, the introduced Amazonian pineapple has become the primary or secondary referent of this term in several languages, including some not cited here, as Tetun and Leti of eastern Indonesia (Blust and Trussel ongoing, sub PAN *paŋudaN "pandanus").
4. Nonetheless, Dempwolff (1934–8: Volume 3) reconstructed disyllables *tulaŋ "bone," and *bənih/binih "seed" for these, so impressed was he with the predominant disyllabic canonical preference of Austronesian languages.

References

Blust, Robert. 1977. A rediscovered Austronesian comparative paradigm. *Oceanic Linguistics* 16.1–51.

Blust, Robert. 1982. An overlooked feature of Malay historical phonology. *Bulletin of the School of Oriental and African Studies* 45.284–99.

Blust, Robert. 2000. Why lexicostatistics doesn't work: The "universal constant" hypothesis and the Austronesian languages. In *Time depth in historical linguistics*, ed. by Colin Renfrew, April McMahon, and Larry Trask, 311–31. Cambridge: The McDonald Institute for Archaeological Research.

Blust, Robert. 2007. Disyllabic attractors and anti-antigemination in Austronesian sound change. *Phonology* 24:1–36.

Blust, Robert, and Stephen Trussel. Ongoing. *Austronesian Comparative Dictionary*. Online: www.trussel2.com/ACD.

Brandstetter, Renward. 1916. *An introduction to Indonesian linguistics*. Translated by C. O. Blagden. London: The Royal Asiatic Society.

Dempwolff, Otto. 1934–8. Vergleichende Lautlehre des austronesischen Wortschatzes. 3 volumes: *Zeitschrift für Eingeborenen-Sprachen*, Special Publication 15, *Induktiver Aufbau einer indonesischen Ursprache* (1934), 17, *Deduktive Anwendung des Urindonesischen auf austronesische Einzelsprachen* (1937), 19, *austronesisches Wörterverzeichnis* (1938). Berlin: Dietrich Reimer.

Fox, Charles E. 1974. *Lau dictionary*. Canberra: Pacific Linguistics (PL C-25).

Grace, George W. 1969. A Proto-Oceanic finder list. *Working papers in linguistics* 1:39–84. Honolulu: Department of Linguistics, University of Hawai'i.

Harrison, S. P. 1973. Reduplication in Micronesian languages. *Oceanic Linguistics* 12.407–75.

Kiparsky, Paul. 1973. Abstractness, opacity and global rules. In *Three dimensions of linguistic theory*, ed. by Osamu Fujimura, 57–86. Tokyo: Taikusha.

Kuhn, Thomas S. 1962. *The structure of scientific revolutions*. Chicago/London: The University of Chicago Press.

Milner, G. B. 1966. *Samoan dictionary*. London: Oxford University Press.

Pawley, Andrew. 1972. On the internal relationships of Eastern Oceanic languages. In *Studies in Oceanic Culture History 3*, ed. by R. C. Green and M. Kelly, 1–142. Pacific Anthropological Records 13. Honolulu: Bernice P. Bishop Museum.

Simons, Gary F., and Charles D. Fennig (eds). 2020. *Ethnologue: Languages of the world*. 22nd edn. Dallas: SIL International. Online: www.ethnologue.com.

Tsuchida, Shigeru. 1976. *Reconstruction of Proto-Tsouic phonology*. Study of Languages & Cultures of Asia & Africa Monograph Series, no. 5. Tokyo: Institute for the Study of Languages and Cultures of Asia and Africa.

Vaihinger, H. [1911] 1968. *The philosophy of "As if": A system of the theoretical, practical and religious fictions of mankind*, translated by C. K. Ogden. New York: Barnes & Noble.

6

The Relationship between Aquitanian and Basque: Achievements and Challenges of the Comparative Method in a Context of Poor Documentation

Joaquín Gorrochategui

1. Introduction

It is a typically held opinion that the Basque language—from its first medieval testimonies confined to the Basque Country, Navarre, and some neighboring areas in Huesca, Burgos, and La Rioja, which were subsequently lost—is a genetically isolated language, in spite of the numerous attempts to relate it to other languages, from the Hamitic to the Caucasian ones, as well Old European, Proto-Indo-European itself and macrofamilies like Dene-Sino-Caucasian and Ural-Altaic (references to these proposals can be found in Trask 1995; Campbell 2011; Lakarra 2018a; Bakker 2020). For a long time it was taken as read, or at least as a null hypothesis, that the Basque language was related to the Iberian language, so that the former was an even later phase of the latter which in ancient times extended throughout the Mediterranean flank of the Iberian Peninsula.[1] The deciphering of the particular writing system used in Iberian inscriptions by Gómez Moreno in the 1920s and subsequent advances in the interpretation and combinatorial analysis of Iberian texts from the 1950s onwards led to the confirmation that, with the exception of some typological similarities in the phonological inventory, of the apparently agglutinative nature of the language and certain striking lexical coincidences, Basque was of no help when it came to understanding them. This is in sharp contrast to what happened with the Celtiberian texts, which have received a fairly satisfactory interpretation with the aid of the linguistic comparison with Celtic and Indo-European.

Aquitanian is understood as the ancient language spoken between the Pyrenees, the Garonne river and the Atlantic Ocean according to a text by Caesar (*Bellum Gallicum* I, 1). We know Aquitanian only by means of onomastic material—around 200 personal names and some sixty names of different gods—transmitted secondarily in Latin inscriptions from the imperial era, mostly between the first and third centuries AD, with a few examples that may date from the fourth or fifth centuries AD. There is, then, no text, however short, written in Aquitanian.

In Luchaire's pioneering study (1877) it was demonstrated that Aquitanian names were different to Gaulish names documented in other parts of Gaul, even in Aquitanian territory itself, while there was a fairly good comparison with quite a few Basque words. Research in the second half of the twentieth century (Michelena 1954; Caro Baroja 1954; Gorrochategui 1984) has demonstrated convincingly that Aquitanian was genetically related to the Basque language, in a much stronger and clearer way than with any other language, including Iberian, thanks to the existence of cognate lexemes and suffixes, which often show an evolutionary phase prior to that established for their Basque correlates (Gorrochategui 1995).[2] This opinion, widely accepted by most scholars, can be summed up in the following quote by Trask (1995: 87): "Aquitanian is so closely related to Basque that we can, for practical purposes, regard it as being the more-or-less direct ancestor of Basque." For Campbell (2011: 25–7), the nature of the relationship is not, however, so clearly identifiable as it was before, suggesting that Aquitanian, more than a direct ancestor of historical Basque, was a close relative that later became extinct. He states that

> although testimonies in Aquitanian are sufficiently detailed as to prove a genetic relationship with Basque, they are also sufficiently distinct from current Basque as to suggest the possibility not of a direct ancestor (as many scholars believe), but rather that of a relative. (p. 26)

Campbell's suggestion is attractive and plausible, bearing in mind not just demonstrable divergences but also the different chronologies and territorial extension of each of the sets compared.

The objective of this work is to evaluate the data and arguments that may support each of the positions briefly described, revealing both the capacity as well as the limitations of the comparative method when applied to secondary linguistic material and to some extent contaminated by contact.

In response to the objectives of this book, attention will be paid here to the analysis and study of the relevant aspects of documentation (including philological, social, and geographical ones) in a multilingual context, in order to obtain valid conclusions for its use in historical and comparative linguistics. There will be discussion about: (a) the comparative method and the establishment of cognates in onomastics, as well as the implications of this for the genetic classification of languages, (b) the inclusion of onomastic material from the territory of Vascones and the Ebro Valley and its consequences for the Basque–Aquitanian relationship, (c) the similarities and differences with the comparison between Rhaetian and Etruscan, and (d) the Aquitanian documentation in the light of new approaches to the reconstruction of Proto-Basque.

2. The comparative method and the onomastic cognates

The comparative method has proven to be a useful and convenient tool for finding genetic relationships between languages, the establishment of linguistic families and the study of linguistic change and its reconstruction. The comparative method is a simple and powerful instrument which extracts consequences of a historical nature, sometimes spectacular, out of the comparison of linguistic elements (whether phonemes, morphemes, lexical items, or syntactic structures) of two or more languages, which the linguist elevates from the category of mere superficial similarities to that of cognates (Joseph 2016). This primordial act of establishing cognates, given the transcendence it has for the success of linguistic comparison, must bring together the greatest number of guarantees to rule out similarities due to mere chance, language contact, or sound symbolism phenomena. Campbell has warned clearly about the defects that many proposals concerning genetic relations and linguistic classification possess owing to these flaws (Campbell 2003; Campbell and Poser 2008: Chapter 7).

The problem is compounded even more in the case of Iberian and Aquitanian, the two languages which, due to their geographic and chronological proximity, offer the most likely probability of being related to Basque. The reason is simple: the comparative method compares linguistic sequences whose meaning or grammatical function is known, circumstances which are not sufficiently evident in the two cases. On the other hand, in the Aquitanian case, we are not dealing with a language but, rather, with a collection of onomastic remains which we may more or less reasonably attribute to the language but, as happens in the case of proper names, they lack a semantic component. One must be very conscious of the fact that onomastics constitutes a particular system within the language, and the parallels and similarities that can be observed between the onomastic elements of two or more languages may be merely superficial, due to the fact that linguists lack the control that semantic correspondence implies. This is a particularly serious problem in badly understood ancient onomastics and toponymy.[3] Nonetheless, when correspondences are well rooted in semantics it is possible to establish and explain the cognacy even in cases of deep etymological opacity, as Blust (this book, Chapter 5) has demonstrated for some Austronesian words.

2.1 Requirements for the establishment of onomastic cognates

Consequently, linguists must collect for each onomastic cognate the greatest possible number of features or characteristics, independent of the form, which may make up for the lack of meaning and serve to control to some extent the statistical ease to which comparisons based solely on the formal part (*signifiant*) of the linguistic sign are so prone. I will mention a couple of Aquitanian examples in order to illustrate this question. One of the most common Pyrenean personal names is *Andosto(n)*, which has been explained by Delamarre (2007: 22) as a Celtic formation *ando-sto- (< PIE. *n̥dʰo-sth$_2$-o- "which is underneath"); the name *Andossus* is considered to be a variant of the previous one and explained as a simplification of the -*st*- cluster, through an intermediary state -*ts*- > -*ss*. The etymology, in abstract terms, appears reasonable and, moreover, the parallel of *An[d]ossie* (dat.) is adduced in an inscription from Lauterecken (Germania Superior). Yet the examination of some details beyond the apparent similarity permits us to make the following two observations. First, Delamarre's morphological analysis does not take into account other Aquitanian names that are clearly related to these, such as *Andoxponni* (dat.) or *Andostenno* (dat.), in which two elements that are well attested in other names from the same geographic area must be separated out, that is, -*bonn* and -*tenn* respectively. This makes an analysis of *Andosto(n)* as *andos-to- very plausible. Second, whereas all Aquitanian names deriving from this base—there are more than twenty—refer without exception to men, the German name refers to a woman. We see that two factors independent of each other, namely geographic distribution and the alignment of names with one or the other sex, point to the existence of two different linguistic realities.[4]

Names based on *seni-/seno-* illustrate how careful morphological analysis together with the geographical factor serve to elucidate the nature of the cognate in an onomastic element. Traditionally, all names in Aquitania formed on these bases *seni-/seno-* were interpreted as derived from the Celtic stem *seno-* "old," which is very common in Gaulish and Brittonic names. However, Michelena (1954) observed that Aquitanian names settled on the invariable base *seni-*, to which suffixes such as *-cco*, *-xso*, *-tenn*, and *-bonn* were added, the latter three unknown in Gaulish. In addition, if we bear in mind that these are men's names, that is, the factor of alignment with sex, one is entitled to assume that this Aquitanian onomastic base *seni-* is a cognate of the Basque dialectal forms *sehi, segi, sei, sein* "boy, servant," whose reconstructed form is precisely *seni. We see, then, that independent factors coincide in pointing to the idea that Aquitanian *seni-* is related to Basque *sehi, sein*: only a specific form of the base is considered, leaving aside alternate forms or variants, such as *Sennacius*; the names consistently refer to males; they display a coherent and single set of suffixes, and all this within specific geographical limits coinciding with the distribution of other names which present identical formal features (word formation, morphological, and phonological structure). This set of elements make up part of what Untermann (1961: 6–7; 1965: 12) defined as Namenlandschaft or an onomastic area. This analysis for Aquitanian based on purely internal arguments is reinforced by the assumption of a Basque protoform *seni reconstructed according to the standard criteria used to reconstruct vocabulary. This protoform *seni is the source of all the Basque dialectal forms historically attested after the change of lenis *-n-* to *-h-* in intervocalic position, a change which Latin borrowings also suffer (e.g., Lat. *anate(m)* "duck" > Bq. *ahate*). The detail of the phonological development is given in (1), according to Igartua (2015: 655ff.):

(1)		-V.nV- >	*-Ṽ.nṼ-	> -Ṽ.h̃Ṽ-	> -Ṽ.hṼ-	> V.hV	> -V:/V-
	Lat.	anate	*ānāte	ãh̃ãte (Soul.)	ãhãte	ahate (L, LN)	a:te, ate (G, B)
	PBq.	*seni	*sēnī	sẽh̃ĩ	sẽhĩ	sehi	sei/sein

(B = Bizkaian; G = Gipuzkoan; L = Labourdin; LN = Low Navarrese; Soul. = Souletin)

The strongest proof for a relationship between Aquitanian and Basque is rooted in the reduced set of lexical cognates which refer to age, sex, and family relations: *Atta-* (Bq. *aita* "father"), *Cisson* (Bq. *gizon* "man"), *Hanna-* (Bq. *anaia* "brother"), *Sembe-* (Bq. *seme* "son"), *Seni-* (Bq. *sehi, sein*, "boy, servant"), *Ombe-* (Bq. *hume* "child") amongst male names and *Andere* (Bq. *andere* "lady"), *Nescato* (Bq. *neskato* "little girl," diminutive of *neska* "girl") amongst those of women. These correspondences are exclusive to Basque and Aquitanian, without any Iberian participation.

To this nucleus of uncontroversial cognates we may add others that are highly likely, and which can be grouped into the following semantic fields. Animals: *Hars-* (Bq. *hartz* "bear"), *Oxson* (Bq. *otso* "wolf"), *Aher-* (Bq. *akher* "billy goat"), *Heraus-* (Bq. *herauts* "boar"). Trees: *Arexo* (Bq. *haretz* "oak"), *Arte* (Bq. *arte* "live oak"). Color or brightness: *Belex, Bels-* (Bq. *beltz* "black"), *Ilunn* (Bq. *ilhun* "dark"), *-gorri* (Bq. *gorri* "red, bare") and still others up to some thirty lexical cognates (Gorrochategui 1984: 359–62; 1995: 40–2).

As one can observe, cognates are of a kind we can consider obvious, given that many of them are identical and others only exhibit a minimal variation, which is sometimes due to a sound change suffered by the Basque form, as in the cases of Aq. *Seni* > Bq. *sehi* (-VnV- > -VhV-) or Aq. *Sembe-* > Bq. *seme* (-VmbV- > -VmV-). As happens often in comparative linguistics, once the nucleus of the comparison has been drawn up more evidence emerges owing to a sharper analysis of the documentation or the discovery of new data.

- The former happens with *Andossus* and its derivatives, already mentioned at the beginning of this subsection, which form the most numerous set of male designations, and which is also used as an epithet of three different divinities (e.g., *Herculi Ilunno Andose*). The name, however, has no obvious Basque parallel. Nevertheless, the similarity with the Aquitanian female name *Andere* "lady" is striking. An analysis of *Andossus* as *(h)an-dots- would permit us to compare the second element with Basque words for male animals like *ordots* "boar" or *bildots* "lamb" and the medieval Bq. *andosco* "a two- or three-year-old ram." That makes it quite plausible that Aq. *Andossus* (i.e., /andots/) was used for "sir," a meaning which is perfectly compatible for both a personal designation for a man and the epithet of a divinity: it would be the Aquitanian counterpart of Lat. *Dominus* which sometimes accompanies Roman deities in Latin inscriptions.
- The discovery of the Hagenbach treasure (Bernhard et al. 1990; Gorrochategui 2003) has provided us with twenty Aquitanian names, most of them already known, and some written with interesting spelling variants. One of these cases is *Xembus* and its derivative *Xembesus*, which can only be considered as written variants of the common *Sembus* (nom.), *Sembi* (gen.), that is, Aq. *Sembe*. One must bear in mind that another of the most persuasive arguments in favor of the Basque–Aquitanian relationship, besides the set of cognate lexemes and suffixes, consists of a coincident distribution of fortes and lenes phonemes in sibilants and sonorants in the noun stem: thus sibilants always present in initial a lenis fricative realization (written via S), in final a fortis affricate realization (typically written -X(S), -SS), whilst in intervocalic position they alternate (*Sosonnis* vs. *Oxson*). The spelling *Xembus* contravened, therefore, the expected distribution. As *Sembus* and *Xembus* are, with full certainty, variants of the same name, the only solution is to think that, by means of X, there has been a desire to mark a significant phonetic feature, which from the Basque point of view can only be an expressive palatalization which is used in certain names in order to give them an affective meaning.

Everything stated to this point has been based upon data and evidence to prove the close relationship of Aquitanian to Basque, a unique and exclusive relationship not shared by any other language. Yet we should not forget that the cognates, although according to widely held opinion they would fulfil the statistical threshold necessary to be considered, in the words of Nichols (1996: 48), "individual-identifying evidence," are limited to lexical units—once the original semantic meanings of the Aquitanian names have been assumed as very plausible—without grammatical correspondences intervening, which are the safer base from which to demonstrate a linguistic relationship. It is illustrative to compare our Basque–Aquitanian case to the research undertaken around the classification of Rhaetian, an extinct ancient language of the Alps (formerly spoken in the area of the Alto Adige and Tyrol), of which there are some 100 short and repetitive inscriptions. Considered a language not understood and without any relations, it was interpreted in the light of Etruscan in a very convincing way by Rix (1998). The inscriptions, although short, present complete sentences in Rhaetian, normally the expression of an act of donation (with the verb *zinake*) of an object to a divinity by an offerer; the sentence contains a verbal form in preterite tense (comparable to other Etruscan preterite forms such as *turuce* "offered" or the cognate form *zinace* "fabricated"), participle forms in the preterite in *-u* with the use of pertinentive cases in both classes to express the beneficiary (Rhaet. *laspa-si eluku pitamnu-ale* "donated by/for Laspa, son of Pitame," cf. Etr. *mi spurieisi teiθurnasi aliqu* "I (was) donated by/for Spurie Teithurna"), the use of the suffix *-nu* with a patronymic value in Rhaetian versus suffix *na* with an evolution towards family name or *gentilicium* in Etruscan, and so on. Grammatical cognates may be established between Rhaetian and Etruscan, such as the endings of preterite in *-ce*, of participle in *-u*, the two endings of gen. sg. in *-s* and in *-l*, on which are created the corresponding pertinentives *-si* and *-ale*, and the suffix in the nasal *-nu* (originally *-na) with a patronymic value, later family name (*gentilicium*) in Etruscan. Besides this grammatical material, the Rhaetian inscriptions have supplied some seventy personal names which, curiously, have no parallels in the abundant corpus of Etruscan names; Rix (1998: 59) only finds one: *remi*, which has an indirect correspondence in Etruscan. This leads to the worrying suspicion that if Rhaetian had been known only by means of an onomastic corpus of proper names transmitted in Latin epigraphy from the area, as Aquitanian is, its genetic relationship to Etruscan would hardly have been sensed, except, perhaps, by a coincident derivative formation in nasal in patronymic or family names.[5]

2.2 The type of linguistic relationship as a consequence of the establishment of cognates

In this confrontation of parallels Basque offers the known part of the equation, whilst Aquitanian, which behaves as if it were an unknown language, represents the unidentified part which is shed light on and clarified through comparison. We are quite sure when the cognates are identical or corresponding, in those which any small difference is explained as a regular phonetic evolution of Basque out of a protoform identical to Aquitanian. However, our certainty wanes quickly when the equations are not identical and the differences enter into territories not so well supported by the history or the standard reconstruction of Basque. For instance, it is highly likely that the male name Aq. *Hanna-* is a cognate of the Bq. *anaia*; the maintenance of the intervocalic fortis -N-, expressed in Aquitanian by means of the geminate nasal, would support the equation, but it still remains to explain the loss of aspiration in initial position, whose maintenance would have been expected, or the final part of the Basque term. Perhaps we could find support in the derivative *Hannabi* (gen.), if we believe that the underlying Aquitanian form is *hannabe, with a suffix *-be*, attested in *Sembe-* "son," *Ombe-* "child," and related to the suffix Bq. *-ba* in certain names which designate a familial relation such as *neba* "brother of the sister," *arreba* "sister of the brother," *osaba* "uncle," *ahizpa* "sister of the sister."

Another case is the relationship assumed by Luchaire between the theonym Aq. *Arixo* (dat.) and Bq. *haritz* "oak," which has gradually been accepted, as an example of tree worship as *Fago deo* in other inscriptions from the same territory; however, this still presents two difficulties for a complete equating: on the one hand, in contrast to the previous case, the lack of aspiration in the Aquitanian form that we find in the Basque cognates, and, on the other, the reduction of the diphthong in the reconstructed form *hareitz (which is at the base of the western dialectal forms *areitz*, *aretx*, and the central-eastern *(h)aritz*) > Aq. /aritz/ for the ancient era, with consequences for the establishment of a chronology of the protolanguage and successive dialectal changes. One inscription recently discovered in Vignec (Hautes-Pyrénées) bears testimony to the name of the inhabitants of a *pagus*, the *Harexvates*, whose name we may understand as formed by *-ates* on the toponym *Harexu* /haretz-zu/ "oak grove,"[6] to which one would have to add a substantial correction to the reading of the theonym on one of the altars from Luchon, which now reads [.]*arexo* or [.]*areîxo* (Gorrochategui 2015). These new testimonies confirm the accuracy of the traditional comparison, at the same time that they establish the possibility of the existence of variants due to processes of adapting indigenous names to Latin perception and to their written shape.

The consequence of all this is that certainty in the accuracy of the cognate depends very directly on the Aquitanian part of the equation receiving a good explanation in the light of the known diachronic development of Basque, which extends fairly certainly across the last two millennia since its contact with Latin. Anything that does not enter into this schema will still be useful, just as paleontological fossils are useful, because they offer us precisely dated testimonies and, what is more, we can describe their external characteristics (morpheme structure, phoneme distribution, combinations, etc.) which, through application of the always necessary Occam's razor, we cannot attribute to other languages different from Aquitanian. However, in the same way as fossils, they will only be explained satisfactorily whenever we can situate them in a coherent evolutionary and phylogenetic history with respect to their Basque cognates.

The idea that Aquitanian is not just a language related to Basque, but "the more-or-less direct ancestor of Basque" is in part a by-product of the method, a result of the necessity itself to be based on cognates whose existence is not independently a given per se, but as the consequence of prior expurgation, that is, of a previous selection of the material made by the linguist(s), so that they do not contradict what is known of the history of the Basque language.

One example may well be the apparent identity between the component *neure-* in the Aq. woman's name *Neureseni* (dat.) and the possessive pronoun of the first person anaphoric-intensive Bq. *neure* "mine," a form of the gen. sg. of the personal pronoun *neur*, *neu*. But these Bq. anaphoric-intensive forms, compared to the simpler forms of the possessive *ene* and the pronoun *ni*, are considered the outcome of the combination of personal pronoun *ni* + proximal demonstrative pronoun *hau(r)*, *nihaur-e (> Ronc. *ñore*, Soul. *nore*, B, L *neure*). Due to its dialectal differentiation, this Bq. formation does not seem to go very far back in time,[7] so that the relationship with the Aq. *Neure-* is far from being clear.

With this procedure, precedence is taken by those comparisons that present plesiomorphic features, that is, those which related languages share and in those on which the notion of a linguistic relationship hinges. In summary, they are the following:

(2) • cognates like those pointed out above
 • parallels in the phonological inventory: lack of /r/ in initial position and existence of /m/ just as an allophonic variant of /b/ and /n/ in certain contexts
 • distribution of fortis and lenis variants depending on their position in the morpheme
 • neutralization of sibilants following a sonorant
 • expressive palatalization of sibilants (*Xembus* vs. *Sembus*).

Besides the above-mentioned shared features, there are also differences between the Aquitanian data and the linguistic traits characterizing all the Basque dialects.[8] Here are the most assured ones (examples in (3)): (a) the Aquitanian intervocalic nasal lenis has disappeared in Basque, giving first an aspiration, which then disappears in some dialects (cf. supra (1)); (b) the *-mb-* cluster, phonologically /nb/, has simplified to *-m-*; (c) Basque restricts aspiration to just one per word, whilst such a restriction did not exist in Aquitanian; (d) in Aquitanian, there is no transformation of the first element in a compound; (e) there is no evidence for the existence of the article in Aquitanian, as opposed to its increasingly frequent use in Basque; and (f) the typical and productive toponymical suffixes *-eta*, *-aga*, which are closely linked to determinate inflection, do not exist in Aquitanian or in the place names transmitted by ancient sources.

(3) a. Aq. -VnV- > Bq. -VhV-: Aq. *Seni-* : Bq. *sehi, sein*
 b. Aq. *Sembe-* : Bq. *seme*; Aq. *Ombe-* : Bq. *(h)ume* (Lerga *Umme*)
 c. Aq. *Hahanten, Hontharris*, etc. : Bq. *ilherri* "cemetery" (*hil+herri)
 d. Aq. *Cisson-bonnis* : Bq. *giza-seme* "(male) human" (*gizon+seme)
 e. Aq. Ø : Bq. *Ochoa* (*otso* "wolf" + article *-a*)
 f. Aq. Ø : Bq. *Harrieta* (*harri* "stone"), *Areizaga, Aretxaga, Harizaga* (*hareitz* "oak")

The differences listed in (3) can all be located chronologically in a period later than that documented for Aquitanian, given that they were phonological processes that also happened in Latin borrowings (cf. Lat. *anatem* > *ahate*; Lat. *ambitione* > *amizioe*, before the change *-mp-* > *-mb-* in Lat. *tempora* > *denbora*) or morphological processes such as the creation of determinate declination by means of the grammaticalization of the definite article out of the distal demonstrative pronoun, as in Romance. As for the toponymical suffixes *-eta*, *-aga*, apart from the fact they do not exist in ancient documentation, their geographical distribution matches perfectly the limits of historical Basque from the Middle Ages on. Notice in this sense the contrast with the situation of the currently not productive suffix in *-otz* (corresponding to Gasc. *-òs* and Aragonese *–ués*), which is documented in place names in the Basque Country and also covers wide-ranging Pyrenean and Aquitanian territories. If the interpretation of the ethnic *Harexu-ates* explained above is correct, we would have a use of the suf. *-zu* coinciding with historical Basque (cf. *Amezu-a* < *ametz-zu "abundant in Pyrenean oaks"). The assumption that in some cases the Aquitanian form is identical to the form reconstructed for Proto-Basque and in others it presents a lack of Basque elements emerging chronologically after the Roman era has led to the conclusion that Aquitanian, "for practical purposes," as Trask (1995: 87) said, represents an ancestor of Basque.

The Aquitanian documentation presents quite a number of personal and divinity names that have no Basque correlate. Some may not be of Aquitanian origin, but instead come from other languages, although these are in practice limited to Gaulish or to some variety of regional Celtic and to Iberian.[9] Nevertheless, theonyms like *Lelhunn, Alar-(dosto), Toli-(andosso), Lahe, Daho, Idiatte, Haloisso*, and *Erge*, and personal names like *Gere-, Silex, Orgo-, Uloho-, Hunnu, Narhon-*, as well as bases such as *Erhe-, Edunn-, Hahann-, Hauten-*, which are specifically used in women's names, present all the formal features to be considered genuinely Aquitanian, even though there is apparently no Basque cognate for them.[10] They may be an indication, therefore, that Aquitanian was a sufficiently distant language from Basque to possess an onomastics with an important number of different names, but perhaps not so far removed as is Rhaetian from Etruscan. It may also be the case that the forerunner of Basque had these names, but that it would have lost them in the passage from antiquity to the Middle Ages; at least the medieval Basque name *Unuso* seems to correspond to Aq. *Hunnu* + suf. *-so*, without that helping us to know its etymology or its "meaning." In the end, there is a geographical difference in the attestation of both languages: Aquitanian documentation is concentrated in the northern valleys of the central Pyrenees with the odd extension towards Gascony, whereas historical Basque occupies a more western territory, which would lead us to think about adjacent languages.

3. New Vasconic documentation

That said, it is necessary to bring to the discussion the situation of Vasconic, that is, the language spoken by the *Vascones* mentioned in the classical sources, who inhabited the lands of present-day Navarre and the western part of Huesca. The indigenous documentation is, in the same way as that in Aquitania, only of an onomastic nature,[11] so that it is subject to the same problems, and even more serious still, for two reasons: (1) the scarcity of the corpus, and (2) the greater difficulty in the formal distinction between the Vasconic and the neighboring Iberian. In spite of the latter, typically Basque features and characteristics have been isolated in the indigenous onomastic material, such as the presence of aspiration (*Larrahe, Serhuhoris*), the distribution of fortes sibilants and sonorants in morpheme-final position (*Ordunets-i, Selaits-e*). In addition to that, one has to mention the name *Ummesahar* in the Lerga inscription, in which the Basque *(h)ume* "child" and *zahar* "old" stand out. A few theonyms in the central zone of Navarre which apparently have acceptable Basque parallels are also worth noting: *Selaitse* (cf. Bq. *zelai* "meadow, field"), *Larrahe* (cf. Bq. *larra* "pasture"), *Itsacurrinne* (cf. Bq. *txakur* "dog"?) and *Urde*[(cf. Bq. *urde* "pig, swine"), all terms attested from the beginning of Basque documentation and even beforehand in medieval documents (Gorrochategui 2018).

It is also significant that the same Lerga inscription documents the name *Narhunges-*, whose first element *Narhun-* has a direct parallel in the Aq. *Narhon-sus*, in the same way that the Vasconic name *Enne-ges* has the parallel Aq. *Enne-box*, which ultimately affirms the ties of unity between both geographical extremes of the ancient common linguistic domain. To which one should add another feature, which is important because it affects a grammatical aspect: a desinence *-(h)e* may be isolated in many theonyms attested in both Aquitania and the Vasconic area, and this morphological element can hardly be interpreted as the Latin gen. sg. desinence *-ae* (of the *a*-stems) > *-e* (Michelena 1954: 424).

I have used the same criteria to characterize the indigenous onomastics attested in the area covering the high Cidacos and Linares valleys, to the south of the Ebro, as a Vasconic (Gorrochategui 2009). Its non-Indo-European character is obvious; but the presence of aspiration on the suf. *-thar* (as in Aq. *Harontharris*, gen.) and the comparison of the elements in the name *Sesenco* with Bq. *zezen* "bull" + diminutive suf. *-ko* suggests a connection with the Basque language. I believe the presence of the suffixal alternation *-so /-se* in names like *Ae(milius) Onso* and *Antestia Onse* is more persuasive, because their use is in line with the expression of sex-based differences, in the same way that in Aquitanian we find many women's names with the suffix *-se* (*Andere-se*, *Hauten-se*, etc.) or pairs like *Uriassi* (gen. male) versus *Uriaxe* (nom. female).

Aquitanian, in the same way as Basque and other languages such as Etruscan, lacked any grammatical gender. But its onomastic system utilized special suffixes to express women's names: in contrast to *Laurco* (m.) there was *Laur-eia* (f.) and in contrast to *Belex* (m.), *Belex-eia*, so that *Lexeia* and *Talseia* are also women's names. It appears that one must seek their origin in a derivative Indo-European suf. *-(e)io-/a* used in neighboring languages.[12] Besides this suf. *-eia*, which is foreign in origin, Aq. had *-se* in order to derive women's names from women's names (*Andere -> Andere-se*), thus with a reinforcing character, but which was applied occasionally to bases that were not strictly female in order to create women's names, giving rise to pairs like **Uriasso* (m.) versus *Uriaxe* (f.). The origin of this suffix seems to lie in the language itself; it is probably an alteration of the suf. *-so*, *-xso*, indifferent when it comes to sex, to *-se*, identical to the ending of the typical female name *andere*. If the alternating suffix in the pair *Onso* versus *Onse*, attested in southern Vasconic areas, is an example of the same procedure, then we have an expression common to the whole Basque-speaking domain in antiquity, older and more extensive than that of the suf. *-eia*, limited to Aquitanian, and it is another indication of linguistic unity.[13] In spite of this apparent general extent, the female suf. *-se* has little or no representation in historical Basque;[14] starting from its medieval testimonies, this language displays both *-so* in names expressing familial relations and *-txo* as well as *-to*, *-ko*, as a diminutive suffix.

Vasconic, therefore, belongs to the Basque language family. In the former analysis we focused on unitary features, those in common with Aquitanian and with Basque, highlighting the parallels with Aquitanian (lexical terms and desinence *-(h)e* in theonyms). But it is also interesting to look at the differences, in spite of the scanty of material. First, it is striking that the most unmistakably Basque anthroponyms, those that refer to designations of sex, age, and family relations, do not stand out in the Vasconic area; we only have *Umme-*, closer to Bq. *(h)ume* than to the Aq. cognate *Ombe-*. One must suppose that the *-mb-* cluster was assimilated into *-mm-* quite early on, forerunning the treatment that would later be more widespread and become common in Basque, whilst in Aquitanian it lasted longer, although it ended up affecting the pronunciation of bilinguals in the area (Lat. *Conuenae* > *Combenas* > *Cummonigo*, current *Comminges*, cf. Chambon and Greub 2002: 480).

Second, noun composition seems significantly more represented in Vasconic anthroponyms than in their Aquitanian counterparts, although the proportion is inverted in theonyms. These are not strictly speaking linguistic but rather cultural differences. In my opinion the preference of Vasconic for composition is due to the influence of Iberian personal onomastics, whose canonical scheme consisted of compound names of two disyllabic members. Iberian cultural influence is also responsible for the use of Iberian names by Basque speakers, such as *Ordunetsi* (dat.) and *Urchatetelli* (dat.), whose spellings demonstrate clearly Basque phonological traits.

Finally, with the exception of a few names, such as the already cited *Umme-*, *Enne-*, and *Narhun-* as well as *Belteso-*, the rest are not reflected in the Aquitanian corpus. Even *Narhun-ges* and *Enne-ges* present a final element *-ges* which is unknown in Aquitanian and is limited to the Vasconic area.

4. Discussion of the similarities and differences

The suggestion by Campbell (2011: 26), which saw a sibling relationship between Aquitanian and Basque rather than the anteriority of the former over the latter, was based on certain differences in detail in the cognates, which could be from an entity comparable to that which separates Gothic from English amongst the Germanic languages. Table 6.1 summarizes the ideas proposed by Campbell.

The first observation refers to the condition of cognates in a pair of correspondences. Although traditionally the ethnic *Ausci* (current Auch) has been related to the name for the Basque language *eusk-ara*, Irigoyen argued persuasively, based on the sixteenth-century form *enusquera*, for an etymology on the verb stem **enausi-* "speak, bark," which was subsequently widely accepted (Lakarra 2011: 695). The relationship between Aq. *Siri-co* and Bq. *zuri* is only supported by the existence of parallels in the semantic field of color and luminosity (see above), but there are no more examples of an Aq. *i* : Bq. *u* correspondence in the corpus, and instead *i* : *i*, *u* : *u* (Aq. *ilun-* : Bq. *ilhun*) is accepted. The difference between western Bq. *u*, on the one hand, and central and eastern Bq. *i* in initial, on the other (cf. the pairs *uri* : *hiri* "town," *ule* : *ile* "hair," *urten* : *irten* "go out") presents a geographical distribution which is not compatible with the proposal (cf. Michelena 1977: 73ff., 479–80; Lakarra 2011: 697, for some explanations).[15]

Table 6.1 Correspondences between Aquitanian and Basque, Gothic and English (Campbell 2011)

Aquitanian	Basque	Gothic	English
Arixo	haritz	(faírguni)	oak
Atta	aita	fadar	father
Belex	beltz	swart-s	black
Bon-	on	goþs	good
Sembe-	seme	sun-us	son
Hanna	anaia	broþar	brother
Seni-	sehi/seiñ	mag-us	boy
Oxson	otso	wulf-s	wolf
Siri(co)	zuri	hweit-s	white
Ausci	euskara	–	basque

As regards the remaining correspondences, in some of them the Aquitanian form is identical to that of Proto-Basque (*seni, *sembe), in the same way as in some cases the Gothic form is identical to the predecessor of the English one, for example Go. *sunus* : E. *son*. In other cases (*wulfs* : *wolf, hweits* : *white*), although we know by other means that the Proto-Germanic forms were *wulfaz and *hwītaz (the Gothic diphthong is graphic), we can operate as if the Gothic forms were predecessors of the English ones. In the same way, too, bearing in mind the lack of *b-* before /o/ in patrimonial words, one can accept a *b- > Ø- change before -*o* (Michelena 1977: 531) in order to explain the Aq. *bon-* : Bq. *on* correspondence. The Bq. *beltz* may also derive from /beletz/, which is understood as a derivative of a root *bel which is attested in Bq. *harbel* "slate" < "black stone." Bq. *aita* is explained as the depalatalization of [at'a], an expressive pronunciation of /ata/. We have already seen that Aquitanian makes use of expressive palatalization to assign affective meaning to certain words.

In other correspondences we would face problems trying to derive Basque from Aquitanian, as we have in order to derive English words with dental consonants out of Gothic ones (Go. *goþs* : E. *good* and Go. *fadar* : E. *father*), because their results do not coincide. Thus, Aq. *Oxson* contains a final -*n* that we do not find in Bq. *otso*, as opposed to that expected by the Aq. *Cisson* : Bq. *gizon* "man" correspondence. We have already pointed out previously that the initial aspiration in Aq. *Hanna-* has not been maintained in Bq. *anaia*, whilst that of the Bq. *haritz* is not documented in Aq. *Arexo* (although it has been in *Harexuates*).

The lexical differences are not too important for the question that concerns us, as one deduces from the fact that OE. had *sweart* "black" and *magu* "boy, servant," substituted in modern English. In the same way one could think that many Aquitanian names lack a Basque correspondence, because Basque substituted ancient or common terms for other new ones from antiquity onwards. We come across an interesting discrepancy in the term for "sir," "dominus," which in Aq. is *andots* and in Bq. is *jaun*, whilst the word for "lady" is *andere* in both languages. Apart from noting the discrepancy, it is difficult to know which of the two languages came up with the innovation in a previous phase or whether they both did, independently. The existence of the medieval term *andosco* "a two- or three-year-old ram" points to the existence of the term in the common language, although with a clear difference of meaning.[16] Very probably, the original meaning referred to an animal, if we take into account that the first element in the compound *an- is the base of Bq. *ahuntz* "goat" (< *an-untz, cf. place name *Anuncibay* "goat river"); as a parallel for a change in semantic meaning one could cite OIr. *ander* "young woman," W. *anneir* "calf," which some take to be the source of Bq. *andere* (De Bernardo Stempel 2006: 14–17; see Matasović 2009: 35). It seems, then, that this semantic change only took place in Aquitanian, without affecting the predecessor in Basque, which preferred *jaun*, a form which has all the appearance of being a nominalization of a verb stem.[17]

Following the review of Basque–Aquitanian correspondences we see that there are similar situations to those that Campbell suggested for Gothic and English. A good number could easily derive from the situation documented in Aquitanian by applying the phonological and morphological rules of post-Roman chronology assured by Latin borrowings. Those correspondences in which we know that Gothic is not really a direct source of English, but with the data furnished may "function in practice" as if they were, are especially interesting for our argument. Given that in the Basque–Aquitanian case we lack information supplied by other members of the family, we cannot resolve this question. And cognates also exist which present contradictory correspondences, especially in the presence of aspiration. Curiously there are also indications of linguistic variation within the same Aquitanian documentation, for example *Handos* with aspiration on a plate from Hagenbach as opposed to the general *Andos*. And lastly, there are Aquitanian elements without any Basque cognation, and discrepancies in semantic evolution as in the case of /andots/. All of this leads one to think that there was a difference between the Aquitanian language and what would be the ancestor of historical Basque, although we cannot measure its scale: if it would be of a scale similar to that presented by the modern Basque dialects amongst themselves, which in spite of their many detailed differences are considered one single language, or of a greater scale. We lack data, especially of the grammatical type, and sequences of texts, to decide on this question.

5. The Basque–Aquitanian relationship within the scope of the new reconstruction of Proto-Basque

The reconstruction of Proto-Basque, whose classical presentation by Michelena we have used up to now, has received a new impulse thanks to the research carried out in the last twenty years by the Basque philologist and linguist J. A. Lakarra. His works are part of the field of internal reconstruction—as it has to be in the case of a language isolate—and aided widely by studies of a diachronic holistic typology and grammaticalization. Starting from the idea that the assumption of the existence of a canonical form of the root is a significant help to reconstruct protolanguages, as happened in Indo-European with post-Saussurean advances, especially on the part of Benveniste, he contended that Proto-Basque possessed a canonical form of the C_1VC_2 root, with restrictions on each C for certain classes of sounds, as opposed to the previous idea of a multiplicity of root patterns (Lakarra 1995). That brought with it certain immediate consequences, such as the fact that the two-syllable pattern of Basque and Aquitanian words, which on account of their abundance in the historical period was considered canonical, was a later evolutionary phase, to which it arrived via the action of certain formative processes, such as reduplication of the root or the addition of suffixes. In recent years Lakarra has conceived an ambitious research program, by means of which he has suggested a remote Proto-Basque with an isolate morphology without verb or noun inflection, with prefixes and sequences of serial verbs, VO word order, typologically opposite to historical Basque. Its reconstruction offers numerous etymologies, some suggestive and acceptable, others highly speculative, based on the application of ideal processes of grammaticalization, sometimes with the assumption of sound changes such as metathesis and other sequential modifications, which have no sufficient independent confirmation. Much of his recent research has centered on morphology, especially on an explanation for the different verb forms, both infinite and finite paradigms, like the union of prior sequences of serial verbs, an explanation that he has also applied to the origin of noun case marks (Lakarra 2018a: 67–78, 2018b: 131–212).

All this part of the reconstruction is outside the reach of the documentation in Aquitanian, which can hardly offer any evidence for the proper morphology of the language, although certain aspects of root theory can be used to approach an analysis of Aquitanian names.

The first observation is that Aquitanian mostly demonstrates two-syllable words or onomastic bases, although a reduced number of monosyllabic ones are also documented; of some sixty different elements in the corpus (Gorrochategui 1984: 359–62), approximately fifty are disyllabic and only ten monosyllabic. Word formation takes place mostly by means of suffixes, whose structure is of the CV(R) pattern, such as *-to*, *-co*, *-se*, *-ten*, *-tar* in which C is normally voiceless. There are root extensions, which consist of a sibilant or a VC structure: thus *Har-* : *Hars-*, *Bel-* : *Bel-ex* : *Belex-enn*. There is only one isolated case of apparent prefixation, *Pi-andosponn-*, whose bilabial voiceless consonant is moreover extraneous to the phonological system of the language. All the documented compounds in personal names, apart from being scarce in number, have been formed by just two elements: *-belex* and *-bon*: *Bon-belex*, *Bon-silex*, *Har-belex*, *Gisson-bonn*, and *Seni-ponn*.

Although in Aquitanian the elements *Sembe-* and *Seni-* always appear as two-syllable without any variation, one could think, accepting a semantic relationship which exist between them, that they are different formations of the same root *sen. We do not know if *-be* in *Sembe* is the same element that we find in *Hannabi* (gen.), derived from *Hanna-*, and in *Harspi* (gen.), derived from *Hars-*, but one can affirm that Aquitanian does not treat the word synchronically as a derivate, with the existence of a morphological boundary, given that according to the example of *Cissson-bonn* we would expect an inexistent *sen-be spelling. The Aq. *Ombe-* behaves in the same way; however, if our analysis of the pair of names *Onso* and *Onse* from Soria is correct, we could isolate a monosyllabic *on*[18] for a previous phase.

On the other hand, some elements with the CVRS pattern, like *Tals-co*, *Tals-eia*, *Hals-co*, which do not alternate in the corpus with other shorter ones, may be considered, according to the parallel of *Har-* : *Hars-*, as extensions of the monosyllabic roots *Tal-*, *Hal-*.

One of the means Lakarra proposes for the formation of two-syllable words from monosyllabic roots is partial reduplication. There are reduplicated words in Basque like *gogor* "hard" versus *gor* "deaf"; the same structure presents words like *zezen* "bull," *odol* "blood" (*do–dol), *adats* "mane" (*da–dats), *ahal* "be able" (*ha-hal < *na-nal), according to Lakarra, although there are no synchronically related words in the language.[19] Some names in the ancient documentation may be interpreted from this perspective, not just the clearly Vasconic name *Sesenco* (Bq. *zezen* "bull" + diminutive suf. *ko*), but also Aq. *Hahan-*, which can be understood as the partial reduplication of *han-, from which the element *Hanna-* is obtained by means of another procedure. The same scheme is presented by the names *Sosonnis* (gen.), *Tottonis* (gen.), and *Cugur*.

One of the consequences that is derived from accepting a reduplicated structure *da-dats, *do-dol, and *de-der as original forms of Bq. *adats, odol,* and *eder* "beautiful" is that one must assume a loss of the initial *d-. This would come to explain the striking lack of initial *d-* on patrimonial words in Basque which has already been observed for some time. Aquitanian demonstrates an example which fits this structure well: if *Andots* can be understood as a compound of *(h)an + dots, the names *Odossi* (gen.) and *Odoxo* (dat.) enter perfectly into the reduplicated structure *do-dots > *odots*.

Michelena (1977: 257–8) was able to propose, thanks to the felicitous comparative connection between Bq. *lohi* "mud, body" and the suffix of abundance in phytonyms *-dui, -di*, that one of the origins of Basque initial *l-* was in the ancient *d-. Michelena thought that the base of the Aq. *Lohi-xsi, -si, -tton* was a cognate of the Bq. *lohi*, so that the *d- > l- change would be prior to Aquitanian documentation. This still does not explain Aquitanian names with initial *d-* like *Derro, Deri*, or the theonym *Daho*. The Hagenbach plates have supplied *Doxxi* (gen.). One solution is to think that it is a question of borrowings or names with non-Aquitanian origins. Delamarre (2007: 89) links the latter with other names from the west of the empire such as *Dosso* (Vinxtbach, Germany), *Dossonius, -ia* (Cologne and Aquileia), and *Dossennus*. Yet this identification also implies certain problems: first, *Dossennus* is a strictly Italic name, with a suffix frequent in Etruscan; *Dossonius* is a Latin name in *-ius* formed out of *Dosson-*, a word on *-n* stem, identical to the testimony of Vinxtbach, whilst one must analyze our Aquitanian name as a sibilant stem, not a *-n*. On the other hand, the Aq. theonym *Lahe* is also attested, which may be related to *Daho*. All these data suggest that the *d- > l- change on initial had begun at a date prior to Aquitanian documentation, but that perhaps did not reach a conclusion, leaving behind still some remains of the previous situation.[20] Whatever the case, it is later than *d- > Ø- in reduplicated stems.[21]

The segmentation of Basque words within the monosyllabic root theory has brought with it as a consequence the identification of initial syllables with the function of prefixes, being *sa-* and *la-* those that apparently have a greater presence. In Aq. we only have the name *Saherossis* (gen.), unfortunately lost, which could have presented this prefix, although there are no good parallels for the rest of the name. One should mention the existence of a clear prefix case in *Pi-Andos-*, which is perhaps repeated in *Bihotarris* versus *Hotarris*, and with less certainty in *Bihotus*. The question is that the supposed prefix *bi-* does not seem to be present amongst the new prefixes detected in

Basque[22] and nor does the root resulting from the analysis *ho-(?) present the canonical structure or semantic parallels in Basque. The apparent relationship of the names cited with *Bihoxus* and *Bihos-cinn*, which have traditionally been related to Bq. *bihotz* "heart," leaves the question of analysis open.

Lakarra has argued that the origin of many Basque morphological markers, both in the verb and in the noun, is to be found in the ancient roots of serial verbs. Intriguingly, he proposes interpreting the morph *da-* in the third person sg. of the present ones (*dator* "is coming," *dakar* "is bringing") as remains of the root *dar "sit," which, used first in a construction of serial verb, was then grammaticalized, in the form of *da-*, as a prefix of imperfect aspect, then present time. Likewise, some infinitive forms receive an attractive explanation as the result of a sequence of prefixes, originally serial verbs. Their application to other areas of Basque morphology seems to me more problematic.[23] In this reconstructive hypothesis he has contended that dative markers, both in one of the auxiliary verbs (*d-i-o* "(s)he it him/her") and in noun inflection (*Jon-i* "to John"), are the result of grammaticalization of the verb *nin "give," documented in a few archaic forms in the sixteenth century.[24] It is difficult to think that the supposed Aquitanian dative marker *-(h)e*, documented in theonyms, has this origin: one would have to accept a *-n-* > *-h-* change prior to that experienced in the step from Aquitanian to historical Basque (*seni* > *sehi*) or major phonetic losses. Apparently, this is one of the points in which Aq. does not coincide with Bq., and it does not seem to be a question of geography because the few Vasconic theonyms (vid. *supra*) coincide in presenting an *-e* desinence. Independently of the question of its etymology, one has to assume that Basque has created a new dative marker in the intermediate period between its ancient Vasconic–Aquitanian phase and its historical texts, whether by supplanting the ancient form or by creating a new case out of a functionally wider previous one, which had to include the semantic roles of possessor and beneficiary.[25]

We have seen, therefore, that the new image of Proto-Basque proposed by Lakarra offers certain guidelines in order to understand the structure of some Aquitanian bases, such as those reduplicated, and establishes bases for the discussion of chronologies. In any event, many of the reconstructions of Proto-Basque, especially those morphological ones obtained through typological reasons, cannot be applied to Aquitanian documentation and cannot be tested. It seems, though, that many of the characteristics of his ancient Proto-Basque, such as the use of serial verbs or prefixation, reach periods not too far removed from historical Basque[26] and would imply a certain contradiction with the Aquitanian documentation. Most of the two-syllable bases are still obscure (*Erhe, Neure-, Edun-, Gere-, Hauten-*)[27] and some of the new etymological explanations undermine traditional approaches, as in the theonym *Baigorri-*, which used to be linked to the Bq. *(h)ibai*, the name *Laur-co*, which was related to the Bq. *lau(r)* "four"[28] and the theonym *Leherenn* associated with Mars which is related to the Bq. *leher* "explode, burst."[29] Lakarra thinks that Basque diphthongs are recent, a creation of so-called Common Basque, contemporaries of the features described *supra* (3), so that the diphthongs attested to by Aquitanian, although not many, but obvious ones like *Bai-, Neure-, Herauts-*, and *Laur-*, remain outside the evolutionary line proposed for Basque. One gets the impression that the new reconstructive hypothesis, which due to its greater time depth should in theory offer a broader frame in which Aquitanian and Basque data could be brought together, in practice raises difficulties for some—not all—of the proposals of traditional cognations.[30] It can be understood as the normal corollary of scientific progress, by which previous assumptions are invalidated, although in return one expects a more extensive explanation of the ensemble, still inexistent. It may also be an indication that the Basque–Aquitanian relationship is not so close as was supposed, or that the concrete proposals of chronology and etymology adopted in the hypothesis are not correct. I see problems in accepting a *-n- > -h- change in the pre-Aquitanian era in order to explain Aq. *Lohi-tton* out of **don-i*. Not only do we have the attested Aq. *Seni-*, but the comparative data demonstrate clearly that their respective results in Basque are different: the former presents a composition form *lot- (*lotin* "wet land," *lokatz* "mud," with the same correspondence as in *behi* "cow" : *betizu* "wild cow") and not the expected *lon- as if it were to come from *doni, in the same way as in *mihi* "tongue" : *mingain* "top of the tongue." The monosyllabic theory must originate /loh-/ in a root with canonical structure and as it does not admit a stop in the position of C_2 (which could be a reasonable origin for /h/), it only has *n. It is a question of circular reasoning, without any comparative base. On the other hand, although the result of the *-VnV- > ṼhṼ change precedes Basque documentation, it does not seem to go back many centuries before, given that we still have in the sixteenth-century variants from the Romance tradition with an -n- maintained, such as *Anuncibay*, cited earlier,[31] and during the Middle Ages there were abundant spellings with geminate to express N fortis. Suggesting the existence of an -n- lenis > -h- change in the prehistoric era, different to the post-Aquitanian one, clashes with the implausibility of accepting twice a change that is really quite infrequent typologically. Detailed research into all these aspects is necessary.

I have just mentioned the notion of Common Basque, whose existence Michelena (1981) considered necessary in order to explain the evident unity of all the Basque dialects (cf. n. 8) and which he tentatively established around the sixth–eighth centuries AD. Lakarra (2015a) highlights the necessity of defining more precisely this linguistic entity, of establishing relationships with the Proto-Basque previous stage, and proposing a hypothesis of fragmentation of unity in the historical dialects. Aquitanian, owing to the characteristics of documentation, cannot contribute much more to this history beyond that pointed out earlier, although its data may be explained coherently within this idea. We have seen that the Basque linguistic domain—which encompassed a wide territory in ancient times—presented noteworthy features of unity alongside areal differences. Amongst the former the coincidences in the distribution of lenes and fortes consonants, the coincidence of the use of the suffix pairs *-so* /-se* to differentiate sex, and the use of the desinence *-(h)e* in datives, together with the identity of some words, especially Vasc. *Umme* : Aq. *Ombe*, are of great interest. The differences are centered around the use of distinct onomastic bases in one or another territory, with special interest in the use of *Andots* in Aquitania meaning "sir," which appears to be a semantic evolution out of a previous and general "male animal." Other differences are, besides the use of the suf. *-eia* to form women's names in Aquitania, the confirmation of different phonetic evolutions or, at least, different chronologies in one or another territory. As regards the *-mb-* cluster, we see that it was assimilated early on to *-mm-* in the Vasconic area (Vasc. *Umme*), whilst throughout the entire Aquitanian documentation *-mb-* is maintained (Aq. *Ombe-*, *Sembe-*). If we link this confirmation to the fact that the Iberian onomastics on the Ascoli bronze (89 BC) shows assimilation of *-nb-* > *m* (*Adimels* < **Adin-bels*), we can assume that the assimilation process began in the Vasconic area of the Basque territory and gradually expanded throughout the latter, embracing the whole territory as demonstrated in the evolution experienced by *-mb-* in Gascon. On the contrary, in the Aquitanian area we find sporadic testimonies of *-nd-* > *-nn-* assimilation, as demonstrated by the spellings *Annereni* (dat.) for *Andere* and *Annosus* for *Andoxus*. This change is also one of the characteristics of Gascon, but not of Basque (cf. Gasc. *làno* : Bq. *landa* "moor"). Common Basque, therefore, which had to develop in the western territory of the ancient domain, formed through a process of convergence out of western Pyrenean dialects. Some of its characteristics were evident in the ancient documentation of the area, like Vasc. *Umme-*, which presents the same initial vocalism as in the Bq. *(h)ume*, as opposed to the Aq. *Ombe-*; one must assume an *o-* > *u-* change before the new /m/ sound.

6. Conclusions

We can sum up the most important aspects taking into account the comparison of Aquitanian and Basque data, as follows:

- The establishment of cognates is a task full of obstacles and difficulties, due to the fact that the Aquitanian documentation is just of an onomastic nature, so that linguists must reinforce the formal parallels with additional factors, such as geographic distribution and the coherent and recurring association or alignment with features independent of form, with the aim of making the most certain cognation possible.
- A reduced but significant number of cognates, as well as phonological distribution features, demonstrate an exclusive relationship with the Basque language, not shared by any other nearby language. The relationship between both languages has been proven, although many other elements whose cognation do not possess the sufficient degree of certainty remain outside the comparison. The methodological limitations in establishing the cognates favor common elements or plesiomorphic features.
- Many of the most reliable cognates exhibit a relationship in which the Basque data are forms derived in an evolutionary way from Aquitanian forms or that show the presence of innovative elements which did not exist in the previous phase. Concluding from them an affiliation rather than collateral family relationship may be a methodological corollary more than a reflection of the reality.
- The new data from the ancient Vasconic territory, thanks to the presence of a few Basque cognates, confirm its belonging to the Basque-language family; as regards its relationship with Aquitanian, besides common features which endorse the idea of linguistic unity between both sides of the Pyrenees,

there are also divergences which point to a dialectalization of the area: some are innovative (as the sound changes in *umme*) with respect to the previous stage and Aquitanian, whilst others are conservative (as the preservation of the animal-like meaning of *andosco*).

Notes

1. For a history of traditional ideas on the ancient nature and origin of the Basque language and its relationship to Iberian, see Tovar (2015). For a current perspective on pre-Roman or Palaeohispanic languages in the Iberian Peninsula, see Sinner and Velaza (2019).
2. This has not stopped the aforementioned researchers from revealing at the same time certain formal similarities between Aquitanian and Iberian onomastics, especially that represented in the Ascoli Bronze, accepting in Michelena's words a kind of onomastic pull in which some elements could have been shared; Gorrochategui (1993: 622–34) addresses in detail this aspect of the relationship between Aquitanian and Iberian names with a critical evaluation of traditional proposals (Gorrochategui 2013: 59–60).
3. Many studies on ancient personal onomastics and toponymy in Europe, both the traditional work of Hubschmid (1960) and Pokorny (1936, 1949) and more recent contributions by Vennemann (1994) and Villar (2005), suffer from these defects.
4. A new reading of the inscription in Lauterecken (*Am*[*m*]*osse*, cf. Kakoschke 2014: 291) has come to confirm the weakness of the parallel, reinforcing the "Aquitanian nature" of the whole set of male names built on *Andoss-*.
5. Rix does not think that this radical divorce between the anthroponyms of both languages can be due to separation after 600 BC, when Celtic tribes settled between Rhaetian and Etruscan by occupying the Po Valley, but instead that it dates to hundreds of years previously ["er muß Jahrhunderte älter sein," 1998: 59].
6. Just as the Lactorates are the inhabitants of Lactora (the current Lectoure) or the Sibylates the inhabitants of the valley of Ziburu or Soule.
7. In the northern tradition, since the first author Dechepare, we find the form *nihaur* as the intensive personal pronoun, with its regular gen. sg. *nihauren*, which should be considered a restored form, taking into account the coetaneous existence of the common form *neure*.
8. Here we are focusing only on those features in common Basque which are of interest to Basque–Aquitanian comparison. Michelena (1981: 301–4) summarized the most important ones: noun inflection, existence of two stems in demonstrative pronouns, proximal articles with syncretism in the plural, anaphoric personal pronouns, general verb structure, and processes of noun composition.
9. In this sense, one could think that the theonym *Sutugio / Suhugio*, despite presenting an alternation, stop (t) / aspiration (h), identical to the correspondence Bq. *aker* "goat" / Aq. *Aher-*, is a Gaulish compound *su-tug-io- (root *(s)teug- "incite, push"); or that the anthroponym *Dannadinn-is* (gen.) may contain the typical Iberian element *-adin*. Possible Iberianisms could be broadened

to some more names (for example Aq. *Gere-* : Ib. *-gere*, in several names in Pech Maho and Ampurias or the theonym *Iluro-* which is identical to the Iberian toponym *Iluro*). In contrast, Aq. *Belex* : Ib. *beleś* constitutes the only correspondence with frequently attested names in both onomastics.

10. Some relationship can always be proposed, although guaranteeing this may be difficult: for *Silex* Michelena (1970: 106; 1979: 38, fn. 35) suggested Bq. *sirats* "destination" (LN), *siracha* "nerve" (old B); *Edunn* is identical to the verb stem *edun "have" and the auxiliary verb, and *Idiatte* resembles Bq. *idi* "ox."
11. The inscription from *Andelo* (Untermann 1997: 718–19) is generally considered to be Iberian, and the testimonies on coins do not offer any clear linguistic facies.
12. Likewise Etruscan presents an onomastic subsystem in which reference is made to the female sex by adding the suf. *-i* or *-a*, of Indo-European origin, at the end of the male name: for example, from the patronym-gentilicium in *-na* one gets *-nai* (tarχna → tarχnai).
13. One should point out the slightly paradoxical nature of a pro-relationship argument which is based on a "quasi-grammatical" cognate that did not refer to any category of protolanguage, but to an innovation restricted to the onomastic subsystem. The same thing happens between Etruscan and Rhaetian as regards the patronymic-gentilicium suffix, although the relationship is based in this case on more cognates of a grammatical kind.
14. Michelena (1954: 442–3) adduced *Totacoje* to be a diminutive of the medieval name *Tota, Toda*, analyzed as *Tota-co-xe*.
15. The name *Suri* (gen.) would be a better correspondence, but one cannot be sure it is Aquitanian.
16. This difference is more significant than that observed in *seni, which in the eastern Basque dialects means "servant," whilst in the western ones it is "child, boy." Because of parallels in semantic changes, but above all because of the existence of *se(h)aska* "cradle" (*sehi* + *aska* "trough, crib") all over Basque-speaking areas, one must assume that the ancient meaning, and also in Aquitanian, was "child, boy."
17. Lakarra (2006, 2011: 697), proposed *e-da-dun (*e-* + *da* durativ + *dun* "have") > *eaun > *jaun*. The verb stem is formally identical to Aq. *Edunn* (see n. 10).
18. The monosyllabic root theory would demand an element in the position of the first consonant in the CVC root, which would have to be reconstructed as *hon-. That could explain the aspirated form of the Bq. *hume*. However, both *Hon-* and *Bon-* are attested in the corpus in several testimonies, although with other suffixes, so that the reasons for the alternation are not clear.
19. Lakarra has on occasion constructed "lexical families" formed out of the same root, for example a root node form *lats* "stream," reduplicated *adats* "mane," compound *aldats* "incline" (*alde+dats*), infinitive verb *jatsi* "descend" (*e-dats-i) (Lakarra 2018a: 71–2) on the root *dats* "hang, slide from top to bottom." Cf. Lakarra (2011: 693–9) for other examples of lexical families, although sometimes it is difficult to accept the quality of cognate for all of them.
20. Lakarra favors thinking that the oldest Proto-Basque did not have *l in initial, so that every *l-* historically attested is the result of an original *d-. The fact that nor did

historical Basque have initial *r-* and certain cases of initial *n-*, even though certain and ancient ones, like Aq. *Nescato*, Bq. *neska*, may be explained as borrowings, could lead one to think that the oldest Proto-Basque consonant system distributed its consonants in the root in a quasi-complementary way: stops *t-*, *k-*, *b-*, *d-*, *g-* and sibilants *s-*, *ś-* initially and sonorants *-n*, *-l*, *-r* and sibilants *-s*, *-ś* in final position of the root. Although this outline offers the elegance of internal reconstructions based on system structures, there are many words with initial *n-*, such as the first person personal pronoun Bq. *ni* as well as Aq. names like *Neure-*, *Narhun-* which oblige one to postulate *n- on initial. In the same way, the *d- > *l-* change does not imply that there was no *l- in initial, so that there was phonological fusion.

21. Lakarra (2015b: 432f.) has suggested a relative chronology of these changes: (1) *d- > Ø- in reduplicated formations of the oldest Proto-Basque, (2) loss of the capacity to create reduplicates, (3) *d- > *l-*, (4) use of prefixes before roots with initial *l-*, (5) loss of the capacity to form words by means of prefixes and typological drift towards suffixation. The problem that emerges is that Aq. had already clearly achieved stage 5 of this chain, which implies a prolonged prior period for the typological drift of a prefixational to a suffixational language, and, yet, the *d- > *l-* step had to be prior to that evolutionary phase, which goes against the existence of supposed Aquitanian terms with initial *D-*, even against the changes suffered by Latin borrowings (Lat. *theca* > *deka > *leka* "sheath").

22. It has always been noteworthy that some parts of the human body, like *begi* "eye," *buru* "head," and *beso* "arm" begin with *b-*, in which it is seen as a remnant of the prefix or class marker. However, Lakarra derives these nouns in another way, cf. *begi* < *goi-hegi "above-corner" (!) (Lakarra 2011: 694).

23. For instance, it is difficult for me to admit that the desinence on the noun inflection *-raino* to indicate direction with the term, which is apparently due to a recent creation out of the simple desinence of the allative *-(r)a*, is the grammaticalization of the sequence of serial verbs -da-+din-+no = "sit-come-go"; the same applies to the idea that the third person pl. marker *-te/-de/-e* (*-de) is the grammaticalization of the verb *den "finish," which also ended up being grammaticalized by another route in the past marker *-en*.

24. I do not see, however, any semantic reason to think that the perfect participle markers in *-i* and in *-n* should be the result of a split of the previous marker *nin (Lakarra 2011: 670, fn. 32); I still think that the argument of Trask (1990) explains the relationship between both markers in an elegant way.

25. One should bear in mind that the archaic marker of gen. sg. is *-e*: pronoun *hire* "yours," medieval name *Ortire* "of Orti." Curiously, Lakarra (2018b: 141–5) conceives said gen. *-e* as an ancient marker of a general locative sense, stemming from the root *her "near." For a relationship between genitive and beneficiary, see above the formation and use of the pertinentive case in Etruscan.

26. Thus the fact that the imperfect marker *da- has the freedom to be placed in initial of the verb sequence in a period following the *d- > *l-* change, so as to be able to explain its form with initial *d-*.

27. The odd one may be considered a borrowing, like *Gere-* (see *supra*), but this explanation for most of them is difficult. Lakarra has used this route a lot, sometimes in

an unconvincing way, in order to explain Latin borrowings in Basque words like *negar* "cry" (*lacrima), *leher* "explode" (*tremere), and *gau* (*cado).
28. For Lakarra (*h*)*ibai* "river" comes from *hur "water" + ban-i "edge" and *lau(r)* "four" < *la-bur, originally the fourth finger starting to count from the index finger, that is, the little finger, cf. *labur* "short"; one has to admit, I suppose, that the Bq. *labur* has been renewed through restoration at a later date to the loss of intervocalic -*b*-, in which *la*- still functions as a living prefix, and in which the final -*r* behaves in a different way.
29. The theonym *Leherenn* can be broken down into *leher-enn*, with the suffix -*enn* also documented in *Belex-enn*, which is formally identical to the Basque superlative suffix; semantically something like "the very destructive" would be a parallel of the epithet for Mars *Sutugio / Suhugio* mentioned in n. 9.
30. Some would still be cognates, like Aq. *Nescato* : Bq. *neska-to* "girl," although it would not be a patrimonial Basque word but a borrowing taken from another language, presumably Celtic.
31. The toponym *Anuncibay* "goat river" keeps the -*n*- from the name for goat *anuntz (Bq. *ahuntz*), but not that for river *ibai* (*hur-iban-i, according to Lakarra). Likewise, some Latin loanwords, like Bq. *zendea*, are very helpful to determine the dating of the borrowing and thereby a *terminus post quem* for the loss of the -*n*-; according to Hualde (2015: 136, 145), if the palatalization process suffered by the initial velar stop in Vulgar Latin (*kentena > *tʃentena > tsentena) was not completed before the seventh century, then the loss of the intervocalic -*n*- occurred necessarily after this date.

References

Bakker, Peter. 2020. Review of the book *Advances in Proto-Basque Reconstruction with Evidence for the Proto-Indo-European-Euskarian Hypothesis* by Juliette Blevins. *Fontes Linguae Vasconum*: 130, 563–92. doi: https://doi.org/10.35462/flv.130.8

Bernhard, Helmut, Heinz-Josef Engels, Renate Engels, and Richard Petrovszky. 1990. *Der römische Schatzfund von Hagenbach*. Mainz: Verlag des römisch-germanischen Zentralmuseums.

Campbell, Lyle. 2003. How to show languages are related: Methods for distant genetic relationship. In *Handbook of historical linguistics*, ed. by B. D. Joseph and R. D. Janda, 262–82. Oxford: Blackwell.

Campbell, Lyle. 2011. La investigación histórica de las lenguas aisladas, o ¿es raro el vasco? In *2nd conference of the Luis Michelena chair*, ed. by J. A. Lakarra, J. Gorrochategui, and B. Urgell, 23–40. Vitoria-Gasteiz: UPV/EHU.

Campbell, Lyle, and William J. Poser. 2008. *Language classification. History and method*. Cambridge: Cambridge University Press.

Caro Baroja, Julio. 1954. *Materiales para una historia de la lengua vasca en su relación con la latina*. Salamanca: Universidad de Salamanca.

Chambon, Jean-Pierre, and Yan Greub. 2002. Note sur l'âge du (proto)gascon, *Revue de Linguistique Romane* 66: 473–95.

De Bernardo Stempel, Patrizia. 2006. Las lenguas célticas en la investigación: cuatro observaciones metodológicas, *Estudios griegos e indoeuropeos* 16: 5–21.
Delamarre, Xavier. 2007. *Noms de personnes celtiques dans l'épigraphie classique*. Paris: Errance.
Gorrochategui, Joaquín. 1984. *Onomástica indígena de Aquitania*. Bilbao: Universidad del País Vasco.
Gorrochategui, Joaquín. 1993. La onomástica aquitana y su relación con la ibérica. In *Lengua y Cultura en la Hispania prerromana, Actas del V Coloquio Int. sobre Lenguas y Culturas prerromanas de la Península Ibérica*, ed. by J. Untermann and Francisco Villar, 609–34. Salamanca: Universidad de Salamanca.
Gorrochategui, Joaquín. 1995. The Basque language and its neighbors in Antiquity. In *Towards a history of the Basque language*, ed. by J. I. Hualde, J. A. Lakarra, and R. L. Trask, 31–63. Amsterdam/Philadelphia: John Benjamins.
Gorrochategui, Joaquín. 2003. Las placas votivas de plata de origen aquitano halladas en Hagenbach (Renania-Palatinado, Alemania). *Revue Aquitania* 19: 25–47.
Gorrochategui, Joaquín. 2009. Vasco antiguo: algunas cuestiones de geografía e historia lingüísticas. *Palaeohispanica* 9: 539–55.
Gorrochategui, Joaquín. 2013. Hispania indoeuropea y no indoeuropea. In *Iberia e Sardegna. Legami linguistici, archeologici e genetici dal Mesolitico all'Età del Bronzo*, ed. by E. Blasco Ferrer, P. Francalacci, A. Nocentini, and G. Tanda, 47–64. Firenze: Le Monnier Università / Studi.
Gorrochategui, Joaquín. 2015. Akitaniera eta Euskara, in *Ibon Sarasola, Gorazarre. Homenatge, Homenaje* ed. by B. Fernández and P. Salaburu, 291–302. Bilbao: Universidad del País Vasco.
Gorrochategui, Joaquín. 2018. La lengua vasca en la antigüedad. In *Historia de la lengua vasca* ed. by J. Gorrochategui, I. Igartua, and J. A. Lakarra, 245–305. Vitoria-Gasteiz: Gobierno Vasco.
Hualde, José I. 2015. Dialektologia dinamikoa. *Lapurdum*, Numéro spécial 3: 125–53.
Hubschmid, Johannes. 1960. *Mediterrane Substrate*. Bern: A. Francke Verlag.
Igartua, Iván. 2015. Diachronic effects of rhinoglottophilia, symmetries in sound change, and the curious case of Basque. *Studies in Language* 39(3): 635–63.
Joseph, Brian. 2016. The comparative method: Simplicity + power = results. *Veleia* 33: 39–48.
Kakoschke, Andreas. 2014. Amossa – nicht Andossa. Neulesung einer Grabinschrift aus Lauterecken/Germania Superior. *Zeitschrift für Papyrologie und Epigraphik* 19: 291–2.
Lakarra, Joseba A. 1995. Reconstructing the root in Pre-Proto-Basque. In *Towards a history of the Basque language*, ed. by J. I. Hualde, J. A. Lakarra, and R. L. Trask, 189–206. Amsterdam/Philadelphia: John Benjamins.
Lakarra, Joseba A. 2006. *Jaun* eta *jabe*, *jaio* eta *herio*, *jin* eta *joan*: etimologiaz eta aditz morfologia zaharraz (hitz hasierez II). In *Andolin gogoan. Essays in honour of Professor Eguzkitza*, ed. by B. Fernández and I. Laka, 575–611. Bilbao: Universidad del País Vasco.
Lakarra, Joseba A. 2011. Teoría de la raíz monosilábica y reconstrucción del protovasco: algunos aspectos y consecuencias. In *2nd conference of the Luis Michelena*

chair, ed. by J. A. Lakarra, J. Gorrochategui, and B. Urgell, 651–99. Vitoria-Gasteiz: Universidad del País Vasco.

Lakarra, Joseba A. 2015a. Gogoetak euskal dialektologia diakronikoaz: Euskara Batu Zaharra berreraiki beharraz eta haren banaketaren ikerketaz. In *Euskal dialektologia: lehena eta oraina*, ed. by I. Epelde, 155–241. San Sebastián/Bilbao: Diputación Foral de Gipuzkoa / Universidad del País Vasco.

Lakarra, Joseba A. 2015b. Saratsola eta (aitzin)euskar(ar)en geruzak. In *Ibon Sarasola, Gorazarre. Homenatge, Homenaje*, ed. by B. Fernández and P. Salaburu, 419–39. Bilbao: Universidad del País Vasco.

Lakarra, Joseba A. 2018a. Basque and the reconstruction of language isolates. In *Language isolates*, ed. by Lyle Campbell, 59–99. Abingdon/New York: Routledge.

Lakarra, Joseba A. 2018b. La prehistoria de la lengua vasca. In *Historia de la lengua vasca*, ed. by J. Gorrochategui, I. Igartua, and J. A. Lakarra, 23–244. Vitoria-Gasteiz: Gobierno Vasco.

Luchaire, Achiles. 1877. Les origines linguistiques de l'Aquitaine. *Bulletin de la Société des Sciences, Lettres et Arts de Pau*, 1876/7: 349–423.

Matasović, Ranko. 2009. *Etymological Dictionary of Proto-Celtic*. Leiden, Boston: Brill.

Michelena, Luis. 1954. De onomástica aquitana. *Pirineos* 10: 409–58.

Michelena, Luis. 1970. *Estudio sobre las fuentes del Diccionario de Azkue*, Bilbao: Euskaltzaindia.

Michelena, Luis. 1977. *Fonética histórica vasca* (2nd edn). In *Obras Completas* VII, ed. by Luis Michelena. San Sebastián: Diputación Foral de Gipuzkoa.

Michelena, Luis. 1979. La langue ibère. In *II Coloquio sobre lenguas y culturas prerromana de la península ibérica*, ed. by A. Tovar, M. Faust, F. Fischer, and M. Koch, 23–39. Salamanca: Universidad de Salamanca.

Michelena, Luis. 1981. Lengua común y dialectos vascos. *Anuario del Seminario Julio de Urquijo* 15, 291–313.

Nichols, Johanna. 1996. The comparative method as heuristic. In *The comparative method reviewed*, ed. by M. Durie and M. Ross, 39–71. Oxford: Oxford University Press.

Pokorny, Julius. 1936. Zur Urgeschichte der Kelten und Illyrier. *Zeitschrift für celtische Philologie* 20: 315–55, 489–522.

Pokorny, Julius. 1949. Zur Urgeschichte der Kelten und Illyrier. *Zeitschrift für celtische Philologie* 21: 55–166.

Rix, Helmut. 1998. *Rätisch und Etruskisch*. Innsbruck: Innsbrucker Beiträge zur Sprachwissenschaft.

Sinner, Alejandro and Velaza, Javier (eds). 2019. *Palaeohispanic Languages and Epigraphies*. Oxford: Oxford University Press.

Tovar, Antonio. 2015. *Mythology and ideology of the Basque language*, with an introduction by J. Gorrochategui, Basque Classics Series, nº 9. Reno: University of Nevada.

Trask, Robert L. 1990. The *-n* class of verbs in Basque. *Transactions of the Philological Society* 88(1): 111–28.

Trask, Robert L. 1995. Origin and relatives of the Basque language: Review of the evidence. In *Towards a history of the Basque language*, ed. by J. I. Hualde, J. A. Lakarra, and R. L. Trask, 65–99. Amsterdam/Philadelphia: John Benjamins.

Untermann, Jürgen. 1961. *Sprachräume und Sprachbewegungen in vorrömischen Hispanien.* Wiesbaden: Harrassowitz.

Untermann, Jürgen. 1965. *Elementos de un Atlas antroponímico de la Hispania antigua.* Madrid: CSIC.

Untermann, Jürgen. 1997. *Monumenta Linguarum Hispanicarum*, IV: *Die tartessischen, keltiberischen und lusitanischen Inschriften.* Wiesbaden: Reichert.

Vennemann, Theo. 1994. Linguistic reconstruction in the context of European prehistory. *Transactions of the Philological Society* 92: 215–84.

Villar, Francisco, and Blanca Prósper. 2005. *Vascos, celtas e indoeuropeos. Genes y lenguas.* Salamanca: Universidad de Salamanca.

7

Evidence, New and Old, Against the Late *k(') > *ch(') Areal Shift Hypothesis

David F. Mora-Marín

1. Introduction

This chaper deals with two topics that have been amply researched by Lyle Campbell: the application of philology to address matters of interest in the historical linguistics of American Indian languages, including Mayan hieroglyphic writing (Campbell 1984, 1990); and the scrutiny of loanwords in order to assess relative chronologies of culture historical and linguistic developments, including evidence of past contacts between different ethnolinguistic groups (Campbell 1970, 1972, 1986, 2000; Campbell and Kaufman 1976; Justeson et al. 1985). More specifically, this chapter addresses the question of the *k(') > *ch(') shift in the Mayan languages, focusing on the problem of its chronology and attestations in Epigraphic Mayan, and the nature of scribal practices and their connection to linguistic ideologies.[1]

This question has recently resurfaced: Law et al. (2014) have put forth a proposal for a late application of this shift among already differentiated Ch'olan and Tzeltalan languages, which they argue is attested in real time primarily from the beginning of Late Classic (600–900 CE) period. Their proposal would revise the previous model, based on both comparative linguistic and epigraphic evidence, that called for the application of the shift among speakers of a largely undifferentiated community of Greater Tzeltalan speakers, by the first half of the Late Preclassic (400 BCE–250 CE) period, possibly by c.200–100 BCE (Kaufman 1976; Kaufman and Norman 1984; Justeson et al. 1985; Justeson and Fox 1989; Kaufman and Justeson 2007), and more conservatively no later than c. 250-400 CE, roughly corresponding to the first half of the Early Classic period (c.200-600 CE), when spellings of **ka-ka-wa** for proto-Ch'olan (pCh') *käkäw "cacao," a loanword from Mixe-Zoquean, are first attested. That etymon presents the right conditions to have experienced the shift, and yet, as Campbell (2000: 5) has noted, it did not, demonstrating that the shift must have occurred prior to its earliest occurrences. Law et al.'s (2014) proposal would revise the timing of shift to between c.600 and 900 CE, and would require that we accept that scribes ignored three phonemic contrasts (*q vs. *k, *q' vs. *k, and *nh vs. n).

This chapter assesses and critiques Law et al.'s (2014) proposal. Section 2 begins by reviewing the models for the phonological history of the Greater Tzeltalan languages, and more specifically, the proposals for the *k(') > ch(') shift by Kaufman and Norman (1984), Justeson et al. (1985), and Law et al. (2014), paying especial attention to loanwords between Greater Tzeltalan and other Mayan languages that are crucial to establishing relative chronologies for several sound changes (*k(') > ch('), *nh > n, *q(') > *k(')). Section 3 focuses on philological evidence, both old and new, from Epigraphic Mayan (ISO 639-3 emy), including examples from early inscriptions containing lexical and grammatical morphemes that experienced the shift (Mora-Marín 2001, 2005, 2009), as well as loanwords that should have experienced the shift if Law et al.'s chronology were correct, but did not (Campbell 2000; Kaufman and Justeson 2007). Finally, Section 4 offers conclusions and discusses their implications.

The chapter concludes that the philological and loanword evidence support the early shift proposal, prior to the earliest attestations of pCh' *käkäw, as previous authors had already established (Campbell 2000; Kaufman and Justeson 2007), and proposes that the sociolinguistic context of the Maya lowlands during the Late Preclassic and Classic periods, which involved interaction between likely bilingual speakers of Ch'olan and Yucatecan varieties, was probably one of interlinguistic literacy, previously proposed by Fox and Justeson (1982) and Justeson and Fox (1989), as a factor that inhibited a more systematic representation of the *k(') > ch(') shift in explicit phonetic spellings. Scribes were not linguists, attentive to capturing "supple" changes in the language, as suggested by Law et al. (2014: 362), despite the fact that their proposal necessitates that the same scribes ignored three sets of phonemic contrasts. Instead, scribes were social actors exercising their sociolinguistic attitudes and ideologies, sometimes in contradictory ways, as contextualized acts of identity. Crucially, this proposal finds support in the differential treatment of grammatical versus lexical morphemes: the former were invariably spelled phonetically and exhibited positive evidence of *k(') > ch(') shift from their earliest attestations; the latter were spelled ambiguously for the most part, and were only rarely specified, mostly during the Late Classic period, and were thus more vulnerable to social manipulation.

2. Background and proposals concerning the *k(') > ch(') shift

2.1 Mayan historical linguistics

I follow Kaufman's (1976, 1990, 2015, 2017) model of the diversification of Mayan: it is the most narrowly defined model of the diversification of the family, and therefore, of the interrelationships between the various groupings and subgroupings, as it calls for a succession of early binary splits.[2] The reader should refer to Kaufman (2017: 66–7, Figs. 4.2A–4.2B) for the illustration of his model, available online in its original, prepublication design by Justeson (n.d.). Kaufman groups Greater Q'anjob'alan and Greater Tzeltalan into a Western Mayan grouping coordinate with Eastern Mayan, and both of these, in turn, into a larger, Central Mayan grouping. He groups Yucatecan and Central Mayan into a Southern Mayan grouping (earlier, "Late Proto-Mayan" or "Core Mayan"), and regards Huastecan (aka Wastekan) as the most divergent grouping, and the first one to depart from the homeland.³ Kaufman's justification for including Yucatecan (aka Yukatekan) as part of Southern Mayan, and for grouping Greater Tzeltalan and Greater Q'anjob'alan into Western Mayan is based more on comparative morphology than phonology, most of which was written down as of 1989, but was not made available until just a few years ago (Kaufman 2015).

I do not assume Kaufman's glottochronological estimates a priori, but instead propose to test them against other lines of evidence, as that author and others have done in the past (Josserand 1975; Kaufman 1976; Justeson et al. 1985; Kaufman with Justeson 2007). Below I discuss Kaufman's proposed diversification and movement scenarios as they become relevant. Table 7.1 provides the language and subgroup names and abbreviations that will be used in this chapter; those in bold letters are the most important.

One more general concern must be addressed before introducing the *k(') > ch(') shift: language contact. Several diffusion zones have been defined within the Maya region. Justeson et al. (1985) established the importance of two areas of close interaction between Mayan languages: the *Greater Lowland Mayan* area (henceforth GLL), primarily involving the Greater Tzeltalan and Yucatecan languages; and the *Lowland Mayan* area (henceforth LL), primarily involving the Ch'olan and Yucatecan languages. Kaufman (1976: 107; 2015: 98, 233, 413) further defined two additional areas: the *Chiapas Sphere* (Tojolob'al, Tzotzil, Ch'ol) and the *Huehuetenango Sphere* (Greater Mamean and Greater Q'anjob'alan minus Tojolob'al and Motozintleko). In addition, Justeson et al. (1985: 9–10, Table 2) and Kaufman (2017: 69) have also identified significant diffusion from LL, but in Kaufman's opinion "mostly from Ch'olan," into "Q'anjob'alan, Ixil, Uspanteko, Q'eqchi7." Wichmann and Hull (2009) focus on the extent of diffusion from LL into Q'eqchi', and indeed, highlight the influx of Ch'olan languages especially. The most recent, systematic work on language contact in the Maya lowlands is Law's (2013a, 2013b, 2014, 2017). An important aspect in his work is the focus on "areal spread," that is, diffusion across language boundaries, of phonological and morphological innovations, not only between Ch'olan and Yucatecan languages, but also between Ch'olan and Q'anjob'alan languages, "in spite of the fact that Yucatecan and Cholan are generally characterized as the core languages of the lowland area" (2017: 122). Nevertheless, this is consistent with prior and recent characterizations by Kaufman (1976, 2015, 2017) and others (Justeson et al. 1985), who have explicitly suggested relevant cases of lexical, morphological, and phonological diffusion into Greater Q'anjob'alan, a matter of relevance in this chapter.

2.2 Initial formulations of the *k(') > ch(') shift and relevant loanword evidence

From this point on I will refer to etyma with pM *k(') that underwent the *k(') > *ch(') shift, as well as those that did not, by the respective item # in Appendices A–D, consisting of four tables comprising 118 etyma in total, for a total of 125 cases of pM *k('). Appendices A–B include etyma that did not experience the shift in GTz, a total of 48 (40.7%), while Appendices C–D include those that did, a total of 70 (59.3%). In addition to GTz data (Ch', Tz), data from GQ' and Yu are also included. The datasets have been collected primarily on the basis of Kaufman and Norman (1984).

Table 7.1 Nomenclature and abbreviations used in this chapter

Proto-Mayan (pM)						
Huastecan (Hua)						Huastec
						Chicomuceltec
Late Proto-Mayan (LpM)	Yucatecan (Yu)					Mopan
						Itzaj
						Yucatec
						Lacandon
	Central Mayan (CM)	Western Mayan (WM)	Greater Tzeltalan (GTz)	Ch'olan (Ch')	Western Ch'olan (WCh')	Ch'ol
						Yokot'an (Chontal)
					Eastern Ch'olan (ECh')	Ch'olti'
						Ch'orti'
				Tzeltalan (Tz)		Tzeltal
						Tzotzil
			Greater Q'anjob'alan (GQ')	Chujean (Chj)		Tojolob'al
						Chuj
				Q'anjob'alan Proper (Q'P)		Popti'
						Akateko
						Q'anjob'al
					Kotoke Complex (KCx)	Mocho'
						Tuzantek
		Eastern Mayan (EM)	Greater Mamean (GM)	Mamean Proper (MP)		Mam
						Teko
				Ixilan (Ixn)		Ixil
						Awakateko
				Uspantek (Usp)		Uspantek
			Greater K'iche'an (GK')	K'ichee'an Proper (K'P)		Kaqchikel
						Tz'utujil
						Sakapulteko
						Sipakapense
						K'ichee'
				Q'eqchi' (Qeq)		Q'eqchi'

Note: Where language and subgroup names are prefixed with "p," it means "proto."

A few items have been revised, rejected, or added based on new evidence primarily from Kaufman with Justeson (2003). Such changes are explicitly remarked upon in the footnotes to the relevant appendices or in the discussion that follows, except for #123 (Appendix C), "to weave," which I identify here for the first time as a possible example of the shift, but which I do not discuss further below.

Kaufman (1976: 109–10) reviewed several innovations of GTz, including the *k > ch shift (with no explicit mention of *k' > ch' at this point), and also proposed that it diffused to GQ', but in his examples he suggests diffusion of etyma, not of a sound change rule. He explains that this GTz shift must have preceded the shift of *q > k, for etyma with reflexes of pM *q were unaffected, and highlighted the fact that "lexical borrowings from Greater Tzeltalan in highland languages" such as "to sell," "peccary," and "fish," indicate that the Greater Tzeltalan *k > ch shift preceded the Greater Tzeltalan *nh > n shift, as well as the Huehuetenango Sphere *t > ch and *ch > tx shifts. These etyma correspond to items #77 (pM *konh, Yu *kon, GTz *chon, Tojolab'al *chon*, Chuj *chonh*, Q'anjob'al *txon*, Akatek *xono7*, Popti' *txonh*, KCx *chonh*), #116 (LL+WM *kitaam, Yu *kitam, Ch' *chitam, Tz *chitam, Chujean *chitam*, Q'Cx *txitam*, KCx *chitaam*) and #65 (pM *kar, Yu *kay, Ch' *chäy, Tz *chay, Chujean chay). Thus, by carefully considering likely GTz loans, Kaufman (1976) established a relative chronology for the *k > ch shift with respect to both the *q > k and *nh > n shifts, which it must have preceded.[4]

To the cases of early diffusion between GTz and GQ' raised by Kaufman (1976), I would also add the following: item #100, pM *k'ajaanh "rope, vine," reflected as pGQ' *ch'ajaanh and pGTz *ch'ajaan; #49, pM *ki7 "sweet," reflected in Chujean *chi7 and Q'Cx *chi7, but absent from KCx in a pattern reproducing proximity to the lowlands, and thus supporting of diffusion; #57, pM *kehj "deer," present in GQ' (minus Mocho') as *chej* or *cheej* or *cheh*, possibly from pre-GTz *chehj > pGTz *chihj, especially given the Chuj term *chej=chan* "boa constrictor," likely borrowed from a pre-GTz form *chehj=chan; and item #84, pM *7iik "chile," reflected in GTz *7iich, appearing in Chujean as *7ich and Q'Cx as *7ich, once again absent from KCx. Like the case of "to sell" (#77), "rope, vine" (#100) further supports the earlier timing of the *k' > ch' shift relative to the *nh > n shift. Item #61 could also provide evidence of such a relative chronology: Tojol-7ab'al *chan-e* "four" and Chuj *chanh-e7* "four" could support diffusion of a pre-GTz form *chanh- "four" prior to the GTz *nh > n shift. Also, note that possible loan evident in Chuj *chej=chan* "boa constrictor" would suggest that the sporadic change of *eh > ih in "deer" followed the *k > ch shift in GTz; this example is discussed in more detail in Section 3.2.

Several years later, Kaufman and Norman (1984: 83–5) characterized the shift as unconditioned and as involving both reflexes of pM *k and *k'. They defined a set of inhibiting environments that prevented the shift in thirty of the eighty-nine etyma in their dataset. Their characterization of the inhibiting environments is cited verbatim and in full next (Kaufman and Norman 1984: 84):

(1) Formulation of the *k(') > ch(') shift by Kaufman and Norman (1984: 83–5)
   a. in initial position before a vowel that is in turn followed by an apical consonant or /p/, unless the vowel is /i/;

b. in final position following a vowel, if the consonant preceding the vowel is an apical or /p/ (*even if* the vowel is /i/);
c. in final position following /h/ (but not following /j/);
d. in intervocalic position within a single root *unless* the vowel that precedes the velar stop is /i/.

Those authors added that out of the thirty items in which the shift did not occur, three should have undergone the shift, for they lacked inhibiting environments (Kaufman and Norman 1984: 85, 89). They argued on such basis that the following three items were diffused into GTz from other Mayan languages subsequent to the shift (and in the process likely replaced the relevant reflexes of the pM forms): pCh' *kab' "earth" (#62b), proposed to be a loan from Yucatecan *kaab' (from pM *kab' ~ *kaab'); *k'ooj "mask" (#35), which the authors suggested was diffused from the Maya highlands to the lowlands; *kok "turtle" (#5); and *kuhkay "firefly" (#8). They also noted that Ch'olti' provides evidence for both the loan as <εo> (i.e. /k'oj/) as well as the native form <choh> (i.e. /ch'oj/) (Kaufman and Norman 1984: 124, entry #263); thus, Ch'olti' retained the original GTz form that underwent the shift of pre-GTz *k'ooj > pGTz *ch'ooj (> pre-Ch' *ch'ooj > pCh' *ch'oj > Ch'olti' /ch'oh/). Law et al. (2014: 359, 363), who do not cite Kaufman and Norman's observation, argue instead that Ch'olti' /ch'oj/ constitutes evidence that the shift occurred late; if Law et al. correct, this would constitute the only case of the shift that did not diffuse identically within Ch' or within GTz.

Elsewhere in their paper, Kaufman and Norman (1984: 143) provided a longer list of likely loans from "Eastern Mayan or Kanjobalan Proper" into GTz, including several additional items that would have masked the application of the shift based on then-available evidence: pM *k'isiis (cf. Tzeltal *k'isis=taj* "cypress," item #26), should have shifted to ch'isiis* > ch'isis*; pM *ko "OK" (item #3) should have shifted to cho* (cf. Ch'olan *ku and Tzeltalan *ko); pM *k'oq "to cut, tear" (item #36) should have shifted to ch'oq* > ch'ok* (cf. Ch'olan *k'ok, Tzeltalan *k'ok); and pM *k'o7 "snail" should have shifted to ch'o7* (cf. Ch'olan *k'o7 and Tzeltalan *k'o7). I have culled the last example from my dataset: Kaufman with Justeson (2003: 657) have revised the reconstruction to WM *q'o7, and therefore constitutes a case that would not have undergone the shift.[5] Lastly, Kaufman and Norman (1984: 118) point to one item that should not have undergone the shift because of its apical final consonant, but which nonetheless did: LL *kyol "to clear a milpa" and the related form *kyool "milpa" (#120), both attested in Ch' as *chol "to clear fields; milpa."

Next, Justeson et al. (1985: 13) offer several important observations and qualifications relevant to the shift, which they refer to as conditioned. First, they conceive of the shift as a two-step process involving palatalization and affrication: *k(') > *ky(') > *ch('). Second, they pointed to ten diffused GLL etyma with *k(') that presented the conditions for the shift, out of which six underwent the shift in GTz but not Yu: *b'uluky "eleven" (#91), pGTz *b'uluch; *kyiiky "older sister" (#88), pGTz *chiich; *kyitaam "peccary" (#116), pGTz *chitaam; *kyonh "to sell" (#77), pGTz *chon; #maniky' "seventh day name" (#117), pGTz #manich'; *weky' "to cast grains, to sprinkle liquid" (#118), pGTz *wech'. These six etyma would have diffused within the GLL area prior to the shift. The remaining four, which retained *k(') in both GTz and Yu even though they fit the conditions for the shift, include the following: *kanan "to guard," *kohk "deaf" (#10), *kohm "short," and *jok' "to dig a well; to dip out a liquid by hand" (#119). Based on these etyma, Justeson et al. (1985: 13) conclude that these four items "all appeared in Cholan-Tzeltalan after it shifted *k(') to *ky(')." Kaufman with Justeson (2003: 710) have since revised the reconstruction of "to guard" to pM as *qanhaanh, based on the Huastec cognat koo7, which points to pM *q (or else Huastec would show tx if from pM *k), which means it would not have undergone the shift, and also that it was not a diffused GLL innovation. Kaufman with Justeson have also revised the reconstruction of "short" to GLL *qohm (2003: 1375). Although they did not revise the reconstruction of "deaf," they did add that it was borrowed from Totonako qo:qo7 "dumb" (2003: 157), making it possible that it could have been borrowed initially as #qohq prior to the *q > k shift. This leaves only *jok' (#119) unaccounted for.

Additionally, Justeson et al. (1985) revisit the aforementioned case of Ch' *chol (presumably Pre-Ch *chol and *chool), and Yu *kol ~ *kool (cf. Yucatec kol and kòol), a LL term (#120)—absent from Tzeltalan, possibly due to lexical replacement. This term did not exhibit the conditions for the shift (or exhibited inhibiting factors against it), which they suggest points to evidence for their proposed two-step process of palatalization, *k(') > ky('), followed by affrication, *k(') > ch('), stating that this case "shows the k/č correspondence while violating the conditions on the sound change, and thus was an innovation after the development of *k > *ky and before *ky shifted further to č" (Justeson et al. 1985: 13). In other words, this term must have been innovated within the GLL area with initial *ky, as *kyol (and *kyool), after the *k > *ky shift had already occurred, but prior to the *ky > ch shift. Kaufman with Justeson (2003: 304) have in fact reconstructed another GLL term with *ky: the root #7iky "facing someone(/something?)" (#121), a likely positional root attested in Yucatecan (Itzaj, Yucatec, Lakantun) and Tzotzil. The Yucatecan form attests to /k/ and the Tzotzil form to /ch/; it is not attested in any Colonial or contemporary Ch'olan language, but it is attested in Epigraphic Mayan as **yi-chi-nal** for y-ich(V)n-al "in his/her presence," as discussed in Section 3.2. Consequently, it is another example of a form that supports the palatalization-before-affrication process, and serves as a counterpart to *kyool/*kyol, which is attested in Ch'olan but not Tzeltalan. Though not mentioned explicitly, Kaufman and Norman (1984) do reconstruct pCh' *chum "seated; dwelling" and propose a LL form *kyum (#79); this form is not attested in Tz, but presumably would have diffused within the GLL area as *kyum prior to the GTz shift, and would have been subsequently replaced in Tz. In Section 3.2 I argue for an additional etymon that was likely innovated with *ky' in the GLL area prior to affrication, and is also attested in Epigraphic Mayan, *ky'al > *ch'al "to tie; to close; to adorn" (#122).

Law et al. (2014) were not the first to consider a later timing for the shift: Justeson et al. (1985: 73, Note 7) had already considered the possibility that the *k(') > ch(') shift "occurred after the separation of the Cholan and Tzeltalan speech communities and then diffused," noting that "such diffusion of sound changes across language boundaries is attested in the case of velar palatalization before unrounded vowels followed by *q(')* or *x* in western dialects of most Quichean languages," as Campbell (1977: 116–18, 122–6) has documented. They immediately countered this possibility: "Such diffusion is unlikely in the case of the Cholan-Tzeltalan shift of **k(')* to *č(')*, however, because both groups inhibited the change under four identical and sometimes complex conditions ...," adding that

> there is no positive evidence of the sound change having postdated the diversification of proto-Cholan-Tzeltalan; loans into the two groups that differ in having *č* or *č'* in one and *k* or *k'* in the other would provide such evidence, but none of about a dozen loans involving these sounds shows such a difference. (Justeson et al. 1985: 73, Note 7)

In Section 3.2 I examine evidence of loans into GTz attested in Epigraphic Mayan precisely to test this idea, the same idea raised by Law et al. (2014).

Like Kaufman (1976) before them, Justeson et al. (1985: 60) also discussed the relevance of the **k > ch* shift with regard to relative chronologies for GQ' and GM. They observed that all the GQ' languages borrowed "to sell" and "peccary" from GTz, and therefore, that this probably happened prior to their diversification, possibly between *c.*300 BCE and 100 CE.[6] As far as GM is concerned, Justeson et al. (1985) also note, the **k > ch* shift took place before the diversification of pGM, for all Mamean languages exhibit evidence of GTz loans **chay* "fish" and **chitaam* "peccary," which then underwent the Mamean **ch > tx* and **t > ch* shifts, resulting in pGM **txay* and **txichaam*, respectively. They argue that the latter changes, which preceded the diversification of GM, occurred around or after 300 BCE. More recently, Kaufman (2017: 67) places the initial differentiation of GM starting around 500 BCE. This places another relative chronology constraint on the GTz **k(') > ch(')* shift. If Kaufman's (1976) estimates of minimal centuries of separation for GTz, GQ', and GM are correct, a Middle-to-Late Preclassic dating for the GTz **k(') > ch(')* shift would be required. But the more important conclusion is that for at least a few etyma ("to sell," "peccary," "fish"), not to mention some of the additional examples I have proposed (certainly "rope, vine," maybe "deer," "sweet," "chile"), the shift and their diffusion must have occurred early, and prior to the differentiation of both GQ' and GM, not just prior to the differentiation of GTz. Additional etyma distributed more narrowly within GQ' and GM would have diffused subsequent to the initial differentiation of these subgroups, but the shift may have been already finalized in GTz by then.

One more contribution by Justeson et al. (1985) was their elaboration on Kaufman and Norman's (1984: 89, 122) observations regarding pCh' **kab'* "earth" (item #62b), proposed to be a loan from Yucatecan **kaab'*. In addition to the evidence for pTz **chab'*, such as Tzeltal *liki-chab'* "earthquake" and Tzotzil *chob'* "milpa," already noted by Kaufman and Norman, Justeson et al. (1985: 14) also presented additional related forms in Tzotzil, as well as an example of the native reflex of pM **kab' ~ *kaab'* "earth" in Ch' in the form of Yokot'an (Chontal) *chab'-an* "earthquake," confirming pGTz **chab'* "earth."

More recently, Kaufman (2015, 2017) proposes that the GTz **k(') > ch(')* shift would have occurred sometime between 1000–200/100 BCE, during the Middle

Preclassic or the Middle-to-Late Preclassic transition. He states that "a shift of *k > ch (but not of *k' to ch') took place in common Chujean, therefore after the Greater Q'anjob'alan diversification, under the same conditions as in Greater Tzeltalan," and likely sometime between 200/100 BCE–400 CE (Kaufman 2015: 1022). And of course, all of these occurred "before the later rule shifting pM *q and *q' to /k/ and /k'/ was also diffused to Chujean" (Kaufman 2017: 66).

Regarding suggestions by previous authors that the *k(') > ch(') shift of GTz be considered a shared innovation with similar shifts observed for other subgroups, including Huastecan, Kaufman (2015: 1024–1025) has remarked the following:

> The change of pM *k to /ch/ and *k' to /ch'/ is not the same in Wastekan, Yukatekan, and Greater Tzeltalan, and should not be viewed as a common development. In Wasteko the change is exceptionless; in Yukatekan the change occurs in only a very few highly specific environments; in Greater Tzeltalan the change occurs in about 50% of the items containing pM *k and *k', according to complex rules. Other languages changing *k and *k' to /ch/ and /ch'/ include tke [sic] Q'anjob'alan Complex, Some [sic] forms of Mam, Awakateko, and some forms of Ixil: in every case the rules are different, and no doubt independently achieved.

Regarding Huastecan specifically, Kaufman and Justeson (2008: 70–2) and Kaufman (2017: 68; 2020: 116–17) have argued that the changes in Huastecan took place after it had already arrived "in the vicinity of the Basin of Mexico or the northern Gulf Coast," given two facts: loanwords from Pre-Huastecan into various languages of Northern and Central Mexico (e.g., Pajalat, Yemé, P'urhepecha, Totonakan, Proto-Oto-Pamean) point to its retention of pM *q('), pM *r, and pM * k('); and the Huastecan *k(') > ch(') shift was significantly more general ("exceptionless") than its Greater Tzeltalan counterpart.

To sum up, prior researchers defined the *k(') > ch(') shift; described a complex set of inhibiting factors; argued that the complexity of such inhibiting factors made it unlikely to have diffused, in identical fashion, between already diversified Ch' and Tz languages, and more likely to have occurred at the GTz stage; that loans from GTz present in the GQ' languages (#77, #116, #65) allow for the definition of a relative chronology of the change with respect to the unrelated and subsequent *q(') > k(') and *nh > n shifts; that some GLL etyma exhibiting *k(') must have avoided the shift either because they can be traced back to earlier *q(') (#10, #36, #119), or because they were innovated with *k(') within the GLL diffusion area after the GTz shift had already occurred (#119); that a few etyma that must have experienced the shift may have subsequently been partly (#35) or completely replaced by cognate loans from other Mayan languages (#3, #5, #8, #26, #62b); that the shift likely proceeded in two steps, *k(') > *ky(') > ch('); and finally, that a few etyma that exhibited inhibiting conditions but nonetheless experienced the shift may have been innovated and diffused early within the GLL area as palatalized *ky(') prior to the second part of the shift, *ky(') > *ch(') (#79, #120, #121, #122). Also worth highlighting, the *k(') > ch(') shift in Huastecan was exceptionless, and thus not the same process as the shift observed in GTz. I have also added a few other cases of likely loans, some of them quite early (#100), between GTz and GQ' languages that provide additional support for the relative chronologies between the *k(') > ch(') and *nh > n shifts proposed by Kaufman (1976).

In what follows, I will cite some of the evidence and arguments just reviewed, and present new cases of etyma that experienced the shift, as well as new cases of likely loanwords that support relative chronologies for sound changes and differentiation events.

2.3 Early work on phonological contrasts in Mayan writing

By the late 1970s several scholars had already marshalled strong evidence in favor of Ch'olan innovations, especially phonological and lexical, to explain major structural properties of Epigraphic Mayan (Campbell 1984). Fox and Justeson (1982), a revised version of which (Justeson and Fox 1989), has been available to me since 1996, carried out a systematic survey of the syllabograms deciphered by then and their implications—phonological and lexical. Those authors reviewed the spellings with k**V** and k'**V** syllabograms to test for evidence of contrasts between pM *k(') and *q('), which proved negative (e.g., **la-ka** for Ch' *lak "plate" from pM *laq, **b'a-ka** for Ch' b'ak from pM *b'aaq); **chV** and **ch'V** syllabograms for evidence of pM *ch(') and cases of the GTz *k(') > ch(') shift, which proved positive (e.g., **7aj-chi**, interpreted by those authors as "drunkard" based on pCh' *chi7 "sweet" from pM *ki7, but evidence of the *k > ch shift even if it represents a reflex of pM *kiih "maguey," pCh' *chih); and n**V** syllabograms for evidence of pM *nh versus *n which proved negative (e.g., **K'AN-na** for Ch' *k'än "yellow" from pM *q'an, **SNAKE-na** for Ch' *chan from pM *kaan, **SKY-na** for Ch' *chan "sky" from pM *ka7nh, **10-na** for Ch' *läjun= "ten" from pM *laajuunh= or *lajunh=) (Justeson and Fox 1989: 13–14, 19). They also identified examples of changes exclusive to Ch'olan, such as the *oo > uu > u shift attested by 445 CE (e.g., **tu-TUN** for *tun "stone" from pM *toonh) (Justeson and Fox 1989: 27).

Many more examples of the lack of orthographic distinction in phonetic spellings of reflexes of pM contrasts *k versus *q, *k' versus *q', and *nh versus *n have emerged since Justeson and Fox (1989). And many more examples of the attestation of sound changes pointing to GTz, Ch', and Yu innovations have been documented since then too (e.g., *k(') > ch(') shift of GTz, *oo > u and *ee > i shifts of Ch'; *t, *ty > ch/__{i, e, #} in Yu) (see review in Mora-Marín 2009). This would suggest that scribes were attuned to the contrasts present in their spoken languages, and were capable of representing them if they chose to do so. In light of their assessment and evidence that scribes could have systematically distinguished between Ch'olan and Yucatecan forms, but most often did not, Justeson and Fox (1989: 39) suggest that "the failure to indicate linguistically distinctive material," that is, material that would have readily distinguished between Ch'olan and Yucatecan cognates in a systematic fashion, "may have been deliberate, for it appears to have functioned to enhance interlinguistic literacy." Thus, interlinguistic literacy, perhaps with sociolinguistic accommodation as a goal, is an option to consider.

2.4 Grube (2010)

A few years prior to Law et al.'s (2014) reassessment, Grube (2010) had drawn attention to a highly interesting pattern, namely, that the use of *preposed* phonetic complements in Mayan texts was more rigidly structured throughout most of the Classic period than previously thought, applying primarily (though not entirely) to three specific phonological contexts.[7] These are cited in full next (Grube 2010: 29):

1) with logographic signs that represent a glottal-initial root (7VC or 7VCVC),
2) with logographic signs that represent a root beginning with one of the semivowels /w/ or /y/,
3) and finally, with roots that were affected by the consonant shift from proto-Mayan *k(') > proto-Ch'olan-Tzeltalan *ch(').

Here I restrict myself to commenting on the last context, the one of relevance to the *k(') > ch shift, for which Grube (2010: 38) concludes that

> The only environment where preposed phonetic complements are clearly motivated by language change is in roots that were related to the shift from proto-Mayan *k(') to proto-Ch'olan *ch('). As far as we know, this was the only consonantal shift in the Cholan languages that coincided with the period in which the script was in use.

This is not correct. If the *k(') > *ch(') shift was taking effect during the period of use of Mayan writing, then both the *q(') > *k(') and *nh > n shifts, also consonantal, would have followed, and would likely have been dealt with by scribes in some manner.

Importantly, Grube (2010: 32) argues that the use of kV preposed phonetic complements in some cases could have been intended "to stress the correct and prestigious old pronunciation," prior to the shift, of certain terms, such as the spelling of SNAKE in the context of the *Kan* emblem glyph, including what might be the earliest occurrence of the ka-SNAKE spelling on La Muerta Monument 1. In other words, rather than argue that scribes were still pronouncing the term "snake" as *kaan, Grube suggests that the act of preposing ka before SNAKE points to the shift having already occurred, and therefore, to scribes emphasizing a conservative rather than innovative pronunciation. This would imply that the script arose prior to the shift, and that evidence of earlier, pre-shift pronunciations was preserved either in older inscriptions, or oral traditions, or both, and that such conservatism may have inspired the linguistic attitudes and ideologies of some scribes.

2.5. Law et al. (2014)

Law et al. (2014: 361) assume that Classic texts were faithful in representing the nuances of a specific spoken language, and that they were sensitive to linguistic variation and changes: "Data from Maya writing, however, are exceptional in showing patent adaptation in supple response to shifts in spoken language." Given this assumption, they regard the pattern of phonetic sign usage involving chV, ch'V, kV, and k'V syllabograms to be indicative of linguistic change in progress, one spreading during the beginning of the Late Classic period. They do see two major alternatives for explaining the pattern: "A simpler explanation is that these terms register either a change in progress or are archaic retentions, maintained from an earlier linguistic stage" (Law et al. 2014: 363). They pursue the change-in-progress option. Such a change, and the complex set of inhibiting factors associated with it, would have spread, as a sound change rule, between already differentiated Ch' and Tz languages, given evidence of exclusive Ch'olan innovations by the beginning of the Classic period, such as the vowel-raising shifts (Fox and Justeson 1982; Justeson et al. 1985; Justeson and Fox 1989). Moreover, if Houston et al.'s (2000) "Classic Ch'olti'an" hypothesis is correct, proposing that Ch' had already differentiated by the beginning of the Classic period and that Classic texts represent a prestige language based on a form of Eastern Ch'olan, the sound change rule would have spread during the Late Classic period between differentiated Ch' varieties (at least between Eastern Ch'olan and Western Ch'olan) in identical fashion, in addition to spreading between Ch' and Tz languages in identical fashion, despite the complexity of the inhibiting factors. All of this, plus the outward diffusion into other Mayan languages (already differentiated Greater Mamean, Greater Q'anjob'alan, Yucatecan subgroups), prior to the *q > k, *q' > k', and *nh > n shifts in GTz and Yu, would be required to have occurred between the Late Classic period and the sixteenth century.

Law et al. (2014) focus on examples of etyma that underwent the shift that were being spelled with **kV** and **k'V** signs during the Late Classic period. They state that "The most common explanation of these unexpected forms is that they represent borrowings from Yukatek Mayan, a neighboring Mayan language that did not undergo this sound change except in a much more limited context ..." (Law et al. 2014: 363). This is a bit of an oversimplification, however, as such an explanation has only been applied to a very few cases based on linguistic evidence, and not attributed to Yucatec, specifically, but to Yu. The only such case, already noted in Section 2.2, is pCh' *kab' "earth" (Kaufman and Norman 1984: 122): it has been observed that both Ch' and Tz have preserved the native form that experienced the shift in compounds or derived lexemes, such as Yokot'an (Chontal) *chab'-an* "earthquake," Tzeltal *liki-chab'* "earthquake," and several related terms in Tzotzil, including *chob'* "cornfield" and *chab'-ah* "to work in a cornfield" (Kaufman and Norman 1984: 124; Justeson et al. 1985: 14). To my knowledge no author has proposed that all etyma subject to the shift that appear with **kV** and **k'V** signs in Epigraphic Mayan constitute cases of Yucatecanisms, borrowings from Yu into Ch'.

However construed, Law et al. dismiss such a possibility for two reasons: because a significant number of spellings with **chV** and **ch'V** signs in etyma that experienced the shift appear in the northern Maya lowlands, very likely inhabited by Yucatecan speakers; and because a large number of what they claim are presumed Yucatecan borrowings spelled with **kV** and **k'V** signs appear in the southern lowlands, from Palenque in the west to Copan in the east, characterized by a "lack of a clear, consistent geographical clustering of the /k(')/ spellings," a fact that they suggest constitutes "another line of evidence supporting the proposal that such forms are conservations of an archaic feature, rather than borrowings" (Law et al. 2014: 363–4). Law et al.

(2014: 363) refer to the northern lowlands **chV** and **ch'V** spellings of etyma exhibiting the shift as "hypercorrection" on the part of what they seem to presume were monolingual Yucatecan speakers; they may very well have been bilingual Ch'olan/Yucatecan speakers, and the **chV** and **ch'V** spellings in question may have been intended to index such an identity.[8] I agree with Law et al.'s assessment that the **kV** and **k'V** signs in the southern lowlands are evidence of archaisms, but perhaps only accidentally so: some scribes may have been motivated less by conservatism than linguistic accommodation via interlinguistic literacy (Justeson and Fox 1989: 39, 47–9). Ch'olan and Yucatecan speakers were in close interaction for centuries, and diffused vocabulary and grammatical morphology between them, a process that was likely promoted by interference in a bilingual context (Hopkins 1984, 1985). In such a context, scribes may have been motivated to use spellings that signaled a Ch'olan identity, archaic or contemporary, or perhaps a Yucatecan identity, or even both: multiple identities could be indexed within a single text.

Regarding the geographic and temporal pattern for first uses of spellings with **chV** and **ch'V** signs, Law et al. provide the following:

(2) Earliest occurrences of **chV** and **ch'V** signs according to Law et al. (2014: 361–2):
   a. **chi-K'IN** "east" in "unprovenienced early lidded tripod vessel" likely from the Peten (Fields and Reents-Budet 2005: 215, Figure 109).
   b. "**chi-hi** as part of a proper name on an Early Classic stone vessel from Santa Rita," Belize.
   c. "**ch'a-CH'AHB'** *ch'ahb'* 'penance, sacrifice' at beginning of Late Classic (Caracol Stela 3:B19, B20; 620s)."
   d. "**ch'a-CH'AM** *ch'am* 'to receive' (Piedras Negras Panel 2:H1; A.D. 667)."
   e. **cha-SKY** "in the final decades of the eighth and early years of the ninth centuries A.D."
   f. **yi-cha-ni** at Yaxchilan Lintel 58:C1 and 9:C2, "at about A.D. 750."
   g. **cho** syllabogram "generated by the early seventh century (Copan Structure 13:D8)."
   h. "**chu** ("breast variant") in the eighth century A.D. (see, for example, the Altar vase ... and Piedras Negras Stela 14, sculptor's signature)."

This list appears to provide evidence for an incremental appearance of **chV** and **ch'V** signs over time, particularly in the spelling of roots that underwent the shift of pM *k(') > *ch('). The pattern, the authors propose, indicates an order of appearance starting with **chi**, then **ch'a**, then **cho**, and so on (2014: 362), perhaps indicating a gradual application of a palatalization and affrication process, starting with the high front vowel.

Finally, Law et al. (2014: 362) admit that their model poses a problem: it would imply that Classic Mayan writing obviated the phonemic distinction between *q(') and *k('), a distinction involving four phonemes (i.e., *q vs. *k, *q' vs. *k'). The problem is actually compounded by Law et al.'s (2014) disregard for the loanword evidence, reviewed in Section 2.2, which shows that the *nh > *n shift of GTz also postdates the *k(') > *ch(') shift, which means that Law et al.'s model requires that Classic Mayan writing also ignore the *nh versus *n contrast.

3. New and old linguistic and philological evidence

3.1 Loans in Epigraphic Mayans

A wide variety of authors have written on the presence of loans in Mayan texts, from other Mayan languages and non-Mayan languages alike (Justeson et al. 1985; Taube and Bade 1991; Bricker 2000; Macri and Looper 2003; Macri 2005; Boot 2006; Kaufman 2007; Kaufman and Justeson 2007; Pallán Gayol and Meléndez Guadarrama 2010). Here I discuss only those cases of relevance to the *k(') > ch('), and then only those whose context allows for a clear determination of their meaning and possible morphological structure. Other cases of potential relevance may exist but their contexts are unclear, and so are their meanings; with more contextualization and research a Mayan etymology may yet be proven to work for them.

I begin with the spellings of pCh' *käkäw "cacao" (Kaufman and Norman 1984: 122), which show substantial variation: **ka, ka-wa, ka-ka-wa, ka²-wa**, and even **ka-ka²-wa**. The second-to-last spelling is illustrated in Figure 7.1. Borrowed from a Mixe-Zoquean language (Campbell and Kaufman 1976), *käkäw is undoubtedly the most prominent loanword from a non-Mayan language attested in Mayan texts. The earliest archaeologically described examples date to the early-to-mid-fifth century CE,

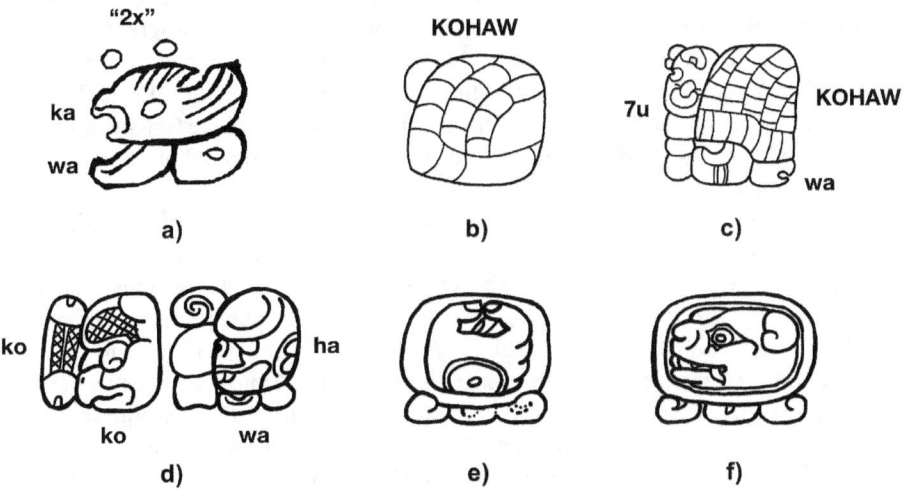

Figure 7.1 Glyphic spellings of proposed non-Mayan loanwords

Notes: a) Spelling **ka²-wa** for pCh' *kakaw > *käkäw "cacao," on lidded tripod vessel from Central Peten, dated to c.250–400 CE. Drawing by the author after Fields and Reents-Budet (2005: 215, Fig. 109). b) Logogram for **KO7HAW** on Piedras Negras Panel 2. Drawing from Macri and Looper (2003: 290, Fig. 5a). c) Logosyllabic spelling **7u-KOHAW-wa** on Middle Panel of Temple of Inscriptions at Palenque. Drawing from Macri and Looper (2003: 290, Fig. 5b). d) Syllabic spelling **ko-7o-ha-wa** on Piedras Negras Panel 2. Drawing from Pallán Gayol and Meléndez Guadarrama (2010: 22, Fig. 8). e) Day sign <MANICH'> or **chi** from Palenque House C, Substructure. Drawing from Thompson (1950: Fig. 7). f) Day sign <OK> from Copan Hieroglyphic Stairway. Drawing from Thompson (1950: Fig. 8).

attested on pottery vessels from sites like Tikal and Rio Azul, and thus predates the period during which Law et al. (2014) argue the *k(') > ch(') shift propagated. Campbell (2000: 5) and Kaufman and Justeson (2007: 199) have observed that if Mixe-Zoquean *kakawa had been borrowed prior to the *k(') > ch(') shift, it would have undergone the shift, and would have resulted in a form like chächäw*, which is not attested in any Mayan language. There exist hundreds of spellings of this term in the Epigraphic Mayan corpus, spanning much of the Early and Late Classic periods: had the *k > ch shift been in progress during this time, there is a very good chance—better than for almost any other lexeme showing the right conditions to experience the *k > ch shift represented in the ancient texts—that we would see at least a few spellings such as **cha-wa*** or **cha-cha-wa***, but none is attested.

Next is the term for a type of headdress or helmet attested eleven times across four texts between 667 and 732 CE. Macri and Looper (2003: 290) have described this term, and spelled once as **KOHAW** (Figure 7.1b), six times as **KOHAW-wa** (Figure 7.1c), once as **ko-ha-wa** (not illustrated), and three times as **ko-7o-ha-wa** (Figure 7.1d), as a possible loanword. These authors note that the term may be attested in Colonial Tzotzil as <kovov> "helmet," showing an initial <k> for /k/. Its very limited distribution within Mayan, restricted to Epigraphic Mayan and Colonial Tzotzil, the authors argue, supports its status as a loanword. They argue for a Nawan sourceword *kwa:-w "head." Kaufman (2007), for his part, proposes a Proto-Zoquean source, *ko7.jap "headgear." Either way, the appearance of this term during the seventh century CE, a time when the *k(') > *ch(') shift would have been in progress according to Law et al. (2014), would have made this term vulnerable to the shift. Since Law et al.'s (2014) model requires that the shift spread between Ch' and Tz, and indeed between already differentiated Ch' varieties, during or after the Late Classic, it is noteworthy that the only possible attestation of this term in a Colonial or contemporary GTz language does not reflect the shift either.

Another case is the Mayan day name corresponding to "deer." Although there are no fully or partly phonetic spellings to confirm a glyphic reading **MANICH'** for the seventh day name, pan-Mesoamerican "deer," it is attested alphabetically as <manik>, that is, #manik', in Colonial Yucatec, and <manich>, that is, #manich', in Colonial Ch'ol baptismal records. Justeson et al. (1985: 15, 21–22) and Kaufman and Justeson (2007: 200) have shown that the term was a loanword from Proto-Zapoteco *mma=ni7 "animal, large quadruped" (itself involving a borrowing from Proto-Zoquean *mu7a "deer") into (Greater) Lowland Mayan, and that it was borrowed into GTz prior to the *k' > ch' shift. I suspect that, prior to the innovation of the use of T671 **chi** to spell this day name, Mayan scribes may have used a DEER logogram, perhaps like the one attested in a Late Preclassic mural fragment at San Bartolo in a spelling 7-DEER (Hurst 2009: 301, Fig. 33e). T671 **chi** would not have worked as a spelling of **MANICH'**. Instead, in Section 3.2 I discuss the use of T671 **chi** and argue that it functioned phonetically to spell pCh' *chihj > *chij.

The term for the Lowland Mayan (Ch'ol, Yucatec) tenth day name, <oc> "dog," that is, #7ok, is very likely a loanword also. Justeson et al. (1985: 23–4) suggested it comes from Proto-Mixean *7uka, reconstructed as "dog," and pointed out that it did not undergo the *k > ch shift, indicating that it was borrowed after the shift had taken effect. More recently, Hopkins (2014: 10) has argued, very persuasively, that the Lowland Mayan loan #7ok reflects the meaning "agouti," not "dog." He follows Wichmann's (1995: 223, 254) reconstruction of Proto-Mixe-Zoquean *7uku as "agouti (*Dasyprocta* spp.)," with Proto-Zoquean preserving the meaning "agouti" and Proto-Mixean shifting the meaning to "dog," and argues that Lowland Mayan borrowed the Zoquean form and meaning.

Kaufman and Norman (1984: 124) and Justeson et al. (1985: 14) proposed that pCh' *kab' "earth," spelled with T529 **KAB'**, T25:501 **ka-b'a**, and T529:501 **KAB'-b'a** in Classic texts, constitutes a loan from another Mayan language, most likely Yucatecan, given the evidence for restricted retentions (see discussion in Section 2.5) in both Ch' and Tz of a form *chab', which confirm that the shift took place for this etymon. Thus, it cannot be doubted that GTz underwent the *k > ch shift for this term. The presence of *kab' as a basic lexeme meaning "earth," in addition to the GLL term *lu7m, requires an alternative explanation: either a loanword from another Mayan language, a neighboring Yucatecan language being the most likely source, or speakers of Ch' retained Pre-GTz *kab' alongside the shifted form *chab', in some registers at least, before it began to displace the shifted form *chab', a process that could have been facilitated by scribal practices. There is one instance, at least, of a spelling **cha-b'a**, cited by Law et al. (2014: 362, Table 1), occurring on Halakal Lintel 1:H7, almost certainly in Yucatecan territory during the Classic period (Justeson and Fox 1989; Lacadena and Wichmann 2002). Such usage could constitute evidence of a loan in the written language of an elite Yucatecan group, or an act of identity by a bilingual Ch'olan/Yucatecan scribe.

I have not discussed the case of **k'o-jo** for pCh' *k'oj "mask" in this section because it is a point of contention. Kaufman and Norman (1984: 85, 124, #263), as already noted in Section 2.2, argued that pCh' *k'oj "mask" (#35) was diffused from the Mayan highlands to the lowlands, along with *kok "turtle" (#5), *kuhkay "firefly" (#8), and a few other etyma that should have experienced the shift if they were native GTz terms. They also proposed that Ch'olti' attests to both the loan from a highland Mayan language, /k'oj/, and the native form /ch'oj/. Law et al. (2014: 359, 363) apparently missed this, for they do not cite Kaufman and Norman's explanation, but posit instead that Ch'olti' /ch'oj/ constitutes evidence that the shift occurred late. I take up this question again in the final section of the chapter.

In summary, at least two loanwords from non-Mayan languages are attested in Classic texts prior or to, or during the time of Law et al.'s (2014) chronology for the *k(') > *ch(') shift: "cacao" and "headgear." These terms should have experienced the shift, if those authors were correct, but they did not.

3.2 Early <chV> and <ch'V> spellings and their sources

Law et al. (2014: 361) begin their chronological review as follows:

> The earliest ch(')V syllabic sign appears to be the syllable **chi**, attested in an early spelling of **chi-K'IN** ("east"—importantly, this is an erosion of *ochi-k'in* "enter sun," which displays the *k* to *ch* sound change *ochi* [from pM **okik*] on an unprovenanced early lidded tripod vessel …

This is example (2a) in the list of earliest occurrences discussed by Law et al. (2014) provided in Section 2.5. The glyphic collocation in question is shown in Figure 7.2, as ʔhi-chi-K'IN for *chik'in* "west." Although Law et al. do not say so, the vessel has been dated stylistically to *c*.250–400 CE by Fields and Reents-Budet (2005: 215, Figure 109). This same vessel also includes the spelling ka²-wa for pCh' *käkäw "cacao" illustrated in Figure 7.1 above, see Section 3.1. Both spellings, ʔ-chi-K'IN and ka²-wa, support the proposition that the shift had already transpired by 250–400 CE. As Law et al. explain, this spelling of "west" represents an already idiomatic, phonetically reduced, and lexicalized version of a phrase they analyze as *7och-i-Ø k'iin* (enter-COMPLETIVE-3SA sun) "the sun entered" > *[7o]chik'iin* > *chik'in* "west," and one showing that item #89, GTz *7ooch from pM *7ook "to enter," that had already experienced the *k > ch shift, by the first half of the Early Classic period.[9] The not-insignificant phonetic reduction of clausal *7och-i-Ø k'iin* to monomorphemic *chik'in*, must have itself taken time to develop; its idiomaticity and lexicalization suggests that speakers and writers were very likely not attending to its phonological form in the written register.

There are certain problems with some of the data Law et al. (2014) present as the earliest uses of **chV** and **ch'V** signs, as cited in (2a–h). For example, they mention the use of T643/HT6 (2h), a sign that resembles a pair of breasts and has been suggested to read **chu**, and note its appearance in the eighth century CE, apparently among their epigraphic evidence for the late appearance of **chV** and **ch'V** spellings. If correctly deciphered, the sign would have to be acrophonically derived from

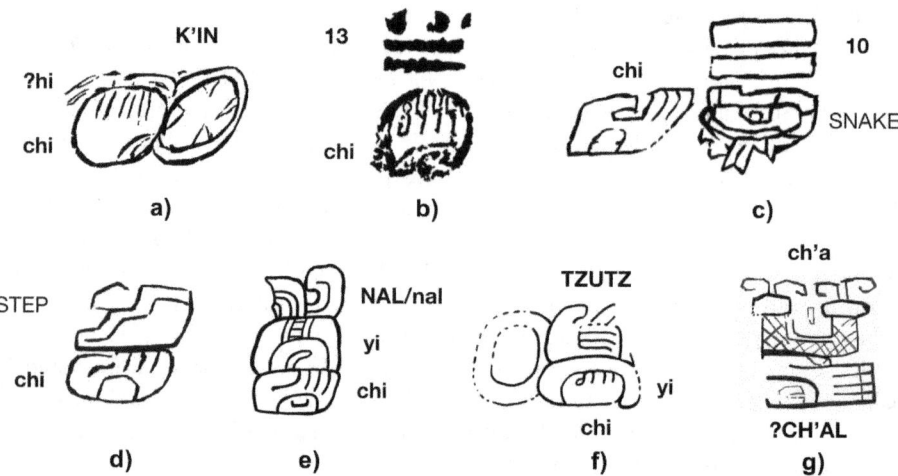

Figure 7.2 Early examples of signs with **chV** and **ch'V** values

Notes: a) Spelling **K'IN-hi-chi** on lidded tripod vessel dated stylistically to *c*.250–400 CE. Drawing by the author based on photograph in Fields and Reents-Budet (2005: 215, Figure 109). b) 13-Deer expression using T671/MR7 **chi** sign. Drawing by Špoták (2017: 78, Fig. 11). c) 10-**chi**-SNAKE expression on Kaminaljuyu Stela 10. Drawing by the author. d) STEP-**chi** expression on Dumbarton Oaks quartzite pectoral. Drawing by the author. e) Detail from Tikal Stela 7:A7. Drawing from Schele (1990: 121).
f) **yi-chi-nal** expression from Tikal Stela 31:C20. Drawing from Schele (1990: 99). g) **ch'a-?CH'AL** expression on K1955. Drawing by the author after photo in Wagner (2001).

pCh' *chu7 "(women's) breast," from pM *chu(u)7, and is thus not relevant to the *k > ch shift at all. They also cite spellings that remain unclear, in their words "opaque," as to their precise lexical, and therefore, historical identification, such as their example (2b), a spelling **chi-hi**. Their example (2e), a spelling **cha**-SKY for pCh' *chan from pM *ka7nh "sky" (item #63), is attested on an inscribed bone from Dzibilchaltun in the northern lowlands, almost certainly in Yucatecan territory, and is more likely an example of Yucatecan or bilingual Ch'olan/Yucatecan scribes associating themselves with the prestige of Ch'olan speech, rather than a case of Ch'olan scribes reflecting a change that is taking place in their speech. Their example (2f), **yi-cha-ni** for *y-ichan* "his mother's brother" (item #82, from pM *7ikaan) on Yaxchilan Lintel 58, dated to 780 CE, is actually the latest-dated of the four inscriptions with this expression, ranging between 734 and 780 CE. Regardless of their late date, it is difficult to assess its significance since there are no prior examples of the "mother's brother" expression, reflecting the shift or not. The same is true of (2d): while it is true that the earliest example of the logosyllabic spelling **ch'a-CH'AM**, for pCh' *ch'äm "to take, grab" (item #101, from pM *k'am), dates to 662 CE, there are no prior examples of this expression with **k'a**, pointing to **K'AM**. In fact, there are fewer than a handful spellings of **k'a-ma**, their context is not very clear and it is not obvious that they represent the same root, not to mention that they postdate the **ch'a-CH'AM** spelling, starting *c*.692 CE. The case of (2c) is again similar: there are no prior or later examples of this logogram involving a **k'a** sign to suggest that it was ever read **K'AB'*** for WM+LL *k'ajb' "to fast, to abstain" (item #104). Lastly, example (2g), the T590/HJ1 **cho** syllabogram, first attested by 652 CE, depicts a jaw with molar teeth, and likely developed acrophonically from pCh' *choh "cheek" (item #70), itself from pM *kooh "molar tooth" or "molar tooth; cheek." This sign actually appears in an Early Classic text, a sixth-century lidded vase, K5509, described by Coe (1973: 84–6), in a spelling **cho-ja**, probably verbal, that remains undeciphered, and thus its status as spelling a reflex of pM *ch('), *k('), or *ty(') cannot yet be tested. However, if one assumes its acrophonic origin is based on pCh' *choh from pM *kooh, it would provide evidence for the *k > ch shift before the vowel *o prior to the Late Classic. Geographically speaking, the data points adduced by Law et al. are too few and scattered to suggest a pattern of spread. At best, what they show is a trend among scribes from different regions to begin to deviate from traditional spellings, mostly logographic spellings.

Table 7.2 presents more examples of early occurrences of **chV** and **ch'V** signs on reliably dated inscriptions that can be associated with etyma that experienced the *k(') > ch(') shift; most examples were collected using the Maya Hieroglyphic Database by Looper and Macri (2011–present. They allow for more detailed assessment of some patterns than the examples by Law et al. (2014). For instance, the **chu** examples at Copan are likely employed in spelling pCh' *chum from (G)LL *kyum "seated" (item #79), which was never spelled with **ku**, and in fact, it was almost invariably spelled logographically, as SEATED. Scribes may very well have read it as **CHUM** from its earliest examples (e.g., Leyden Plate, *c*.320 CE), but the only syllabogram used in its spelling was postposed **mu**, typically infixed graphically within the logogram (i.e., CHUM/KUM[mu]), to spell the final consonant of the root, instead of a preposed syllabogram **chu** or **ku** that would have easily disambiguated the

Table 7.2 Earliest-dated occurrences of chV and ch'V signs in Maya Hieroglyphic Database representing examples of *k(') > ch(') shift

Sign	Site	Text	Date	CE	Spelling	Proto-Ch'olan	Gloss	Proto-Mayan
cha	El Zapote	Stela 1	8.19.10.0.0	426	CHA7 7AJAW	*cha7	metate	*kaa7
cha	Tikal	Stela 31	9.0.10.0.0	445	chi-CHA7	*chih / *cha7	agave / metate	*kiih / *kaa7
chi	Tikal	Stela 31	9.0.10.0.0	445	yi-chi-nal	—	in his presence	GLL *7iky-an-al
chi	Tikal	Stela 9	9.2.0.0.0	475	7i-TZUTZ-yi[chi]	*-ich	already	*-ik
che	Copan	Papagayo Step	9.3.0.0.0	495	che-7e-na	*che7	quotative particle	*kih
che	Copan	Stela 34	9.3.0.0.0	495	che-7e-na	*che7	quotative particle	*kih
chi	Collection	Panel	9.3.3.16.04	498	7OCH-chi-K'AK'	*7och	enter	*7ook
che	Arroyo de Piedra	Stela 01	9.9.0.0.0	613	che-7e	*che7	thus	pCM *hek ~ *hik
che	Chactun	Stela 01	9.16.0.0.0	751	che-he-na	*che7	quotative particle	*kih
ch'a	Seibal	Tablet 09	9.16.0.0.0	751	che-he-na	*che7	quotative particle	*kih
chu	Copan	CPN 40/Stela 02	9.11.0.0.0	652	chu-ni-ya (chu-*mu-*wa-ni-ya)	*chum	seated	GLL *kyum
chu	Copan	CPN 61/Stela 12	9.11.0.0.0	652	chu-wa-ni-ya (chu-*mu-wa-ni-ya)	*chum	seated	GLL *kyum

linguistic affiliation as either Ch' or Yu. What we see at Copan by 652 CE are probably incomplete spellings aimed not at representing a change-in-progress, but at asserting, after centuries of ambiguity, a specific linguistic identity.

It is important to highlight that the spellings of the pCh' *che7 "thus" (item #124), first attested by 613 CE, and *che7 "quotative particle" (item #53), appearing by 495 CE, are *only* spelled with **che**; perhaps these grammatical morphemes, which could probably only be spelled phonetically, were not tied to sociolinguistic attitudes and ideologies—there are no cases of **ke-he/7e-na** or **ke-7e**.

The glyphic expression **yi-chi-nal** (Figure 7.2), listed in Table 7.2, attests to a positional root that was innovated within the GLL area as *7iky* "facing someone (/something?)" (Kaufman with Justeson 2003: 304). It is not attested in any Colonial or contemporary Ch'olan language, but it is attested in Yucatecan (Yucatec, Itzaj), as in Yucatec *t-uy-iknal* "in his/her presence" (PREPOSITION-3SINGULAR.ERGATIVE-presence) (Bricker et al. 1998: 11), and Tzeltalan, as in Tzotzil *ta k-ichon* "in front of me" (PREPOSITION-1SINGULAR.ERGATIVE -presence/front) (Laughlin 2010: 113). The earliest attestation is found on Tikal Stela 31, dedicated on 445 CE, spelled **yi-chi-nal**, for *y-ich(V)n-al* "in his/her presence" (3SINGULAR.ERGATIVE-presence-ABSTRACTIVIZER), a relational noun. It is never spelled with **ki**.

Table 7.2 also includes the spelling **7i-TZUTZ-yi[chi]** (Figure 7.2f), for *7i tzutz-uy-Ø+ich* "and.then it was finished already" (and.then finish-INCHOATIVE/VERSIVE-3SINGULAR.ABSOLUTIVE + already), on Tikal Stela 9, dated 495 CE. The **yi-chi** sequence spells two morphemes: a -V₁y "inchoative/versive/ingressive" suffix (Mora-Marín 2007), and a reflex of pM *+ik "already" (Kaufman 2015: 208) corresponding to item #29 in Appendix C, and its GTz reflex *+ich (Kaufman and Justeson 2007: 199). This suffix is attested in dozens of Classic texts, most of them portable ones, spelled either **ji-chi** or **yi-chi** depending on the preceding suffix (whether it is -*aj*, with final *j*, or -*Vy*, with final *y*), with Tikal Stela 9 being the only case I know of on a stela. There are earlier texts that bear relevant data, though they lack archaeological context and calendrical data. One such case is the Dumbarton Oaks pectoral, dated stylistically to *c.*300–1 BCE (Coe 1966; Mora-Marín 2001) or 100 BCE–100 CE (Fields and Tokovinine 2012). On it is found a spelling of a dedicatory verb, **STEP-chi** (Figure 7.2d), as proposed in Mora-Marín (2001: 256, n. 180), that closely parallels instances on later texts (e.g., **STEP[yi]-chi, GOD.N-yi-chi, K'AL-la-ja-ji-chi, ya-ja-ji-chi**). In this way, from the Late Preclassic through the Late Classic, the consonant of this enclitic was only ever represented with **chi**, reflecting the shift.

Consequently, the sociolinguistic neutrality apparent in the spellings of *che7 "thus" and *che7 "quotative particle" would also seem to apply to the relational noun *y-ichVn-al* "in his/her/its presence," the **ji/yi-chi** spellings of the enclitic +*ich* "already," and the **chi-K'IN** spelling for *chik'in* "west": whether due to their nature as grammatical constructions (*che7₁, che7₂, y-ich(V)n-al, +ich*) or as phonetically eroded lexicalized idioms (*chik'in*), scribes did not vary their spelling, representing them phonetically and doing so reflecting only the forms exhibiting the shift.

More tentative is the case of "metate," item #67, also on Table 7.2. Stuart (2014) presented preliminary arguments in favor of a logographic value of sign ZE5 (Macri and Looper 2003) as **CHA7** or **KA7**, representing a reflex of pM *ka7 "metate," pCh' *cha7. Shortly afterward, Stuart (2018) presented evidence for the use of ZE5 as a word-final substitution for the T671 syllabogram **chi** in the **K'INICH-chi** expression, as **K'INICH-ZE5**, suggesting that ZE5 does in fact have an initial consonant value /ch/. Stuart narrowed down the logographic value of ZE5 as **CHA7**. He further suggested that T671 **chi** functioned to spell pCh' *chih "maguey" from pM *kiih (item #51), and that together, **chi-CHA7** yields *chih cha7* "maguey metate." If proven correct, the earliest example of the ZE5 logogram on El Zapote Stela 1, dated to 426 CE, would support the *k > ch shift both for "metate" and "maguey."

In addition to the Peten-style lidded tripod vessel with the **?-chi-K'IN** and **ka²-wa** spellings from *c*.250–400 CE, there exist spellings involving **chV** and **ch'V** signs that predate the examples discussed so far. Law et al. (2014: 362) dismiss one of the earliest uses of T671/MR7 **chi**, arguing that it may have functioned logographically instead[10]:

> While this sign itself is not iconographically transparent, early use of this sign within a cartouche for the day sign "manik" or "deer" in the pan-Mesoamerican calendar suggests that this sign takes its value from the word *chij* "deer" (from proto-Mayan *keeh*). Since the earliest uses of this sign are logographic, representing a day in the calendar round, however, it is entirely possible that it indicated "deer" prior to the sound change (**kiih* or **keeh*) but was only recruited as a syllabic sign after the sound change had affected that word.

By "the earliest uses of this sign are logographic, representing a day in the calendar round," the authors seem to be referring, though not explicitly, to the early Uaxactun Structure B-XIII murals (Smith 1950), discussed in connection to the *k(') > ch(') shift by Kaufman and Justeson (2007: 199). On the murals, recently studied by Špoták (2017: 81–2), who dates them to either 378 or 402 CE, T671/MR7 **chi** is used in the spelling of the seventh day name in the ritual calendar, "deer," in a 13-Deer day count (Figure 7.2b).[11] Law et al. (2014) dismiss its significance by arguing that it may have been used logographically, via some indirect and unexplained association left unresolved. Nevertheless, there is evidence that the use of the **chi** syllabogram may have in fact been phonetic. At the site of San Bartolo, Beltrán (2008: 43) briefly reports on the discovery of a text fragment topped with the expression "seven deer"; a photograph of the fragment illustrated by Hurst (2009: 301, Fig. 33e) shows a DEER.HEAD sign used as a day sign logogram topped by a bar-and-dot numeral "7." This 7-DEER collocation from San Bartolo, presumably of Late Preclassic date (*c*.100 BCE?), supports the likelihood that the spellings from Uaxactun are indeed phonetic—instances of the syllabogram **chi** used to spell pCh' *chihj > *chij "deer." In other words, since Late Preclassic period scribes had access to a thoroughly iconic logogram for that day name, the early use of T671/MR7 **chi** at Uaxactun makes more sense as a purely phonetic sign usage.

There are instances of T671/MR7 **chi** in Late Preclassic texts that suggest a phonetic function and also correspond to cases of the *k > ch shift (Mora-Marín 2001, 2008). Perhaps the earliest one is present on Kaminaljuyu Stela 10, previously dated stratigraphically to *c*.400–200 BCE (Shook and Popenoe de Hatch 1999), but more recently to *c*.100 BCE (Inomata and Henderson 2016). In it is found a spelling of **10-chi-**SNAKE (Figure 7.2) that likely spells '10 Chicchan' (Mora-Marín 2005: 71).

This term involves the etymon "deer" as the first term of a compound for "boa constrictor": Ch'orti' *chijchan* and Colonial Yucatec <chicchan> ~ <chijchan> "boa constrictor," literally "deer=snake." The term for "deer" is reconstructed as pM *kehj and underwent the *k > ch shift in the GTz languages, as well as a sporadic vocalic change of *eh > ih > i, unrelated to the *ee, *e7 > ii > i shift characteristic of Ch'olan languages. Prior to this sporadic vocalic change, but after the *k > ch shift, it was borrowed as *chej* into Chujean and Q'Cx. Mocho' alone retains the reflex of pM *kehj as *keej*. The pGTz term *chihj=chaan* "boa constrictor" is attested in Chuj as *chej=chan* (Hopkins 2012: 51): it must have been borrowed from a Pre-GTz form *chehj=chaan*. One may wonder whether the GQ' languages borrowed *chej from GM instead: Ixil, Awakatek, and most varieties of Mam in fact show *cheej* or *chej*, with two varieties of Mam showing *kyeej/kyej*. However, no GM language shows *chan* or *chaan* for "snake"; thus, a loan like Chuj *chej=chan* is much more likely to have come from GTz. Consequently, the Kaminaljuyu Stela 10 spelling likely postdates not only the *k > ch shift, but also the sporadic vocalic change of Pre-GTz *chehj > pGTz *chihj > pCh' *chij, and the Chuj loan must predate such spelling, as it preserves the vowel *e*.

The example in Figure 7.2g is part of a "Protoclassic" text inscribed on a stone sculpture of Goddess O, K1955, described by Wagner (2001) and also by Fields and Reents-Budet (2005); the latter authors describe the sculpture as dating to *c.*100–350 CE. This text bears the spelling T93/2G2:T713/MR2, the first sign being a syllabogram **ch'a**, the second the logogram **K'AL** "to bind." Interestingly, Kaufman with Justeson (2003: 1000) document the reflexes of pM *k'al, generally with meanings related to "amarrar (to tie (up), to bind)," in Yu, GK', and GM; this distribution would make it a LpM (aka Southern Mayan) term. However, they do not provide attestations in any of the GTz languages. I believe that Yokot'an (Chontal) *ch'äl* "enredar (to tangle (up))" (Keller and Luciano 1997: 98, 100), Ch'ol *ch'äl* "adornar" (Aulie and de Aulie 2009: 31), Tzeltal *ch'al* "adornar" (Slocum et al. 1999: 36), and Tzotzil *ch'al* "amarrar (to tie (up), to bind)" (Laughlin 2007: 83) are the relevant cognates. These cognates point to pGTz *ch'al "to tie (up), to bind; to adorn," which could explain the Early Classic spelling **ch'a-FLAT.HAND** in question: the spelling could point to a reading **ch'a-CH'AL** for *ch'al* "to bind; to adorn." Pictorial imagery in Mayan art associated with dedicated objects often appear to refer to the binding, but occasionally the binding appears to be a type of adornment, as with the case of the imagery on the Copan peccary skull, a detail of which is seen in Figure 7.3. This presumed GTz term, *ch'al "to bind; to adorn," would then join Ch' *chol "to clear fields; milpa" as exceptions to the first inhibiting environment proposed by Kaufman and Norman (1984: 84), in word-initial position before a vowel other than /i/ followed by an apical consonant. It points to a GLL etymon *ky'al that likely diffused far and wide, beyond the GLL area, preserved as *k'al outside of GTz. It is worth noting that after the **ch'a-CH'AL** spelling, the next example with a phonetic complement is found in the Po Panel, dated to 521 CE, an Early Classic spelling **k'a-ja-K'AL** for *k'a[h]l-aj-Ø-Ø* (close[(MEDIO)PASSIVE]-INTRANSITIVIZER-COMPLETIVE-3SINGULAR.ABSOLUTIVE) "it was/got closed/wrapped." Scribes were thus making a choice when favoring **k'a**, and this choice would likely be based on sociolinguistic accommodation, to promote interlingual literacy of logographic or logosyllabic spellings.

Figure 7.3 Detail of incised peccary skull from Copan Tomb 1
Note: Photo and line drawings by the author.

Finally, Table 7.3 presents examples of **chV/ch'V** signs spelling etyma that can be traced back to pM *ch, *ch', *ty, *ty', or whose history cannot be confirmed, as they are attested only in Ch', lacking outside cognates. One such case is the root *chok "to throw down," the root represented in the so-called "to scatter" verbal expression. Its preposed phonetic complement, T590/HJ1 **cho**, is first *confirmed* on a reliably dated inscription at 652 CE. Law et al. (2014) highlight this sign because it is acrophonically derived from pCh' *choh "cheek," traced back to pM *kooh (item #70); in pM it may have meant "molar tooth" or possibly "molar tooth; cheek." Although its earliest, reliably dated example is Late Classic, it also appears in an unprovenienced Early Classic text, a sixth-century lidded vase described by Coe (1973: 84–6), in a spelling **cho-ja** that remains undeciphered (perhaps an abbreviated spelling of **cho-*ka-ja** for *cho[h]k-aj-Ø-Ø* "it was thrown down" (throw.down[PASSIVE]-PASSIVIZER-COMPLETIVE-3SINGULAR.ABSOLUTIVE). Even if this means that its use as spelling a reflex of pM *ch('), *k('), or *ty(') in such context cannot yet be tested, it does support the *k > ch shift in pCh' *chok having already occurred no later than the Early Classic, by *c.*600 CE.

To summarize, there is evidence from Late Preclassic and Early Classic texts supporting an early date for the *k > ch shift (Justeson et al. 1985; Kaufman and Justeson 2007, 2009). Some of these examples include grammatical morphemes and idiomatic/lexicalized expressions, which were only spelled in Mayan texts in a manner reflecting the shift. I propose that scribes lacked strong sociolinguistic attitudes associated with

Table 7.3 Earliest-dated occurrences of **chV** and **ch'V** signs in Maya Hieroglyphic Database not relevant to *k(') > ch(') shift (from pM *ch, *ch', *ty, *ty')

Sign	Site	Text	Date	CE	Spelling	Proto-Ch'olan	Gloss	Proto-Mayan	*k > ch shift?
ch'a	Tikal	Ballcourt marker-Marcador	8.19.0.0.0	416	ch'a-CH'AMAK	Yucatecan *ch'umak > Yucatec ch'omak ~ ch'amak	fox	—	Not known
chi	Collection	Jade Museum plaque	8.19.10.14.0	426	TUN-chi	Yuc. tùunich	stone	—	Not known
ch'o	Uaxactun	Structure B-13 Mural	9.2.0.0.0?	475?	ch'o-ko	*ch'ok	unripe, young child	—	Not known
ch'o	Pacbitun	Stela 06	9.2.10.0.0	485	ch'o-ko	*ch'ok	unripe, young child	—	Not known
ch'a	Quirigua	Monument 26	9.3.0.0.0	495	ch'a-ho-ma	?ch'aj-om	dripper	*ty'aj- 'dripping, splattered'	Irrelevant
chu	Yaxchilan	Lintel 18	9.4.12.0.0?	526?	[ku]chu-TE7	*kuch	to carry	WM+LL *kuch	Irrelevant
chi	Nim Li Punit	NMPJP Monument 13	9.6.14.10.0	568	K'IN-ni-chi	Yuc. <kinich>	Sun God	—	Not known
chu	Dzibanche		9.7.0.0.0	573	chu-?-ja, chu-?ka-?	*chuq	to capture	*chuq	Irrelevant
che	Caracol	Stela 06	9.8.10.0.0	603	che-ka-ja	*chek	visible	WM+LL *chik, WM *chek.el	Irrelevant
chu	Coba	Stela 11	9.10.0.0.0	633	chu-ja	*chuk	to capture	*chuq	Irrelevant
cho	Copan	CPN 62/Stela 13	9.11.0.0.0	652	7u-cho-ko-?wa	*chok	to throw down	—	Not known
chu	Calakmul	Stela 09	9.12.0.0.0	672	chu-ka-ja	*chuk	capture	*chuq	Irrelevant

grammatical markers, unlike the case of lexical roots/stems, such as GLL *ky'al > pGTz *ch'al.

4. Conclusions and implications

The philological evidence, both new and old, reviewed and presented in this chapter allows for the following conclusions:

(1) Positive evidence points to the spellings of several examples of the *k(') > *ch(') shift by the Late Preclassic and beginning of Early Classic periods, in spite of the fact that logographic spellings were the norm for most lexical items that experienced the shift.
(2) Crucially, loanwords with /k/ into Epigraphic Mayan attested during the Early Classic and Late Classic periods did not experience the *k(') > *ch(') shift, which can only be the case if the shift had already occurred prior to their earliest attestations (e.g., 250–400 CE for pCh' *käkäw "cacao" from Mixe-Zoquean *kakawa).
(3) Ambiguities and oscillations in spelling patterns were likely responses to sociolinguistic attitudes and ideologies by scribes, including accommodation through interlingual literacy, appeals to conservatism through archaic spellings, and instantiations of distinct phonological markers as acts of identity perhaps by Ch'olan/Yucatecan bilinguals.
(4) A model based on sociolinguistic attitudes and ideologies is better suited to explaining the fact that spelling ambiguities are evident in lexical roots and stems, some of which would have been highly culturally and politically salient (e.g., pCh' *chum "seated"), whereas grammatical particles and constructions (e.g., inflectional and derivational affixes, enclitics, relational nouns) and phonetically reduced and lexicalized expressions (*chik'in* "west") that experienced the shift, and which may not have been as salient, were consistently spelled phonetically in such a way as to display the shift from their earliest attestations.
(5) A few of the signs and spellings adduced by Law et al. (2014) are irrelevant to the shift (instead reflecting pM *ch(') or *ty(')); those that are relevant, most of which date to the Late Classic period, lack a pattern of geographic spread, and in several cases are restricted to sites in the northern lowlands, where Yucatecan-speaking scribes were likely showing off their knowledge of Ch'olan pronunciations of words, or perhaps indexing their Ch'olan/Yucatecan bilingual identities by code-switching. Several of these items became incorporated, as loans, into the modern Yucatecan languages (e.g., *cháak* "rain; thunder").

In light of the data and conclusions, Kaufman and Norman's (1984: 85, 125, entry #263) proposal that pCh' *k'oj "mask" is a loan from a highland Mayan language (one that did not undergo the *k' > ch' shift), and that it must have coexisted with a native pCh' *ch'oj form, can be given additional support, much like the case of pCh' *kab' "earth," borrowed from Yucatecan, but not entirely replacing GTz *chab'. In fact, pTz *k'oj "mask" can also be argued to be a loan, which means that a hypothetical GTz *ch'ooj can be proposed, one that was ultimately replaced almost completely, except in Ch'olti', which exhibits both the reflex and the loan (i.e., <εo> for /k'oj/ and <choh> for /ch'oj/). This case also highlights the difficulty of identifying loans in Mayan writing that originate in other Mayan languages, for the spelling **k'o-jo** for pCh' *k'oj "mask" has not been treated in recent discussions of loans in Mayan writing (Macri and Looper 2003; Macri 2005; Boot 2006; Pallán Gayol and Meléndez Guadarrama 2010) despite Kaufman and Norman's (1984) proposal.

Finally, I return to Law et al.'s (2014: 362) claim that the "Data from Maya writing, however, are exceptional in showing patent adaptation in supple response to shifts in spoken language." I do not dispute that Mayan scribes were capable of representing the important phonemic contrasts of their linguistic varieties, or to adapt the script to real-time changes. In fact, as noted by Campbell (1990: 100–1) with regard to Colonial K'ichee' scribes, it is likely that ancient Mayan scribes were capable of isolating and representing non-contrastive, allophonic details of their speech. Nevertheless, Law et al.'s hypothesis for a very late spread of the *k(') > ch(') shift calls for an unnecessarily complex scenario. It requires that we assume that scribes were in fact interested in reflecting their spoken language accurately, at all times and places, throughout the two-millennium history of the script, instead of behaving like people with sociolinguistic attitudes and ideologies, concerned with prestige and stigma, political and social alliances, which often lead them to use language and writing in prescriptive and contradictory ways that may themselves shift radically over time as social valuations of linguistic practices themselves change. It also requires that we assume that the scribes ignored three phonemic contrasts that were retained in the Greater Tzeltalan languages for some time after the *k(') > ch(') shift had taken effect, namely, */k/ versus */q/, */k'/ versus */q'/, and */nh/ versus */n/. From the perspective of historical linguistics, the late *k(') > ch(') shift model also places a great deal of strain on our credulity: timing the *k(') > ch(') shift almost a millennium later than previously proposed (Kaufman 1976; Justeson et al. 1985; Kaufman and Justeson 2007) requires that it have spread to many already differentiated speech communities (Ch'olan languages, Tzeltalan languages) *in identical fashion* in spite of the complexity of the inhibiting factors, between the time when the shift was supposedly completed in the spoken language of Mayan scribes sometime in the middle-to-late Late Classic period, and outward, in the form of isolated loanwords at least, into a possibly still unified Yucatecan subgroup, and the already-by-this-time differentiated Greater Q'anjob'alan (Chujean, Q'anjob'alan Complex, Kotoke Complex) and Greater Mamean (Mamean Proper, Ixilan) languages.

The evidence presented in this chapter, both philological and comparative, along the same vein as was already explored by Lyle Campbell, and including some of the very same data and arguments he has advanced in the past (Campbell 2000: 5), suggests that the shift had already occurred prior to the early attestations of loanwords such as *käkäw "cacao," starting *c*.200–450 CE, and probably by the time of the earliest attestations of the shift itself, as early as 100 BCE. Such constraints allow for the possibility that the shift could have in fact spread areally within a largely undifferentiated Greater Tzeltalan speech community by the Late Preclassic period, and then outward, in the form of loanwords or at best limited sound change rules, or both, onto largely undifferentiated Greater Q'anjob'alan, Greater Mamean, and Yucatecan speech communities as well starting in the Late Preclassic period and continuing into the Early Classic periods. It would also allow for enough time for the necessarily subsequent shifts and mergers (i.e., *q(') > k(') and *nh > n) to take place before phoneticism mainly in the form of phonetic complementation would become increasingly common during the Early Classic period.

Indeed, the data support Grube's (2010: 32) suggestion that the kV and k'V complements may have actually served to promote a more prestigious, archaic pronunciation—one that, in my opinion, may have been preserved by this time only in written texts, and perhaps ritual spoken registers. Such archaisms suggest a significant amount of institutionalization of scribal practices, one that promoted the retention of conservative spellings, one scribe after another, one generation after another, while innovations in the earliest texts from the Late Preclassic, and occasional departures from archaic spellings during the Early Classic and Late Classic, could be suggestive of occasional disruptions or changes in institutional practices (e.g., shrinking or expanding of scribal networks; political events leading to reorganization of scribal institutions), akin to the patterns of spelling variation described by Bricker (2015) in Colonial Maya testaments. Alternatively, instead of archaisms, many scribes may have been guided by a principle of interlingual literacy (Justeson and Fox 1989), implying a strategy of sociolinguistic accommodation between Ch'olan and Yucatecan scribes, many of whom were likely bilingual (Hopkins 1984, 1985). Among such bilinguals, in fact, code-switching in speech and writing may have been common.

Mayan scribes were not linguists, dedicated to documenting their speech varieties as faithfully as possible, apathetic to worldly matters, just like they were not peaceful astronomers dedicated to observing the heavens, mystified by their endless cycles. They were social and political agents motivated by complex and even contradictory linguistic attitudes and ideologies, exhibiting at times innovative tendencies, and at times conservative tendencies, depending on the changing patterns of social and cultural valuation of linguistic practices.

Acknowledgments

I am indebted to John Justeson for reading an earlier draft of this chapter and discussing some of the details relevant to several etyma. I am also very grateful to Victoria Bricker for her comments on specific glyphic examples and the problem of scribal practices more generally. I have also benefited from comments by Nicholas Hopkins and Martha Macri, and want to thank both Martha Macri and Matthew Looper for their generosity with access to the Maya Hieroglyphic Database. I would also like to thank Diana Zlatanovski, Collections Steward at the Peabody Museum of Archaeology and Ethnology at Harvard, for facilitating access to study several artifacts, and Jakub Špoták for permission to use one of his drawings. Finally, many thanks to W. D. L. Silva, Nala Lee, and Thiago Costa Chacon for their patience and assistance throughout the submission and editing process starting in 2017.

Appendices: Datasets for the *k(') > ch shift.

Appendices A–D are based on data from Kaufman and Norman (1984), Kaufman with Justeson (2003), and Boot (2009) unless otherwise stated. Due to space limitations, the appendices *will be available on the Edinburgh University Press website*: edinburghuniversitypress.com/languagechange.

Notes

1. I would like to thank John Justeson for correspondence on some of the data items relevant to this chapter, including proto-Ch'olan *wich' "wing," and for directing me toward the entry in Kaufman with Justeson (2003) relevant to the positional root *7iky- "facing someone" of relevance to the yi-chi-nal expression. Any mistakes in the citation of the data are entirely my own.
2. Campbell (2017: 45) states: "It has generally been accepted that Ch'olan-Tseltalan and Greater Q'anjob'alan belong together in a single branch (sometimes called Western Mayan), though this has never been completely confirmed."
3. Kaufman (1976: 106) argued that Eastern Mayan departed from the homeland after Huastecan and before Yucatecan. Subsequently, Kaufman (1990, 2015, 2017) posits that Yucatecan broke off after Huastecan and before Eastern Mayan.
4. Robertson (1977: 113–14), who in the process of carrying out a comparison of Popti', Q'anjob'al, Chuj, Tojolabal, Tzotzil, and Tzeltal, defined the *k > ch shift as a trait shared by Chuj, Tojolabal, Tzotzil, and Tzeltal. He did not address the Ch'olan languages in connection to this shift.
5. Another such item is the Lowland Mayan term *k'aab'aa7 "name," which likely replaced pM *b'ih "name" in Ch'olan (cf. Tzotzil b'i "name"). It is likely that it diffused from Yucatecan into Ch'olan after the *k > ch shift, or else it is possible that it could have been originally *q'aab'aa7, in which case it would not have undergone the shift. Similarly, the Tzeltal term k'intun ~ k'inton "rainbow" is attested also in Tojolab'al as k'intum and in Mocho' as k'emtum; Kaufman with Justeson (2003: 470) propose a reconstruction to WM as *k'intum but note that it has been diffused. It is also possible that it avoided the shift in GTz because of diffusion into GTz subsequent to the occurrence of the shift; but given that Mocho' preserves pM *q', it did not avoid the shift because of the presence of earlier *q'.
6. Interestingly, Justeson et al. (1985: 60) have also observed that while Q'P retained pM *xiik' "wing," and Chuj innovated a unique form, k'axi7il "wing," Tojolab'al exhibits a form wech' "wing," corresponding to Ch' as *wich'; since this form is suggestive of the *ee > ii > i shift of Ch'olan, it may have been borrowed as *weech' into Tojolab'al (or possibly Chujean more generally), or vice versa, from Tojolob'al (or Chujean) into Ch'olan, prior to the *ee > ii > i shift in Ch'olan, which would place the Ch'olan *ee > ii > i shift after the *k' > ch' shift. This in turn would mean that the earliest spellings attesting to the *ee > ii > i shift in Epigraphic Mayan, documented in the adverbial enclitic sequence +ij+iy "since," from pM *+eej+eer, on the Tikal Ballcourt Marker (416 CE), would also serve as absolute anchors for the *k' > ch' shift. However, since there are no cognates of

pCh' *wich' in Mayan languages that did not experience the shift or borrow etyma including evidence the shift, this cannot be confirmed.
7. Although Law et al. (2014) do not cite Grube's (2010) work, it is likely that multiple epigraphers were becoming aware of the pattern of preposed phonetic complements with chV and ch'V signs around the same time.
8. "Hypercorrection" would imply that the Ch'olan terms were used "incorrectly" or outside their normal context by the likely Yucatecan scribes, but this was not the case: the spellings in question were being used in their proper contexts. Instead of hypercorrection we are probably witnessing borrowings or cases of code-switching.
9. Hopkins and Josserand (2011: 7–8) describe the etymological derivation carried out by them in conjunction with Terrence Kaufman in 1990; they proposed an expression *7och-ib' k'in "the door of the house of the Sun (where the Sun enters)" as a metaphor for "west," which eventually became reduced: *7och-ib' k'in > [7o]ch-i[b'] k'in > chik'in. In Yucatec and Itzaj, at least, this would constitute another loan. In Mayan languages, Hopkins and Josserand (2011) show, the terms for "east" and "west" are typically based on the terms for "exit" and "enter," respectively, plus an instrumental/locative. Thus, *7och-ib' k'in, with *-ib' "instrumentalizer," is a more likely origin for chik'in "west."
10. The evidence for reconstructing the pM "deer" root as *kehj, rather than *keej, is quite strong (cf. Yucatec kéeh < *kehj; Tzeltal chihj). Pre-Greater Tzeltalan likely had *kehj, not *kij, as a reflex of Proto-Mayan *kehj prior to the *k(') > ch(') shift.
11. The Uaxactun murals bear at last one instance of a non-calendrical T671/MR7 **chi**, which is regrettably largely erased, and its potential function thus unclear.

References

Aulie, Wilbur H., and Evelyn W. de Aulie. 2009. *Diccionario Ch'ol-Español, Español-Ch'ol*. 3rd edn. Mexico City: Instituto Lingüístico de Verano.
Beltrán, Boris. 2008. Excavaciones de la tercera etapa constructive del complejo arquitectónico Las Pinturas (Pinturas Sub-6). In *Proyecto arqueológico regional San Bartolo: Informe anual no. 7, Séptima temporada 2008*, ed. by Mónica Urquizú and William Saturno, 42–60. Informe entregado al Instituto de Antropología e Historia de Guatemala.
Boot, Erik. 2006. Loanwords, 'foreign words', and foreign signs in Maya writing. Paper presented at the symposium *The Idea of Writing III: Loanwords in Writing Systems*. Research School CNWS, Leiden University, Leiden, the Netherlands, June 7–9, 2006.
Boot, Erik. 2009. The updated preliminary classic Maya – English, English – Classic Maya vocabulary of hieroglyphic readings. *Mesoweb Resources*. <http://www.mesoweb.com/resources/vocabulary/Vocabulary-2009.01.pdf> (last accessed January 2017).
Bricker, Victoria. 2000. Bilingualism in the Maya codices and the Books of Chilam Balam. *Written Language and Literacy* 3:77–115.

Bricker, Victoria. 2015. Where there's a will, there's a way: The significance of scribal variation in colonial Maya testaments. *Ethnohistory* 62.421–44.
Bricker, Victoria, Eleuterio Po'ot Yah, and Ofelia Dzul de Po'ot. 1998. *A dictionary of the Maya language as spoken in Hocabá, Yucatán*. Salt Lake City: University of Utah Press.
Campbell, Lyle. 1970. Nahua loan words in Quichean languages. *Chicago Linguistic Society* 6.3–13.
Campbell, Lyle. 1972. Mayan loan words in Xinca. *International Journal of American Linguistics* 38. 187–90.
Campbell, Lyle. 1977. *Quichean linguistic prehistory*. University of California Publications in Linguistics, no. 81. Berkeley: University of California.
Campbell, Lyle. 1984. The implications of Mayan historical linguistics for glyphic research. In *Phoneticism in Maya hieroglyphic writing*, ed. by John S. Justeson and Lyle Campbell, 1–16. Institute for Mesoamerican Studies, Publication No. 9. Albany: State University of New York.
Campbell, Lyle. 1986. Cautions about loan words and sound correspondences. In *Linguistics across historical and geographical boundaries: In honor of Jacek Fisiak on the occasion of his fiftieth birthday, Vol. 1: Linguistic theory and historical linguistics*, ed. by D. Kastovsky and A. Szwedek, 221–5. Berlin: Mouton.
Campbell, Lyle. 1990. Philological studies and Mayan languages. *Historical linguistics and philology* ed by Jacek Fisiak, 87–105. Berlin: Mouton de Gruyter.
Campbell, Lyle. 2000. Time perspective in linguistics. In *Time depth in historical linguistics*, ed. by Colin Renfrew April McMahon, and Larry Trask, 3–32. Cambridge: The McDonald Institute for Archaeological Research.
Campbell, Lyle. 2017. Mayan history and comparison. In *The Mayan languages*, ed. by Judith Aissen, Nora C. England, and Roberto Zavala Maldonado, 43–61. London/New York: Routledge/Taylor & Francis Group.
Campbell, Lyle, and Terrence Kaufman. 1976. A linguistic look at the Olmecs. *American Antiquity* 41.80–9.
Coe, Michael D. 1966. An early stone pectoral from southeastern Mexico. *Studies in Pre-Columbian Art and Archaeology, Number 1*. Washington, DC: Dumbarton Oaks, Trustees for Harvard University.
Coe, Michael. 1973. *The Maya Scribe and His World*. New York: The Grolier Group.
Fields, Virginia, and Dorie Reents-Budet. 2005. *Lords of creation: The origins of sacred Maya kingship*. London: Scala Publishers Limited.
Fields, Virginia M., and Alexandre Tokovinine. 2012. Belt Plaque [PC.B.586]. In *Ancient Maya Art at Dumbarton Oaks: Pre-Columbian Art at Dumbarton Oaks, Number 4*, ed. by Joanne Pillsbury, Miriam Doutriaux, Reiko Ishihara-Brito, and Alexandre Tokovinine, 184–9. Washington, DC: Dumbarton Oaks Research Library and Collection, Trustees for Harvard University.
Fox, James A., and John S. Justeson. 1982. Hieroglyphic evidence for the languages of the classic Maya. Unpublished manuscript.
Grube, Nikolai. 2010. Preposed phonetic complements in Maya hieroglyphic writing. In *Linguistics and Archaeology in the Americas*, ed. by Eithne B. Carlin and Simon van de Kerke, 27–43. Leiden: Brill.

Hopkins, Nicholas A. 1984. La influencia del yucatecano sobre el cholano y su contexto histórico. *Investigaciones recientes en el área maya; XVII Mesa Redonda; 21-27 junio 1981*, 191–207. San Cristóbal de Las Casas, Chiapas: Sociedad Mexicana de Antropología.

Hopkins, Nicholas A. 1985. On the history of the Chol language. In *Fourth Palenque Round Table 1980, Vol. VI*, ed. by Elizabeth P. Benson, 1–5. San Francisco: Center for Pre-Columbian Art Research.

Hopkins, Nicholas A. 2012. *A dictionary of the Chuj (Mayan) language, as spoken in San Mateo Ixtatán, Huehuetenango, Guatemala, ca. 1964-1965*. <http://www.famsi.org/mayawriting/dictionary/hopkins/dictionaryChuj.html> (last accessed October 2014).

Hopkins, Nicholas A. 2013. Mayan Words for "Market" and Related Concepts. Paper presented at the Chac Mool Conference, Calgary, Alberta, November 2013.

Hopkins, Nicholas A. 2014. The classic Maya day name Oc and its origins. <https://www.academia.edu/6413833/On_a_Wing_and_a_Prayer_A_Reconsideration_of_a_Glyphic_Reading_T77_> (last accessed January 2018).

Hopkins, Nicholas A., and J. Kathryn Josserand. 2011. Directions and partitions in Maya world view. <http://www.famsi.org/research/hopkins/directions.html> (last accessed January 2020).

Houston, Stephen D., John Robertson, and David S. Stuart. 2000. The language of classic Maya inscriptions. *Current Anthropology* 41.321–56.

Hurst, Heather. 2009. *Murals and the ancient Maya artist: A study of art production in the Guatemala Lowlands*. Yale University unpublished Ph.D. dissertation.

Inomata, Takeshi, and Lucia Henderson. 2016. Time tested: Re-thinking chronology and sculptural traditions in preclassic southern Mesoamerica. *Antiquity* 90.456–71.

Josserand, J. Kathryn. 1975. Archaeological and linguistic correlations for Mayan prehistory. *Actas del XLI Congreso Internacional de Americanistas, México, 2-7 de septiembre de 1974*, vol. 1, 501–10.

Justeson, John. n.d. *Justeson-Mayan classification-for Kaufman 2017 fig2*. PDF file. <https://www.academia.edu/37842946/Justeson_Mayan_classification_for_Kaufman_2017_fig_2_pdf> (last accessed August 12, 2021).

Justeson, John S., and James A. Fox. 1989. Hieroglyphic evidence for the languages of the Lowland Maya. Unpublished manuscript.

Justeson, John S., William M. Norman, Lyle Campbell, and Terrence Kaufman. 1985. *The Foreign Impact on Lowland Mayan language and script*. Middle American Research Institute, Publication 53. New Orleans: Tulane University.

Kaufman, Terrence. 1976. Archaeological and linguistic correlations in Mayaland and associated areas of Mesoamerica. *World Archaeology* 8.101–18.

Kaufman, Terrence. 1990. Algunos rasgos estructurales de los idiomas Mayances. In *Lecturas sobre la lingüística maya*, ed. by N. England and S. Elliott, 59–114. Antigua/Guatemala: CIRMA.

Kaufman, Terrence. 2007. Northern Mije-Sokean: The elite language of the Basin of Mexico from 1000 BCE to 600 CE. Conference paper, October 2007.

Kaufman, Terrence. 2015. Mayan comparative studies. <https://www.albany.edu/ims/pdlma/2015%20Publications/Kaufman-Mayan%20Comparative%20Studies.pdf> (last accessed January 2017).
Kaufman, Terrence. 2017. Aspects of the lexicon of Proto-Mayan and its earliest descendants. In *The Mayan languages*, ed. by Judith Aissen, Nora C. England, and Roberto Zavala Maldonado, 62–111. London/New York: Routledge/Taylor & Francis Group.
Kaufman, Terrence. 2020. Olmecs, Teotihuacaners, and Toltecs: Language history and language contact in Meso-America, <https://www.researchgate.net/publication/340721651_MALP_2020> (last accessed September 2, 2021).
Kaufman, Terrence, with John Justeson. 2003. *Preliminary Mayan etymological dictionary*. <http://www.famsi.org/reports/01051/index.html> (last accessed January 2017).
Kaufman, Terrence, and John Justeson. 2007. The history of the word for cacao in ancient Mesoamerica. *Ancient Mesoamerica* 18.193–237.
Kaufman, Terrence, and John Justeson. 2008. The Epi-Olmec language and its neighbors. In *Classic Period Cultural Currents in Southern and Central Veracruz*, ed. by Philip J. Arnold, III, and Christopher A. Pool, 55–83. Washington, DC: Dumbarton Oaks Research Library and Collection.
Kaufman, Terrence, and John Justeson. 2009. Historical linguistics and pre-Columbian Mesoamerica. *Ancient Mesoamerica* 20.221–31.
Kaufman, Terrence, and William Norman. 1984. An outline of Proto-Cholan phonology, morphology, and vocabulary. In *Phoneticism in Maya hieroglyphic writing*, ed. by John S. Justeson and Lyle Campbell, 77–166. Institute for Mesoamerican Studies Publication No. 9. Albany: State University of New York.
Keller, Kathryn C., and Plácido Luciano G. 1997. *Diccionario Chontal de Tabasco*. Tucson, AZ: Summer Institute of Linguistics.
Lacadena, Alfonso, and Søren Wichmann. 2002. The distribution of lowland Maya languages in the Classic period. In *La organización social entre los mayas; memoria de la Tercera Mesa Redonda de Palenque vol. II*, ed. by Vera Tiesler Blos, Rafael Cobos, and Merle Greene Robertson, 275–319. México: Instituto Nacional de Antropología e Historia, and Mérida: Universidad Autónoma de Yucatán.
Laughlin, Robert M. 2007. *Mol cholobil k'op ta sotz'leb; El Gran Diccionario Tzotzil de San Lorenzo Zinacantán.*, México: CIESAS/CONACULTA.
Laughlin, Robert M. 2010. *Mol Cholobil K'op ta Sotz'leb, El gran diccionario tzotzil de San Lorenzo Zinacantán*. San Cristobal las Casas, Chiapas, Mexico: Sna Jtz'ibajom.
Law, Danny. 2013a. Mayan historical linguistics in a new age. *Language and Linguistics Compass* 7.141–56.
Law, Danny. 2013b. Inherited similarity and contact-induced change in Mayan languages. *Journal of Language Contact* 6.271–99.
Law, Danny. 2014. *Language contact, inherited similarity and social difference: The story of linguistic interaction in the Maya lowlands*. Amsterdam: John Benjamins.
Law, Danny. 2017. Language contacts with(in) Mayan. In *The Mayan languages*, ed. by Judith Aissen, Nora C. England, and Roberto Zavala Maldonado, 112–27. London/New York: Routledge/Taylor & Francis Group.

Law, Danny, John Robertson, Stephen Houston, Marc Zender, and David Stuart. 2014. Areal shifts in Classic Mayan phonology. *Ancient Mesoamerica* 25.357–66.
Lenkersdorf, Carlos. 2010. *B'omak'umal tojol'ab'al-kastiya = Diccionario tojolabal-español: idioma mayense de Chiapas*. Mexico City: Plaza y Valdés.
Looper, Matthew G., and Martha J. Macri. 2011–present. Maya Hieroglyphic Database. Beta version available with permission of authors. University of California, Davis.
Macri, Martha J. 2005. Nahua loan words from the Early Classic period: Words for cacao preparation on a Río Azul ceramic vessel. *Ancient Mesoamerica* 16.321–26.
Macri, Martha J., and Matthew G. Looper. 2003. *The new catalog of Maya hieroglyphs, Volume One, The Classic period inscriptions*. Norman: University of Oklahoma Press.
Mora-Marín, David F. 2001. The grammar, orthography, and social context of late Preclassic Mayan texts. University at Albany, Albany, New York, doctoral dissertation.
Mora-Marín, David F. 2005. Kaminaljuyu Stela 10: Script classification and linguistic affiliation. *Ancient Mesoamerica* 16.63–87.
Mora-Marín, David F. 2007. The identification of an ingressive suffix in Classic lowland Mayan texts. In *Proceedings of the CILLA III Conference, October 2007, Austin, Texas*, ed. by Nora England, 1–14. Austin: Archive of the Indigenous Languages of Latin America, Linguistics Department, University of Texas. <https://ailla.utexas.org/sites/default/files/documents/MoraMarin_CILLA_III.pdf> (last accessed January 2017).
Mora-Marín, David F. 2008. Análisis epigráfico y lingüístico de la escritura maya del período Preclásico Tardío: Implicaciones para la historia sociolingüística de la region. In *XXI Simposio de Investigaciones Arqueológicas en Guatemala, 2007*, ed. by Juan Pedro Laporte, Bárbara Arroyo, and Héctor E. Mejía, 853–76. Ciudad de Guatemala: Museo Nacional de Arqueología y Etnología.
Mora-Marín, David F. 2009. A test and falsification of the "Classic Ch'olti'an" Hypothesis: A study of three proto-Ch'olan markers. *International Journal of American Linguistics* 75.115–57.
Pallán Gayol, Carlos, and Lucero Meléndez Guadarrama. 2010. Foreign influences on the Maya script. In *Acta Mesoamericana 22: The Maya and Their Neighbors: Internal and External Contacts through Time*, ed. by Laura van Broekhoven, Rogelio Valencia Rivera, Benjamin Vis, and Frauke Sachse, 9–28. Munich: Verlag Anton Saurwein.
Polian, Gilles. 2015. *Diccionario Multidialectal del tseltal*. Mexico City: CIESAS.
Robertson, John S. 1977. A proposed revision in Mayan subgrouping. *International Journal of American Linguistics* 43.105–20.
Schele, Linda. 1990. *Notebook for the XIVth Maya hieroglyphic workshop at Texas, March 10-11, 1990*. The University of Texas at Austin.
Shook, Edwin M., and Marion Popenoe de Hatch. 1999. Las tierras altas centrales: períodos Preclásico y Clásico. In *Historia general de Guatemala, Tomo 1: época pre-colombina*, ed. by Marion Popeneo de Hatch, 289–318. Guatemala: Fondo para la Cultura y el Desarrollo.
Slocum, Marianna C., Florencia L. Gerdel, and Manuel C. Aguilar. 1999. *Diccionario Tzeltal de Bachajón, Chiapas*. México: Instituto Lingüístico de Verano.
Smith, A. Ledyard. 1950. *Uaxactun, Guatemala: Excavations of 1931-1937*. Washington, DC: Carnegie Institution of Washington.

Špoták, Jakub. 2017. Maya timeline in Uaxactun: Calendric notations on the mural paintings at structure B-XIII. *Ethnologia Actualis* 17.60–88.

Stuart, David. 2014. A possible sign for Metate. *Maya Decipherment: Ideas on Ancient Maya Writing and Iconography*. Blog. <https://mayadecipherment.com/2014/02/04/a-possible-sign-for-metate/> (last accessed August 12, 2021).

Stuart, David. 2018. An update on CHA', "Metate." *Maya Decipherment: Ideas on Ancient Maya Writing and Iconography*. Blog. <https://mayadecipherment.com/2018/07/27/an-update-on-cha-metate/> (last accessed August 12, 2021).

Taube, Karl A., and Bonnie Bade. 1991. An appearance of Xiuhteathtli in the Dresden Venus Pages. *Research Reports on Ancient Maya Writing* 35. Washington, DC: Center for Maya Research.

Thompson, John Eric S. 1950. *Maya hieroglyphic writing: An introduction*. Washington, DC: Carnegie Institution.

Wagner, Elizabeth. 2001. Some notes on Kerr 1955, an Early Classic stone sculpture representing goddess 0. <http://www.mayavase.com/com1955.html> (last accessed January 2017).

Wichmann, Søren. 1995. *The Relationship among the Mixe-Zoquean Languages of Mexico*. Provo, UT: University of Utah Press.

Wichmann, Søren, and Kerry Hull. 2009. Loanwords in Q'eqchi', a Mayan language of Guatemala. In *Loanwords in the world's languages: a comparative handbook*, ed. by Martin Haspelmath and Uri Tadmor, 873–96. Berlin: Mouton de Gruyter.

8

Are All Language Isolates Equal? The Case of Mapudungun

Willem F. H. Adelaar and Matthias Pache

1. Introduction

A recent volume published by Lyle Campbell (2018) provides a comprehensive overview of the language isolates in the world and highlights the situation in South America, where such isolates are found to be particularly numerous. This extreme linguistic diversity is unexpected considering the relatively short history of human occupation in the South American subcontinent (possibly less than 15,000 years) and the comparatively high genetic uniformity of its indigenous population. So far, no convincing explanation has been found for the process of diversification underlying this state of affairs. It may appear that, for reasons not yet understood, linguistic differentiation occurred in an accelerated, possibly chaotic manner during early stages of human occupation in the Americas. In more recent time periods accessible to inspection, there are relatively few signs of unusually rapid historical change. The overall pattern is one of gradual diversification similar to that of other, better known linguistic areas in the world, such as, for instance, Europe.*

A possible method to obtain a greater understanding of the genesis and past of some of the language isolates in South America may consist in a systematic study of lexical and structural properties that might link each of them to other documented language families and isolates in the subcontinent. In the absence of obvious genealogical connections based on a classic comparative approach, the evidence of prehistoric contact as well as areal features deserves special attention (e.g., Adelaar 2012; Pache 2018a). It appears that some South American language isolates fit more or less well the typological signature of the ethnolinguistic environment in which they are situated, whereas other isolates seem to be typologically alien to the areas in which they continue to exist. Several small families and isolates of the Amazonian region may

---

* Research of the second author was funded by the Deutsche Forschungsgemeinschaft (DFG, German Research Foundation)—Project number UR 310/1-1.

belong to the former category, whereas notorious typological outliers, such as Mochica in the Andean Pacific area, but also Nambikwaran, Trumai, and Yathê, in the South American lowlands may represent the latter category.

In the present chapter we intend to look at another intractable isolate, namely, Mapudungun, the language of the Mapuche ("people of the land") in southern Chile and Argentina.[1] The name Mapudungun ("language of [the people of] the land") refers to a relatively homogeneous language with local dialects that are in general mutually understandable. A possible exception is formed by its southernmost variety, spoken by the Huilliche ("people of the South"). For practical reasons, "Mapudungun" can be used as a cover term for all varieties, including the somewhat divergent Huilliche. Situated in the far south of the South American subcontinent (the so-called "Cono Sur"), originally in central and central-southern Chile, and later on in central-southern Chile and parts of Argentina, the Mapudungun language figures as an isolate from a genetic and typological point of view, as it does not exhibit a significant number of similarities with the surrounding indigenous languages, as far as these are known or recoverable. A convincing genealogical relationship of Mapudungun with geographically more distant languages or language families has never been established.

The wide geographical distribution of Mapudungun in early contact times, covering most of central and southern Chile as far south as the island of Chiloé, in combination with its linguistic uniformity, is suggestive of a relatively recent genesis of the language. It stands in contrast to the fact that the southern Chilean mainland harbors some of the oldest permanently inhabited settlements of the continent (Dillehay 1989–97). It would seem that Chile may have been the scene of subsequent invasions that eventually resulted in a linguistically homogeneous population of which the different components are nowadays difficult to tell apart. Around 1540, Mapudungun, known in colonial times as *Chile dugu* "language of Chile," was the dominant language in most of the territory of modern Chile.

Although Mapudungun certainly has its own defining and unique characteristics (inter alia, a distinction between alveolar and interdental stops; five different nasal consonants, which can be combined in sequences seldom recorded in other natural languages), the existence of historical connections with other New World languages, in South America and possibly beyond, can hardly be denied. Interestingly, these connections mostly point at areas situated in locations featuring a very different natural environment, which are relatively remote from the Mapuche heartland. A relatively straightforward case is the presence of lexical forms derivable from the Arawakan language family or some of its subbranches (Croese 1991). These lexical similarities are not limited to the domain of cultural vocabulary, and some of them belong to the more basic lexicon of a language which is normally seldom borrowed (e.g., Proto-Arawakan (PA, as reconstructed by Payne 1991) *waja{na}, Mapudungun (M) *wiṇ* "mouth"; PA *uhbana, M *pana* "liver"; PA *du{tʰi}, Chamicuro *tolo* (Parker et al. 1987), M *tol̯* ~ *tol̯* "forehead"; PA *kahitʰi, M *kijeṇ* "moon"; PA *na{tʰu} "sister-in-law, cousin," M *ɲaθo* "female cross-cousin"; color names such as PA *kʰuere, M *kuṯi* "black," and PA *kira, M *keli* "red"; PA *kheime, M *kime* "good"; the verb "to sleep": PA *imaka, M *umauɥ-*, etc.).[2] Although it is clear that the existence of such shared vocabulary items is not sufficient to ascertain a genealogical relation between Mapudungun and Arawakan, the similarities are too numerous and too specific to be assigned to mere coincidence.

Arawakan is not the only lowland South American language family that may have played a role in the formation of Mapudungun. Languages of the (Brazilian) Jê family, including its northern and southern (Kaingáng) branches, may also have contributed to the Mapuche lexical inventory (Proto-Jê (PJ) <*ŋgre>, Mapudungun *kuɹam* "egg"; PJ <*paj'>, M *lipaŋ* "arm"; PJ <*ñiji ~ jiji>, M *(ɯ)ɨj* "name").[3] Further research focused on other lowland and Amazonian language families and isolates may reveal further lexical correspondences with Mapudungun, as for instance, in Tupi–Guarani, words for "house," Proto-Tupi–Guarani (PTG) *ok, modern Paraguayan Guarani, *oɰa*, Mapudungun *ɹuka*, and "tobacco/to smoke," PTG *petɨm "smoke, tobacco," M *pit͡sem* "tobacco."

Among the languages of the central Andean highlands, Aymara exhibits a number of close lexical resemblances with Mapudungun which may not be due to recent borrowing (Tarata [Tacna] Aymara (A) *aŋanu* "face, jaw," Mapudungun *aŋe* "face"; A *t͡ʃara*, M *t͡ʃaŋ* "leg"; interrogative pronouns A *kam(a)*-, M *t͡ʃem* "what," and A *kaw-*, M *t͡ʃew* "where"). In the Quechuan languages (Q), many lexical resemblances with Mapudungun can be attributed to relatively recent borrowing by the latter (Q, M *wampu* "boat," Q *minka, mink'a* "hired labor," M *minka-* "to look for hired laborers," the number "hundred" Q *pat͡sak*, M *pataka* [borrowed through Aymara]). However, this does not hold for every case (for instance, Quechua I *pat͡sa*, M *pit͡sa* "belly/stomach"; Q *inti*, M *antɨ* "sun"; Q *pani*, M *peɲi* "sister/brother of male ego"; and the verb "to burn," Q *rupa-*, M *lɨf-*). With the extinct and scarcely documented Puquina language (possibly an Andean–Arawakan hybrid), originally spoken in the Titicaca Basin and its surroundings, some further curious lexical similarities with Mapudungun obtain in words referring to quantification (Puquina <coma>, Mapudungun *kom* "all"; Puquina <uin>, Mapudungun *fiʎ* "every").

Nevertheless, in terms of possible links with central Andean languages, structural and morphological correspondences with Mapudungun are more likely to draw the attention (see, for instance, Pache 2013: 210–11). The way in which affixes are selected and used in verbal inflection for the expression of grammatical person in agent–patient combinations reveals structural parallels between Mapudungun and central Andean languages. It implies the use of inverse markers, possibly to make up for the scarcity of dedicated affixes for specific pronominal functions. This highly specialized strategy is not only found in Mapudungun and in Quechuan, but also in Puquina. It is suggestive of a shared structural adaptation to the more complex model of pronominal markers found in the Aymaran languages (Adelaar 2009). Further similarities between Mapudungun and the Andean languages concern semantic and functional categories expressed by verbal derivation.

In a wider continental perspective, Mapudungun appears to align with the characteristic *n/m* pattern for the expression of first and second person, which is also found in most of the Californian languages. Furthermore, the existence of two co-occurring non-speech act participants that can be characterized as "proximate" and "obviative" (Zúñiga 2000: 24) has often been compared with the Algonquian obviative system (cf.

Arnold 1996). Finally, the morphological expression of centripetal and centrifugal motion ("hither/thither") in the verb form is curiously similar, both in shape and in function, in Mapudungun, Quechuan, and Tarascan or Purepecha, a Mesoamerican language isolate.

Surprisingly, Mapudungun does not exhibit a particularly close relationship with the languages of its immediate surroundings. Some possible shared words may have been borrowed from its eastern neighbors, the extinct Huarpean languages Allentiac and Millcayac. For instance, the word for "bread" or an equivalent starchy food is <cupi> in both Allentiac and Millcayac (Tornello et al. 2011: 173) and *kofke* in Mapudungun, and the verbal inflectional paradigms of Mapudungun show some formal and structural similarities with those of Günün-a Yajich, an equally extinct language of the Argentinian pampas and a possible member of the Chon family (cf. Viegas Barros 1992). The expression of dual number in verbal morphology is another characteristic of Mapudungun that has its parallels in Günün-a Yajich and in the Yaghan language, an isolate of Tierra del Fuego. Possible connections with the Matacoan languages, in which words for "name," for instance, Mak'á *-ii* (Gerzenstein 1999), and Nivaclé *ei* (Seelwische 1980; cf. Campbell et al. 2020) are nearly identical with Mapudungun *(uɟ)ij* "name," require further attention.

2. Documentary status of Mapudungun

The Mapuche or Araucanian nation has a long and eventful history of contact with Spanish invaders, which harks back to the second quarter of the sixteenth century (Bengoa 2007). For almost two and a half centuries, until their final defeat in the 1880s, the Mapuche people established in the Araucanía region of southern Chile and in the Argentinian territories of the pampas and Patagonia, succeeded in maintaining their independence against Spanish conquistadors, colonial administrators and missionaries, and subsequently against Chilean and Argentinian nation-building efforts. In these southern regions, attempts to Christianize and Hispanicize the non-subjugated Mapuche were successfully resisted, and the Mapudungun language continued to develop in a situation of limited interaction, in which occasional non-native elements were borrowed selectively, rather than imposed. Meanwhile, in other regions, such as the island of Chiloé, Spanish control was powerful from the beginning of colonization, and its effects on local (*Huilliche*) culture and language were presumably stronger.

Documentation of Mapudungun began in the early seventeenth century with Luis de Valdivia's *Arte* and dictionary of the Chilean language (1606), one of the best classic studies of a South American indigenous language, with remarkable attention for phonetic detail (distinction between interdental and alveolar consonants), as well as for morpho-syntactic peculiarities (noun incorporation). Several grammatical descriptions followed during the colonial period (Febrés 1765; Havestadt 1777), as well as Hervás's grammatical notes which provided the basis for a reanalysis and evaluation of the Mapudungun language by Wilhelm von Humboldt (Ringmacher and Tintemann 2011). At the end of the nineteenth century, Lenz (1895–7) published extensive materials on Mapudungun and its geographical variation. Capuchin missionaries active in the area of Temuco (Augusta 1903, 1916a, 1916b; Moesbach 1962) published authoritative grammars and dictionaries in close collaboration with traditional Mapuche leaders. One of them was Pascual Coña, whose account of the traditional life of the Mapuche, their last stand against the Chilean military, and the subsequent defeat and repression is an impressive document, both for its contents and the rhetoric of its language (Moesbach 1930; Coña 1984).

The twentieth century witnessed a steady decline of Mapuche society and language, which culminated with the military takeover in 1973, as many Mapuche ceased to transmit their language to the generations of their children and grandchildren. As a result, the number of fluent Mapuche speakers diminished steeply. Nevertheless, this decline did not stand in the way of a surge in modern linguistic research on the Mapuche language (Salas 1992; Zúñiga 2007; Smeets 2008), henceforth renamed Mapudungun ("speech of the land"). Since the beginning of the twenty-first century a strong revival movement has been underway, inciting Mapuche youngsters to relearn their language. Conflicting orthographies, a comprehensive inventory of Mapuche lexicon, and the interpretation of traditional terms and concepts have become important issues, which are discussed in workshops and language courses set up by grass roots organizations, occasionally with academic or governmental support. The need for expansion and modernization of the Mapudungun lexicon among Mapuche organizations and academics is illustrated by a renewed interest in neologisms (Villena Araya 2016).

Due to this unique combination of factors, Mapudungun continues to present a productive and promising field of research. The long period covered by the different stages of its documentation, the diversity of available sources, and the varied geographical background in which data were obtained and continue to be recorded offer possibilities for detailed studies of the historical evolution and development of the language, which eventually may also shed light on its earliest contacts and genetic origins. The geographical diversity of extant material is partly correlated with chronology, as the focus of attention moved from the (extinct) variety once spoken in the surroundings of Santiago (cf. Valdivia 1606), to the Araucanía heartland in the south (Lenz 1895–7; Augusta 1903, 1916a, 1916b; Moesbach 1962), and eventually to more outlying areas, such as the Argentinian pampas and Patagonia, the Upper Biobío valley (*Pehuenche*), and the southern region of the Huilliche subgroup (Chiloé and the areas of Valdivia and Osorno).

The current reappraisal of the Mapudungun language is closely linked with societal changes that have occurred in recent decades. As a result of massive migration from the Araucanía heartland to major Chilean cities, a substantial part of the Mapuche people is currently established in the metropolitan area of Santiago, where many young migrants seek to renew contact with their heritage language by relearning it or improving their knowledge of it. Issues of standardized orthography and the creation of a linguistic norm are the object of many debates. This process, which is crucial for the current situation of Mapudungun, deserves the attention and engagement of all linguists interested in this unique language, with the understanding that only the Mapuche themselves are entitled to decide about the future of their hereditary language.

3. Parallels of Mapudungun with other languages

The descriptive materials, compiled since the early seventeenth century and briefly presented in the previous section are the basis for the quest of Mapudungun external relations. Among the first authors to compare Mapudungun data with data from other languages was Imbelloni (1928, cited in Ramírez 1990: 53). He observed that Mapudungun *toki*, the term for a stone axe and symbol of a war-leader, formally and semantically resembles its counterpart in languages of Polynesia. Since then, several parallels between Mapudungun and other languages have been observed and interpreted in terms of prehistory and contact scenarios, for instance, by Jolkesky (2016: 376–7, 429–30, 479, 503–5, 508–12). The following subsections will give an overview of some of them. We shall look at languages of the Pacific coast (3.1), languages of lowland South America (3.2), those of the central Andean highlands (3.3), and some *Wanderwörter* (3.4).

3.1 Coastal languages

Several coincidences have been identified between Mapudungun and other languages of the Pacific coast. This subsection will present some of them, from south to north. One such corresponding form is Mapudungun *ketsu* or *kitsu* "steamer duck," Chono (extinct, unclassified) <quetu> "birds from which [the Chonos] extracted feathers to dress warmly" (Urban 2018: 42). Only few parallels indicate direct language contact between speakers of Mapudungun (or Huilliche) with other coastal languages of the Southern Cone, such as Qawasqar or Yaghan. Among the few lookalikes is, for instance, Mapudungun *alka* "male" (Augusta 1916a: 5) and Qawasqar *areq* "male" (Clairis and Viegas Barros 2015). Further to the north, there is Mapudungun *lame* "sea-lion" (Augusta 1916a: 110), sixteenth-century coastal Quechua <thome> "sea-lion" (Santo Thomas 1560: 71r), and Mochica <chommi> "seal" (Middendorf 1892: 60). There are more parallels of Mapudungun with Mochica, the extinct native language of the Lambayeque region in northern Peru, as shown in Table 8.1 (the parallels in the two first rows were first identified by Hovdhaugen 2000).

Table 8.1 Some Mapudungun–Mochica lookalikes

English	Mapudungun	Mochica
I want to go!; Let's go!	*amutʃi* "let me go! I want to go!" (Augusta 1903: 256)	<amoch> "let's go!" (Hovdhaugen 2000: 135)
to carry in arms/ to carry	*meta-* "to carry in arms"	<met-> "to carry" (Hovdhaugen 2000: 135)
to die	*la-*	<läm> [laʊm] (Middendorf 1892: 87)
I [1st pers. sing.]	*iɲ-tʃe* (*tʃe* "person")	<mo-iñ> (*mo-* demonstrative) (Middendorf 1892: 70)

Source: If not indicated otherwise, Mapudungun data are from Augusta (1916a).

In terms of the phoneme inventories of Mapudungun and Mochica, it is interesting to notice the existence of a velar nasal <ng> [ŋ] in intervocalic position in Mochica (in Mapudungun, the velar nasal can occur in any position), of what was possibly a dental fricative <d> [θ] or [ð], and, presumably, of a labiodental or bilabial fricative (<f> [f] or [φ]) in Mochica. The dental fricatives are also found in Mapudungun and, except for Yaghan and coastal Barbacoan, they are unusual in the languages of the Andean area (cf. Adelaar and Muysken 2004). A rather specific lexical parallel between Mochica and Mapudungun, which may be mentioned here, is found in the words <fichillko> "small intestine" and <fitako> "colon" (Middendorf 1892: 59). These Mochica forms suggest the existence of a fossilized morpheme <ko> "intestine" and two elements <fichill> [fit͡ʃiʎ] "small" and <fita> "large," which are strikingly similar to Mapudungun *pit͡ʃi* "small" and *fita* "large."

Parallels with Mapudungun attested in languages that are spoken still further to the north of course do not necessarily reflect direct language contact. Two examples are Mapudungun *piɻu* "worm" or *filu* "snake" and Mapudungun *maʃew* "shrimp" (Augusta 1916a: 132), which may be compared with Ulwa (Misumalpan) *biru* "worm, earthworm" (Green 1999: 174) and *wadau* "lobster, crayfish" (ibid.: 272). Indirect contact may also explain a parallel of Mapudungun with Mixe-Zoquean languages: Mapudungun *t͡ʃakaŋ*, *t͡ʃakantu* "a kind of seashell," and Proto-Mixe-Zoquean *saːka "shell" (cf. Wichmann 1995: 557), which has been interpreted as a coastal *Wanderwort* (Urban 2018: 48–9).

3.2 Eastern Lowlands

Several authors have noticed remarkable coincidences of Mapuche culture with cultures of the eastern Lowlands. Links with Amazonian cultures have been noticed by Menghin (1962: 11–12; cited in Croese 1991: 287) and Steward (1949: 711). Parallels with Amazonian cultures include the existence of shamanism, urn burial, and the consumption of cremated ashes with chicha among the Mapuche (Steward 1949: 711). Also, there are some similarities in oral traditions: The Mapuche myth of Latrapai, recorded by Lenz (1895: 225–34), contains several elements that recur in myths of the Tupi-speaking Mundurukú (Ehrenreich 1905: 49) and other Lowland South American peoples.

For instance, the theme of the night which is kept in a pot is attested both in this Mapuche myth, and among the Tupi (Ehrenreich 1905: 14).[4] Typological similarities between Mapudungun and Lowland South American languages occur, such as the widely distributed six-vowel system and noun incorporation. A semantic coincidence is the equation or interchange of "head" and "hair" in several Lowland South American languages (Adelaar 2013: 124) and in Mapudungun *loŋko*. This form likewise has the two meanings "hair (of the head)" and "head."

As for specific lexical coincidences between Mapudungun and languages of the eastern slopes or lowlands, Adelaar and Muysken (2004: 470) and Jolkesky (2016: 479) observe parallels between Mapudungun and Cholón (belonging to the small Hibito–Cholón family of the upper Huallaga valley in northern Peru). Some Mapudungun–Cholón lookalikes are shown in Table 8.2.

Table 8.2 Some Mapudungun–Cholón lookalikes

English	Mapudungun	Cholón
two	*epu*	*ip*
to kill	*ḻaŋim-*	*lam(a)*
light, clarity; moon	*pelo* "light, clarity"	*pel* "moon"
to find; to meet	*peθa ~ peʃa* "to find"	*pele/peʎ* "to meet"
to lay down	*kuθu*	*kule/kuʎ*
young girl; woman	*iʎĩʃa* "young girl"	*ila* "woman"

Sources: Mapudungun data from Augusta (1916a). Cholón data from Alexander-Bakkerus (2005). Except for "to kill" and "to lay down," these parallels have been identified by Jolkesky (2016: 479).

Some lexical parallels have been noticed between Mapudungun and Kaingáng, as well as other (Macro-)Jê languages (Adelaar 2008: 11). Macro-Jê is a stock, comprising Jê proper, Bororoan, Chiquitano, Jabutían, Karajá, Kariří, Krenák, Maxakalí, Ofayê, Rikbáktsa, and several extinct languages, all spoken in present-day Brazil, with the exception of Chiquitano.[5] Table 8.3 shows some coincidences of Mapudungun in Proto-Southern Jê.

Table 8.3 Some Mapudungun–Proto-Southern Jê lookalikes

	Mapudungun	Proto-Southern Jê
to see	*pe-*	*we
to say; to speak	*pi-* "to say"	*wĩ "to speak"
flower, to flower	*ḻaji-* "to flower," *ḻajen* "flower"; Huilliche *ʃaiŋen* "flower"	*sej "flower, to flower"
egg	*kuḻam* "egg", cf. also *kuḻa* "stone"	*grɛ
arrow; needle	*pilki* "arrow"	*prɛj "needle"
den; pot	Huilliche *kuḻko (θewɨ)* "den (of mice)," Huapi island: *kuḻkuḻ*, "the den of certain quadrupeds"	*kukrũ ~ *kukrũw "pot"

Sources: Mapudungun data from Augusta (1916a). Proto-Southern Jê data from Jolkesky (2010).

More Mapudungun lookalikes can be identified in Jê languages than in Proto-Macro-Jê (cf. Nikulin 2015, 2020). In some cases, Mapudungun shares the form in question with both Cholón and Southern Jê, for instance, Mapudungun *lolo* "hole," Cholón *lol* "mouth," Proto-Southern Jê *ror* "round." In addition, some rather surprising parallels can be found between Mapudungun and (Macro-Jê) Bororo (Augusta 1916a: 5–6; Bezerra Nonato 2008: 211): Mapudungun *ale* "moonshine," Bororo *ari* "moon," and, astoundingly, Mapudungun *alwe* "soul of the deceased" ("el alma del muerto"), Bororo *aroe ~ aloe* "soul of the deceased" ("almas dos mortos").

Further Mapudungun coincidences are found in Tupi–Guarani languages; some of them are shown in Table 8.4.

Table 8.4 Mapudungun–Chiriguano–Proto-Tupi–Guarani lookalikes

	Mapudungun	Chiriguano (Bolivian Guarani)	Proto-Tupi–Guarani
tobacco	pitsem	pẽti	*petim "smoke, tobacco"
parrot	tʃoɻoj	ajuru	*ajuru
monkey	maltʃinᵃ	maĩʃi	—
house	ɻuka	ʃé-ro "my house"	*ok
louse; chigoe flea	tiŋ "louse"	—	*tuŋ "chigoe flea (*Tunga penetrans*)"

Sources: Mapudungun data from Augusta (1916a), if not indicated otherwise. Chiriguano data from Dietrich (2015). Proto-Tupi–Guarani data from Mello (2000).

Note: ᵃ We only found this form in Fernández Garay et al. (2015), but not in Augusta (1916a, 1916b).

Whereas the term for "tobacco" might be a borrowing from a (Tupi–)Guarani language other than Chiriguano, the form for "monkey" seems to be exclusively shared with Chiriguano. (It is not attested, for instance, in Paraguayan Guarani.)

More parallels between Lowland South American languages and Mapudungun can be found in Jivaroan and Arawakan. These coincidences are dealt with in the following subsections (3.2.1 and 3.2.2).

3.2.1 Jivaroan

Jivaroan or Chicham is a small language group consisting of four languages: Shuar (or Jívaro), Achuar-Shiwiar (or Achual), Awajun (or Aguaruna), and Huambisa. Mutual intelligibility between them is considerable (Overall 2018: 22; see also Kohlberger 2020). According to Wise (1999: 312), Aguaruna is the most deviant Jivaroan language in terms of phonology. Jivaroan languages are spoken in northern Peru and eastern Ecuador, that is, in northwestern Amazonia. Aguaruna has several loans from Quechuan (Overall 2018: 34–5, 126), whereas Jivaroan languages as a whole also have some formal parallels in Aymaran, in the morphology and the lexicon (Gnerre, personal communication; Adelaar and Muysken 2004: 436, 442), and also in the fact that both Jivaroan and Aymaran have morphologically conditioned rules of vowel suppression. Some lookalikes of Mapudungun forms in Aguaruna and Huambisa are shown in Table 8.5.

In terms of morphological parallels, only a few coincidences between Mapudungun and Jivaroan languages can be found—for instance, a verbalizing suffix -*tu* in Aguaruna (Overall 2018: 255–7), which is reminiscent of the Mapudungun verbalizing suffix -*tu* (Smeets 2008: 126–7). Finally, compounds of the modifier–modified type (e.g., "deer-dog" for "cougar") are right-headed both in Jivaroan and in Mapudungun, whereas compound forms that are actually possessive constructions (of the type "dung-whale" for "amber") are left-headed in both language groups (Adelaar and Muysken 2004: 436, 520; for Mapudungun, see also Loncon 2017: 103).

Table 8.5 Mapudungun–Jivaroan lookalikes

	Mapudungun	Aguaruna	Huambisa
mouth	wiŋ	winu	wini
to hug, embrace	paŋko[a]	'paŋku-	paŋku-
leaf; wing	tapɨl "leaf"[b]	nanap(i) "wing"	nanap "wing"
to dress, put on (clothes)	tɨku-tu- "to dress, put on (clothes)"	nuŋ'ku- "to put on clothes above the belt";[c] du'ku- "to cover"	nuku- "to cover"
skin; naked	wiɻu-loŋko "bald"[d] (loŋko "head")	wi'su "naked"	misu "naked"
to jump	ɻɨŋkɨ	'tsɨkɨ-	tsɨkɨ-
clay, mud	ɻauɻ "clay"	tsa'kus "mud"	tsakus "mud"
round	tʃinkɨθ	tin'ti	tinti, tintitʃ
braid; braided rope	tʃape "braid"	'tʃapik "braided rope, braid"[c]	tʃapik "braided rope"
foot	ɲamuɲ	'dawi	nawi
darkness; night	θumiɲ "dark(ness)"	'suwi "obscure, darkness"	suwi "night"

Sources: Mapudungun data from Augusta (1916a), if not indicated otherwise. Aguaruna data from Wipio Deicat (2015). Huambisa data from Jakway (2008).

Notes:
[a] We only found this form in Fernández Garay et al. (2015), but not in Augusta (1916a, 1916b).
[b] Compare also Quechua tʃapra "leaf" and related forms (Pache 2014).
[c] Simon Overall, personal communication.
[d] We only found this form in Fernández Garay et al. (2015), but not in Augusta (1916a, 1916b). An anonymous Mapudungun dictionary (Anonymous 2002: 197) gives wiɻuwe "foreskin." The final element -we is a frequent derivational ending in Mapudungun (see below).

3.2.2 Arawakan

This subsection presents and discusses some correspondences between Mapudungun and Arawakan, one of the largest language families of South America. Its homeland has been argued to be in north-western or western Amazonia (Walker and Ribeiro 2011). Croese (1991) argued a genealogical connection between Mapudungun and Arawakan languages (for a discussion, see Díaz-Fernández 2011). Indeed, when the vocabularies of Mapudungun and Arawakan languages are compared, several lookalikes can be identified, not only in Arawakan languages spoken close to the Andes, such as Ashéninca, Piro, or Trinitario and Ignaciano, but also in languages further afield (cf. Croese 1991). In Table 8.6 several lookalikes are shown which can be found when Mapudungun data are compared with Payne's (1991) Proto-Arawakan reconstructions.

Table 8.6 Mapudungun–Arawakan lookalikes

English	Mapudungun	Proto-Arawakan
sky	wenu	*jenuh{kɨ}
fat, grease	jiwiɲ	*jui{n}{ka}
liver	pana	*uhbana
black	kuɻi	*kʰuere
red	keli	*kɨra
grass	kat͡ʃua	*kat͡ʃau
good	kime	*kʰeime
salty, sour; sour	kot͡si "salty, sour"	*kat͡so{ri} "sour"
fire; smoke	kit͡sal	*kit͡ʃa{li}
to sleep	umaɰ-	*imaka

Sources: Mapudungun data from Augusta (1916a). Proto-Arawakan data from Payne (1991).
Note: ᵃ Compare also Cuzco Quechua q'at͡ʃu "grass, fodder" (Cusihuamán 1976a: 117).

In addition to the correspondences with these reconstructed forms, there are also very telling lexical resemblances with individual Arawakan languages, for instance, the parallel between Mapudungun ɲaθo, Ashéninca o-nato-to, Lokono re-netʰo, and Parecís natʲo-lo, all meaning "sister-in-law, cross-cousin (f) of a woman" (Croese 1991: 288). Another notable correspondence is between Mapudungun toḻ ~ ṯoḻ and Chamicuro tolo "forehead" (Parker et al. 1987: 44); Mapudungun peʎke "anxiety, worry" (Fernández Garay et al. 2015) resembles Proto-Arawakan *pinka "to fear" (Payne 1991: 403).[6]

3.3 Highlands

Coincidences between Mapudungun and languages of the central Andes (Quechuan, Aymaran) have been observed for a relatively long time (see, for instance, Englert 1936). Havestadt (1777: 188) explicitly attributes some lexical parallels with Quechua to trade contacts, for instance the corresponding terms for "sun" and "chicken." In cultural terms, there are a number of parallels between Mapudungun-speaking groups and Quechuan/Aymaran-speaking populations of the central Andes in the domain of material culture, for instance in the production of textiles, including weaving terminology, and the practice and use of messages conveyed in knotted threads ("quipus," Mapudungun piɻonfiw "knotted thread," cf. Coña 1984: 271). There is also a common element in agriculture (potatoes). Furthermore, there are coinciding story themes of Mapuche oral traditions with those of the central Andes further north. In both Mapuche and Andean folktales, the fox prominently appears as a trickster, and there are sometimes identical themes (cf. Pache 2007, 2012). Both areas also have an elaborate native account of a prehistoric diluvium (Ehrenreich 1905: 31).

Some general parallels between Mapudungun and Quechuan and/or Aymaran have briefly been mentioned in the introduction above. They indicate intense, early contact between speakers of Mapudungun and of central Andean languages (for a more elaborate account see Pache 2014). Given the long periods in which Proto-Quechuan,

Proto-Aymaran, as well as individual Quechuan and Aymaran languages mutually influenced each other (cf. Adelaar 2012; Emlen 2017), it comes as no surprise that in several cases, Mapudungun shares forms with both Quechuan and Aymaran. Compare Quechua *ana'naw*, Aymara *ana'naj* (de Lucca 1983: 26), and Mapudungun *ananaj, aninij* "how painful!" (Augusta 1916a: 8–9).[7] Similar cases are Mapudungun *ʎaθki-* "to get sad, upset" and Quechuan/Aymaran *ʎaki-* "to get sad," or *t͡ʃaʎwa* which means "fish" in all three languages. In the domain of bound morphology, there is a non-productive suffix *-ka*, attested in both Quechuan and Aymaran, which seems to correspond to an element *-ke* in Mapudungun, as shown in Table 8.7. Once more, it is impossible to argue that Mapudungun borrowed this element from either Quechuan or Aymaran.[8] The fact that it only occurs in one or two, but not in all forms shown in Table 8.7 suggests that *-ka* and *-ke* were still productive elements when borrowing occurred.

Table 8.7 Mapudungun *-ke* and its counterpart *-ka* in Quechua and Aymara

Mapudungun	North Junín Quechua	Aymara
pit͡sa "stomach, belly"	*pat͡sa* "belly, inner part"	*puraka* "stomach"
t͡ʃaw "father"	*t͡ʃakwa* "old lady"	*tajka* "mother"
ʎifke "lightning"	*ʎip(j)a ~ lip(j)a* "lightning"	–
t͡ʃaŋ "leg"	*t͡sanka* "leg"	*t͡ʃara* "leg"
ɲuke "mother, mother's sister"	*ɲuɲu* "woman's breast" (Ayacucho Quechua, Parker 1969: 167)	*ɲuɲu* "breast"

Sources: Mapudungun data from Augusta (1916a), North Junín Quechua data from Adelaar (1977), and Aymara data from de Lucca (1983).

A somewhat similar case is found in terms referring to the components of the weaving loom. In Mapudungun such terms characteristically end in *-we* (e.g., *θipiʎwe* "arched stick used in order to pick up the thread," Augusta 1916a: 32), whereas in Quechua they end in *-wa* (e.g., Ayacucho Quechua *iʎawa* "instrument for separating the warp strands one by one," Parker 1969: 136). The etymology of these weaving terms is otherwise generally obscure in both languages. The element *-wa* has no other productive use in Quechua. However, Mapudungun *-we* is also a productive nominalizing suffix for reference to names of places and instruments, for instance, *i-we* "eating place" (Augusta 1916a: 70), from *i-* "to eat." In this respect, it bears a close resemblance with the ending *-(:)wi* in Aymara, which has a similar function.

As we mentioned earlier, a significant case of early borrowing or possible cognacy may be reflected in Mapudungun *lif-* "to burn," transitive *lip-im-* "to light (a fire)" (Augusta 1916a: 114), as compared to Quechua *rupa-* "to burn" (Cuzco Quechua *rupʰa-*) and Aymara *lupi* "sunshine," "sunheat" (de Lucca 1983: 279).

3.3.1 Aymaran

As argued above, there are several forms shared by Mapudungun and both Quechuan and Aymaran. Some, however, are clearly shared with Aymara, and there are sometimes recurrent sound correspondences, for instance between the Mapudungun velar nasal *ŋ* and the Aymaran rhotic *r*. Some cases are illustrated in Table 8.8.

Table 8.8 Some forms illustrating the correspondence of Mapudungun *ŋ* with Aymara *r*

English	Mapudungun *ŋ*	Aymara *r*
leg	t͡ʃaŋ	t͡ʃara
star	waŋi̯len	warawara
ball-shaped	moŋkol	muruq'u

Sources: Mapudungun data from Augusta (1916a) and Aymara data from de Lucca (1983).

It must be noted, however, that a more straightforward correspondence between Mapudungun *ŋ* and Aymara intervocalic *ŋ* can be observed in the word for "face," Mapudungun *aŋe*, Tarata (Tacna) Aymara *aŋanu* "face, jaw."

In the domain of interrogatives, the Mapudungun postalveolar affricate t͡ʃ seems to correspond to an Aymara velar stop *k*. The Mapudungun interrogative pronouns t͡ʃem "what" and t͡ʃew "where" correspond, in Aymara, to *kam(a)-* and *kaw-*, respectively. The form *kam(a)-* is not the current term for "what" in Aymara (which is *kuna*), but it occurs in derived expressions such as *kamisa* "how," *kam-sa-* "to say what," and *kama-t͡ʃa-* "to do what"; *kaw-* is found in the word *kawki* "where," in which the element *-ki* probably represents a restrictive marker (*-ki* "just"). In the domain of morphology, the third person hortative (imperative) ending of the verb shows a close resemblance between both languages: *-pe* in Mapudungun, as in *amu-pe* "may he go!," and *-pa* in Aymara, as in *sar-pa* (same meaning). Another formal coincidence of Aymaran and Mapudungun is found in the domain of numbers: Mapudungun "nine" is *aʎʎa*, which resembles Aymara *ʎaʎa* in *ʎaʎatunka* "nine" (cf. de Lucca 1983: 774), literally "almost ten" (cf. ibid.: 588) (*tunka* "ten").

In terms of semantics, there is a parallel in that both in Mapudungun and in Aymaran, teeth are conceived of as the bones of the mouth. Mapudungun *foɻo* has two meanings: "bone" and "tooth." The latter is probably secondary since there is also a form *wiɲfoɻo* "tooth" (*wiɲ* "mouth," Augusta 1916b: 52, 120, 188). Likewise, in Aymara, t͡ʃ'aqʰa means "bone" whereas the teeth are referred to as "bones of the mouth," *laka* t͡ʃ'aqʰa (*laka* "mouth," de Lucca 1983: 261).

3.3.2 Quechuan

Several formal parallels can be identified in the case of Mapudungun and Quechuan (e.g., Díaz-Fernández 1992, 2008). Occasionally, there are recurring sound correspondences, for instance between the Mapudungun rhotic *ɻ* and Quechua *s*, as in the terms for "eight," Mapudungun *puṯa* (Augusta 1916a: 190) and Cuzco Quechua *pusaq* (Cusihuamán 1976a: 106), or in the narrative past markers: Mapudungun *-ṯke*⁹ (Smeets 2008: 112, 246–7), Cuzco Quechua *-sqa* (Cusihuamán 1976b: 160). Above all, it is non-basic vocabulary in Mapudungun that is clearly related to Quechuan, as illustrated in Table 8.9.

Table 8.9 Some Quechua borrowings in Mapudungun

English	Mapudungun	Southern Quechua
"enemy, rebel"	*awka*	*awqa*
"dried meat"	*tʃaṯki*	*tʃarki*
"letter, inscription"	*tʃiɻka*	*qilqa* "writing"
"stone wall"	*piṯka* (Valdivia 1606)	*pirqa*

Sources: Mapudungun data from Augusta (1916a), if not indicated otherwise. Quechua data from Cusihuamán (1976a). Some of these parallels have previously been noticed by Díaz-Fernández (1992).

The semantics of the Quechua terms shown in Table 8.9 suggest that the forms in question were probably introduced into Mapudungun from Quechua at the time of Inca conquest in the late fifteenth/early sixteenth century (cf. León 1983) or later. Two different contact situations seem to be reflected by competing forms in Mapudungun such as <quillca> "letter ('*carta papel, cedula, escriptura*')" and <chilca> "letter ('*carta*')," both recorded in Valdivia (1606) and ultimately derived from Quechuan *qiɻqa* "drawing, scribble, letter" (cf. Cusihuamán 1976a: 114; Rosat Pontacti 2004: 865). Other possible Quechuan loans in Mapudungun seem to be older, such as, for instance, *kaḻ* "body hair" (cf. Quechua *qara* "skin, leather, fur"), and *kaḻku* "witch" (cf. Quechua *qarqu* "evil omen"), given that they underwent some formal and semantic changes. Other forms not belonging to cultural vocabulary and shared by Mapudungun and Quechuan are Mapudungun *peɲi* "brother (of a male ego)," Quechuan *pana, pani* "sister or (female) cousin of a male ego" (compare also Proto-Arawakan *peri{pe} "brother" (Payne 1991: 397)), or the Mapudungun relative/comitative suffix *-wen* (Smeets 2008: 109–10), corresponding to Quechuan instrumental/comitative *-wan* (Rosat Pontacti 2004: 1189–90).

3.4 Wanderwörter

In South America, as in other parts of the world, it has been observed that several words are very widespread and shared by otherwise unrelated languages through a chain pattern or a radial pattern/star pattern. These words are referred to as *Wanderwörter* and are usually found in the vocabulary referring to culturally salient entities (Haynie et al. 2014; Pache 2018b: 547). The first author to observe some *Wanderwörter* that also occur in Mapudungun was Englert (1936: 81–2; however, Englert did not use the term "*Wanderwort*"). He observed a similarity between Mapudungun "lightning" terms (Huilliche of Panguipulli *ɻifke*, Huapi Island dialect *lifke* "lightning"; compare also Mapudungun *ḻemḻem-uw-* "to suddenly glare") and words with similar meanings in languages of South America and Mesoamerica, such as Mayan (cf. Proto-Mayan *lem "shiny, flashing," Kaufman with Justeson 2003: 472), Quechuan (cf. ǩip(j)a ~ lip(j)a "lightning," see above), Yaghan (lam "sun," Guerra Eissmann 2015), Kunza (<liplipna-> "to glare," "to flash," Vilte Vilte n.d.), Allentiac (<lepchap> "light," Valdivia 1607), and Lule (<lipitip> "lightning," <lipit-> "to flash," Machoni 1732: 114).

A typical *Wanderwort* is the term for "maize"; compare Mapudungun *uwa* (Huapi Island variety), *iwa* (Huilliche variety of Panguipulli), and *wa* (in other Mapudungun varieties; Augusta 1916b: 228), <abo> in Timucua <abo pahama> "corn crib" (<paha> "house, dwelling,"[10] Granberry 1993: 191), Ulwa (Misumalpan) *am* (Green 1999: 151), Proto-Chibchan *aBi ~ *aiB (Pache 2018b: 145), Proto-Tupi–Guarani *aβati "maize" (Mello 2000: 151; for other widely shared maize terms, cf. Chacon and Hammarström n.d.; Zamponi 2020).[11] Another Mapudungun crop term which has parallels in several Native American languages is t͡sapi "chili pepper" (cf. Pache 2018b: 71)—compare Cabécar (Chibchan) *dapa* "chili pepper" (Margery Peña 1989: 50), Proto-Macro-Jê <*ndap° ~ *ndâp°> "sour, bitter," Proto-Tupian <*ndəp> "bitter" (Nikulin 2020: 183, 568), Aguaruna and Huambisa (Jivaroan) *japau* "bitter" (Jakway 2008: 122; Wipio Deicat 2015), Wichí (Matacoan) *ta 'paj* "bitter" (Braunstein 2015), Nivaclé (Matacoan) <tʔapɔʔy> "bitter" (Seelwische and Stell 2015). Words for "dog," "jaguar," and "puma" in Mapudungun, t͡sewa "dog," *nawel* "jaguar," and t͡sapial "cougar" are reminiscent of Proto-Chibchan *ⁿdaᵐba "feline" (Pache 2018b: 100), Proto-Northern Jê <rop> "jaguar" (Nikulin 2020: 499), Aguaruna (Jivaroan) *ja 'wa*, Huambisa (Jivaroan) *jawa* "dog" (Jakway 2008: 123; Wipio Deicat 2015), and Proto-Tupi–Guarani *jawar "jaguar" (Mello 2000: 167; for further similar "jaguar" terms, see Zamponi 2020).[12] Finally, two *Wanderwörter* that may be mentioned here are %kaka and %kuku (Pache 2018b: 98). These forms most frequently refer to parents' opposite sex siblings (mother's brother, father's sister) or a grandmother, and one may venture that originally, %kaka and %kuku may have meant "father-in-law" and "mother-in-law," respectively. The existence of two similar forms differing only in vowel quality suggests that one of them may originally have referred to a male and the other to a female person. In South American languages, forms approximating %kaka are Quechua *kaka* "mother's brother or cousin, father's sister, father-in-law of a man, brother-in-law" (Steinen 1886: 292–3; Rosat Pontacti 2004: 370), possibly also Kaingáng *kãkra* "mother's brother; father-in-law" (Key 2015), and different forms for "mother's brother": Páez <kakka>, Zuñi <kaka>, Nisenan (Maiduan) <kaka>, Central Miwok <kaka> (Swadesh 1957: 33). The last three forms are from North language groups. As to %kuku and related forms in South and Mesoamerican languages, compare Proto-Cariban *kuku (Meira 2017), Purepecha <kuku> (Swadesh 1957: 31), both "grandmother"; in North American languages, there is, for instance, Zuñi <kuku> "father's sister" (Swadesh 1957: 31), to mention just a further example. These terms may eventually turn out to reflect old networks that spread across North and South America (Pache 2018b: 98). Both *kaka* and *kuku* occur in Mapudungun: Valdivia (1606) gives <caca> "sister-in-law of a woman," and there is Huilliche (Panguipulli dialect) *kaka piɲiɲ* "niece-in-law" (a mocking term, Augusta 1916a: 74); *piɲiɲ* is a kinship term that can refer to the son or the daughter of a female ego. There is no form <caca> in the dictionary of Febrés (1765). As to forms resembling %kuku, Augusta (1916a: 98) gives Mapudungun *kuku* as a term for the paternal grandmother and her grandchildren, and Febrés (1765: 463) mentions a form <cucu> for the maternal grandmother and her grandchildren. No form <cucu> could be found in Valdivia (1606).

4. Conclusion

This chapter has discussed several lexical correspondences between Mapudungun and languages of the eastern Lowlands and the Andean Highlands. It has shown that although Mapudungun must be considered a language isolate from a strictly genealogical point of view, it is by no means free of lexical and structural influences from other linguistic lineages, some of which cover considerable geographical distances and unknown temporal depths. The traces left by these different sources of impact are varied and well integrated in the Mapudungun language in its present form. At the moment it appears to be impossible to establish a hierarchy of importance of the linguistic contacts that have contributed to the formation of this language and of which probably only a few could be identified at present.

The formal inventory of Mapudungun appears to contain several different layers, associated with languages of the central Andes, eastern Brazil, and western Amazonia. In the case of *Wanderwörter*, it could be shown that Mapudungun shares some kinship terms with languages all over the Americas, whereas in other cases (words for "dog/jaguar" and for "maize"), the network reflected by the *Wanderwörter* spreads across the tropical Lowlands rather than across the Andes. Concerning specific formal coincidences, forms shared by Mapudungun and some of the major stocks/language families of lowland South America (Macro-Jê, Tupi–Guarani) appear to be relatively few, although significant. The parallels clearly betray contact but no genealogical connection in the cases of Southern Jê and Chiriguano/Guarani. Parallels of Mapudungun in Quechuan reflect two subsequent periods of contact, one in pre-Inca times, and the other in Inca and post-Inca times. Parallels with Aymaran may reflect a similar situation of different waves of language contact. The largest amount of parallels, including several coincidences in basic vocabulary, could be identified in a lowland South American language family, Arawakan and, to a lesser extent, in Jivaroan. Their geographic localization suggests an original homeland of Pre-Mapudungun further north than today, in the Andean foothills or in western Amazonia.

Notes

1. The number of Mapudungun speakers has been estimated at 260,000 people located in southern central Chile and parts of Argentina (cf. Eberhard et al. 2019). Nevertheless, the language has suffered a steep decline during the last four decades, and intergenerational transmission is seriously endangered. Knowledgeable sources now estimate the number of fluent traditional speakers in Chile at $c.$120,000 (Loncon 2017) and a much lower number in Argentina. Nevertheless, a powerful revitalization movement is currently underway.

2. Transcriptions of indigenous language data are phonemic and use IPA symbols. Other symbols used here are: x/y = alternating segments; x ~ y = segments in free variation; <...> = graphemic (orthographic) representation; (...) = optional segment; {...} = grammatical morpheme, for example a classifier; /.../ = phonemic representation; [...] = phonetic representation; - = unknown segment (in reconstructed forms); morpheme boundary; feature not present; % = generalization across similar forms found in genealogically unrelated languages (cf. Zamponi 2020); B stands for a bilabial stop [^{M}b, b, m, p].
3. Proto-Jê forms from Nikulin (2020).
4. Also among eastern Tucanoan peoples (Thiago Costa Chacon, personal communication).
5. The inclusion of Guató and Yathê is debated.
6. Augusta (1916a: 19) attributes to the verb peŕke- the meaning "to be in a hurry" in Huilliche of Panguipulli and the meaning "to get very much scared, frightened" in the Huapi Island variety. Compare also Quechua p'inqa "to be ashamed" (Rosat Pontacti 2004: 739), and Puquina penka "to be ashamed."
7. Febrés (1765: 90) also gives some related forms, such as <alùlùy> "how painful!" (stinging pain, itch); <athù, athùthùy> "how painful, how cold!," and Valdivia (1606: 54v) mentions the exclamative <atú atútúy>, expressing pain (<ù, ú> = [ɨ]).
8. In Mapudungun there is also an affix -ke which functions as a plural or distributive marker on adjectives. The equivalent in Quechuan is -kama.
9. Neither this suffix nor a related form are mentioned by Valdivia (1606).
10. Timucua is an unclassified language from northern and central Florida and southeastern Georgia.
11. There is no trace of this "maize" Wanderwort in languages of the central Andes (Aymaran, Puquina, Quechuan, and Uru–Chipayan).
12. Once more, no trace of a related term is found in Andean languages; words for "dog" are prone to being borrowed in the Americas (Pache et al. 2016).

References

Adelaar, Willem F. H. 1977. *Tarma Quechua: Grammar, texts, dictionary*. Lisse: Peter de Ridder Press.

Adelaar, Willem F. H. 2008. Relações externas do Macro-Jê: o caso do Chiquitano. In *Topicalizando Macro-Jê*, ed. by Stella Telles and Aldir Santos de Paula, 9–28. Recife: Nectar.

Adelaar, Willem F. H. 2009. Inverse markers in Andean languages: A comparative view. In *The linguistics of endangered languages: Contributions to morphology and morphosyntax*, ed. by W. Leo Wetzels, 171–85. (LOT Occasional Series, 13.) Utrecht: Landelijke Onderzoekschool Taalwetenschap.

Adelaar, Willem F. H. 2012. Modeling convergence: Towards a reconstruction of the history of Quechuan–Aymaran interaction. *Lingua* 122.461–9.

Adelaar, Willem F. H. 2013. Searching for undetected genetic links between the languages of South America. In *Historical Linguistics 2011: Selected papers from the 20th International Conference on Historical Linguistics, Osaka, 25–30 July 2011*, ed.

by Ritsuko Kikusawa and Lawrence A. Reid, 115–28. (Current Issues in Linguistic Theory, 326.) Amsterdam/Philadelphia: John Benjamins.

Adelaar, Willem F. H., with Pieter C. Muysken. 2004. *The languages of the Andes.* Cambridge: Cambridge University Press.

Alexander-Bakkerus, Astrid. 2005. *Eighteenth-century Cholón.* Utrecht: Landelijke Onderzoekschool Taalwetenschap.

Anonymous. 2002. *Diccionario mapudungun–español, español–mapudungun.* San Ignacio, Chile: Editorial Centro Gráfico Limitada.

Arnold, Jennifer. 1996. The inverse system in Mapudungun and other languages. *Revista de Lingüística Teórica y Aplicada* 34.9–48.

Augusta, Felix José de. 1903. *Gramática araucana.* Valdivia: Imprenta Central, J. Lampert.

Augusta, Felix José de. 1916a. *Diccionario araucano–español y español–araucano, vol. 1: araucano–español.* Santiago de Chile: Imprenta Universitaria.

Augusta, Felix José de. 1916b. *Diccionario araucano–español y español–araucano, vol. 2: español–araucano.* Santiago de Chile: Imprenta Universitaria.

Bengoa, José. 2007. *Historia de los antiguos mapuches del sur.* 2nd edn. Santiago: Catalonia.

Bezerra Nonato, Rafael. 2008. *Ainore Boe egore: um estudo descritivo da língua bororo e conseqüências para a teoria de caso e concordância.* Campinas: Universidade Estadual de Campinas master's thesis.

Braunstein, José A. 2015. Wichí dictionary. In *The intercontinental dictionary series*, ed. by Mary Ritchie Key and Bernard Comrie. Leipzig: Max Planck Institute for Evolutionary Anthropology, <http://ids.clld.org> (last accessed August 16, 2021).

Campbell, Lyle R. (ed.). 2018. *Language isolates.* London/New York: Routledge.

Campbell, Lyle, Luis Díaz, and Fernando Ángel. 2020. *Nivaclé grammar.* Salt Lake City: University of Utah Press.

Chacon, Thiago Costa, and Harald Hammarström. n.d. Análisis de la diversidad léxica en el Noroeste de Suramérica, <https://www.academia.edu/35119269/An%C3%A1lisis_de_la_diversidad_l%C3%A9xica_en_el_Noroeste_de_Suram%C3%A9rica> (last accessed August 16, 2021).

Clairis, Christos, and José Pedro Viegas Barros. 2015. Qawasqar dictionary. In *The intercontinental dictionary series*, ed. by Mary Ritchie Key and Bernard Comrie. Leipzig: Max Planck Institute for Evolutionary Anthropology, <http://ids.clld.org> (last accessed August 16, 2021).

Coña, Pascual. [1930] 1984. *Testimonio de un cacique mapuche.* Santiago: Pehuen Editores.

Croese, Robert A. 1991. Evidencias léxicas y gramaticales para una posible filiación del mapudungun con la macro-familia arawaka. *Revista Latinoamericana de Estudios Etnolingüísticos* 6.283–96.

Cusihuamán Gutiérrez, Antonio. 1976a. *Diccionario quechua Cuzco-Collao.* Lima: Ministerio de Educación/Instituto de Estudios Peruanos.

Cusihuamán Gutiérrez, Antonio. 1976b. *Gramática quechua Cuzco-Collao.* Lima: Ministerio de Educación/Instituto de Estudios Peruanos.

Díaz-Fernández, Antonio Edmundo. 1992. Contactos del mapudungun con dos lenguas principales del Tawantinsuyu: el quechua y el yunga. *Actas de Lengua y Literatura Mapuche* 5.193–201.

Díaz-Fernández, Antonio Edmundo. 2008. Transferencias léxicas del quechua en el mapuzungun. II Congreso Internacional de Lenguas y Literaturas Indoamericanas and XIII Jornadas de Lengua y Literatura Mapuche. Temuco: Universidad de La Frontera, Facultad de Educación y Humanidades, 22–24 October 2008.

Díaz-Fernández, Antonio Edmundo. 2011. Relaciones genéticas del mapuzungun: aportes para su ubicación dentro del stock equatorial. In *Investigaciones sobre lenguas indígenas sudamericanas*, ed. by Ana Fernández Garay and Antonio Díaz-Fernández, 69–113. Santa Rosa: Editorial de la Universidad Nacional de La Pampa.

Dietrich, Wolf. 2015. Chiriguano dictionary. In *The intercontinental dictionary series*, ed. by Mary Ritchie Key and Bernard Comrie. Leipzig: Max Planck Institute for Evolutionary Anthropology, <http://ids.clld.org> (last accessed August 16, 2021).

Dillehay, Tom D. 1989–97. *Monte Verde: A Late Pleistocene settlement in Chile*. Washington, DC: Smithsonian Institution Press.

Eberhard, David M., Gary F. Simons, and Charles D. Fennig (eds). 2019. *Ethnologue: Languages of the world*. 22nd edn. Dallas: SIL International. <http://www.ethnologue.com> (last accessed August 16, 2021).

Ehrenreich, Paul. 1905. *Die Mythen und Legenden der südamerikanischen Urvölker und ihre Beziehungen zu denen Nordamerikas und der Alten Welt*. Berlin: A. Asher & Co.

Emlen, Nicholas Q. 2017. Perspectives on the Quechua–Aymara contact relationship and the lexicon and phonology of Pre-Proto-Aymara. *International Journal of American Linguistics* 83.307–40.

Englert, Sebastián. 1936. Lengua y literatura araucanas. *Anales de la Facultad de Filosofía y Educación* 1.62–190.

Febrés, Andrés. 1765. *Arte de la lengua general del Reyno de Chile*. Lima: Calle de la Encarnación.

Fernández Garay, Ana V., María Catrileo, and Mary Ritchie Key. 2015. Mapudungun dictionary. In *The intercontinental dictionary series*, ed. by Mary Ritchie Key and Bernard Comrie. Leipzig: Max Planck Institute for Evolutionary Anthropology, <http://ids.clld.org> (last accessed August 16, 2021).

Gerzenstein, Ana. 1999. *Diccionario etno-lingüístico mak'á–español*. Buenos Aires: Instituto de Lingüística, Facultad de Filosofía y Letras, Universidad de Buenos Aires.

Granberry, Julian. 1993. *A grammar and dictionary of the Timucua Language*. 3rd edn. Tuscaloosa: The University of Alabama Press.

Green, Thomas Michael. 1999. *A lexicographic study of Ulwa*. Cambridge, MA: Massachusetts Institute of Technology, dissertation.

Guerra Eissmann, Ana María. 2015. Yagán dictionary. In *The intercontinental dictionary series*, ed. by Mary Ritchie Key and Bernard Comrie. Leipzig: Max Planck Institute for Evolutionary Anthropology, <http://ids.clld.org> (last accessed August 16, 2021).

Havestadt, Bernardus. 1777. *Chilidúgú sive res chilensis*. Münster: Aschendorff.

Haynie, Hannah, Claire Bowern, Patience Epps, Jane Hill, and Patrick McConvell. 2014. Wanderwörter in languages of the Americas and Australia. *Ampersand* 1.1–18.
Hovdhaugen, Even. 2000. A loanword from Mapudungun in Mochica? In *Essays in honour of Arne Skjølsvold, 75 Years*, ed. by Paul Wallin and Helen Martinsson-Wallin, 133–8. Oslo: The Kon-Tiki Museum, Institute for Pacific Archaeology and Cultural History.
Imbelloni, José. 1928. La première chaine isoglossématique océano-américaine: le nom des haches lithiques. In *Festschrift/Publication d'hommage offerte au P. W. Schmidt: 76 sprachwissenschaftliche, ethnologische, religionswissenschaftliche, prähistorische und andere Studien/Recueil de 76 études de linguistique, d'ethnologie, de science religieuse, de préhistoire et autres*, ed. by Wilhelm Koppers, 324–35. Vienna: Mechitharisten-Congregations-Buchdruckerei.
Jakway, Martha. [1987] 2008. *Vocabulario huambisa*. (Serie Lingüística Peruana, 24.) Lima: Summer Institute of Linguistics, <http://repositorio.cultura.gob.pe/handle/CULTURA/472> (last accessed August 16, 2021).
Jolkesky, Marcelo Pinho De Valhery. 2010. *Reconstrução fonológica e lexical do Proto-Jê meridional*. Campinas: Universidade Estadual de Campinas master's thesis.
Jolkesky, Marcelo Pinho De Valhery. 2016. *Estudo arqueo-ecolinguístico das terras tropicais sul-americanas*. Brasília: Universidade de Brasília dissertation.
Kaufman, Terrence S., with John Justeson. 2003. Preliminary Mayan etymological dictionary, <http://www.famsi.org/reports/01051/pmed.pdf> (last accessed August 16, 2021).
Key, Mary Ritchie. 2015. Kaingáng dictionary. In *The intercontinental dictionary series*, ed. by Mary Ritchie Key and Bernard Comrie. Leipzig: Max Planck Institute for Evolutionary Anthropology, <http://ids.clld.org> (last accessed August 16, 2021).
Kohlberger, Martin. 2020. *A grammatical description of Shiwiar*. Amsterdam: Landelijke Onderzoekschool Taalwetenschap.
Lenz, Rodolfo. 1895–7. *Estudios araucanos: materiales para el estudio de la lengua, la literatura y las costumbres de los indios mapuche o araucanos*. (Anales de la Universidad de Chile, 97.) Santiago de Chile: Imprenta Cervantes.
León, Leonardo. 1983. Expansión inca y resistencia indígena en Chile, 1470–1536. *Revista Chungará* 10.95–115.
Loncon Antileo, Elisa del Carmen. 2017. *El poder creativo de la lengua mapudungun y la formación de neologismos*. Leiden: Leiden University dissertation.
Lucca, Manuel de. 1983. *Diccionario aymara–castellano, castellano–aymara*. La Paz: Comisión de Alfabetización y Literatura en Aymara.
Machoni de Cerdeña, Antonio. 1732. *Arte y vocabulario de la lengua lule y tonocoté, part 2: vocabulario de la lengua toocoté y lule*. Madrid: Herederos de Juan García Infanzón.
Margery Peña, Enrique. 1989. *Diccionario cabécar–español, español–cabécar*. San José: Editorial de la Universidad de Costa Rica.
Meira, Sérgio. 2017. Lexical reconstruction in Cariban: What we don't know and would like to. Paper presented at International Workshop: Socio-Cosmologies in the Isthmo–Colombian Area; Toward an Understanding of Relationships

among Chibchan and Neighboring Cultures and Languages, January 25–27, 2017, Collegium de Lyon.

Mello, Antônio Augusto Souza. 2000. *Estudo histórico da família lingüística Tupí-Guaraní: aspectos fonológicos e lexicais*. Florianópolis: Universidade Federal de Santa Catarina dissertation.

Menghin, Osvaldo. 1962. *Estudios de prehistoria Araucana*. Acta Praehistorica 3.49–120.

Middendorf, Ernst W. 1892. *Die einheimischen Sprachen Perus, vol. 6: Das Muchik oder die Chimu-Sprache; mit einer Einleitung über die Culturvölker, die gleichzeitig mit den Inkas und Aimaràs in Südamerika lebten, und einem Anhang über die Chibcha-Sprache*. Leipzig: F. A. Brockhaus.

Moesbach, Ernesto Wilhelm de. 1930. *Vida y costumbres de los indígenas araucanos en la segunda mitad del siglo XIX, presentadas en la autobiografía del indígena Pascual Coña*. Santiago de Chile: Imprenta Cervantes.

Moesbach, Ernesto Wilhelm de. 1962. *Idioma mapuche*. Padre Las Casas, Chile: Imprenta y Editorial 'San Francisco'.

Nikulin, Andrey. 2015. *On the genetic unity of Jê–Tupí–Karib*. Moscow: Lomonosov Moscow State University master's thesis.

Nikulin, Andrey. 2020 *Proto-Macro-Jê: um estudo reconstrutivo*. Brasília: Universidade de Brasília dissertation.

Overall, Simon E. 2018. *A Grammar of Aguaruna (Iiniá Chicham)*. (Mouton Grammar Library, 68.) Berlin/Boston: de Gruyter Mouton.

Pache, Matthias. 2007. *Der Fuchs als Tricksterfigur in den Anden: Grenzgänger und Vermittler zwischen Gegensätzen*. Bonn: Rheinische Friedrich-Wilhelms-Universität Bonn master's thesis.

Pache, Matthias. 2012. The fox in the Andes: An alternative interpretation of the trickster. *Anthropos* 107.481–96.

Pache, Matthias. 2013. Surprise!... and its encoding in Kamsá and other languages of western South America. In *Wege im Garten der Ethnologie. Zwischen dort und hier: Festschrift für María Susana Cipolletti*, ed. by Hanna Heinrich and Harald Grauer, 203–21. (Collectanea Instituti Anthropos, 46.) Sankt Augustin: Academia.

Pache, Matthias. 2014. Lexical evidence for pre-Inca language contact of Mapudungun (Mapuche) with Quechuan and Aymaran. *Journal of Language Contact*, 7.345–79.

Pache, Matthias. 2018a. Lengua X: An Andean puzzle. *International Journal of American Linguistics* 84.265–85.

Pache, Matthias. 2018b. *Contributions to Chibchan historical linguistics*. Leiden: Leiden University dissertation.

Pache, Matthias, Søren Wichmann, and Mikhail Zhivlov. 2016. Words for "dog" as a diagnostic of language contact in the Americas. In *Language contact and change in the Americas: Studies in honor of Marianne Mithun*, ed. by Andrea Berez-Kroeker, Diane Hintz, and Carmen Jany, 385–409. (Studies in Language Companion Series, 173.) Amsterdam/Philadelphia: John Benjamins.

Parker, Gary J. 1969. *Ayacucho Quechua grammar and dictionary*. The Hague/Paris: Mouton.

Parker, Stephen G., with Gregorio Orbe Caro and Alfonso Patow Chota. 1987. *Kana acha'taka ijnachale kana chamekolo: vocabulario y textos chamicuro*. (Comunidades y Culturas Peruanas, 21.) Lima/Yarinacocha: Ministerio de Educación, Instituto Lingüístico de Verano.

Payne, David L. 1991. A classification of Maipuran (Arawakan) languages based on shared lexical retentions. In *Handbook of Amazonian languages*, ed. by Desmond C. Derbyshire and Geoffrey K. Pullum, vol. 3, 355–499. Berlin/New York: Mouton de Gruyter.

Ramírez, José Miguel. 1990. Transpacific contacts: The Mapuche connection. *Rapa Nui Journal* 4.53–5.

Ringmacher, Mannfred, and Ute Tintemann (eds). 2011. *Wilhelm von Humboldt: Südamerikanische Grammatiken*. Paderborn/Munich/Vienna/Zurich: Ferdinand Schöningh.

Rosat Pontacti, Adalberto A. 2004. *Diccionario enciclopédico quechua–castellano del mundo andino*. Cochabamba: Verbo Divino.

Salas, Adalberto. 1992. *El mapuche o araucano: fonología, gramática y antología de cuentos*. Madrid: MAPFRE.

Santo Thomas, Domingo de. 1560. *Lexicon, o vocabulario de la lengua general del Perú*. Valladolid: Francisco Fernández de Córdova.

Seelwische, José. 1980. *Diccionario nivacle–castellano*. Mariscal Estigarribia, Chaco, Paraguay: UCNSA.

Seelwische, José, and Nélida N. Stell. 2015. Nivaclé dictionary. In *The intercontinental dictionary series*, ed. by Mary Ritchie Key and Bernard Comrie. Leipzig: Max Planck Institute for Evolutionary Anthropology, <http://ids.clld.org> (last accessed August 16, 2021).

Smeets, Ineke. 2008. *A Mapuche grammar*. (Mouton Grammar Library, 41.) Berlin/New York: Mouton de Gruyter.

Steinen, Karl von den. 1886. *Durch Central-Brasilien: Expedition zur Erforschung des Schingú im Jahre 1884*. Leipzig: F. A. Brockhaus.

Steward, Julian H. 1949. South American cultures: An interpretative summary. In *Handbook of South American Indians, vol. 5: The comparative ethnology of South American Indians*, ed. by Julian H. Steward, 669–772. (Smithsonian Institution, Bureau of American Ethnology, Bulletin 143.) Washington, DC: United States Government Printing Office.

Swadesh, Morris. 1957. *Términos de parentesco comunes entre tarasco y zuñi*. (Cuadernos del Instituto de Historia, Serie Antropológica, 3.) Mexico City: Universidad Nacional Autónoma de México.

Tornello, Pablo José, Arturo Andres Roig, Nora Díaz, and Luis Aguirre. 2011. *Introducción al millcayac: idioma de los huarpes de Mendoza; textos de Luis de Valdivia*. Mendoza: Zeta.

Urban, Matthias. 2018. Maritime loanwords in languages of Pacific Meso- and South America? An explorative study. In *New perspectives on the peopling of the Americas*, ed. by Katerina Harvati, Gerhard Jäger, and Hugo Reyes-Centeno, 27–60. Tübingen: Kerns.

Valdivia, Luis de. 1606. *Arte y gramática general de la lengua que corre en todo el Reyno de Chile, con un vocabulario y confesionario*. Lima: Francisco del Canto.

Valdivia, Luis de. 1607. *Doctrina cristiana y catecismo en la lengua allentiac, que corre en la ciudad de S. Juan de la Frontera, con un confesionario, arte, y vocabulario breves*. Lima: Francisco del Canto.

Viegas Barros, José Pedro. 1992. La familia lingüística tehuelche. *Revista Patagónica* 12.39–46. Ushuaia.

Villena Araya, Belén. 2016. *Innovación léxica en mapudungún: genuinidad, productividad y planificación*. Barcelona: Universitat Pompeu Fabra dissertation.

Vilte Vilte, Julio. n.d. *Diccionario kunza–español, español–kunza: kunza, lengua del pueblo lickan antai o atacameño*. Santiago de Chile: Codelco.

Walker, Robert S., and Lincoln A. Ribeiro. 2011. Bayesian phylogeography of the Arawak expansion in lowland South America. *Proceedings of the Royal Society B* 278.2562–7.

Wichmann, Søren. 1995. *The relationship among the Mixe–Zoquean Languages of Mexico*. Salt Lake City: University of Utah Press.

Wipio Deicat, Gerardo. 2015. Aguaruna dictionary. In *The intercontinental dictionary series*, ed. by Mary Ritchie Key and Bernard Comrie. Leipzig: Max Planck Institute for Evolutionary Anthropology, <http://ids.clld.org> (last accessed August 16, 2021).

Wise, Mary R. 1999. Small language families and isolates in Peru. In *The Amazonian languages*, ed. by R. M. W. Dixon and Alexandra Y. Aikhenvald, 307–40. Cambridge: Cambridge University Press.

Zamponi, Raoul. 2020. Some precontact widespread lexical forms in the languages of Greater Amazonia. *International Journal of American Linguistics* 86.527–73.

Zúñiga, Fernando. 2000. *Mapudungun*. Munich: LINCOM EUROPA.

Zúñiga, Fernando. 2007. *Mapudungun: el habla mapuche*. Santiago de Chile: Centro de Estudios Públicos.

9

The Historical Linguistics and Archaeology of Ancient North America: "A Linguistic Look" at the Hopewell

Eve Okura Koller

1. Introduction

There are many examples of archaeological and linguistic evidence each corroborating hypotheses of the other discipline. Scholars have explored this relationship between archaeology and historical linguistics in the Americas, where much of what we know about diachronic language change prior to European contact has come from thorough documentation of daughter languages. This thorough documentation enables historical reconstructions in the absence of written documents for societies that had no known writing systems. Most of the Indigenous languages of North America fall into this category, including the languages of this chapter: Algonquian languages, Mobilian Jargon, and its lexifiers (for example, Natchez). Our knowledge of Algonquian language change stems from the documentation efforts of early scholars like Leonard Bloomfield (1946). Campbell and Kaufman (1976) determined that the archaeological civilization known as the Olmec included speakers of Mixe-Zoquean languages (see also Campbell 1997: 12). Aztec (Hill 2017), Mayan, and Andean archaeological findings have also been connected to known language families, and are discussed further in Section 2. For some reason that remains unexplained, the ancient archaeology of North America has received less public attention than have the ancient histories and archaeology of Mesoamerica and South America. However, some of the ancient civilizations of Mesoamerica and adjacent regions in southern North America—for example, Aztec, Maya, and Zapotec—were contemporaneous with the complex interaction spheres of North America, including the Adena, Hopewell, and the Cahokia (Townsend 2004: 12). While extensive valuable scholarship has been done on the historical linguistics of North America (Goddard 1996; Campbell 1997; Mithun 1999), and the archaeology of North America (Theler and Boszhardt 2003; Carr and Case 2005; Spence and Fryer 2005; McCoy et al. 2017), there has yet to be much discussion attempting to connect the two fields.

Denny (1989: 91) proposed that speakers of Algonquian languages were connected to the mound-builder archaeological sites in the Northeast of North America. He cites Goddard (Denny 1989: 92) as proposing Proto-Algonquian to have split approximately 1000–500 BCE (Denny 1989: 91). This would place Proto-Algonquian speakers at the time of the Middle Woodland Hopewell. Drechsel (1997) has been one of the few to engage in this important discussion. He proposed that Mobilian Jargon, a trade language of North America, was originally spoken in pre-European contact situations (1997: 292). Drechsel observed that the locations where Mobilian Jargon was historically spoken coincided with archaeological sites of the Cahokia, also known as the "Mound Builders," suggesting that Mobilian Jargon was a trade language of the Cahokia (1997: 292). He also noted that Central Algonquian languages likely had a more significant role in the lexicon of the trade language historically. Archaeological evidence supports Drechsel's proposal (Drechsel 1997: 286–309).

Little scholarly discussion has attempted to connect languages with the earlier Hopewell archaeological complex of the Middle Woodland period. In this chapter, it is proposed that speakers of Central Algonquian languages[1] were one of the linguistic groups involved in the Hopewell interaction sphere, which was most likely a multilingual network.

In the Americas, one of the prominent connections of linguistic identity to an ancient archaeological culture was that of the Olmec. In "A linguistic look at the Olmecs,"[2] Campbell and Kaufman demonstrated that:

> the archaeological Olmecs, at least in part, were speakers of Mixe-Zoquean languages. The hypothesis is supported by not only geographical and temporal correlation, but by Mixe-Zoquean loan words in other Mesoamerican languages, many of which refer to things diagnostic of the Mesoamerican culture area. Also the cultural inventory revealed in Proto-Mixe-Zoquean vocabulary provides additional support. (Campbell and Kaufman 1976: 80)

Likewise, this chapter hypothesizes that the archaeological Hopewell, at least in part, were speakers of Central Algonquian languages. In addition, Central Algonquian loanwords in other North American languages refer to "things diagnostic" of the Hopewell interaction sphere. Archaeological, linguistic, geographic, and genetic evidence are presented to support this hypothesis.

2. The tradition of archaeology and historical linguistics in the Americas

There is a tradition of connecting languages and/or language families to the archaeological record across various cultures in the Americas, primarily in southern North America, Mesoamerica, and South America. These include the Olmecs, Aztec, Maya, Andean, and Cahokia.

2.1 Olmec

Campbell and Kaufman noted that:

> The geographical distribution of speakers of Mixe-Zoquean (henceforth MZ) languages corresponds closely to that of the Olmec archaeological sites ... suggesting as a hypothesis for further investigation that the archaeological Olmecs, at least in part, may have been speakers of Mixe-Zoquean languages. (Campbell and Kaufman 1976: 80)

The idea that the Olmecs may have involved Mixe-Zoquean speakers was first proposed by Terrence Kaufman (1969, 1973, 1974; Campbell and Kaufman 1976). Campbell and Kaufman provide convincing linguistic evidence supporting the case. In the archaeological record, they note, it is clear that the Olmecs had a significant cultural influence over a wide geographic area throughout Mesoamerica (1976: 81). It is presumed that items unique to the Olmec culture or predominantly associated with Olmec culture would be borrowed by other languages.

> The Mixe-Zoquean speakers were the inventors of the Mesoamerican calendar and hieroglyphic writing, and Mixe-Zoquean has recently been shown to be the language of the Epi-Olmec writing system associated with the La Mojarra stela (Justeson and Kaufman 1993). Campbell and Kaufman presented some reconstructed Mixe-Zoquean vocabulary, finding the cultural inventory reflected in it to be consistent with that revealed in the archaeology of that period, and they identified Mixe-Zoquean loanwords in many other Mesoamerican languages. (Campbell 1997: 162)

Campbell and Kaufman (1976) provide fifty loanwords of Mixe-Zoquean origin borrowed by other Mesoamerican languages. These loanwords were determined based on etymology or morphological complexity, geographical and ecological clues, cognates, semantic domains, and phonology. They point out that typically when two or more languages share a word, if it is morphologically complex in one language and monomorphemic in another or the other languages, the language in which it is morphologically complex is the source language. For example, *tsunami* in English is monomorphemic, whereas in Japanese *tsu-nami* literally means "harbor" + "wave," revealing Japanese as its etymological source. Words for plants, animals, or minerals that are native to one area but not to another would more likely originate from the language spoken in the area with that ecology. If there are cognates for a word in several related languages and in one unrelated language, the source language was probably the ancestral language of the sister languages with cognate forms (Campbell and Kaufman 1976: 83). Lexical items containing aberrant phonological or morphological features relative to the rest of the language are likely borrowings. Returning to the example of the word *tsunami*, a word-initial *ts* cluster is atypical of native English and is common in Japanese, further clearly identifying it as a loan from Japanese to English.

2.2 Aztec

Through linguistic scholarship in combination with archaeology, it is estimated that the Aztecan archaeological culture involved forty or more languages (Hill 2017: 129). In addition, the existence of a Nahuatl lingua franca spoken throughout the empire is known from historical documents (Hill 2017).

2.3 Maya

A multidisciplinary approach has also been used to reconstruct Mayan ancient history. As Kaufman stated: "historical-comparative linguistic, archaeological, and ethnohistorical studies may be integrated to provide a fuller reconstruction of the culture history of a particular area than each could independently" (Kaufman 1976: 101). He also points out that historical linguistic work must "be fitted into a broad historical framework involving places, objects, time, and all the kinds of inferences of which historical disciplines are capable" (Kaufman 1976: 102). From this multifaceted approach, he notes that Cholan was the "one language group" in the "Maya region" which "had vastly more lexical and phonetic influence than any other" (Kaufman 1976: 113). While Kaufman demonstrates a more detailed reconstruction of ancient Maya movement and locations of particular varieties than will be done in this chapter for Middle Woodland peoples in North America, the approach is similar in an attempt to ground the historical linguistics of Eastern North America in time and physical space.

2.4 Andean

Beresford-Jones and Heggarty (2012) focus on the archaeology and linguistics of the Andes to create a fuller picture of the past. They also mention the role of genetic research in retracing migrations (Beresford-Jones and Heggarty 2012: 2). Beresford-Jones and Heggarty (2012) refer to an integration of disciplines in order to gain greater understanding of ancient Andean peoples as a "much-needed conversation" (2012: 1).

2.5 Cahokia

Drechsel (1997) proposes a connection of Mobilian Jargon to the Cahokia.

> An elegant answer to this problem would be the use of Mobilian Jargon as the Mississippian lingua franca, whether in trade or other interlingual interactions ... The pidgin in some form comparable to attestations in early documents would have suited well as a contact medium among pre-Columbian Mississippians speaking different languages, and could have served in other contexts than just those mentioned. As attested historically, Mobilian Jargon would clearly qualify in this role if one could take the listing of Choctaw and Muskogee words related to subsistence, economy, sociopolitical organization, and world view by Mochon (1972) as a reliable linguistic indicator for the Mississippian Complex. Out of the total of 108 terms in Mochon's list, the pidgin's historically attested vocabulary (with a smaller number of entries than the other languages except Ofo) could match a majority of words and in

many instances with two or multiple entries—at least seventy-six corresponding or equivalent terms, in contrast to the lower numbers of comparable entries in Osage (seventy), Ofo (thirty-nine), and Biloxi (forty-six) as listed by Mochon (1972: 483–98). (Drechsel 1997: 292)

The vocabulary of the contributing languages to Mobilian Jargon aligns with characteristics of the Mississippian Complex. Here Drechsel specifies the roles of Chocktaw and Muskogee in Mobilian Jargon. Section 4 contains a discussion of Algonquian-derived parts of the Mobilian Jargon lexicon that were noted by Drechsel.

3. An interdisciplinary approach

As with the Olmec, Aztec, Maya, and Andean examples in Section 2, this chapter uses archaeology, genetic data, geography, historical linguistics, and ethnography to connect linguistic groups with the archaeological Middle Woodland Hopewell interaction sphere. This chapter is intended to be a preliminary exploration to open further discussion on the linguistics of the Middle Woodland Hopewell. The archaeological data in this study are derived primarily from Turff and Carr (2005) and Spence and Fryer (2005). Genetic data come from Mills (2003). Linguistic data come from Goddard (1994), Campbell (1997), Drechsel (1997), and Mithun (1999).

While this chapter discusses a few other Indigenous languages of North America, much of the discussion involves Central Algonquian languages. It is important to keep in mind that these are not necessarily a genetic subgroup, but the similarities demonstrated between these languages may have ensued due to prolonged contact (Mithun 1999: 333). The term is used here for convenience to refer to this group of languages. The fact that shared similarities across Central Algonquian languages are a result of contact rather than genetic subgrouping further supports the hypothesis that speakers of historical forms of Central Algonquian languages were involved in the Hopewell interaction sphere. This is consistent with the level of contact needed to produce the level of linguistic similarity these languages exhibit. The genetic subgroups of the Algonquian language family are displayed in Figure 9.1.

4. Who were the "mound builders"?

The term "mound builders" is somewhat ambiguous, because various ancient North American peoples from more than one geographic region and more than one archaeological time period built prominent mounds. These include the Adena (approximately 800 BCE to 100 CE), the Hopewell (approximately 100 CE to 500 CE), and the Cahokia (approximately 800 CE to 1500 CE) (Hall 2000: 8; Mills 2003: 15).

4.1 Linguistic evidence

Linguistic and geographic evidence suggest that Mobilian Jargon was used by the Cahokia. In addition, Mobilian Jargon has linguistic connections to Eastern and Central Algonquian languages. The type of lexical items from Eastern and Central

Algonquian (Algonkian)
    Blackfoot *Montana, Alberta*
    Cheyenne *Wyoming*
    Arapaho (Group)
        Arapaho Wyoming, *Oklahoma*
        Atsina [moribund] *Montana*
        Besawunena
        Nawathinehena
    Menominee (Menomini) *Wisconsin*
    Ojibwa-Potawatomi(-Ottawa) *Michigan, Ontario*; Algonquin (Algonkin), Salteaux *Ontario, Quebec*
    Fox
        Fox *Iowa, Oklahoma, Kansas*
        Sauk
        Kickapoo *Kansas, Oklahoma, Texas, Coahuila (Mexico)*
        †Mascouten
    Shawnee *Oklahoma*
    Miami-Illinois [awakening] *Oklahoma*
    Cree-Montagnais(-Naskapi) *eastern Canada*
    Eastern Algonquian
        Micmac *Nova Scotia, New Brunswick, Quebec, Newfoundland*
        Abenaki(-Penobscot) *Quebec, Maine*
            Eastern Abenaki [moribund] *Quebec*
            Western Abenaki [moribund] *New England*
        Narragansett
        Powhatan
        Delaware (Munsee, Unami) [moribund] *Oklahoma*
        †Massachusett *Massachusetts*
        Maliseet(-Passamaquoddy) *Maine, New Brunswick*
        †Nanticoke-Conoy
        †Etchemin *Maine*
        † "Loup B" *New England*
        †Christanna Alogonquian *Virginia, North Carolina*

Goddard 1972, 1979a, 1994c.

Figure 9.1 The Algonquian language family

Source: Adapted from Campbell (1997: 153).

Algonquian languages into Mobilian Jargon also suggest ancient trade (see Figure 9.2 for a map of the Algonquian languages).

4.1.1 Mobilian Jargon

Drechsel highlights linguistic evidence that Mobilian Jargon was spoken as a trade language by the Cahokia pre-European contact.

> Linguistically, Mobilian Jargon closely matched the sociopolitical integration of paramount chiefdoms—by nature dynamic and flexible, but also rather fragile societies; the pidgin provided a common medium, while allowing its speakers to maintain their native languages and with them their social identities, just as in colonial and recent periods. (Drechsel 1997: 294)

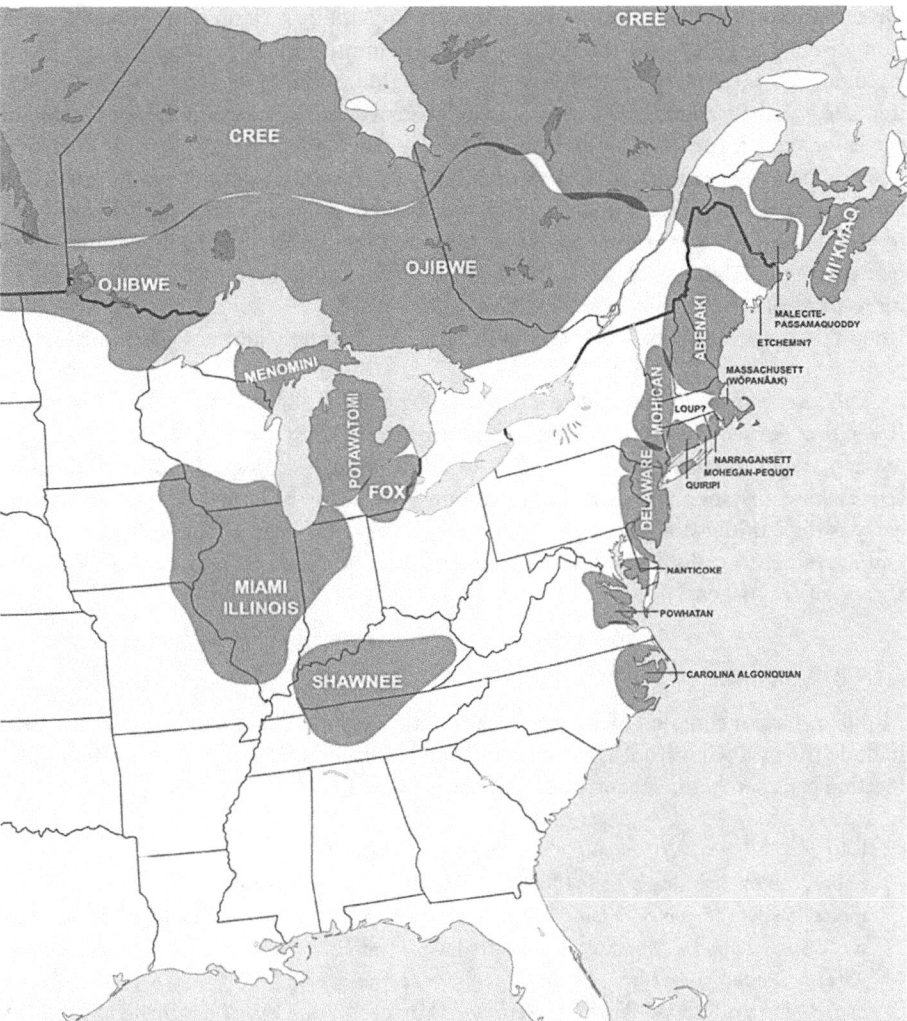

Figure 9.2 Historical locations of Central Algonquian languages superimposed on twenty-first century states and provinces

Note: Languages along the East Coast are Eastern Algonquian languages. The original version of this map is credited to Noahedits at https://commons.wikimedia.org/wiki/File:Algonquian_language_map_with_states_and_provinces.svg. It is licensed under CC BY-SA 4.0, https://creativecommons.org/licenses/by-sa/4.0/deed.en. Adaptations made by the author, Eve Koller, to the map include changing it to grayscale and cropping off the left and top of the image, including cropping out Western Algonquian languages.

Drechsel refers to the Algonquian lexicon in Mobilian Jargon as "loan-words" (Drechsel 1997: 83). Campbell (2018: personal communication) notes that if viewed as a pidgin, the vocabulary of Mobilian Jargon would be completely composed of lexical items from other languages, so rather than "loan-words," they would be the lexicon of the language with an etymology from other languages.

Pending better comparative data or actual historical records, the most convincing explanation is the direct transmission of words from adjoining Algonquian languages in the Great Lakes area into Mobilian Jargon. What speaks for such a route is the fact that most Algonquian loans in Mobilian Jargon apparently derived from one or more Central Algonquian languages and, in a few instances, specifically from Miami-Illinois, whose speakers were the immediate northern neighbors of Southeastern Native Americans (Drechsel 1997: 95).

This pre-European language exchange is logically probable due to the Mississippi River that served as a type of water highway connecting seemingly distant groups, making travel much more convenient. In addition, archaeological evidence demonstrates long distance traveling for obtaining goods (for example, silver), at least as early as the Middle Woodland period, far before any European contact. Physical travel and movement would likely result in interpersonal interactions between speakers of a variety of languages.

4.1.2 Algonquian words in Mobilian Jargon

Mobilian Jargon contains many words originating from Algonquian languages. These include the following from Drechsel (1997). Drechsel's spelling conventions and formatting are used here, except where otherwise noted.

> 'baby', 'child': *papo(s)* ("papoose" (Dormon)) ~ *papoš*
> 'bobcat', 'lynx', 'wildcat': ‡*pešo* ("pishu" (Gatschet); "pishu" (Read))
> 'money', 'silver': ~ *šonak* ~ *šone*; Ojibwa *šuniawa:bi:k* (*zhooniyaawaabik*), *šunia* (*zhooniyaa*)[3]
> 'moccasin, shoe' ‡*māgasin* (reconstructed) Cree *maskisin*, Menomini *mahkɛ:sen*, Ojibwa *makkisin*, Penobscot *maksən*, Miami-Illinois ‡*mahkisini* ('shoe')
> 'eye': Ojibwa *niški:nšik*; Powhatan *neski:nsek* 'my eye' (Haas 1958:245;[4] Siebert 1975:338); Munsee *nəski:nčəkw* 'my eye' (Goddard 1982:45); Delaware *nə'škinkw* 'my eye';
> 'hominy' ('sagamité'): cf. Nipissing *–agami*. (Drechsel 1997: 87–91)

Others included "pecan nut": ‡*pakan*, "persimmon": ‡*peakemena*, and "hominy" *sakamete* sacamité.

Two of these lexical items are of particular interest: words for "silver" and "eye." The Mobilian Jargon term for "silver" or "money" can be traced to Algonquian words for silver and money. Although there has been some difference of opinion as to the origin of the word and some have argued for European borrowings (Drechsel 1997: 88), there had to have been native words for silver pre-European contact as there were already silver mines and silver cultural objects. Archaeological evidence reveals that ancient peoples involved in the Hopewell trade network were also involved in silver mining (see Section 4.2.3). Hopewellian people along the Mississippi and throughout the Southeast traveled as far north as Michigan and Canada for raw copper and silver to manufacture their own cultural silver products (Turff and Carr 2005: 675, 692). Ojibwa was traditionally spoken in these areas. It would be logical for speakers of other languages to adopt the word for silver from the language that was spoken at the location of the silver mines, here possibly Ojibwa or another closely related Algonquian language (which then over time may have semantically broadened to also refer to money following European contact).

The Mobilian Jargon word for "eye" also appears to have been derived from Algonquian languages. It seems unusual that a people would borrow a basic vocabulary word, such as a body part that would be referred to with relatively high frequency. If Mobilian Jargon were a pre-European contact trade language between the mound-building peoples, it would make sense for the term for "eye" to be borrowed from the primary influencers of mound-building culture. Some archaeological Moundville artifacts depict an eye icon or motif in unexpected contexts, suggesting the eye was deictic, and that there may have been a cultural symbolic meaning conveyed by the borrowed word for "eye" as opposed to the physical everyday "eye" in the speakers' native language. For example, an artifact known as the "Rattlesnake Disk" depicts an eye on the palm of a hand at the center of the disk, bordered by bound serpents (see Townsend 2004: 166–7). Eye themes were common in Mississippian rock art (Diaz-Granados 2004: 142).

Drechsel also proposes that the lexical composition of Mobilian Jargon may have shifted over time, having been more Algonquian-heavy in earlier times.

> What complicates the assessment of Algonquian loan-words in Mobilian Jargon is the fact that, as a pidgin, it could substantially change the composition of its vocabulary over time, depending on the speakers' first languages, their sociopolitical status, and their influence on the pidgin. Possibly, Algonquian Indians once had a greater impact on Mobilian Jargon, with additional words from their native languages in its vocabulary, than the evidence indicates today. As the Algonquians' impact waned over time, speakers of other languages could easily have replaced Algonquian loans with equivalent words of their own by partial relexification. For this reason, some early Algonquian loans need not have survived in modern recordings of Mobilian Jargon, just as but a few words of Chickasaw origin endured. (Drechsel 1997: 98)

The types of vocabulary words from Algonquian languages in Mobilian Jargon also suggest a possible Hopewellian cultural connection, which will be explored further in Section 4.2.

4.2 Archaeological evidence

There is a variety of archaeological evidence that could suggest (1) that, as Drechsel (1997) proposed, Mobilian Jargon was likely a pre-European mixed language used as a trade language between speakers of different Native American languages; (2) that Mobilian Jargon may have been a descended and altered form of an earlier trade language used by the Hopewell; and (3) that speakers of Algonquian languages (particularly Eastern Algonquian and Central Algonquian languages, although not a genetic subgroup) were involved in the Hopewell interaction sphere.

4.2.1 Mobilian Jargon and Cahokia

Drechsel (1997) comments on the linguistic nature of the later mound builders (900 CE onwards). He proposes that a regional lingua franca would be necessary for the complex interactions between a variety of language groups (see Section 2.5). This is supported by the fact that the geographic locations where Mobilian Jargon was traditionally spoken coincide with the Mississippian mound-builder sites.

4.2.2 Burial mounds and the influence of Hopewell on the Cahokia

From an archaeological perspective, the Hopewell seem to have been influenced by the earlier Adena peoples. Likewise, the Cahokia seem to have been influenced by the Hopewell, as they practiced a similar culture of constructing monumental mounds. Even stronger evidence now exists, with DNA linking the Adena to the Hopewell and the Hopewell to the Cahokia (Mills 2003). If the Cahokia spoke Mobilian Jargon, and they were related to the Hopewell both culturally (as evidenced archaeologically) and genetically (which has also been established), then it would be reasonable to think that a similar trade language was used during the period of the Hopewell—perhaps even an earlier, more Algonquian-heavy form of Mobilian Jargon. As with much of what we "know" about history, this cannot be proven, but it can be strongly supported with archaeological, linguistic, and ethnographic evidence.

4.2.3 Hopewell silver trading

The Hopewell archaeological record from the Middle Woodland period includes silver artifacts. Spence and Fryer tested and sourced the silver from Middle Woodland period artifacts from the Royal Ontario Museum, Field Museum of Natural History, Ohio Historical Center, and the Peabody Museum of Archaeology and Ethnology (Spence and Fryer 2005: 714). The provenience of the over fifty artifacts consisted of various Middle Woodland sites, including (1) Terra Ceia in Florida; (2) Mandeville and (3) Tunacunnhee in Georgia; (4) Esch, (5) Mound City, (6) Marietta, (7) Turner, (8) Hopewell, (9) Robinson, (10) Fort Ancient, (11) North Benton, and (12) Seip in Ohio; (13) Knight and (14) Liverpool in Illinois; (15) Irvine in Pennsylvania; (16) Pharr in Mississippi; (17) McRae in Louisiana; (18) Squawkie Hill and (19) Lewiston in New York; (19) Converse in Michigan; (20) Pachuca in Mexico; (21) Cameron's Point and (22) LeVesconte in Ontario. Object types included earspools, beads, panpipes, blended sheets, buttons, sheet fragments, pendants, and an inclusion in copper. These silver artifacts were analyzed with inductively coupled plasma mass spectrometry (ICP-MS) (Spence and Fryer 2005: 719).

Only the silver from artifacts from Terra Ceia in Florida did not match any of the silver mines tested in this study. Silver from the remaining artifacts were sourced to two ancient silver mines, both from the north: Keweenaw, Michigan and Cobalt,

Ontario, both generally geographic areas where Central Algonquian languages have traditionally been spoken. Silver from sites in the Tunacunnhee and Mandeville areas in Georgia are solely from the Cobalt, Ontario mine (Spence and Fryer 2005: 731). However, some of the sites between Cobalt and Tunacunnhee/Mandeville contain silver solely from Keweenaw. It appears that some Hopewell people may have traveled to Cobalt, Ontario to procure silver directly for themselves, and returned to the Southeast. Spence and Fryer also note a "long lapse in its [silver] use throughout the Late Woodland period," observing a cessation of silver use after the Middle Woodland period (Spence and Fryer 2005: 724).

The regions where these ancient silver mines were located, mines that supplied the Hopewell complex with its silver, were historically Algonquian-speaking areas (Figure 9.3). For example, Ojibwa is a Central Algonquian language historically spoken in Ontario and Michigan, among other areas (for example, Wisconsin, Minnesota, southern Manitoba, and southern Saskatchewan) (Mithun 1999: 222, 334); Potawatomi, another Central Algonquian language, was historically spoken in Michigan (Mithun 1999: 334). In the case of the Olmecs, Mixe-Zoquean vocabulary was borrowed by other languages, showing that they were the social influencers of the region, and that the Olmecs were at least in part likely speakers of Mixe-Zoquean languages. Likewise, the widespread borrowing of Central Algonquian loanwords across the vast Hopewell complex, including the word for silver, along with the fact that the sources of silver were located in Central Algonquian-speaking areas, strongly suggests that speakers of Central Algonquian languages were among those who participated in the Hopewell interaction sphere.

4.2.4 Middle Woodland panpipes

A "uniquely Hopewellian" (Turff and Carr 2005: 648 citing Seeman 1979: 327) category of artifacts were metal panpipes, found only in Middle Woodland period sites—not in any earlier or later periods. Turff (1997) analyzed 105 panpipes from fifty-five sites covering all of the major Hopewell. The geographic distribution of Hopewellian panpipes range from the Mississippi River to "western ... Appalachians, and from northern Wisconsin and south-central Ontario to the Gulf Coast" (Turff and Carr 2005: 650). Although there were more accessible copper sources from which Hopewellian people could have mined, copper used to manufacture Hopewellian panpipes primarily originated from the "Upper Great Lakes ... (Bastian 1961; Clark & Purdy 1982; Goad 1978, 1979; Rapp et al. 1990; Schroeder & Ruhl 1968)" and even though some copper from Southeast artifacts originated from the Southeast, "Upper Great Lakes copper predominates (8 or 14 panpipes [Goad 1978:136–148])" (Turff and Carr 2005: 689). According to Turff and Carr:

> It is possible that during the Middle Woodland period, Northeastern religious ideas such as those described above and Northeastern copper symbolism spread through various forms of Hopewellian interaction ... into the Southeast, later to be replaced by or fused with Southeastern concepts and symbolism evident in Mississippian art and historic lore. (Turff and Carr 2005: 675)

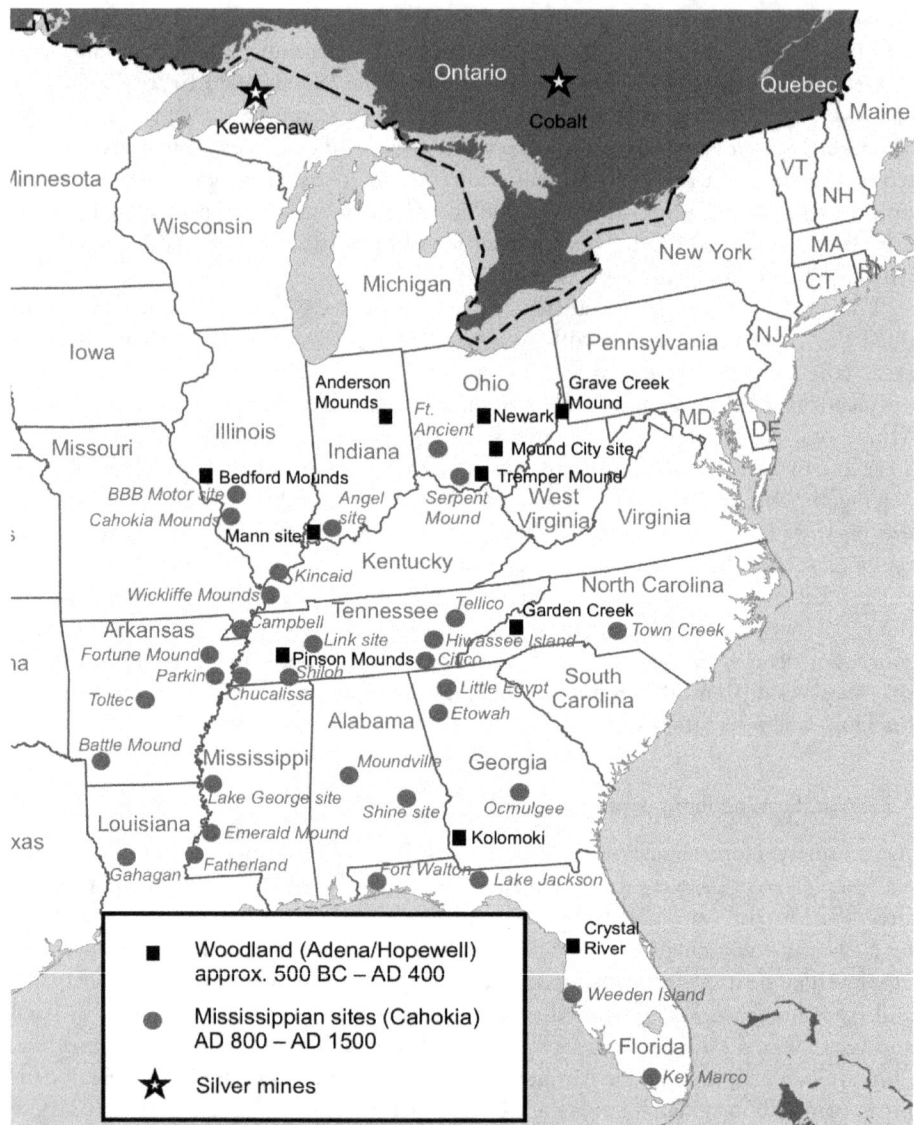

Figure 9.3 Map of Hopewell, Cahokia, and ancient silver mine sites

Note: The site locations are general approximations. The original map image was a textless political map of the USA and Canada and is credited to https://en.wikipedia.org/wiki/File:Map_of_USA.png, under the GNU license: https://www.gnu.org/licenses/fdl-1.3.en.html and CC BY-SA 3.0 https://creativecommons.org/licenses/by-sa/3.0/deed.en. Modifications made by the author, Eve Koller, consist of the addition of: the legend, site markers (squares, circles, and stars), and all text (state names and site names), as well as changing the map to grayscale. Hopewell and Cahokia site names and approximate locations are derived from the map in *Hero, Hawk, and Open Hand* (Townsend 2004: 13). The approximate locations of the silver mines are based on Spence and Fryer (2005).

They also note that "Hopewellian interregional exchange involved primarily raw materials and stylistic concepts and seldom finished goods" (Turff and Carr 2005: 692). This suggests that people from Ohio, the Southeast, and other regions traveled to the Upper Great Lakes region to trade for copper and silver which they brought back to their respective local regions to manufacture finished goods. "It is possible that copper, the concept of panpipes, and beliefs about the Horned Serpent all were brought back hand-in-hand from the Upper Great Lakes by Hopewellian people who journeyed there" (Turff and Carr 2005: 290).

4.2.5 Meteorite beads

Ancient beads found in Havana, a Hopewell site in Illinois, were sourced to Anoka, a meteorite fall site in Minnesota (McCoy et al. 2017). The chemical composition of the metal beads matched that of the meteorite in Anoka. In addition, the Anoka site is located along the Mississippi River, which connects to the Illinois River, along which the Havana site is located. The connecting rivers make it even more likely that there was direct travel between the two sites anciently (McCoy et al. 2017: 21).

4.3 Ethnographic findings

An earlier form of Natchez, one of the languages that compose Mobilian Jargon, was also likely spoken by participants in the Hopewell mound-building culture. Ethnographic evidence reveals that the Natchez traditionally used Middle Woodland Period burial mounds for their chiefs. The chief would be buried on the west end of a mound, facing east, his house would be burned to the ground, and they would build the next chief's house on top of it (Kent T. "Hutke" Fields 2017: personal communication). Some Natchez continue to return to the mounds annually to practice much of the same cultural traditions as their ancestors have done for centuries. The only significant difference between the way their ancestors practiced the culture and the way they currently practice the culture is that they no longer build mounds due to insufficient funding, human resources, and land (Kent T. "Hutke" Fields 2017: personal communication).

The geographic location of the Natchez people in Middle Woodland Hopewell mound areas, along with cultural practices related to the mounds, and ethnographic oral histories of ancestors having built the mounds, further solidify the link between the earlier archaeological Hopewell interaction sphere of the Middle Woodland Period with Natchez. In addition, the Natchez language is a contributor to Mobilian Jargon, likely a pre-European contact Native American trade language.

4.4 Genetic evidence

While genetics and language do not necessarily coincide—as genetically related people can and often do speak mutually unintelligible languages, and genetically unrelated people can and do speak the same language—there is mitochondrial DNA (mtDNA) data linking Adena people to the Hopewell (Mills 2003: 111, 137), and linking the Hopewell to the Cahokia (Mills 2003: 123). This genetic evidence reveals that at least some of the individuals in the Cahokia culture were descendants of some of those who were part of the Hopewell interaction sphere, who in turn were descended—at least in part—from Adena peoples. Archaeological evidence mentioned in Section 4.2.2 suggested that the Cahokia mound-builder culture was influenced by the earlier Hopewell complex. With additional DNA evidence we now know that some of the individuals in the Cahokia culture were also genetically—and not just culturally—related to the earlier Hopewell.

Furthermore, the Cahokia individuals who shared DNA with individuals from the Hopewell burial sites were presumed to be "high status" based on their type of burial (Mills 2003: 123). This suggests that Hopewell culture and ancestry were viewed as socially prestigious. Often socially prestigious languages are those that are adopted when two cultures interact, or are maintained when a people moves into a new area. Even if not preserved in entirety, contact languages borrow from languages viewed as prestigious, as has happened with French loanwords into English.[5] Long after migrations have moved people far from the land of the prestige culture and language, centuries after immediate language contact, much of the borrowed lexicon from the prestige language is maintained in the recipient language. These "high status" Cahokia individuals are logical vehicles for the transmission of cultural revitalization of Hopewell mound-building practices, although the temporal gap between the two remains a mystery.

5. Discussion

There is geographic, ethnographic, and linguistic evidence that the Cahokia spoke Mobilian Jargon (Drechsel 1997). In addition, there is archaeological and genetic data linking the Hopewell to the Cahokia. There is also significant archaeological evidence linking the Hopewell to traditionally Algonquian-speaking language areas, primarily areas where speakers of Central Algonquian languages lived.

Drechsel (1997) proposed that the role of the Algonquian lexicon in Mobilian Jargon may have been more significant in the past, but weakened over time. This is supported geographically and archaeologically, as the center of the Hopewell interaction sphere was further north. Later, the Cahokia center was further southeast. Artifacts found in the Southeast of North America were made of silver sourced to a mine in Cobalt, Ontario (Spence and Fryer 2005: 731). In addition, panpipes made from copper and silver from the north were no longer developed in the Late Woodland period (Turff and Carr 2005: 650; Spence and Fryer 2005: 724).[6] I argue that this loss of metal trading reveals weakening ties between the Southeast and northern Central Algonquian-speaking areas, which would reflect in decreasing amounts of Algonquian vocabulary in Southeast regional languages. The extensive traveling, mining, trading, and production occurring across a vast geographic range during the Hopewell culture suggest a multilingual society with some type of trade language or languages. If Mobilian Jargon were the remnant of a trade language of the Cahokia, it would be possible that the trade language of the Cahokia was also a remnant of a trade language of the Hopewell which had retained a few lexical items from its more Central-Algonquian influenced predecessor.

Regardless of whether Mobilian Jargon was a trade language of the Cahokia and a remnant of an earlier trade language, archaeological and linguistic evidence suggest that speakers of Central Algonquian languages were involved in the Hopewell interaction sphere. Speakers of Iroquoian languages and Natchez were also likely participants in the Hopewell culture, as evidenced by geography and ethnographic accounts (Kent T. "Hutke" Fields 2017: personal communication).

Most of the lexical items in Mobilian Jargon from Algonquian languages are primarily from Eastern and Central Algonquian languages. Although Central Algonquian languages do not form a genetic subgroup of Algonquian languages, they do share linguistic similarities due to language contact. However, the known geographic locations of some of the Central Algonquian languages do not account for the degree of linguistic similarity, suggesting prolonged and repeated language contact historically. Contact through trade networks in the Hopewell culture would account for the close linguistic similarities across the Central Algonquian languages that are attributed to language contact. This is consistent with the assertion that the similarities are due to contact rather than being members of a genetic subgroup.

6. Conclusion

Speakers of Algonquian languages were likely among those who participated in the Hopewell interaction sphere, and perhaps Eastern and Central Algonquian languages in particular. Central Algonquian languages may not compose a genetic subgroup, as it has been argued that their linguistic similarity is due to contact over time (Mithun 1999: 333). Being part of the Hopewell interaction sphere may have been the reason for the amount of contact that resulted in the current degree of linguistic similarity among the Central Algonquian languages. This is similar to Walworth's (2014) conclusion regarding Polynesian languages—that the Tahitic and Marquesic subgroups were not linguistic genetic subgroups, but that the seemingly shared innovations were a result of "waves of contact" and that "PCEP[7] developed as a wide-ranging interaction sphere, with Rapa Nui developing in isolation" (Walworth 2014: 270). They appeared to have split more recently, with a shorter time depth, and to be more closely genetically related because of linguistic similarities due to repeated, long term language contact. In addition to speakers of Eastern and Central Algonquian languages, Natchez speakers were also likely participants in the Hopewell interaction sphere, as suggested by geographic location, ethnographic evidence, and linguistic evidence (the role of Natchez in Mobilian Jargon) (Drechsel 1997). Other contributing languages to Mobilian Jargon may also have had speakers involved in the Hopewell complex, as perhaps Mobilian Jargon is a remnant of an even more ancient trade language that lost some Algonquian vocabulary over time as its center moved further southeast, gaining greater Muskogean linguistic influence during the Cahokia period.

Furthermore, descendants of Hopewellian speakers of Central Algonquian languages may have been the leaders in the Cahokian civilization. This proposal is supported by archaeological evidence that connects the prestigious burials in the later Southeastern burials with the Hopewell burials further north centuries earlier. This is also supported by linguistic evidence in which words were borrowed by Southeastern/

Muskogean languages from Algonquian, and the geographic distribution in which the appearance of ceremonial mounds moved southeastward over time.

This current hypothesis is not intended to be all-encompassing. Further research is necessary to arrive at a more definitive understanding of the linguistic nature of the Hopewell and the speakers of many languages and language families that likely participated in it. At this initial stage of hypothesizing, much more data are needed. Possibilities for future research that would inform various aspects of this question include: an ethnographic study across Central Algonquian tribes to determine if there are any oral traditions, cultural practices, and/or vocabulary related to the mounds and/or artifacts from the Hopewell interaction sphere; a more comprehensive survey of Algonquian borrowings in other Indigenous languages of eastern North America, and possibly historical attestations of loanwords in the other direction—from Natchez and Muskogean languages into Algonquian languages. When we limit our understanding of ancient peoples to being in isolation from other contemporaneous groups prior to European contact, we do them a great disservice. Ancient peoples were capable of long-distance travel across oceans and continents, as shown by archaeological evidence in North America.[8] This demonstrates that there was farther and more frequent distant travel and interaction than had previously been considered.

Notes

1. There is division on whether Central Algonquian languages constitute a linguistic subgroup or a linguistic subarea. Goddard (1994) and Mithun (1999) state that Central Algonquian is not a genetic linguistic subgroup. Proulx (2003) states that Central Algonquian languages do constitute a genetic linguistic subgroup.
2. The phrase, "A linguistic look," in the title of this chapter is derived from Campbell and Kaufman's 1976 paper.
3. *The Ojibwe People's Dictionary*, https://ojibwe.lib.umn.edu/main-entry/zhooni yaa-ni.
4. Haas 1958 proposed that Muskogean languages were genetically related to the Algonquian language family. Muskogean languages are the substrate languages for Mobilian Jargon. I propose that at least some of the participants of the Hopewell interaction sphere were speakers of Central Algonquian languages, and that Mobilian Jargon borrowed lexical items from Algonquian languages, rather than proposing a genetic relationship between Algonquian and Muskogean languages.
5. It is important to note here that I do not personally view any language as superior or inferior to another language. This is merely describing linguistic and social phenomena that are direct results of speakers' language attitudes.
6. "Temporally, all of the site components with panpipes belong to the Middle Woodland period" (Turff and Carr 2005: 650). Referring to silver, Spence and Fryer state: "The greatest obstacle is the long lapse in its use through the Late Woodland period" (2005: 724).
7. Proto-Central Eastern Polynesian.
8. Celestial navigation, also known as "wayfinding" in Oceania, is further evidence of the vast interaction spheres and deliberate long-distance travels of ancient peoples.

The Hōkūleʻa is a double-hulled canoe that was constructed using traditional Pacific Islander methods as an experiment to demonstrate that ancient Oceanic people were adept seafarers and could navigate accurately to islands across thousands of miles of ocean using purely traditional navigational methods (the stars, wind directions, birds, and so on). Knowledge of traditional Pacific Island celestial navigation had almost disappeared when Mau Piailug from Satawal Island of Micronesia taught these methods to Nainoa Thompson of Hawaiʻi. Mr. Thompson then taught a new generation of seafarers who have since been able to sail across the world solely using celestial navigation. Hawaiʻiloa was the predecessor canoe to the Hōkūleʻa. Due to deforestation in Hawaiʻi, no tree was large enough to construct a hull from a single trunk. SeAlaska (owned by the Tlingit, Haid, and Tsimshian tribes in Alaska) donated two trees for the building of these canoes to revitalize the practice. See: Polynesian Voyaging Society, <http://archive.hokulea.com/ike/kalai_waa/hawaiiloa.html> (last accessed August 24, 2021).

References

Bastian, Tyler. 1961. Trace element and metallographic studies of prehistoric copper artifacts in North America: A review. In *Lake Superior copper and the Indians: Miscellaneous studies of Great Lakes prehistory, anthropological papers*, ed. by James B. Griffin, 17.151–75. Ann Arbor, MI: University of Michigan, Museum of Anthropology.

Beresford-Jones, David, and Paul Heggarty. 2012. Introduction: Archaeology, linguistics, and the Andean past: A much-needed conversation. *Archaeology and Language in the Andes*. New York/Oxford: Oxford University Press.

Bloomfield, Leonard. 1946. Algonquian. In *Linguistic structures of Native America*, ed. by Harry Hojier, 6. New York: Viking Fund Publications in Anthropology.

Campbell, Lyle. 1997. *American Indian languages: The historical linguistics of Native North America*. Oxford: Oxford University Press.

Campbell, Lyle, and Terrence Kaufman. 1976. A linguistic look at the Olmecs. *American Antiquity* 41.80–9.

Carr, Christopher, and D. Troy Case (eds). 2005. *Gathering Hopewell: Society, ritual, and ritual interaction (interdisciplinary contributions to archaeology)*. Boston: Springer.

Clark, David, and Barbara Purdy. 1982. Early metallurgy in North America. In *Early pyrotechnology: The evolution of the first fire-using industries*, ed. by Theodore Wertime and Steven Wertime, 45–58. Washington, DC: Smithsonian Institution Press.

Denny, J. Peter. 1989. Algonquian connections to Salishan and Northeastern archaeology. In *Actes du Vintième Congrès des Algonquinistes (Papers of the Twentieth Algonquian Conference)*, ed. by William Cowan, 20.86–107. Ottawa: Carleton University.

Diaz-Granados, Carol. 2004. Marking stone, land, body, and spirit. In *Hero, hawk, and open hand*, ed. by Richard F. Townsend, 139–49. New Haven/London: Yale University Press.

Drechsel, Emanuel. 1997. *Mobilian jargon, Oxford studies in language contact*. Oxford: Clarendon Press.
Goad, Sharon iowa. 1978. *Exchange networks of the prehistoric southeastern United States*. Athens, GA: University of Georgia, Department of Anthropology unpublished dissertation.
Goad, Sharon iowa. 1979. Middle Woodland exchange in the prehistoric southeastern United States. In *Hopewell archaeology: The Chillicothe Conference*, ed. by David S. Brose and N'omi Greber, 239–46. Kent, OH: Kent State University Press.
Goddard, Ives. 1982. The historical phonology of Munsee. *International Journal of American Linguistics* 48(1).16–48.
Goddard, Ives. 1994. The west-to-east Cline in Algonquian dialectology. In *Actes du Vingt-Cinquième Congrès des Algonquinistes*, ed. by William Cowan, 187–211. Ottawa: Carleton University Press.
Goddard, Ives. 1996. *Handbook of North American Indians*, 17.290–323. Washington, DC: Smithsonian Institution Press.
Haas, Mary R. 1958. A new linguistic relationship in North America: Algonkian and the Gulf languages. *Southwestern Journal of Archaeology*. 14(3).231–64.
Hall, Robert L. 2000. Cahokia identity and interaction models of Cahokia Mississippian. In *Cahokia and the Hinterlands: Middle Mississippian Cultures of the Midwest*, ed. by Thomas E. Emerson and R. Barry Lewis, 3–34. Chicago: University of Chicago Press.
Hill, Jane. 2017. The languages of the Aztec Empire. *The Oxford handbook of the Aztecs*, ed. by Deborah L. Nichols and Enrique Rodríguez-Alegría, 129–42. Oxford: Oxford University Press.
Justeson, John, and Terrence Kaufman. 1993. A decipherment of Epi-Olmec hieroglyphic writing. *Science* 259(5102):1703–11.
Kaufman, Terrence. 1969. Some recent hypotheses on Mayan diversification. *Language Behavior Research Lab, Working Paper* 26. Berkeley: University of Berkeley.
Kaufman, Terrence. 1973. Areal linguistics and Middle America. In *Current trends in linguistics*, ed. by T. Sebeok, 11.459–84. The Hague: Mouton.
Kaufman, Terrence. 1974. Mesoamerican Indian languages. *Encyclopedia Britannica*. 15th edn (Encyclopedia Britannica 3). Chicago: Encyclopedia Britannica Educational Corporation.
Kaufman, Terrence. 1976. Archaeological and linguistic correlations in Mayaland and associated areas of Meso-America. *World Archaeology* 8(1).101–18.
McCoy, Timothy J., Amy E. Marquardt, John T. Wasson, Richard D. Ash, and Edward P. Vicenzi. 2017. The Anoka, Minnesota iron meteorite as parent to Hopewell meteoritic metal beads from Havana, Illinois. *Journal of Archaeological Science* 81.13–22.
Mills, Lisa A. 2003. *Mitochondrial DNA analysis of the Ohio Hopewell of the Hopewell Mound Group*. Athens, OH: Ohio University dissertation. <https://etd.ohiolink.edu/apexprod/rws_etd/send_file/send?accession=osu1054605467&disposition=inline> (last accessed September 4, 2021).
Mithun, Marianne. 1999. *The languages of Native North America*. Cambridge: Cambridge University Press.

Mochon, Marion Johnson. 1972. Language, history and prehistory: Mississippian lexico-reconstruction. *American Antiquity* 37(4).478–503.

Proulx, Paul. 2003. The evidence on Algonquian genetic grouping: A matter of relative chronology. *Anthropological Linguistics*, 45(2).201–25. <http://www.jstor.org/stable/30028885> (last accessed January 23, 2018).

Rapp, George Jr., Eiler Hendrickson, and James Allert. 1990. Native copper sources of artifact copper in pre-Columbian North America. In *Archaeological Geology of North America*, Centennial Special Volume, ed. by N. P. Lasca and J. Donahue, 479–97. Boulder: Geological Society of America.

Schroeder, David L., and Katharine C. Ruhl. 1968. Metallurgical characteristics of North American prehistoric copper work. *American Antiquity* 33(2).162–9.

Seeman, Mark F. 1979. Hopewell interaction sphere: The evidence for interregional trade and structural complexity. *Prehistory Research Series* 5(2).235–438. Indianapolis: Indian Historical Society.

Siebert, F. T. 1975. Resurrecting Virginia Algonquian from the dead: The reconstituted and historical phonology of Powhatan. In *Studies in Southeastern Indian Languages*, ed. by James M. Crawford, 285–458. Athens, GA: University of Georgia Press.

Spence, Michael W., and Brian J. Fryer. 2005. Hopewellian silver and silver artifacts from eastern North America: Their sources, procurement, distribution, and meanings. In *Gathering Hopewell: Society, Ritual, and Ritual Interaction (Interdisciplinary Contributions to Archaeology)*, ed. by Christopher Carr and D. Troy Case, 714–33. Boston: Springer.

Theler, James L., and Robert F. Boszhardt. 2003. *Twelve millennia: Archaeology of the Upper Mississippi River Valley*. Iowa City: University of Iowa Press.

Townsend, Richard F. 2004. *Hero, hawk, and open hand: American Indian art of the ancient Midwest and South*. New Haven/London: Yale University Press.

Turff, Gina. 1997. *A synthesis of middle woodland panpipes in eastern North America*. Peterborough: Trent University unpublished master's thesis.

Turff, Gina, and Christopher Carr. 2005. Hopewellian panpipes from eastern North America: Their social, ritual, and symbolic significance. In *Gathering Hopewell: Society, Ritual, and Ritual Interaction (Interdisciplinary Contributions to Archaeology)*, ed. by Christopher Carr and D. Troy Case, 648–95. Boston: Springer.

Walworth, Mary. 2014. Eastern Polynesian: The linguistic evidence revisited. *Oceanic Linguistics* 53(2).256–72.

10

The Lenguas de Bolivia Project: Background and Further Prospects

Mily Crevels and Pieter Muysken

1. Background

Bolivia, a country with more than 11 million inhabitants, has no less than thirty-six languages.[1] A large number of these languages are only spoken by small ethnic groups and are becoming less and less used. Before the small Bolivian languages become extinct, it is important they are documented in reference books and recordings. For the Bolivians this is of cultural historical and cultural political importance, while for the international linguistics community such a description is important because it gives insight into issues such as language development and what happens when languages are in contact with each other.

Bolivia is not only one of the poorest countries of Latin America, it is also a country with a huge cultural and linguistic diversity. In addition to Spanish, the thirty-six indigenous languages are or were recently spoken, with speaker numbers ranging from several million to less than five (Crevels and Muysken 2009, 2012, 2014, 2015). There are not only many languages, but these languages also belong to many different, genetically completely unrelated families. So far, geographical obstacles, the lack of roads, and the isolation of large parts of Bolivia have led to the preservation of parts of the cultural and linguistic heritage. Nonetheless, the majority of the languages of Bolivia are critically endangered. It is expected that only 10–20% will survive in the next century, and in fact all indigenous languages are under pressure or severe threat in the country (Crevels 2012).

Despite the great cultural and linguistic wealth, the knowledge of Bolivian languages and cultures was very limited until recently. There is no national tradition of linguistic research, there are hardly any trained Bolivian linguists, and native speakers of indigenous languages with training and interest in their own language belong mostly to the two largest groups, the Quechua and the Aymara. Most of the research was and is done by foreigners, and the results, in so far as they have been published, are hardly available in Bolivia itself, since they are mostly written in English. They contain, moreover, a lot of technical linguistic terminology. Unfortunately, while

Western scholars often achieve excellent research results with data acquired in the Third World, the local population, and particularly the people who collaborated in the projects, seldom get to see any results.

With the Lenguas de Bolivia (LB) book publication project we hope to have put a stop to this situation, offering the general public brief descriptions in Spanish of the languages and linguistic situation of Bolivia. By mapping the highly threatened and remarkable linguistic diversity of Bolivia and editing this series of books, the interest of local students and scholars in these languages may be sparked, and the attention to cultural and linguistic diversity stimulated.

This chapter reports on the LB project (Section 2), places the project in the Bolivian cultural context (Section 3), and illustrates the prospects of the research reported on for areal linguistics, typology, language documentation, and language change (Sections 4 and 5). As such it hopes to contribute to the exciting ongoing debates on these issues in the South American context, briefly addressed in our concluding Section 6.

2. The Lenguas de Bolivia project

To carry out this project, all or almost all the specialists in this field were brought together; more than twenty authors from more than thirteen countries contributed to the series and wherever Bolivian and other South American experts could be included, this was done.[2]

LB tries to cover the entire Bolivian linguistic landscape and consists of four volumes, containing chapters of approximately forty to fifty pages for thirty still spoken and—as far as there is still something known—extinct languages of Bolivia, written in a clear and easy-to-read way. The books are aimed at a wide audience, so certainly not only at experts and they have been placed in public and university libraries; in addition, the work is available for sale in Bolivian bookstores.

While the first three volumes are dedicated to the languages of the Altiplano and foothills (I), the Bolivian Amazonian lowlands (II), Moxos, Oriente, and Chaco (III), volume IV concerns more general topics related to the linguistic diversity of Bolivia, such as the standardization of alphabets or the relation between language and culture, as well as varieties of Bolivian Spanish.

The first volume, *Ámbito andino* "The Andean Sphere," presents nine languages from the Altiplano and the Andean foothills. For the Altiplano, three representatives of the ancient Uru-Chipayan linguistic family are described: Chipaya, Uchumataqu (Uru) of Irohito, and Chholo of the Murato of Lake Poopó. A description of the extinct Puquina language and the Kallawaya language, the ritual language spoken by itinerant herbalists and healers living in Charazani and Curva, is also offered. Apart from these languages, the varieties of the two most important linguistic families of the Andean region, Quechuan and Aymaran, are described. For the foothills, a description of the isolated Mosetenan family (Mosetén and Chimane) and the isolate Leko can be also found in this volume.

The second volume, *Amazonía* "The Amazonian Sphere," presents six Pano-Tacanan languages from the northwestern part of the Bolivian Amazon, that is, the Panoan languages, Chácobo (and Pacahuara), and the Tacanan languages, Ese Ejja, Cavineña, Araona, and Maropa; and five languages from the northeastern part, that is, the four isolates: Itonama, Cayubaba, Movima, and Canichana, and the Baure language (Arawakan). An introduction to the current linguistic situation of Amazonian Bolivia is presented in the first chapter.

The third volume, *Oriente* "The oriental sphere," contains the description of seven languages from the Moxos area, the Santa Cruz plains and the Chiquitanía: the Arawakan languages Ignaciano, Trinitario, and Paunaca, the Tupi–Guaraní languages Sirionó and Yuki, the isolate Yurakaré, and Chiquitano (Macro-Gêan); and three languages from the Bolivian Chaco, that is, Guaraní (Tupi–Guaraní), Ayoreo (Zamucoan), and 'Weenhayek (Matacoan). An introduction to the linguistic situation in this region of Bolivia is presented in the first chapter.

The fourth volume, *Temas nacionales* "National issues," discusses general issues with respect to the linguistic diversity of Bolivia, such as the sociolinguistic situation, the history of linguistic description, language policy, the standardization of writing systems, and so on. The volume also contains a study about Bolivian Spanish in general and a chapter on Afro-Yungueño. At the end, a sixty-page technical terminology section offers a (certainly for the Spanish-speaking world) unique contribution to the field. For about 450 technical terms, ranging from *ablativo* to *yuxtaposición*, the gloss employed in the books is listed, followed by a typological definition, and glossed examples from one to three languages analyzed in the volumes. This section is followed by an index of authors, an index of languages, ethnic groups and language families, and, finally, an index of subjects.

Since the volumes were primarily for a Bolivian audience, we decided to publish in Spanish and through a leading Bolivian publisher, Plural editores. Books in Bolivia have limited editions, however, and distribution is mainly limited to the three major cities of La Paz, Cochabamba, and Santa Cruz. This implies that speakers of most of the languages included in *Lenguas de Bolivia* and other interested parties may not have direct access to the books. Therefore, there is also a website (https://www.ru.nl/lenguasdebolivia/) with basic information and PDF copies of the chapters.

The four volumes consist of thirty-nine chapters, most of which are descriptions of single languages according to a specific model. A textual example here is taken from Cerrón-Palomino and Carvajal Carvajal (2009: 191) on Aymara (translated from the original Spanish):

---

allative: *-kama* (marks spatial, temporal or circumstantial limit)
(21) *jawir-kama-wa   pur-i   lunis-kama   suy-t'a-ñäni*
     river-ALL-EVI   arrive-3   Monday-ALL   wait-INCH-HORT
     "It reaches as far as the river." "Let's wait until Monday."

Another one from Dahl (2014: 109–10) on Sirionó:

Often, there is one or more other morphemes in the sentence that also express the repeated action meaning. Examples:
(3) *a-so-be   ra   se   reae*
    1SG-walk-REP   FUT   PRO:1SG   seems
    "I will go there again."

---

3. The place of LB in the Bolivian cultural context

In Bolivia, major changes have been occurring in terms of policy and the attitudes towards indigenous languages. The Bolivian Ministry of Education would like to develop programs, but does not have the necessary background knowledge of the languages. Anthropologists, rural leaders, students, journalists, and so on are becoming more and more interested in the languages but, again, until recently little reliable information could be found in the country. Thus, by making LB accessible through the web, it can turn into an important and lasting tool in support of the country's critically endangered languages.

The multiethnic and multicultural character of the country as well as various indigenous collective rights were first recognized after the 1994 reform of the Bolivian Constitution. Subsequently, in September 2000, all indigenous languages were recognized as official languages, and their use has since been promoted in the educational system. Finally, all Bolivian indigenous languages were recognized—together with Spanish—as official languages of the State in the Constitution of November 2007.

On August 19, 2009, the official presentation of the first volume of LB, *Ámbito andino*, took place at the National Museum of Ethnography and Folklore (MUSEF) in La Paz in the presence of a large audience. However, there is a big step up from the preparation and publication of the four volumes, difficult as this had been, to the actual social embedding of the material contained in them, so that they reach their intended audience and have their intended cultural and political effects.

Today law 269—the General Law of Linguistic Rights and Policies,[3] issued on August 2, 2012—together with law 070—Law of Education "Avelino Siñani and Elizardo Pérez,"[4] issued on December 20, 2010—regulate the use, learning, and teaching of the languages in the Plurinational Education System and in the various areas of public administration; predominantly, they enable the recovery, revitalization, and normalization of all the languages spoken in the plurinational territory. Against this background, the Plurinational Institute of the Study of Languages and Cultures (Instituto Plurinacional de Estudio de Lenguas y Culturas [IPELC]) was founded in 2013, which then led to the *in situ* creation of an Institute of Language and Culture (Instituto de Lengua y Cultura [ILC]) for each of the ethnic groups in Bolivia. The main goal of these local institutes is to "decolonize" the existing linguistic and cultural scene, thus enabling the country to manifest its plurinational, multicultural, and multilingual character.

We can only hope that with the implementation of IPELC and the ILCs, attention to the indigenous languages of Bolivia will keep growing and that local students and scholars interested in working on these languages will benefit from our LB series.

4. The LB project and the Amazonian Fringe

In addition to supporting the survival and development of the indigenous languages and cultures of Bolivia, the LB project contributes to our understanding of linguistic diversity on the South American continent, particularly that of the Amazonian

Fringe. While for the purposes of supporting educational and cultural policies, a national, in our case Bolivian, perspective is appropriate, such a national perspective is not fit for scholarly historical and comparative purposes. There a broader perspective is needed, and we argue that the Amazonian Fringe offers a good starting point.

The indigenous languages of South America until recently were relatively unknown. Not only was the majority not at all or poorly documented, the complex relations among them also remained obscure. Currently there is consensus for around 110 separate language families for the continent, but larger subgroupings can probably be established. A crucial role is played by the (highly) endangered languages of the Amazonian Fringe, the area between the Andean range and the Amazon Basin, covering part of Colombia, Ecuador, Peru, Bolivia, Paraguay, Argentina, and adjacent areas of Brazil. This fringe includes the Andean region's eastern foothills and foci of extreme linguistic diversity, such as the Upper Rio Negro region in the Northwestern Amazon (e.g., Epps and Stenzel 2013), the Guaporé-Mamoré region (see Crevels and Van der Voort 2008) in the Southern Amazon, and the Gran Chaco region further to the south (see Comrie et al. 2010). The Amazonian Fringe is characterized by considerable language variation, with a large number of language isolates and small language families. Whereas some languages belong to well-known stocks like Arawakan and Tupian, many represent minor families and isolates. The region harbors, among others, languages that belong to families/ stocks such as Guahiban, Tukanoan, Makuan, Witotoan, Peba-Yaguan, Zaparoan, Mosetenan, Pano-Tacanan, Chapacuran, Nambikwaran, Zamucoan, Enlhet-Enenlhet, Matacoan, Guaycuruan, and Araucanian; or that represent isolates, such as Kamsá, Kofán, Nasa Yuwe, Andoke, Waorani, Aikanã, Kwazá, Kanoê, Itonama, Cayubaba, Movima, Yurakaré, and Leko. This fragmentation contrasts with the more homogeneous central and eastern plains, where most languages belong to large stocks like Macro-Gêan, Arawakan, Cariban, and to the Tupi–Guaraní subbranch. Similarly, in the Andes itself, we find larger language families such as Quechuan and Aymaran. Therefore, the fundamental questions here are: How, when, and why did all these hundreds of languages and peoples emerge and spread throughout this region? Consider these four possible hypotheses:

1. The present fragmentation is the original situation for all of South America. The ethnically and linguistically more homogeneous areas in the center and in the Andes itself are simply the result of more recent expansions of certain linguistic families due to demographic expansion made possible by superior technology or crops.
2. The fragmentation in the fringe zones arose because these areas functioned as zones of refuge, to which many smaller groups fled when pushed out of richer areas by stronger groups.
3. The fragmentation along the eastern flanks of the Andes, the so-called *montañas*, is due to the fact that this was the oldest inhabited zone of South America, the path along which groups moved southward as they came through the Isthmus of Panama.

4. The languages are spoken in quite diverse ecological niches which are near to each other. People maintain separate identities in a specific niche but interchange and trade with other groups.

In the last two decades, there has been a tremendous effort directed towards language documentation, sponsored by European national funding agencies, the Volkswagen Stiftung, and the Rausing Foundation. Dozens of high-quality documentation projects have led to important new insights in the fields of historical comparative and typological linguistics, calling for re-evaluation of the linguistic relationships in the area and further investigation of concrete evidence to reconstruct the language relations of this zone.

These new insights, however, require new efforts at synthesis and comparison, tackling the following questions: What are the lexical and grammatical correspondences and differences between the diverse languages? Which traits point to ancient genetic relationships? Which are the oldest linguistic families of a certain region and which ones can be dated later? Which traits form evidence for ancient contacts and areal diffusion? What kind of cultural and ecological vocabulary points to migration or innovation? What time depths do botanists estimate for domesticated plants in various regions? What are the correspondences and differences with archeological findings?

The linguistic diversity in the Amazonian Fringe is highly threatened, with the majority of languages seriously endangered, moribund, or extinct. As an example, in the Guaporé-Mamoré region, over half of the fifty+ languages have less than fifty speakers, and a third have less than ten speakers. Fortunately research initiatives have contributed to their documentation and have led to new insights and data that at times challenge received ideas about what is possible in language and in contact-induced language change. A new development is the establishment of large language corpora, based on naturalistic recordings.

5. Prospects

What is much needed is systematic research on specific properties of the languages of the Amazonian Fringe and beyond to identify patterns of descent and contact. Surveys of features for large language samples need to be combined with detailed text studies for languages with available corpora. These results should be linked to ethno-historical, archeological, botanical, and genetic findings and would ultimately serve to reconstruct the Western Amazon region's interconnected prehistoric past. Even though apparently unrelated, typologically the languages in this region share a number of highly interesting features, including positional deictics (standing, sitting, lying, etc.), nominal and verbal classifiers, verbal number, directional verbal affixes, reference marked on the verb, and hierarchical alignment. The frequency of the inclusive–exclusive distinction in the languages of the Amazonian Fringe (Crevels and Muysken 2005) seems slightly higher (57%) than the worldwide distribution sampled by Siewierska and Bakker (2005) (46%). Furthermore, there are at least five cases of genderlects reported (Rose 2015), a number of languages with switch reference distinctions (Van Gijn 2016), and a split between verb final orders (often on the Andean side of the country) and other orders.

A few of the topics that require further study are covered below.

5.1 Nominal classification, posture verbs, and deixis

Different types of nominal classification in the Amazonian Fringe, such as noun classes, classifier systems, and classificatory verbs, need to be identified and compared, their functions in discourse studied, and the basic semantic distinctions in noun classification established. Specific questions concerning classifiers that should be addressed include: Where do classifiers come from? What are their grammaticalization paths and functions (see also Grinevald and Seifart 2004; Seifart and Payne 2007)? Nominal classification is a known indicator for language contact (Nichols 2003; Seifart 2010) and often a mechanism for diffusion in macro areas, but how these features are diffused and what constraints there may be on borrowability remains unclear. How do verbal classifiers link up to nominal classifiers?

There are unique solutions for diagramming mental space in the area covering part of Bolivia and the Chaco. We will illustrate this with Itonama (isolate; Bolivian Amazon) posture verbs/classifiers, Movima (isolate; Bolivian Amazon) positional demonstratives, and the Toba (Guaycuruan; Argentinean Chaco) deictic system.

The semantics of Itonama posture verbs/classifiers correspond to the three basic positions of the human body, *standing* (vertically extended), *sitting* (three-dimensional) and *lying* (horizontally extended), and to *hanging*, which is an additional position added by many Amazonian languages (Grinevald 2006). To express these positions, Itonama generally uses verbal/deictic classifiers that attach to existential, possessive, and a reduced number of other predicates (1). These classifiers have been derived from posture verbs that rarely occur on their own, as in (2).

(1) *nik'abï* *o-si-le* *ni-k'a'ne* *biluwa*
DEM:ADV:DIST DV-EX-CLF:hanging CLF:flexible-one snake
"There is a snake hanging (from a branch) over there."

(2) *weta'-te'-ka* *biluwa*
be.standing.SG-CONT-F.SG snake
"The snake is standing upright (ready to attack)."

These posture verbs/classifiers are often combined with locative prefixes, as shown in (3).

(3) *chï-kis-ba* *biluwa* *k'abï*
inside-down-be.flexible snake DEM:ADV:DIST
"There is a snake over there (in the grass)."

The same set of classifiers that attach to verbs also appear on demonstratives (4).

(4) *no'o-so*   *o-pi*   *lowo'-tya*   *k-a'-ki-maku-mu*   *chuk'a'te*
    DEM:PROX-CLF:lying.PL   DV-fish   rotten-STAT   F-2SG-IMP-give-1   other
    "These fish are rotten, give me others!"

Compare this with the following examples (5–6) from Movima (isolate; Haude 2006: 178, 191).

(5) *kinede:*   *as-łabał*
    DEM.NST.F   sit-BE.earth
    "She is sitting on the ground."

(6) *koro'*   *toje:łe*   *kos*   *kara'a*
    DEM.AB.N   pass.AG   ART.N.AB   red.macaw
    "The red macaw is flying by." (we don't see it anymore)

In Movima, six sets of positional demonstratives describe the referent in terms of its location and/or position when "the referent is out of reach of both the speaker and the addressee" (Haude 2006: 177).

In Toba, the deictic system includes three basic positions of the human body that are also used for the classification of objects (standing, sitting, and lying), and three relative distances (proximal, distant, and absent). While the first three (*da*, *ñi*, and *ʒi*) are referential, the last three (*na*, *so*, and *ka*) have a deictic nature. With human and animate referents, *da*, *ñi*, and *ʒi* encode body posture (standing, sitting, and lying), while *na*, *so*, and *ka* encode the relative distance of the referent with respect to the speaker (7).

(7) Positional/deictic classifiers in Toba (Klein 1979; Messineo 2003)
    da yape?   "my grandpa, standing"
    ñi yape?   "my grandpa, sitting"
    ʒi yape?   "my grandpa, lying or dead"
    na yape?   "my grandpa, approaching"
    so yape?   "my grandpa, moving away"
    ka yape?   "my grandpa, absent"

As discussed further on in 5.4, the deictic systems encountered in the Guaycuruan and Matacoan languages, just like the Movima articles, play an important role in the marking of nominal tense, which sometimes is limited to the noun phrase and other times has scope over the whole clause.

5.2 Reference tracking

Crosslinguistically there are four major types of reference tracking in discourse: (1) gender and noun class, (2) grammatical switch reference, (3) grammatical function switch, and (4) pragmatic inference. Van Gijn (2016) provides a thorough overview of the switch-reference structures found in Western South America, but what is still lacking is a survey of the different reference-tracking strategies used in the languages of the Amazonian Fringe, with special focus on noun classes and classifiers, which are particularly common. Furthermore, some languages (e.g., Mosetén [Mosetenan], Sakel 2002) have well-established gender agreement systems. Such a survey of reference-tracking systems would be innovative, since, as far as we know, no discourse-based areal/typological comparison has been undertaken before. Moreover, the comparative analysis of reference-tracking strategies would provide an interesting and new tool for linguistic research.

5.3 Hierarchical alignment

In her sample of 380 languages, Siewierska (2013) finds hierarchical verbal person marking to be the least frequent alignment type, occurring in only eleven (3%) of the languages, of which eight are spoken in the Americas. She observes that, like active alignment, hierarchical alignment is found primarily in the languages of the Americas. Although Siewierska's sample only features three South American languages with hierarchical alignment, this type of verbal person marking is far more common and found throughout the Amazonian Fringe and the adjacent Chaco area. We will illustrate this with a few examples from Itonama (isolate), Sanapaná (Enlhet-Enenlhet), and Mapudungun (Araucanian). Note that languages are subject to different indexability hierarchies.

In independent clauses, Itonama shows accusative alignment in combination with an inverse subsystem, which is subject to the hierarchy 1/2 > 3, in which first and second person outrank third person. In (8a–c), we see that while S and A arguments are indexed on the verb as prefixes, the O argument is indexed as a suffix. Third person singular and plural are not indexed pronominally on independent verb forms, neither as S or A, nor as O (8d). The feminine singular marker -*ka*, however, indicates a feminine third person singular S or A.

(8) Itonama (isolate)
    a. *si-yalïs-na*
       1SG-be_hungry-NEUT
       "I am hungry."

    b. *si-ka-mo'-ke-we*
       1SG-face-grab-PL-2
       "I'm going to hit you (in the face)."   (1.A > 2.O)

    c. wase'wa   *de'-kewa-na-he-mo*
       yesterday 2PL-face-see-NEUT-DISTR-1
       "Yesterday you guys saw us."   (2.A > 1.O)

    d. *ka-mo'-ka*   *ah-may-maye'-ne'-ka*   *pa-nay-'e*
       face-grab-F.SG 3-SUB-parent-NEUT-F.SG 3SG.F-SUB-offspring
       "The mother hit her son in the face."   (3.A>3.O)

Examples (8a–d) show that verbal person marking is strictly accusative in local (1.A/2.A > 2.O/1.O) and direct (3.A > 1.O/2.O) configurations, but in (9a–b) we see that in inverse constructions, in which a third person acts upon a first or second person, the latter (object) is indexed as a prefix in the canonical subject slot; this dedicated prefix is followed by the inverse marker *k'i-* (see Crevels 2010, 2011 for further details on verbal person marking in Itonama).

(9) a. *sih-k'i-ma-doh-ne*   *u-pa'u*
　　　1PL.EXCL-INV-hand-bite-NEUT   DV-dog
　　　"The dog bit us on the hand."　　　(3.A > 1.O)

　　b. *dih-k'i-tes-cha'ke*   *ya-dïlï*   *u-buwa*
　　　2PL-INV-call-MULT   DEM:MED-CLF:standing.PL   DV-person
　　　"Those men called you all."　　　(3.A > 2.O)

In Sanapaná, verbal person marking distinguishes between first person and non-first person arguments; for non-first person arguments, the language distinguishes gender rather than number (Gomes 2013: 284; Van Gysel 2017: 33). Sanapaná verbs obligatorily take one person marking prefix, which usually refers to the S or A argument (10a–b). However, when a non-first person acts upon a first person, the latter (object) is indexed in the canonical subject slot (10c–d) (Van Gysel 2017: 33).

(10)　Sanapaná (Enlhet-Enenlhet; Van Gysel 2017: 33)
　　a. *koʔo*   *as-tjene-ʔaw*   *lejap*
　　　PRO:1SG   1SG-look-INTS   PRO:2/3SG.M
　　　"I am watching you (M.SG)/him."　　　(1.A > 2.O/3.O)

　　b. *lejap*   *ap-tjene-ʔaw*   *semhen*
　　　PRO:2/3SG.M   2/3.M-look-INTS   dog(F)
　　　"You (M.SG) are/he is watching the dog."　　　(2.A/3.A > 2.O/3.O)

　　c. *a-semhen*   *e-tjene-ʔaw*
　　　2/3F-dog   1SG.O-look-INTS
　　　"The dog is watching me."　　　(2.A/3.A > 1.O)

　　d. *lejap*   *e-tjene-ʔaw*
　　　PRO:2/3SG.M   1SG.O-look-INTS
　　　"You (M.SG) are/he is watching me."　　　(2.A / 3.A >1.O)

In Mapudungun, verbal person marking is subject to a 1 > 2 > 3 proximate > 3 obviative hierarchy (Arnold 1994, 1996). As Zúñiga (2002: 26) points out, in the case of two equally animate third persons, both direct and inverse configurations are available, depending on the prominence of the third persons. In (11a) the first clause is direct because a more prominent third person (the proximate) acts upon a less prominent one (the obviative). In (11b), a less salient third person acts upon a more prominent one, resulting in an inverse construction marked by the *-e* suffix.

(11) Mapudungun (Araucanian; Zúñiga 2002: 26)
    a. *mütrüm-fi-i-Ø*   b. *mütrüm-e-i-Ø-mew*
        call-3.O-IND-3   call-INV-IND-3-3.A
        He$_{PROX}$ called him$_{OBV}$ He$_{OBV}$ called him$_{PROX}$ (3.A > 3.O)

Features pointing at hierarchical alignment are also found in other languages and language families in or adjacent to the Amazonian Fringe, such as extinct Puquina (Puquinan; Adelaar 2009; Adelaar and Van de Kerke 2009); Quechua (Quechuan; Adelaar 2009); Mosetén (Mosetenan; Sakel 2011); Reyesano (Pano-Tacanan; Guillaume 2009, 2011); Movima (isolate; Haude 2009, 2011a); the Tupi–Guaraní languages Sirionó (Dahl 2007, 2014), Yuki (Villafañe 2014), Bolivian Guaraní (Dietrich 1986; Gustafson 2014), and Paraguayan Guaraní (Velázquez-Castillo 2008); Karitiana (Tupi-Arikem; Storto 2005); Mekens (Tupi-Tupari; Galucio 2001; Storto 2005); Karo (Tupi-Ramarama; Gabas 1999; Storto 2005); the Guaycuruan languages (Van Gysel 2019), Kadiweu (Sandalo 2005, 2009), Mocoví (Grondona 1998; Carrió 2015), Pilagá (Vidal 2001; 2009–10), and Toba (Censabella 2006; Carpio 2007, 2012); the Matacoan languages Maká (Gerzenstein 1994; Fabre 2008: personal communication), Chorote (Carol 2014), and Nivaclé (Fabre 2016); and Enlhet (Enlhet-Enenlhet; Kalisch 2009–2010).

5.4 Nominal tense

As far as is currently known, nominal tense is strongly rooted in the Cariban language family, and may have spread from there to individual members of other families, such as Tariana and Chamicuro (Arawakan), Wari' (Chapacuran), Nambikwara (Nambikwaran), Movima (isolate), Mosetén (Mosetenan), but also to Tupi–Guaraní, Enlhet-Enenlhet (Kalisch 2007: personal communication; Van Gysel 2017), Matacoan (Vidal and Gutiérrez 2010; Campbell and Grondona 2012; Carol 2015), and Guaycuruan (Vidal and Gutiérrez 2010) languages. Further study of the specific geographical distribution of the features involved is called for, also in light of the possible grammaticalization of lexical suffixes referring to "deceased" and "future." Previous research (Nordlinger and Sadler 2004; Haude 2004, 2006, 2011b; Tonhauser 2007) shows that nominal tense is more pervasive in South America than elsewhere. The study of nominal tense is significant for various fields of research (cognitive linguistics, psycholinguistics, and psychology) but there is still a void in linguistic theory (Muysken 2008).

Nordlinger and Sadler (2004), in an exploratory cross-linguistic article, distinguish two groups of languages in which temporal distinctions are marked on the noun phrase. In the first group, with Independent Nominal Tense, the temporal reference of the nouns themselves is specified by one of a set of suffixes (often past and future). Guaraní would be a typical example. In the second group of languages, with Propositional Nominal Tense, the tense is marked on the noun but has sentential scope. This type is found in Australia, with Kayardild as an example (Evans 1995). However, in Bolivia, there is at least one language, with a category which may be called Extended Nominal Tense, namely the Bolivian isolate Movima (Haude 2006). Here the same marker is sometimes interpreted with respect to the noun phrase, as in (12), and sometimes with respect to the clause, as in (13).

(12) Aj<a>lo:maj   loy   os   no:no   di'   pa:ko.
     narrate<DR>   INTL   ART.N.PST pet   REL   dog
     "I'll tell you about my (former, deceased) dog."   (Haude 2006: 162)

(13) jayna   n-os   imay-ni   jayna   tivij-ni   os   chodo:wi
     DSC   OBL-ART.N.PST night-PRC   DSC   pain-PRC   ART.N.PST   stomach
     "Then at night, my stomach hurt."   (Haude 2006: 165)

In (12) the neuter past article *os* indicates that the speaker's dog does not live any more, while in (13) the marker indicates that the hurting of the speaker's stomach took place in the past. This suggests that the two types of nominal tense (or rather propositional nominal tense, aspect, and mood [TAM]) are not entirely unrelated. It should be noted that Haude herself uses the term "nominal tense" in her 2004 article, but adopts a more complex analysis in her (2006) thesis, where it is assumed that the element glossed PST in (12) and (13) in fact marks the non-existence of the entity denoted.

The data in Movima may be interpreted in such a way that Propositional Nominal Tense is a discursive extension of Independent Nominal Tense in that language, through some kind of conventionalized implicature. In other words, the logical impossibility of the non-existence of my stomach in (13) at the moment of speaking is interpreted as indicating that the hurting took place at some moment in the past. This line of thinking is similar to the analysis presented in Haude (2011b).

While admittedly the evidence from one single language, Movima, is perhaps not convincing, there is evidence that in at least four South American language families, both types of nominal tense occur: Arawakan, Tupi–Guaraní, Matacoan, and Guaycuruan (see Nordlinger and Sadler 2004; Muysken 2008; Vidal and Gutiérrez 2010), and that Pilagá (Guaycuruan) and Nivaclé (Matacoan) seem to exhibit the same type of Extended Nominal Tense as Movima does (Vidal and Gutiérrez 2010). In the case of Tupi–Guaraní, the languages are quite closely related, including Yuki and Sirionó in Bolivia. If we accept the Movima scenario of extension from the independent to the propositional domain, this would suggest that the situation in Sirionó (listed by Nordlinger and Sadler 2004 in the group of languages with Propositional Nominal TAM), if reported correctly, is an innovation, since Yuki displays Independent Nominal TAM.[5] Thus the two types of nominal tense must be at least historically related in some instances. In the future, the inventory of languages in South America may well be further expanded as more data become available and are systematically investigated. There is a likely areal effect in the distribution of the nominal tense markers, at least in Amazonia (see further Muysken 2008). As mentioned, the most likely scenario on the basis of the currently known descriptive facts is that the phenomenon is strongly rooted in the Cariban language family, and has spread from there to individual members or subbranches of other language families. Further study of these families, as well as the specific geographical distribution of the features involved, is needed, however, both in the Amazonian Fringe and in the adjacent Chaco area.

Other topics that should be studied further are verbal categories such as NEGATION (Krasnoukhova and van der Auwera 2018), VERBAL NUMBER (Crevels and Van der Voort 2008; Krasnoukhova forthcoming), and ASSOCIATED MOTION (Guillaume 2016). Though central, these topics remain understudied. The linguistic diversity and abundant contact situations make the Amazonian Fringe an excellent testing ground for the study of these domains, leading to the establishment of directions of borrowing, contact-induced changes, and past contacts.

6. Concluding remarks

The Lenguas de Bolivia project was preceded by a very large single-volume presentation of the languages of Colombia (González de Pérez and Rodríguez de Montes 2000) and a volume on the languages of Suriname (Carlin and Arends 2002). Haboud and Toapanta (2014) provide a modest survey for Ecuador with limited information. However, there are no similar projects that we know of for countries such as Peru, Brazil, or Argentina. Indeed, the amount of work involved is significant. Currently, Patience Epps and Lev Michael are editing a massive collection of sketches of Amazonian language families and isolates (Epps and Michael forthcoming), but this project has a primarily or exclusively academic purpose.

Possibly, websites will fill some of the gaps. For Colombia there is a website maintained by the Instituto Caro y Cuervo (https://lenguasdecolombia.caroycuervo.gov.co/), with five categories: Indigenous languages, Creole languages, Romani, Colombian Sign Language, and Colombian Spanish. In Peru several short films have been produced and are available on YouTube, but no systematic online resource is available. Similarly, in Argentina, Venezuela, and Brazil, there are fragmentary websites, but nothing systematic except for the Brazilian sociolinguistic website *Povos Indígenas no Brasil* (https://pib.socioambiental.org/). In Chile, the Museo de Arte Precolombino has a website with some videos, but again no systematic information.

With the publication of *Lenguas de Bolivia* we have tried to contribute a piece to the puzzle of South American linguistic diversity that we are all so eager to complete, and we hope that it may provide an incentive, especially for local scholars, to continue contributing to the completion of this puzzle. The fact that there are a number of very specific shared features between languages in the Southern Amazonian Fringe and the Chaco area points at historical contact scenarios that need to be further researched.

Notes

1. This chapter is respectfully dedicated to Lyle Campbell, a scholar who has contributed greatly to our understanding of the linguistic diversity of South America and to its complex history. Some of the material in the chapter was earlier presented at meetings in La Paz, Bogotá, Leipzig, and Nijmegen.
2. Research for Lenguas de Bolivia was funded most directly through various Dutch granting agencies, including Radboud University Nijmegen, the Netherlands

Foundation for the Advancement of Research (NWO), the Royal Netherlands Academy of Arts and Sciences (KNAW), and the Royal Dutch Embassy in La Paz. In addition, numerous granting agencies in Argentina, Australia, France, Germany, Italy, Sweden, and elsewhere funded part of the fieldwork that went into the volumes.
3. Ley General de Derechos y Políticas Lingüísticas.
4. Ley de la Educación "Avelino Siñani y Elizardo Pérez."
5. See Dahl (2014) for a completely different analysis of the Sirionó data.

References

Adelaar, Willem F. H. 2009. Inverse markers in Andean languages: A comparative view. In *The linguistics of endangered languages: Contributions to morphology and morphosyntax*, ed. by Leo Wetzels, 171–85. Utrecht: LOT Publications.

Adelaar, Willem, and Simon van de Kerke. 2009. Puquina. In *Lenguas de Bolivia, vol. I Ámbito andino*, ed. by Mily Crevels and Pieter Muysken, 125–46. La Paz: Plural editores.

Arnold, Jennifer. 1994. Inverse voice marking in Mapudungun. *Berkeley Linguistics Society* 20.28–41.

Arnold, Jennifer. 1996. The inverse system in Mapudungun and other languages. *Revista de Lingüística Teórica y Aplicada* 34.9–48.

Campbell, Lyle, and Verónica Grondona. 2012. The languages of the Chaco and Southern Cone. In *The indigenous languages of South America: A comprehensive guide* (The World of Linguistics 2), ed. by Lyle Campbell and Verónica Grondona, 625–68. Berlin: De Gruyter Mouton.

Carlin, Eithne B., and Jacques Arends (eds). 2002. *Atlas of the languages of Suriname*. Leiden: KILTV Press.

Carol, Javier. 2014. *Lengua chorote (mataguayo). Estudio fonológico y morfosintáctico* (LINCOM Studies in Native American Linguistics 72). Munich: LINCOM.

Carol, Javier. 2015. TAM marking on nominals in Chorote (Mataguayo, Argentine, and Paraguayan Chaco). *Linguistics* 53(4).877–930.

Carpio, María B. 2007. *Sistemas de alineación en toba (familia guaycuru, Argentina)*. Hermosillo, Sonora: Universidad de Sonora MA thesis.

Carpio, María B. 2012. *Fonología y morfosintaxis de la lengua hablada por grupos tobas en el oeste de Formosa (Argentina)* (LINCOM Studies in Native American Linguistics 67). Munich: LINCOM.

Carrió, Cintia. 2015. Alternancias verbales en Mocoví (familia guaycuru, Argentina). *Lingüística* 31(2).9–26.

Censabella, Marisa. 2006. Relaciones gramaticales en lengua toba (flia. guaycurú, Argentina). In *VIII Encuentro Internacional de Lingüística en el Noroeste. Memorias. Tomo I*, ed. by Zarina Estrada Fernández, 81–104. Hermosillo, Sonora: Editorial Unison.

Cerrón-Palomino, Rodolfo and Juan Carvajal Carvajal. 2009. Aimara. In *Lenguas de Bolivia, vol. I Ámbito andino*, ed. by Mily Crevels and Pieter Muysken, 169–213. La Paz: Plural editores.

Comrie, Bernard, Lucía A. Golluscio, Hebe González, and Alejandra Vidal. 2010. El chaco como área lingüística. In *Estudios de lenguas amerindias 2: Contribuciones al estudio de las lenguas originarias de las Américas*, ed. by Zarina Estrada Fernández and Ramón Arzápalo Marín, 85–132. Hermosillo, Sonora: Editorial Unison.

Crevels, Mily. 2010. Ditransitives in Itonama. In *Studies in ditransitive constructions: A comparative handbook*, ed. by Andrej L. Malchukov, Martin Haspelmath, and Bernard Comrie, 678–709. Berlin: De Gruyter Mouton.

Crevels, Mily. 2011. Who did what to whom in Magdalena (Itonama). *International Journal of American Linguistics* 77(4).577–94. (Special issue ed. by Antoine Guillaume and Françoise Rose.)

Crevels, Mily. 2012. Language endangerment in South America: The clock is ticking. In *The indigenous languages of South America: A comprehensive guide* (The World of Linguistics 2), ed. by Lyle Campbell and Verónica Grondona, 167–234. Berlin: De Gruyter Mouton.

Crevels, Mily, and Pieter Muysken. 2005. Inclusive–exclusive distinctions in the languages of central-western South America. In *Clusivity: Typology and case studies of the inclusive–exclusive distinction* (Typological Studies in Language 63), ed. by Elena Filimonova, 313–39. Amsterdam: John Benjamins.

Crevels, Mily, and Pieter Muysken (eds). 2009. *Lenguas de Bolivia, vol. I Ámbito andino*. La Paz: Plural editores.

Crevels, Mily, and Pieter Muysken (eds). 2012. *Lenguas de Bolivia, vol. II Amazonía*. La Paz: Plural editores.

Crevels, Mily, and Pieter Muysken (eds). 2014. *Lenguas de Bolivia, vol. III Oriente*. La Paz: Plural editores.

Crevels, Mily, and Pieter Muysken (eds). 2015. *Lenguas de Bolivia, vol. IV Temas nacionales*. La Paz: Plural editores.

Crevels, Mily, and Hein van der Voort. 2008. The Guaporé-Mamoré region as a linguistic area. In *From linguistic areas to areal linguistics* (Studies in Language Companion Series 90), ed. by Pieter Muysken, 151–79. Amsterdam: John Benjamins.

Dahl, Östen. 2007. Argument coding in Sirionó. Paper presented at the *Workshop on Argument-Coding Systems in Bolivian Lowland Languages*, CELIA, Villejuif, April 5–7, 2007.

Dahl, Östen. 2014. Sirionó. In *Lenguas de Bolivia, vol. III Oriente*, ed. by Mily Crevels and Pieter Muysken, 99–133. La Paz: Plural editores.

Dietrich, Wolf. 1986. *El idioma chiriguano. Gramática, textos, vocabulario*. Madrid: Instituto de Cooperación Iberoamericana.

Epps, Patience, and Lev Michael (eds). Forthcoming. *Amazonian languages* (HSK 44/1 and 44/2.). Berlin: De Gruyter Mouton.

Epps, Patience, and Kristine Stenzel (eds). 2013. *Upper Rio Negro: Cultural and linguistic interaction in Northwestern Amazonia*. Rio de Janeiro: Museu do Índio – FUNAI, Museu Nacional.

Evans, Nicholas. 1995. *A grammar of Kayardild. With historical-comparative notes on Tangkic* (Mouton Grammar Library 15). Berlin: Mouton de Gruyter.

Fabre, Alain. 2016. *Gramática de la lengua nivacle (familia mataguayo, Chaco paraguayo)* (LINCOM Studies in Native American Linguistics 78). Munich: LINCOM.
Gabas Jr., Nilson. 1999. *A grammar of Karo, Tupí (Brazil)*. Santa Barbara, CA: University of California dissertation.
Galucio, Ana Vilacy. 2001. *The morphosyntax of Mekéns (Tupi)*. Chicago: University of Chicago dissertation.
Gerzenstein, Ana. 1994. *Lengua Maká. Estudio descriptivo*. Buenos Aires: Instituto de Lingüística, Facultad de Filosofía y Letras, Universidad de Buenos Aires.
Gomes, Antonio Almir Silva. 2013. *Sanapaná uma língua Maskoy: aspectos gramaticais*. Campinas: Universidade Estadual de Campinas dissertation.
González de Pérez, María Stella, and María Luisa Rodríguez de Montes (eds). 2000. *Lenguas indígenas de Colombia: una visión descriptiva*. Bogotá: Instituto Caro y Cuervo.
Grinevald, Colette. 2006. The expression of static location in a typological perspective. In *Space in languages: Linguistic systems and cognitive categories* (Typological Studies in Language 66), ed. by Maya Hickmann and Stephane Robert, 29–58. Amsterdam: John Benjamins.
Grinevald, Colette, and Frank Seifart. 2004. Noun classes in African and Amazonian languages: Toward a comparison. *Linguistic Typology* 8(1).59–131.
Grondona, Verónica. 1998. *A grammar of Mocoví*. Pittsburgh: University of Pittsburgh dissertation.
Guillaume, Antoine. 2009. Hierarchical agreement and split intransitivity in Reyesano. *International Journal of American Linguistics* 75(1).29–48.
Guillaume, Antoine. 2011. Third-person agreement and passive marking in Tacanan languages: A historical perspective. *International Journal of American Linguistics* 77(4).521–36. (Special issue ed. by Antoine Guillaume and Françoise Rose.)
Guillaume, Antoine. 2016. Associated motion in South America: Typological and areal perspectives. *Linguistic Typology* 20(1).81–177.
Gustafson, Bret. 2014. Guaraní. In *Lenguas de Bolivia, vol. III Oriente*, ed. by Mily Crevels and Pieter Muysken, 307–68. La Paz: Plural editores.
Haboud, Marleen, and Jesús L. Toapanta (eds). 2014. *Voces e imágenes: lenguas indígenas del Ecuador*. Quito: Centro de Publicaciones, Pontífica Universidad Católica del Ecuador.
Haude, Katharina. 2004. Nominal tense marking in Movima: Nominal or clausal scope? In *Linguistics in the Netherlands 2004* (Linguistics in the Netherlands 21), ed. by Leonie Cornips and Jenny Doetjes, 80–90. Amsterdam: John Benjamins.
Haude, Katharina. 2006. *A grammar of Movima*. Nijmegen: Radboud University Nijmegen dissertation.
Haude, Katharina. 2009. Hierarchical alignment in Movima. *International Journal of American Linguistics* 75(4).513–32.
Haude, Katharina, 2011a. Argument encoding in Movima: The local domain. *International Journal of American Linguistics* 77(4).559–75. (Special issue ed. by Antoine Guillaume and Françoise Rose.)

Haude, Katharina. 2011b. Tense marking on dependent nominals in Movima. In *Tense across languages*, ed. by Renate Musan and Monika Rathert, 189–206. Berlin: De Gruyter Mouton.

Kalisch, Hannes (2009–10). Los constituyentes de la cláusula enlhet (enlhet-enenlhet). Esbozo de una cláusula omnipredicativa. *Amerindia* 33/34.109–50. (Special issue ed. by Lucía A. Golluscio and Alejandra Vidal.)

Klein, Harriet E. M. 1979. Noun classifiers in Toba. In *Ethnolinguistics: Boas, Sapir and Whorf revisited* (Contributions to the Sociology of Language 6), ed. by Madeleine Mathiot, 85–95. The Hague: Mouton.

Krasnoukhova, Olga. Forthcoming. Number in South American languages. In *Handbook of Number*, ed. by Michael Daniel and Paolo Acquaviva. Berlin: De Gruyter Mouton.

Krasnoukhova, Olga, and Johan van der Auwera. 2018. Negation in the languages of the Eastern foothills: Towards some patterns and their explanations. Paper presented at *Amazonicas VII*, Baños, Ecuador, May 28–June 1, 2018.

Messineo, Cristina. 2003. *Lengua toba (guaycurú). Aspectos gramaticales y discursivos.* (LINCOM Studies in Native American Linguistics 48). Munich: LINCOM.

Muysken, Pieter. 2008. Nominal tense. Time for further Whorfian adventures. Comments on Casasanto. In *Time to speak: Cognitive and neural prerequisites for time in language*, ed. by Peter Indefrey and Marianne Gullberg, 81–8. Oxford: Blackwell.

Nichols, Johanna. 2003. Diversity and stability in language. In *The handbook of historical linguistics*, ed. by Brain D. Joseph and Richard D. Janda, 283–310. Malden: Blackwell.

Nordlinger, Rachel, and Louisa Sadler. 2004. Nominal tense in cross-linguistic perspective. *Language* 80(4).776–806.

Rose, Françoise. 2015. Male and female speech and more: Categorical gender indexicality in indigenous South American languages. *International Journal of American Linguistics* 81(4).495–537.

Sakel, Jeanette. 2002. Gender agreement in Mosetén. In *Current Studies on South American Languages*, ed. by Mily Crevels, Sérgio Meira, Simon van de Kerke, and Hein van der Voort, 287–305. Leiden: CNWS Publications.

Sakel, Jeanette. 2011. Mosetén and Chimane argument coding: A layered system. *International Journal of American Linguistics* 77(4).337–57. (Special issue ed. by Antoine Guillaume and Françoise Rose.)

Sandalo, Filomena. 2005. Case and agreement: Person hierarchy in Kadiwéu. *Estudos Lingüísticos* 34.44–58.

Sandalo, Filomena. 2009. Person hierarchy and inverse voice in Kadiweu. *Línguas Indígenas Americanas* (LIAMES) 9.27–40.

Seifart, Frank. 2010. Nominal classification. *Language and Linguistics Compass* 4(8).719–36.

Seifart, Frank, and Doris L. Payne. 2007. Nominal classification in the North West Amazon: Issues in areal diffusion and typological characterization. *International Journal of American Linguistics* 73(4).381–7. (Special issue ed. by Frank Seifart and Doris L. Payne.)

Siewierska, Anna. 2013. Alignment of verbal person marking. In *The World Atlas of Language Structures Online*, ed. by Matthew S. Dryer and Martin Haspelmath. Leipzig: Max Planck Institute for Evolutionary Anthropology, <http://wals.info/chapter/100> (last accessed June 24, 2019).

Siewierska, Anna, and Dik Bakker. 2005. Inclusive and exclusive in free and bound pronouns. In *Clusivity: Typology and case studies of the inclusive–exclusive distinction* (Typological Studies in Language 63), ed. by Elena Filimonova, 151–78. Amsterdam: John Benjamins.

Storto, Luciana. 2005. Caso e concordância nas línguas Tupi. *Estudos Lingüísticos* 34: 59–72.

Tonhauser, Judith. 2007. Nominal tense? The meaning of Guaraní nominal temporal markers. *Language* 83(4).831–69.

van Gijn, Rik. 2016. Switch reference in Western South America. In *Switch Reference 2.0* (Typological Studies in Language 114), ed. by Rik van Gijn and Jeremy Hammond, 153–206. Amsterdam: John Benjamins.

Van Gysel, Jens. 2017. *Temporal predicative particles in Sanapaná and the Enlhet-Enenlhet Language family (Paraguay): A descriptive and comparative study*. Leiden: Leiden University MA thesis.

Van Gysel, Jens E. L. 2019. Hierarchical alignment and comparative linguistics in the Guaykuruan languages: An exhaustive alignment approach. *International Journal of American Linguistics* 85(1).123–61.

Velázquez-Castillo, Maura. 2008. Voice and transitivity in Guaraní. In *The typology of semantic alignment*, ed. by Mark Donohue and Søren Wichmann, 380–95. Oxford: Oxford University Press.

Vidal, Alejandra. 2001. *Pilagá grammar (Guaykuruan family, Argentina)*. Eugene: University of Oregon dissertation.

Vidal, Alejandra. 2009–10. Las dimensiones semántica y pragmática de las relaciones gramaticales en pilagá (guaycurú). *Amerindia* 33/34.151–84. (Special issue ed. by Lucía A. Golluscio and Alejandra Vidal.)

Vidal, Alejandra, and Analía Gutiérrez. 2010. La categoría de 'tiempo nominal' en las lenguas chaqueñas. In *La renovación de la palabra en el Bicentenario de la Argentina: los colores de la mirada lingüística*, ed. by Victor Castel and Liliana Cubo de Severino, 1348–55. Mendoza: Editorial FFyL.

Villafañe, Lucrecia. 2014. Yuki. In *Lenguas de Bolivia, vol. III Oriente*, ed. by Mily Crevels and Pieter Muysken, 175–219. La Paz: Plural editores.

Zúñiga, Fernando. 2002. *Inverse systems in indigenous languages of the Americas*. Zurich: University of Zurich dissertation.

11

The Typology of Grammatical Relations in Tuparian Languages with Special Focus on Akuntsú

Carolina Coelho Aragon and Fabrício Ferraz Gerardi

1. Introduction

This chapter investigates aspects of grammatical relations in five Tuparian languages (Akuntsú, Makuráp, Mekéns (Sakurabiat), Tuparí, and Wayoró), with special focus on Akuntsú, in order to compare and discuss their respective alignment patterns and the relationship between these patterns and word order.[1]

Van Valin and LaPolla (1997) have shown that grammatical relations and/or semantic roles are essential to well-formed clauses, to how speakers create meaning, and how hearers interpret it.[2] Coding of grammatical relations varies across languages, ranging from morphological case marking and word order to the discourse-pragmatic features.

The present work addresses the similarities and unique characteristics of grammatical relations in Tuparian languages. In addition, this chapter presents some of the special characteristics of Akuntsú, where the presence of an inanimate patient of a transitive construction was said to trigger a change in the alignment pattern. This study sheds light on the grammatical organization of Akuntsú, and raises the hypothesis that this language does not differentiate between possessive and intransitive constructions due to the character of its lexical roots. The lack of case marking in core arguments in the Tuparian languages indicates that grammatical relations are sensitive to verb semantics and verb categories, such as voice, word order, person markers, and animacy.

The rest of this chapter is organized as follows: the remainder of Section 1 outlines the current status of some languages in Rondônia, their historical background, and typological features of Akuntsú; Section 2 offers an overview of grammatical relations in Tuparian languages; Section 3 introduces the relationship between grammatical relations, word order, and animacy hierarchy; Section 4 discusses nominal and verbal syntax in Akuntsú; and Section 5 presents concluding remarks.

1.1 Languages of Rondônia

The term Tupian, designating a language family, has been employed since Rodrigues (1955) to refer to a linguistic family which includes the Tupi–Guarani subfamily and other smaller and lesser-known subfamilies. In 1986, Rodrigues revised the internal relationships within the Tupian family, accounting for ten subfamilies: Arikém, Aweti, Juruna, Mawé, Mondé, Mundurukú, Puruborá, Ramarama, Tuparí, and Tupi–Guaraní (Rodrigues 1986). Recent studies on genetic relationship and internal classification of the Tupian family have improved our understanding of this language family (Cabral and Rodrigues 2012; Galucio et al. 2015).

The Tupian languages have a peculiar geographic distribution (Rodrigues 2007). Five of these subfamilies (Arikém, Mondé, Puruborá, Ramarama, and Tuparian) are found in the state of Rondônia. The largest concentration of these subfamilies near tributaries of the Guaporé and Aripuanã rivers points to an origin in that area (see, for example, Rodrigues 2000 and Gerardi and Reichert 2021). The Arikém subfamily is the only one located outside the Guaporé–Aripuanã area, on the tributaries of the Madeira River. The Guaporé and the Mamoré regions are considered one of the most diverse linguistic regions in the world, with a linguistic area which includes, among others, Tupian languages and isolates (Crevels and van der Voort 2008). The languages investigated in this chapter are spoken by indigenous groups situated on the right bank of the Guaporé River, and all are endangered, either severely or critically (Languages Project 2020).

Lévi-Strauss (1948) was the first to mention the cultural similarities between the Rondonian Indians, especially those located near the Guaporé River (including speakers of Tuparian languages). He divided the Guaporé into two parts: the Chapacuran area, located to the west of Branco River (left side of the Guaporé), and the Tupian area to the east (right side of the Guaporé). Accounting for cultural similarities on both sides, such as the preparation of *marico* (baskets of various sizes made with tucum fiber), the lack of manioc cultivation, the construction of round houses, and the preparation of *chicha*, Maldi (1991) speaks of a "Marico Cultural Complex," which includes not only speakers of Tupian languages, but also speakers of isolated languages, such as Kanoé and Kwazá.

1.2 Akuntsú history

The Akuntsú live adjacent to the Omerê river, on the left bank of the Corumbiara River in the southeast of Rondônia. Nowadays, this language is spoken by only three women, the only survivors of a genocide. Based on their own stories, they were forced to abandon their homeland years ago (Aragon and Algayer 2020). The map in Figure 11.1 shows the "Rio Omrê" Indigenous Territory where the Akuntsú live.

The present location of the Akuntsú, their reduced number, and current situation can only be explained in the light of the colonization process of Rondônia. Indigenous life in Rondônia was drastically impacted by the Amazon rubber boom and intense extraction of latex, which took place from 1879 to the end of the Second World War (Trubiliano 2017). The settlement of the southeastern region of Rondônia during

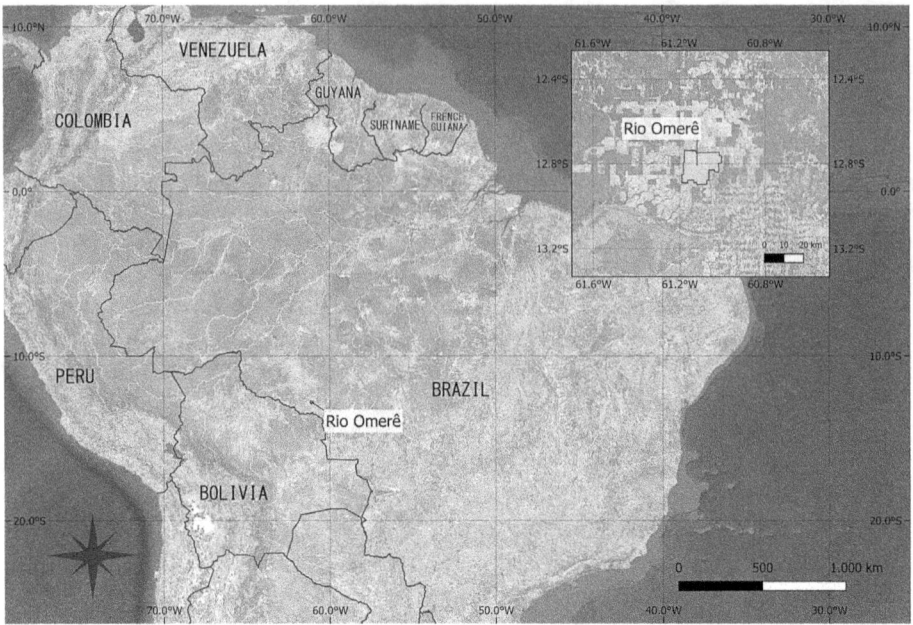

Figure 11.1 Map of the location of the Akuntsú in the "Rio Omerê" Indigenous Territory

the last three decades of the twentieth century was also devastating for the remaining indigenous groups who resisted the massive process of colonization (Valadão 1986), of which Akuntsú and Kanoé of the Omerê are representative.

These groups could only stop fleeing eminent death as late as 1995, when FUNAI (the National Indian Foundation) finally contacted them[3] (Santos and Algayer 1995). By that time, cattle ranchers had destroyed most of the rainforest where vestiges of indigenous people had previously been found. By then, the Akuntsú consisted of only one consanguineal group, seven people out of a larger population in the past.

The three Akuntsú women are all monolingual. Pugapia is in her eighties, her daughter Aiga in her sixties, and her other daughter Babawru in her forties. Konibu (or Kʷatin atʃo) and Pupak, the only men in the group, passed away in 2016 and 2017, respectively. The Kanoé of the Omerê shaman woman Txiramanty gave birth to Konibu's son, Bukwa, in 2002. Bukwa, a native speaker of Kanoé, began learning Portuguese and Akuntsú when he was around six years of age.

1.3 Typological features of Akuntsú

Akuntsú is a mildly agglutinative language, with some degree of synthesis. It is mostly a suffixing language with a single open class of lexical roots. Closed classes include postpositions, quantifiers/numerals, demonstratives/deictics, particles, and interjections.

The open word class lexically expresses objects, actions, and properties. The arguments may codify a subject or an object. Verbal roots may be syntactically transitive or intransitive. There are no copulas. Verbal morphology items include, among others, valence-changing morphemes, such as antipassives and causatives. There is also a subclass of auxiliary verbs and directional morphemes. Negation is either expressed by particle or/and by suffix.

Any lexical root and pronouns may function as a possessor. When a possessor is present, the syntactic construction formed requires a relational prefix (*t-* or *ø-*). Morphemes coding functional information on nominal lexical items include, for example: locatives, datives, essives/translatives, instrumentals, and inessives. Derivational operations include compounding, reduplication, and affixation.

Akuntsú, as a Tupian language, is predominantly head-final. Objects tend to precede verbs, with SOV as the most frequent word order. Clause combining may occur through parataxis and subordination.

2. Grammatical relations

In Tuparian languages each syntactic role is marked by one set of indexes.[4] All five Tuparian languages present two sets of indexes: (1) bound that mark subject, object, and possessor in possessive constructions;[5] and (2) free that mark the agent, as exemplified in Table 11.1.[6]

In Akuntsú,[7] as in other Tuparian languages, there is no overt case marking on nouns to distinguish actor and undergoer. This language, according to Aragon (2014), codes S and O with bound indexes[8] and A with free indexes. This is illustrated by the examples (1a–d):

Table 11.1 Set of personal pronouns across Tuparian languages

	Akuntsú (Aragon 2014)		Makuráp (Braga 2005)		Mekéns (Galucio 2001)		Tuparí (Singerman 2018)		Wayoró (Nogueira 2019)	
	Bound	Free	Bound	Free	Bound	Free	Bound	Free	Bound	Free
1SG	o=	on	o	on	o-	õt	o-/w-	on	m-/mb- ~o-	on
2SG	e=	en	e	en	e-	ẽt	e-	en	e-	en
3SG	i=/t=	te	Ø/e	tʃeke	i-/s-	te	i-~y- ~s-~Ø-	—	j-~dj- ~Ø- /te	ndeke
3COR	te=	—	—	—	se-	sete	te-	—	te	—
1PL.INC	ki=	kitʃe	ki	kitẽjã	ki-	kise	ki-	kit	tʃi-	tʃire
1PL.EXC	otʃe=	otʃe	te	tẽjã	ose-	ose	ote-	ote	ote-	ote
2PL	iat=	iat	eki	ekitẽjã	eyat	eyat	wat-	wat	djat-	djat
3PL	—	kejat	Ø/e	tʃekejã	teyat	teyat	—	—	j-~dj- ~ Ø- /te	ndeat
3PL.COR	—	—	—	—	seteyat	seteyat	—	—	—	—

S
(1) a. *o=atʃop-a*
    1SG=shower-THV
    "I shower."[9]

S
   b. *o=pip*
    1SG=afraid.of
    "I am scared." (Aragon 2014: 286)

A/O
   c. *tʃatʃakop o=pia*
    ant (sp.)   1SG=sting
    "Ant (sp.) stung me."

A/O
   d. *on   i=maã   kete*
    1SG 3=store there
    "I am storing it there."

Makuráp does not differ from Akuntsú in this respect. S and O are coded by bound argument indexes whereas A is marked differently from both S and O (Braga 2005), as can be seen in (2):

S
(2) a. *o=atet-a   on*[10]
    1SG=walk-IMPERF 1SG
    "I walk." (Braga 2005, 147)[11]

S
   b. *o=apitet-a   on*
    1SG=think-IMPERF 1SG
    "I think." (Braga 2005)

A/O
   c. *xeke o=peat-a*
    3SG   1SG=look.for-IMPERF
    "He looks for me." (Braga 2005, 111)

A/O
   d. *xop   me   eko   on   axexu   op-a*
    DEM.PROX LOC today 1SG towels wash-IMPERF
    "Today, I was washing the towels." (Braga 2005, 264)

In Mekéns, one set of bound argument indexes codes the absolutive arguments (S/O) whereas another set, free indexes, codes A:

S
(3) a. *o-ser-a-r=õt*
        1sg-leave/go-THV-?=1sg
        "I'm going (Lit. I leave)." (Galucio 2001: 160)

S
   b. *o-apitaka   o-yẽt*
       1sg-think   1sg-AUX.sitting.PRES
       "I am thinking." / "I am sitting thinking." (Galucio 2001: 84)

O/A
   c. *o-so-a-t   ẽt*
       1sg-see-THV-PAST   2sg
       "You saw me." (Galucio 2001: 130)

O/A
   d. *e-so-a-t   **õt***
       2sg-see-THV-PAST   1sg
       "I saw you." (Galucio 2001: 130)

In Tuparí, S and O are coded by the same set of argument indexes, whereas A is marked differently from both S and O:

S
(4) a. ***o-tet-a***   *ʔon*[12]
        1sg-go.SG-THV   1sg
        "I went." (Singerman 2018: 126)

S
   b. *w-apsitkat-a   ʔon   ʔẽn-o   Ø-maʔẽ-a   ʔen   herõwap   hem*
       1sg-think-THV 1sg   2sg-INS 3-speak-THV 2sg yesterday HE.INS
       "I thought about you, about the thing that you said yesterday." (Singerman 2018: 27)

O/A
   c. *o-top-a   ʔen*
       1sg-see-THV   2sg
       "You saw me." (Singerman 2018: 182)

O/A
   d. *e-top-a   ʔon*
       2sg-see-THV   1sg
       "I saw you." (Singerman 2018: 182)

Finally, the alignment in Wayoró is the same as in the other languages:

S
(5) a. *o-ter-Ø-a-t*
    1SG-go-VERBLZR-THV-PAST
    "I went." (Nogueira 2011: 70)

S
  b. *o-piako-õn*
    1SG-hot-1SG
    "I am hot." (Nogueira 2011: 58)

O/A
  c. *o-piri-g-a-t*   *ẽn*
    1SG-pierce-VERBLZR-THV-PAST   2SG
    "You pierced me." (Nogueira 2011: 155)

O/A
  d. *e-po-kw-a-t*   *õn*
    2SG-burn-kw-THV-PAST   1SG
    "I burn you." (Nogueira 2011: 102)

In light of the above examples, Tuparian languages can be said to exhibit an ergative–absolutive pattern and express grammatical relations by two different sets: bound indexes coding S and O, and free coding A. Recent studies on Tuparian languages have argued that the arguments of transitive and of intransitive verbs code similar properties in simple clauses (Galucio and Nogueira 2018). Based on the fact that free pronouns appear obligatorily in transitive clauses and optionally in intransitive ones (with the exception of Tuparí), these languages display a nominative–absolutive pattern, rather than an ergative–absolutive pattern. It has also been shown that besides this alignment pattern, Tuparian languages display "a divergent ergative pattern restricted to object focus clauses" (Galucio and Nogueira 2018: 123). Moreover, in Mekéns (Galucio 2001, 2014) and in Tuparí (Singerman 2018),[13] the nominative–accusative pattern is used with auxiliary verbs. Akuntsú will be discussed in Section 4.

A question that remains to be discussed concerns the identification of grammatical relations with arguments coded by full noun phrases (NPs), as in (6):

Makuráp
(6) *amengko*   *pok-ng-a*   *awa*
    jaguar   kill-EFF-IMPERF   **dad**
    "Daddy killed (the) jaguar." (Braga 2005, 255)

The next section discusses the above example, as well as other relevant examples that illustrate the role of syntax in defining grammatical relations in these languages.

3. The relationship between grammatical relations, word order, and animacy

It has been often said that grammatical relations are usually coded by word order (Van Valin and LaPolla 1997; Givón 2001). The analysis of argument indexes on predicates, seen in the previous sections, suggests that they are not the only property defining grammatical relations in Tuparian languages.

In all Tuparian languages, O tends to precede the predicate, and A and S can both precede or follow the predicate, a pattern that fits the typological parameter proposed in Dryer (1997): OV versus VO and SV versus VS, as seen in the following examples from all five Tuparian languages.

Akuntsú
(7) a. *Buko te=Ø-ti tʃop-a* (SOV)
Bukwa 3COR-R-mother see-THV
"Buquá is going to see his mother."

b. *pero õpa Konibu* (OVS)
macaw beat Konibu
"Konibu beat the macaw." (Aragon 2014: 221)

Makuráp
(8) a. *yã mame tut-a* (SOV)
mom pancake toast-IMPERF
"Mom toasts the pancake." (Braga 2005, 115)

b. *yiam amok-ng-a João (Marisa pe)* (OVS)
door open-EFF-IMPERF João Marisa DAT
"João opens (the) door (for Marisa)." (Braga 2005, 108)

Mekéns
(9) a. *ikwaay ameko õpa-a-t* (SOV)
tapir jaguar/dog beat/kill.by clutching-THV-PAST
"The tapir killed the jaguar." (Galucio 2001: 219)

b. *Ameko mi-a-r-ap Pedro* (OVS)
dog/jaguar kill-THV-PAST-NEG Pedro
"Pedro did not kill the jaguar." (Galucio 2001: 93)

Tuparí
(10) a. *Daltina-n i-memsit-et top-a* (SOV)
Daltina-NUC 3-child.of.woman-NUC see-THV
"Daltina saw her child." (Singerman 2018: 46)

b. i-aʔup-et   erote-pek-a-t   e kire-ʔeat-et   (OVS)
    3-son.of.man-NUC   all-buy-THV-NEAR.PAST   3   person-many-NUC
    "The people bought all of his sons." (Singerman 2018: 144)

Wayoró
(11) a. mbogop   aβẽko   õmba-Ø-a-t   (SOV)
         child   dog   hit-VERBLZR-THV-PAST
         "The child hit the dog." (Nogueira 2011: 71)

     b. aβi   k-a-t   ɲã   (OVS)
         daddy   ingest-THV-PAST mommy
         "Mommy ate daddy." (Nogueira 2011: 72)

Since in these languages argument indexes seem to control the morphological coding of grammatical relations and the unmarked word order can be either SOV or OVS, the issue is how to identify the A and O when both are full NPs, as in sentences such as "X_A kills Y_O" or "X_O kills Y_A" below:

Makuráp
(12) amengko   pok-ng-a   awa
     jaguar   kill-EFF-IMPERF   daddy
     "Daddy killed (the) jaguar." (Braga 2005, 255)

Akuntsú
(13) ameko   mi-a   Konibú
     jaguar   kill-THV   Konibú
     "Konibú killed (the) jaguar."

In Akuntsú, despite the fact that the subject can be placed before or after the predicate, the object directly precedes the predicate in unmarked sentences. The object is usually preverbal and, when it is placed after the predicate (and the pragmatic situation is not clear to the hearer), either a focus marker or prosody indicates its movement:

(14) a. mi-a   te   poka
         kill-THV   FOC   tortoise
         "Kill the tortoise." (Aragon 2014: 283)

     b. pero   tʃok-a   te   Kani Ø-po
         macaw   bite-THV   FOC   Kani R-hand
         "Macaw bite Kani's hand." (Aragon 2014: 284)

When A is placed after the predicate, it is because O is the topic of the conversation:

(15) Tʃiramanti t-ek   poka   i=ko   Bawro
     Tʃiramanti R-house   burn   3=BE.IN.MOVEMENT   Paulo
     "Paulo is burning Txiramanty's house."

In Akuntsú, animacy is reflected in the semantic relation between the predicate and its arguments when the arguments are full noun phrases, but not free indexes. When both arguments are [+animate], a noun that is [+human] is preferred as A over nouns that are [-human] (see Croft 2003: 111–17):

(16) tatakaw   õpa   Konibú
     lizard   kill   Konibú (proper name)
     "Konibú killed the lizard." (Aragon 2008: 119)

When both A and O are [+human] and in clauses where the theme is not the focus, O precedes the verb and A is placed before the predicate (17), whereas OV is not a separable unit.

(17) Etʃinawdo   [Ururu   tʃop-a   kom]
     Reginaldo   Ururu   see-THV   PROJ
     "Reginaldo will see Ururu."

As for word order in other Tuparian languages, Braga (2005) argues that in Makuráp the basic word order is OVS and the object is placed immediately before the predicate in any situation. She shows that it is possible to identify grammatical relations both through word order and through pragmatics. The object retains a fixed position relative to the verb, either preceding or following it according to the pragmatics of the context. In other words, it is the "thematic relation" (Braga 2005: 146) which determines the SOV and OVS word orders in this language.

In Mekéns, A of transitive clauses can be placed before OV (SOV) or after it (OVS) (as shown above for Makuráp and Akuntsú). O has a fixed position that always precedes the verb. Hence, the same question applies to Mekéns: What happens when O and A of the clause are expressed by full NPs instead of by free or bound indexers, since the word order can be both OVS and SOV? For Galucio (2002), there is a difference between a clause which has a nominal subject and a clause with a subject expressed by a free index. She argues that in a clause that has a pronominal subject the word order is usually OVS, and when it has a nominal subject, the order is SOV. She found in her corpus that SOV amounts to 71% of the clauses that have a nominal subject and only 29% with pronominal subject. Wayoró clauses are predominantly SOV or OVS, whereas OV is the fixed order (Nogueira 2011). Regarding Tuparí, both word orders (SOV and OVS) are attested and, according to Singerman (2018), direct objects must precede the transitive verbs.

4. From verbal to nominal syntax in Akuntsú

Aragon (2014) states that the ergative–absolutive pattern may be neutralized in the case of O expressed by [-human] NP with A coded by a bound index (first and second person only). In this case, the word order becomes OSV, as in examples (18–19):

1 (AGENT) > 3 (NON-HUMAN PATIENT)
(18) a. *pitoa   o=kõj-ka   kõj-kõj-kõj*
tobacco   1SG=pound-TR   pound-RED-RED
"I'm going to pound the tobacco, kneading (intensively)." (Aragon 2014: 282)

Literally: (There is) my pounding (of) tobacco[14]

　　b. *kɨpkap   o=paj-a*
annatto   1SG =clean-THV
"I clean the annatto (by removing the leaves from the fruit)." (Aragon 2014: 203)

　　c. *kɨp   t-ep   o=ĩ-a*
tree   R-leaf   1SG=smell-THV
"I smell the leaf of the tree." (Aragon 2014: 203)

2 (AGENT) > 3 (NON-HUMAN PATIENT)
(19) a. *orobaj   e=ãmana*
bird (sp.)   2SG=put.away
"You put away the bird."

Literally: (There is) your putting away (of the) bird

　　b. *o=Ø-jã + po   e=õ-a*
1SG=R-teeth + hand   2SG=give-THV
"You gave my spoon." (Aragon 2014: 203)

　　c. *komãta   e=at-a*
bean   2SG=get-THV
"You've picked beans." (Aragon 2014: 203)

Reanalyzing the data in Aragon (2014), another interpretation is proposed here. Observe that the bound indexes used to cross-reference S and O are also used for marking the possessor in possessive constructions (20a–b). The reanalysis considers bound indexes to be possessor, but not argument indexes.

(20)　a. *e=Ø-ãpita   tam*
2SG=R-nose   Full
"Your nose is congested." (Aragon 2014: 181)

b. *e=Ø-ãpita*
    2SG=R-nose
    "(There is/it is) your nose/You have a nose."

The hypothesis put forward here is that Akuntsú intransitive predication is expressed by existential predicative possession, that is, nominal instead of verbal syntax. This is a case of acategoriality in function indication, as proposed by Haspelmath (forthcoming). Taking the speech act function of predication, for example, it can be expressed by any semantic root class without a function indicator, as in (21).

OBJECT-DENOTING WORD
(21) a. $k^w ak^w a$ *i=t-et*
         $k^w ak^w a$ 3=R-name
         "$k^w ak^w a$ is her name / $k^w ak^w a$, there is her name." (Aragon 2014: 272)

PROPERTY-DENOTING WORD
    b. *i=petʃe*
        3=good
        "It is good / There is its good(ness)."

ACTION-DENOTING WORD
    c. *kete en   i=ma*
        there 2SG 3=place/put/spill
        "You put it there / There is its placing of/by you there." (Aragon 2014: 247)

Example (20b) is thus an existential predicate similar to what has been suggested by Dietrich (2017) for Guaraní.[15] The original verbal construction is replaced by a predicative possessive (nominal) construction, but this terminology is unnecessary since lexical roots are acategorial (see Haspelmath forthcoming). This idea becomes clearer by comparing the "verbal construction" in (22) which uses the free index *en* against its "nominal counterpart" in (19a) with a bound index *e=*.

(22) *En   orobaj   ãmana*
     2SG   bird (sp.) put.away
     "You put away the bird."

The use of bound indexes in a possessive construction and, according to the interpretation in Aragon (2014), in a construction marking the absolutive argument of a verbal predicate only differs in the presence or absence of the relational prefix. While examples (23a–b) do not take relational morphemes, (23c–d) require them. This could be due to the semantics of "more noun-like words" (see Givón 2001: 49—4). As it will be shown below, other morphemes that would be expected to occur with one specific root class, do, in fact, combine with roots of other classes, blurring the word classes' distinctions.

(23) a. *koɾo   o=eɾe-kʷa*
    bowl   1SG =speak-TR.PL
    "Bowl, I say." (Aragon 2014: 150)

  b. *apaɾapia   o=tʃop-a*
    non.Indian   1SG=see-THV
    "The non–Indian saw me." (Aragon 2014: 202)

  c. *o=ø-mapi ete?*
    1SG=R-arrow REL
    "What about my arrow?" (Aragon 2014: 156)

  d. *o=t-it   jẽ   it*
    1SG=R-buttocks   DEM   buttocks
    "(It is) my buttocks, this buttocks." (Aragon 2014: 132)

Positing a single function for the bound person markers, that of possessor— instead of possessor and absolutive marker—simplifies the system as a whole and keeps it coherent. We do not want to categorically exclude a line between root classes in Akuntsú, but one should not consider structures of one language in terms of the categories of another (see Haspelmath 2007). In spite of the absence of a relational prefix between the bound person marker and the action-denoting root (23a–b) it is still possible to consider this construction one of the "nominal type."

Roots in Akuntsú may, on the one hand, perform different syntactic functions without a function indicator (see Haspelmath forthcoming). On the other hand, morphemes may apply to roots of any class, emphasizing root acategoriality as far as speech–act functions are concerned (Croft 1991, 2021; Haspelmath forthcoming). For example, the transitivizer morphemes *-ka* (24) and *-kʷa* (25), and the projective morpheme *kom* (26) can be combined with object-denoting roots (24a, 25a, and 26a) or action-denoting roots (24b, 25b, and 26b):

(24) a. *kap   e=pit-ka*
    wasp   2SG=hole-TR
    "Wasp stung you." (Aragon 2014: 181)

  b. *o=Ø-anam   ãpi-pi-ka*
    1SG =R-head   pull-RED-TR
    "I am pulling and pulling my head." (Aragon 2014: 228)

(25) a. *apaw   i=t-et-kʷa*
    grub (sp.)   3=R-name-TR.PL
    "I call it grub / Grub is its name." (Aragon 2014: 274)

  b. *Enotej   iki   kiɾam-kwa*
    Enotéj   water   pour-TR.PL
    "Enotéj is pouring water." (Aragon 2014: 216)

(26) a. pebo   at-a kom   Pura   kom   pebo   kom
         feather   get-THV PROJ   Purá   PROJ feather PROJ
         "He will get the feather, it will be Purá, it will be the feather." (Aragon 2014: 228)

   b. tekarap   ita-a   kom
       rain   arrive-THV   PROJ
       "The rain will arrive (soon)." (Aragon 2014: 227)

Just as relational prefixes only combine with the object-denoting root, the "thematic vowel" -a/-Ø (see Aragon 2014) optionally attaches to action-denoting roots and it seems to be context dependent (27a). It also never appears with negation (27b).[16]

(27) a. apara   ko-a   apara   ko   apara   ko   wen
         banana   ingest-THV   banana   ingest   banana   ingest   finish
         "(She) is eating bananas over and over, (they are) gone." (Aragon 2014: 229)

   b. en   i=o-kit   ko-a   orẽ=bõ   nõm   iwe
       2SG   3=R-seed   ingest-THV   1SG.EM=DAT   no   INTERJ
       nõm   i=o-kit   ko
       no   3=R-seed   ingest
       "You eat the seed, I don't, it hurts, (I) don't eat the seed." (Aragon 2014: 231)

Furthermore, what was asserted as an "innovative A-alignment" based on the morpheme -i- "object nominalizer" (sometimes referred to as "(object) focus marker") in Tuparian languages (Galucio and Nogueira 2018), occurs in Akuntsú exclusively in "nominal constructions," combining, for example, with oblique clitics (28a). In fact, "nominalized constructions" may also combine with aspectual markers (28b), a category usually associated with verbal morphology (see Croft 2021: Chapter 1).[17]

(28) a. arop   i-tʃop=na?
         who   OBJ.NMLZ-see=ESS
         "For whom (whose) is the seen (thing)?" (Aragon 2014: 293)

   b. e=i-mi   tawtʃe   nika
       2SG =OBJ.NMLZ-kill peccary   UNC
       "It may be your hunted thing, peccary." (Aragon 2014: 253)

The analysis presented here seems to suggest that, due to the fact that monovalent predicates only exist as possessive existential predication, it would be irrelevant to talk about alignment patterns.

5. Final remarks

This chapter briefly surveyed the alignment patterns in languages of the Tuparian subfamily and explored the peculiarities of Akuntsú. In addition, it examined the relationship between argument indexes (bound and free) with different alignment types, shedding light on how the different word orders interact with animacy of full NPs. Word order and discourse organization play an important role in defining grammatical relations in Tuparian languages. In Akuntsú, bound indexes are better seen as possessor indexes, thus making the discussion of alignment type superficial. Whether this analysis can be extended to other Tuparian languages will depend on the results of investigations of lexical roots in these languages in the light of Haspelmath (forthcoming) and Croft (2021).

Again, what was previously regarded as a change in the alignment pattern due to animacy constraints is better explained as a change from verbal to nominal syntax, excluding intransitive verbs in favor of possessive predication. It was also suggested that semantic categories of roots, object, action and property are expressed by a single word class in Akuntsú. This class can function syntactically as argument or predicate without function indicator (Croft 2021). A comprehensive diachronic study of lexical roots in Tuparian languages would be invaluable for throwing light on the hypothesis suggested here.

Notes

1. Carolina Aragon would like to thank her colleagues who organized this book, providing the opportunity to honor the career of Professor Lyle Campbell, to whom she is grateful. We both thank Professor Wolf Dietrich, Stanislav Reichert, and Frederic Blum for their comments and suggestions.
2. Of particular interest in the approach to grammatical relations in Role and Reference Grammar is the fact that these are not regarded as universal, that is, not all languages possess them (see Van Valin 2005: 89–127).
3. These peoples were considered isolated before the contact.
4. We employ the terms argument indexes and possessor indexes following Haspelmath (2013).
5. Possessive constructions in Akuntsú will be analyzed in Section 4.
6. For Proto-Tupian, two different sets of person markers, bound and free, have been reconstructed (Rodrigues and Cabral 2012).
7. The Akuntsú data used in this study are from casual discourse. All the examples for Tuparian languages in this chapter deal with simple clauses and no auxiliary verbs were analyzed. The original glossings of each source have been maintained.
8. It will be shown below that the bound indexes code neither S nor O, but possessors.
9. All examples without a quoted source are from Aragon's field notes.
10. The free pronoun is optional in intransitive clauses for Akuntsú, Makuráp, Mekéns, and Wayoró.
11. The examples from Braga (2005) are from a Word document (.docx), and the numbers refer to the example number (when mentioned in the original) and not to the page. The original examples have been translated from French to English by the authors of this chapter.
12. The glottal stop in the Tuparí examples substitutes the apostrophe (') in the original source. Unlike the other Tuparian languages, there is another set of

pronouns called weak nominative pronouns: ʔon (1SG), ʔen (2SG), ʔokit (1INCL. DUAL), ʔokitwat (1INC.PL), ʔote (1EXCL), wat (2PL), e ~Ø- (3). These pronouns are not optional in intransitive clauses. Their use is conditioned by tense marking, rather than by the valency of the lexical verb (Singerman 2018: 296–7).
13. Singerman (2018:180) questions this alignment system with auxiliaries in Tuparí, referring to it as a "(superficial) nominative-accusative one."
14. This is the appropriate translation suggested for the examples (18–19).
15. Meira (2006: 212) also discussed the "lack of sharpness of the verb-noun distinction" for Sateré-Mawé. See also Queixalós (2006) regarding the omnipredicative type of Tupi–Guaraní languages, which could perhaps be extended to (some) Tupian languages.
16. Aragon (2014) suggests that this thematic vowel may be now a crystalized morpheme whose function can neither be traced nor predictable from the phonological context.
17. It is possible for languages that do not have function-indicator markers that substantive markers shape the behavior of roots (see Croft 1991, 2021; Haspelmath forthcoming). In Akuntsú the relational morphemes and the thematic vowel should be associated with "behavioral potential" of roots as far as word class is concerned. Substantive markers, as Haspelmath (forthcoming: 21) observes, "contribute to semantic substance, and do not … point to an atypical propositional act function."

References

Aragon, Carolina Coelho. 2008. *Fonologia e aspectos morfológicos e sintáticos da língua Akuntsú.* University of Brasília master's thesis.
Aragon, Carolina Coelho. 2014. *A grammar of Akuntsú, a Tupian language.* University of Hawai'i, Manoa Ph.D. thesis.
Aragon, Carolina Coelho, and Altair Algayer. 2020. A história contada pelos Akuntsú: ocupação territorial e perdas populacionais. *Linguística Antropológica* 12(1).223–34.
Braga, Alzerinda de Oliveira. 2005. *Aspects morphosyntaxiques de la langue Makuráp/ Tupi.* University of Toulouse, Mirail Ph.D. thesis.
Crevels, Mily, and Hein van der Voort. 2008. The Guaporé-Mamoré region as a linguistic area. In *From linguistic areas to areal linguistics* (Studies in Language Companion Series 90) ed. by Pieter Muysken 151–79. Amsterdam/Philadelphia: John Benjamins.
Croft, William. 1991. *Syntactic categories and grammatical relations: The cognitive organization of information.* Chicago: University of Chicago Press.
Croft, William. 2003. *Typology and universals.* 2nd edn. Cambridge: Cambridge University Press.
Croft, William. 2021. *Morphosyntax: Constructions of the world's languages.* Draft version (January). New Mexico: University of New Mexico.
Dietrich, Wolf. 2017. Word classes and word class switching in Guaraní Syntax. In *Guarani linguistics in the 21st century*, ed. by Bruno Estigarribia and Justin Pinta, 158–93. Leiden: Brill.

Dryer, Matthew S. 1997. On the six-way word order typology. *Studies in Language* 21(1).69–103.
Endangered languages Project. Catalogue of endangered languages 2020, <http://www.endangeredlanguages.com> (last accessed August 16, 2021).
Ferraz Gerardi, Fabricio, and Stanislav Reichert. 2021. The Tupí-Guaraní language family: A phylogenetic classification. *Diachronica* 38(2).151–88.
Galucio, Ana Vilacy. 2001. *The morphosyntax of Mekéns*. University of Chicago Ph.D. thesis.
Galucio, Ana Vilacy. 2002. Word order and constituent structure in Mekéns. *Revista da ABRALIN* 1(2).51–73.
Galucio, Ana Vilacy. 2014. Estrutura argumental e alinhamento gramatical em Mekéns. In *Sintaxe e Semântica do verbo em línguas indígenas do Brasil*, ed. by Luciana Storto, Bruna Franchetto, and Suzi Lima, 167–96. Campinas: Mercado de Letras.
Galucio, Ana Vilacy, and Antônia Nogueira. 2018. From object nominalization to object focus. *Journal of Historical Linguistics* 8(1).95–127.
Galucio, Ana Vilacy, Sergio Meira, Joshua Birchall, Denny Moore, Nilson Gabas, Sebastian Drude, Luciana Storto, Gessiane Picanço, and Carmen Rodrigues. 2015. Genealogical relations and lexical distances within the Tupian linguistic family. *Boletim do Museu Paraense Emílio Goeldi: Ciências Humanas* 10(2).229–74.
Givón, Talmy. 2001. *Syntax: A functional-typological introduction, vol. 2*. Amsterdam: John Benjamins.
Haspelmath, Martin. 2007. Pre-established categories don't exist: Consequences for language description and typology. *Linguistic Typology* 11(1).
Haspelmath, Martin. Forthcoming. *Word class universals and language-particular analysis*.
Lévi-Strauss, Claude. 1948. Tribes of the right bank of the Guaporé River. In *Handbook of South American Indians*, ed. by Julian Steward, vol. 3, 371–9. Washington, DC: United States Government Printing Office.
Maldi, Denise. 1991. O complexo cultural do Marico: sociedades indígenas dos rios Branco, Colorado e Mequéns, afluentes do médio Guaporé. *Boletim do Museu Paraense Emílio Goeldi* 7(2).209–69.
Meira, Sergio. 2006. Stative verbs vs. nouns in Sateré-Mawé and the Tupian family. *LOT Occasional Series* 5.189–214.
Nogueira, Antonia. 2011. *Wayoró ẽmẽto: fonologia segmental e morfossintaxe verbal*. University of São Paulo Master's thesis.
Nogueira, Antonia. 2019. *Predicação na língua Wayoró (Tupi): propriedades de finitude*. University of São Paulo Ph.D. thesis.
Queixalós, Francisco. 2006. The primacy and fate of predicativity in Tupi-Guarani. In *Lexical categories and root classes in Amerindian Languages*, ed. by Ximena Lois and Valentina Vapnarsky, 249–87. Bern, Switzerland: Peter Lang CH.
Rodrigues, Aryon Dall'Igna. 1955. As línguas "impuras" da família Tupi-Guarani. In *Anais do XXXI Congresso Internacional de Americanistas*, 1055–71. São Paulo.

Rodrigues, Aryon Dall'Igna. 1986. *Línguas brasileiras: para o conhecimento das línguas indígenas*. São Paulo: Loyola.
Rodrigues, Aryon Dall'Igna. 2000. Hipótese sobre as migrações dos três subconjuntos Meridionais da família Tupí-Guarani. *Atas do II Congresso Nacional da Abralin e XIV Instituto Lingüístico*, Florianópolis, CD-ROM, 1596–1605.
Rodrigues, Aryon Dall'Igna. 2007. Tupí languages in Rondônia and in Eastern Bolívia. In *Language endangerment and endangered languages: Linguistic and anthropological studies with special emphasis on the languages and cultures of the Andean-Amazonian border area*, ed. by Leo Wetzels. Leiden: Universiteit Leiden.
Rodrigues, Aryon Dall'Igna, and Ana Suelly Arruda Câmara Cabral. 2012. Tupían. In *The indigenous languages of South America: A comprehensive guide*, ed. by Lyle Campbell and Verónica Grondona, 495–594. Berlin: Mouton de Gruyter.
Santos, Marcelo, and Altair Algayer. 1995. Índios Isolados do Vale do Corumbiara. Technical Report. Fundação Nacional do Índio, Brasília. Ms.
Singerman, Adam. 2018. *The morphosyntax of Tuparí, a Tupían language of the Brazilian Amazon*. University of Chicago Ph.D. thesis.
Trubiliano, Carlos Alexandre Barros. 2017. Apontamentos sobre a economia da borracha e a exploração da mão de obra indígena em Rondônia. *Revista Ñanduty* 5(7).45–63.
Valadão, Virgínia. 1986. *Relatório de avaliação: Área Indígena Igarapé Omeré*. Technical Report. Fundação Nacional do Índio. Ms.
Van Valin, Robert D. 2005. *Exploring the syntax-semantics interface*. Cambridge: Cambridge University Press.
Van Valin, Robert D., and Randy J. LaPolla. 1997. *Syntax: Structure, meaning, and function*. Cambridge: Cambridge University Press.

12

Meskwaki (Algonquian) Evidence against Basic Word Order and Configurational Models of Argument Roles

Ives Goddard and Amy Dahlstrom

The syntax of Meskwaki (Algonquian; spoken in Iowa) is sensitive to grammatical relations such as subject, object, secondary object, and oblique, but word order is not used to distinguish subject from object.[1] In other words, Meskwaki is an example of the type of language proposed by Mithun (1987) in which none of the six permutations of subject, verb, and object familiar from Greenberg (1966) can be identified as the basic word order. Instead, Meskwaki word order is sensitive to a template including positions specialized for discourse functions such as topic and focus. The word order template is largely flat, with no verb phrase (VP) constituent grouping together a verb and its direct object and excluding the subject. We here present a corpus-based study of a set of clauses in which word order might be predicted to play a role in distinguishing subjects from objects: clauses in which the subject and object are both marked as obviative, used for third persons peripheral to the discourse. We show below that even in this context word order is not determined by grammatical relations. Instead, word order is sensitive to the relative ranking of the two obviatives in the discourse, rather than functioning to indicate which argument is subject and which is object.

A secondary goal of the chapter is to emphasize the value of older written texts for language documentation. For Meskwaki there is an extraordinary corpus of nearly 27,000 pages of traditional narratives and ethnographic information, written during 1911–18 in the Meskwaki syllabary (Goddard 1996) by mostly monolingual speakers of Meskwaki for Smithsonian ethnologist Truman Michelson. This corpus is stored at the Smithsonian Institution's National Anthropological Archives (NAA). As discussed in Goddard (1990b), these texts constitute a remarkably accurate record of connected speech by fluent speakers who were skilled narrators: they preserve an oral culture on paper. For linguists, the NAA corpus is invaluable for discovering the discourse conditions influencing the order of constituents in Meskwaki, a language with extremely flexible word order, or for investigating the discourse-based opposition within third person known as OBVIATION (Thomason 2003). Both obviation and word order are extensively discussed below. Most examples in the present chapter are drawn from this corpus; some simple elicited sentences from fieldwork illustrate basic descriptive facts.[2]

1. Background on Meskwaki

Meskwaki verbs are subcategorized for grammatical relations including subject, (primary) object, secondary object, and oblique, with relation-changing syntactic processes such as causative and antipassive sensitive to these grammatical relations. Verbs exhibit inflectional morphology that encodes the following features of the subject and (primary) object: person, number, gender (animate vs. inanimate), and OBVIATION. Obviation is a discourse-based opposition within third person: the third person most central to the discourse is referred to by unmarked third person forms, called PROXIMATE; other, more peripheral third persons are referred to by marked OBVIATIVE forms. The opposition of proximate and obviative is overtly marked on animate gender nouns and demonstrative pronouns, and it also appears in verb inflection. For example, in (1) the man is the third person participant of central interest so the noun stem *neniw-* "man" is inflected with the unmarked third person animate singular suffix *-a*. The drum, grammatically animate in Meskwaki, is of less interest and is marked obviative singular with the suffix *-ani* (underlyingly *ahkohkw-ani*). The verb is inflected with a complex string of suffixes indicating that an animate singular proximate third person subject is acting on an animate obviative third person object (here in the aorist conjunct verbal mode).[3]

(1) ôni='pi neniw-a êh=anwêwêhw-âči   ahkohkôni.
  and=HRSY man-SG AOR=make.O.sound.by.beating-3>3'/AOR drum.OBV
  "and the man (proximate), it's said, would beat the drum (obviative)."
  (K-MFLA 190)

In (1) we see that the inflection on the verb for subject and object functions as agreement with the external arguments. In the absence of an external subject or object, the inflection on the verb is interpreted pronominally:

(2) êh=anwêwêhw-âči
  AOR=make.O.sound.by.beating-3>3'/AOR
  "he or she (proximate) beats it (obviative)."

The marking of proximate and obviative third persons is subject to certain syntactic constraints. For example, nouns possessed by a third person possessor are obligatorily obviative:[4]

(3) o-kwis-ani "his or her son (obviative)"
  3-son-OBV

  *o-kwis-a
  3-son-SG

Furthermore, it is impossible to have a transitive verb for which both subject and object are third person proximate: only one proximate argument is permitted per clause. In fact, the system of verb inflection (discussed further below) is incapable of expressing that both subject and object are proximate. It is possible, however, for both arguments of a transitive verb to be third person obviative if there is a third person proximate present in the context (often as possessor of one of the obviative noun phrases (NPs)):

(4) ôs-ani   ašâh-ahi   êh=nes-ekoniči
     3.father-OBV Sioux-OBV.PL   AOR=kill-3″>3′/AOR
     "The Siouxs (obviative) killed his (proximate) father (obviative)." (K-MBES 1)

The proximate third person of (4) is a young boy, the possessor of *ôsani* 'his father,' and both the father and the Siouxs are obviative. More examples of this type are presented in (37–47) in the discussion of word order.

Although in the narrowest contexts—bare-minimum possessed noun phrases and transitive verb clauses—there cannot be two proximates, speakers have considerable latitude in assigning proximate and obviative status within more complex clauses and sentences and in connected discourse. Proximates may co-occur if they are conjoined, but alternatively one of a pair of conjoined nouns may be obviative. A third-person-possessed obviative that is central to the narrative may immediately show agreement as a proximate. A temporarily highlighted proximate can be followed in the same sentence by a higher ranked or more central proximate. It is a fundamental characteristic of the proximate and obviative categories that to a significant extent they are not dictated by grammatical considerations but are deployed for discourse purposes. The speaker has the option to manipulate both who or what is proximate and the length of the narrative span over which proximate status is maintained, which may extend over many sentences (Goddard 1990a; Thomason 2003). In informal narratives as opposed to story-telling, Thomason (1995) found "a different (less elaborate) set of criteria for establishing relative discourse prominence." And a speaker may also assign obviative status in the absence of an overt proximate to indicate a point of view outside the narrative, especially one that has shifted (see (38–9, 41, 44 below). It is not possible to account for the use of proximate and obviative in Meskwaki by referring only to inflectional morphology within sentences, as proposed, for example, for Potawatomi by Halle and Marantz (1993).

Meskwaki verbs indicate features of subject and object in relation to a hierarchical ranking of person and animacy categories. That is, the person and number features of both subject and object are expressed by affixes which are unspecified for grammatical function; a separate suffix on transitive verbs, known as a THEME SIGN, indicates which cluster of person and number features is to be interpreted as the subject and which as the object. Consider the following pair of verbs inflected in the independent indicative mode, used for main clause assertions, with the theme signs in boldface:

(5) a. *newâpamâwa*   "I looked at him or her."
         ne-wâpam-â-w-a
         1-look.at-DIRECT-3-(3)SG

b. *newâpamekwa* "He or she looked at me."
   ne-wâpam-**ekw**-w-a
   1-look.at-INVERSE-3-(3)SG

The verb forms in (5a–b) are identical except for the theme sign, labelled DIRECT in (5a) and INVERSE in (5b). Both verbs bear a first person prefix *ne-*, and both exhibit a third person suffix *w* followed by a third person singular suffix *-a*. The direct suffix in (5a) indicates that the subject outranks the object on the following hierarchy:

(6) non-third person > third person proximate > third person (first) obviative > third person second obviative > inanimate

Since the subject outranks the object, in (5a) the cluster of non-third person features must be associated with subject and the cluster of third person features must be associated with object. Conversely, the inverse suffix in (5b) imposes the opposite interpretation: the object of (5b) outranks the subject on the hierarchy so the third person features are mapped onto subject and the non-third person features are mapped onto object. Note, however, that in the glosses of examples other than (5) in this chapter the theme signs are not separately glossed. Instead, the cumulative information about subject and object features is expressed in glosses such as "1>3," to be read "first person singular subject acting on a third person singular object."

The opposition of direct and inverse morphology on transitive verbs holds not only for verbs involving one third person argument and one non-third person argument, as in (5), but also for verbs in which both arguments are third person. (Verbs with two non-third person arguments are expressed with different theme signs.) If a proximate subject acts upon an obviative object, a direct theme sign is used; if an obviative subject acts upon a proximate object, an inverse theme sign is used. When both arguments are obviative third person a ranking must be imposed upon the two obviatives, making one a FIRST OBVIATIVE (also called "nearer obviative") and the other a SECOND OBVIATIVE (or "further obviative"). In (4) above, the father, as a relative of the proximate character and as a Meskwaki, is higher on the scale of empathy. The Siouxs, on the other hand, were the traditional enemies of the Meskwaki. The father in (4) is therefore the first obviative and the Siouxs are the second obviative, and the verb contains an inverse theme sign.

It must be emphasized that the opposition of direct and inverse is a morphological phenomenon associated with the hierarchical type of case marking system, and it does not reflect a change of grammatical relations. That is, the agent argument of the inverse verbs in (4) and (5b) are subjects and the theme or patient arguments are objects.

Only subjects and (primary) objects trigger agreement on the verb; secondary objects and obliques do not. Ditransitive verbs encode the recipient or beneficiary as primary object and the theme or patient argument as secondary object, as in (7).

(7) nehtamaw-i   k-ôhkomesêh-enân-a   mâhani   kîhčêw-ani
    kill.O2.for-2>3/IMP 2-grandmother-1P-SG   this.OBV turkey-OBV
    "Kill this turkey for our (inclusive) grandmother" (K-W 189)

Pronominal third person secondary objects are expressed by zero anaphora:

(8) ke-mîn-ene   "I gave him, it, them (anim., inan.) to you (sg.)"
    2-give-1>2/IND

A subset of verbs in Meskwaki require a subject and a "secondary" object, with no primary object, as in (9). See Dahlstrom (2009) for discussion of the syntax of these verbs.

(9) ahpênemo-wa   o-sîmêh-ani
    rely.on.O2-3/IND 3-younger.sibling-OBV
    "He relies on his younger brother." (K-W 712)

As with ditransitives, pronominal third person secondary objects are expressed by zero anaphora:

(10) wêpâhkê-wa   "he threw him, it, them (anim., inan.)"
     throw.O2-3/IND

Note that the verb of (10) does not have an intransitive meaning such as "engage in throwing": it requires a second argument expressing the object thrown.

OBLIQUE arguments in the Lexical Functional Grammar (LFG) inventory of grammatical functions are ones in which a thematic role is explicitly encoded, perhaps by choice of preposition, as in English, or by semantic case marking, as in Finnish. In Algonquian languages it is special morphology (known as RELATIVE ROOTS) in verb stems and preverbs which typically encodes the thematic role associated with particular oblique arguments. For example, in (11) the initial morpheme of the verb stem (underlying form |ot-|, with mutation of the *t* to *č* by the following high front vowel) signals that the verb requires an oblique argument expressing source.

(11) menes-eki   êh=očiwen-ekoči,
     island-LOC   AOR=carry.O.from.{somewhere}-3'>3/AOR
     "It (an eagle) carried him from the island" (K-MFLA 161)

Further examples of obliques may be found below in (13, 15, 26); see Dahlstrom (2014) for more discussion of this grammatical relation.

2. Word order template

We are assuming here an informal version of LFG in which grammatical relations such as subject and object are represented separately from constituent structure (cf. Bresnan et al. 2015). This is a departure from theories such as Chomsky's Minimalist Program (Chomsky 1995) and earlier proposals in which grammatical relations are a secondary notion, derived from a universal asymmetry in phrase structure in which a verb and its direct object form a constituent which excludes the subject. A consequence of divorcing the grammatical relations of a clause from the constituent structure expression of that clause is that there is no need to assume a universal configuration of phrase structure. Instead, LFG analyses require that constituent structure represent only those categories and constituents for which positive evidence can be found in the language under investigation. As a consequence, a wide variety of constituent structures is permitted within the LFG framework.[5] With that in mind we argue that Meskwaki constituent structures are sensitive to the template in (12):

(12) [$_{S'}$ TOPIC [$_S$ NEG FOCUS (FOCUS) OBL V {SUBJ, OBJ, OBJ2, COMP}]]

The schema in (12) indicates that if an overt topic is present it appears in initial position, followed by a comment which is a full clause (S). Within the clause proper, a negative element, if present, will be leftmost, followed by slots for focused elements, such as contrastive focus or the answer to a question-word question. To the immediate left of the verb is the unmarked position for arguments bearing the syntactic relation of oblique. Other syntactic types of arguments, such as subject, object, second object, and complement clauses (COMP), appear to the right of the verb unless they are in topic or focus position. In contrast to the generalizations that can be made about relative order of elements to the left of the verb, it is difficult to predict the relative order of the right-hand elements when more than one argument follows the verb, as will be seen in the word order discussion below. The template in (12) indicates only that any number of constituents may occur in postverbal position, and that they may be associated with the grammatical functions listed in the curly brackets.

Note that the structure of (12) is largely flat, except for the topic position, which is outside the clause proper. Evidence that the topic position is higher in the structure than the remaining portion of the utterance comes from coordination, placement of adverbial clauses, and placement of second position enclitics (Dahlstrom 1993). For example, in (13) a second position enclitic appears after the first phonological word in the complex topic NP, and other second position enclitics appear after the first phonological word in the clause following the topic. The enclitics are underlined in (13).

(13) [[TOP îniyêka=kêhi   kîh–kočawi-čiki   wîh=čâkih-âwâči
       those.ABSENT=moreover   IC.PERF–try-3P/PART/3P   FUT=kill.all-3P>3'/AOR
      apenôh-ahi],
      child-OBV.PL

      [$_S$ waninawe=meko='pî='ni   êh=inoh~inotê-wâči.]]
      all.directions=EMPH=HRSY=then   AOR=REDUP~move.{thither}-3P/AOR

"As for those aforementioned ones who had tried to kill all the children, they then moved away in all directions, it's said." (K-W 250)

Analyzing the material following the topic as a clause provides an explanation for the appearance of second-position enclitics attached to *waninawe* "all directions."

Comparable evidence cannot be found to justify placing the negative element of the template or focus in a similarly asymmetric position, higher than what follows. For example, a single negative word cannot be used to negate two conjoined clauses, nor can a single question word be used to question two conjoined clauses:

(14) * âkwi   [[nîmi-čini]   nâhkači [nakamo-čini]]
      not   dance-3/NEG   also   sing-3/NEG
      ("He didn't dance and sing")

(15) * kêswi=čâhi   [[îinahi awi-waki]   ôni [nîmi-waki]]?
      how.many=so there be.{somewhere}-3P/IND and dance-3P/IND
      ("How many people were there and danced?")

If the material following the negative *âkwi* "not" in (14) or the question word *kêswi* "how many?" in (15) were a constituent, it should be able to be conjoined. (14) and (15) demonstrate that those strings are not constituents.

It should also be noted that the template in (12) contains no constituent corresponding to a VP in which a verb and its object form a constituent, excluding the subject. There are a number of justifications for positing such a template for Meskwaki. First of all, there is no positive evidence for a VP constituent. In English, for example, the existence of a VP constituent is shown by a number of tests: two VPs may be conjoined to form a single VP constituent; the verb and its object may be moved together to the front of the sentence; a VP may be deleted, or replaced by the pro-form *do so*. However, none of these phenomena is found in Meskwaki: there is no anaphor comparable to English *do so* which stands for a verb plus object; nor does a verb plus object function as a constituent in any other construction.

Furthermore, it must be emphasized that any putative verb–object collocation in Meskwaki can be interpreted as a full clause with a pronominal subject. For example, suppose we wanted to test whether the Meskwaki equivalent of the English VP "see a bear" is a VP constituent. Meskwaki has no infinitive form of the verb—no bare form of the stem which lacks subject agreement. We must therefore choose one of the inflected forms to use for constituency tests, such as *wâpamêwa mahkwani*, with third person animate proximate singular subject agreement, as well as third person animate obviative object agreement, since the verb is transitive. But in the absence of an external subject the subject agreement is interpreted pronominally. That is, *wâpamêwa mahkwani* in isolation will always be interpreted as a clause "he or she (proximate) sees a bear (obviative)," and can never be forced to have a reading as only a VP "see a bear." As a consequence, the fact that the collocation *wâpamêwa mahkwani* behaves as a constituent reveals only that the full clause is a constituent, a trivial result.

The fact that the tests in favor of a VP constituent in English do not work in Meskwaki does not, in itself, argue against there being a VP node in Meskwaki; it simply means that the tests do not provide evidence one way or the other. However, clear evidence against a VP may be found in examining weak crossover constructions in Meskwaki. The weak crossover constructions show that subject and object NPs stand in a symmetrical relationship to the verb, rather than following the English pattern in which the verb and object form a constituent which is sister to the subject. In other words, both (16) and (17) are grammatical in Meskwaki, in contrast to the ungrammaticality of the English gloss of (17) with the pronoun *his* interpreted as bound by *anyone*.

(16) âkwi owiyêh-a kakâčim-âčini ôhkom-ani
 not anyone-SG tease-3>3′/NEG 3.mother-in-law-OBV
 "No one$_i$ teases his$_i$ mother-in-law."

(17) âkwi owiyêh-a kakâčim-ekočini ôhkom-ani
 not anyone-SG tease-3′>3/NEG 3.mother-in-law-OBV
 As if: "His$_i$ mother-in-law doesn't tease anyone$_i$."
 [but meaning "No one$_i$ is teased by his$_i$ mother-in-law."]

The symmetry in Meskwaki between subject and object is exactly what we would expect from a language with symmetrical clause structure.[6]

3. Word order of subject and object

With the above background we now turn to a detailed examination of Meskwaki word order, starting with the relative order of subjects and objects. All permutations of S, V, and O are possible: Thomason (2004) found twenty-two clauses with three overt arguments and 1,279 clauses with two overt arguments in edited texts from the NAA corpus and determined the order to be most frequently SVO, followed in order by VOS, SOV, VSO, the rare OVS, and the very rare OSV. (To make clear the variability in word order, we refer to the familiar S, O, and V, not the discourse relations in (12).)

Examples (18–21) have all four possible orders of subject and object after a verb with the two different assignments of proximate and obviative status. In both (18) and (19) the subject is proximate, the object is obviative, and the verb exhibits direct inflection (here -*âči*, with direct theme sign |-â|). The word order of (18) is VSO, while that of (19) is VOS.

(18) êh=môših-âči=kêhi meškwahkîh-a môhkomân-ani.
 AOR=have.a.vision.of-3>3′/AOR=moreover Meskwaki-SG American-OBV
 "What's more, the Meskwaki (prox.) had a vision of the American (obv.)."
 (K-CDWP 13)

(19) êh=pakin-âči ot-ôhpwâkanimotêh-ani kwîyesêh-a, ...
 AOR=throw.down-3>3′/AOR 3-tobacco.bag-OBV boy-SG
 "the boy (prox.) threw down his tobacco bag (obv.)" (C-G 19)

In both (20) and (21) the assignment of proximate and obviative status is the reverse of that of (18–19): the subject is obviative and the object is proximate, so the verb exhibits inverse inflection (here -*ekoči*, with inverse theme sign |-ekw|). The word order of (20) is VOS, while that of (21) is VSO.

(20) takâwi=meko êh=nâ~nôtêhkwam-ekoči ihkwêw-a anemôh-ani.
a.little=EMPH AOR=REDUP~miss.biting-3′>3/AOR woman-SG dog-OBV
"The dog (obv.) was barely missing the woman (prox.) with its bites." (JP-GTF 43)

(21) ... êh=kîmâh-ekoči ašâh-ahi neniw-a.
AOR=watch.unseen-3′>3/AOR Sioux-OBV.PL man-SG
"some Siouxs (obv.) spied on the man (prox.)" (K-IML 2)

4. Word order of demonstrative, quantifier, and noun

The flexibility seen in the relative ordering of verb, subject, and object is also exhibited within noun phrases. A demonstrative or quantifier may either precede or follow its head noun. For example, in (22) the demonstrative *îniki* "those" (animate proximate plural) precedes the head noun *neniwaki* "men"; in (23) the demonstrative mani "this" (inanimate singular) follows the head noun *mâtesi* "knife."

(22) îniki neniw-aki "those men" (K-O 1F)
those.ANIM man-PL

(23) mâtes-i mani "this knife" (K-EGC 1)
knife-INAN.SG this.INAN

(24) and (25) demonstrate that the position of quantifiers is also flexible, with *nîšwi* "two" appearing before the head noun in (24) but following the head noun in (25):

(24) nîšwi neniw-aki "two men" (K-O 1E)
two man-PL

(25) mahkw-aki nîšwi "two bears" (K-FC 306)
bear-PL two

Meskwaki, like other languages of the Algonquian family, exhibits discontinuous noun phrases (cf. Reinholtz 1999). The order of a quantifier and a noun is also free if the noun phrase is discontinuous. In (26) the quantifier *nîšwi* "two" appears before the verb while its head noun *mahkwaki* "bears" appears to the right of the verb; in (27) the head noun *ihkwêwahi* "women (obv.)" precedes the verb while *nîšwi* "two" follows. (Discontinuous noun phrases involving demonstratives are not free in order, however; see below.)

(26) ayôh=čâh nîšwi awi-waki mahkw-aki.
here=so two be.{somewhere}-3P/IND bear-PL
"Well, two bears live here." (K-MWL 14)

(27) ayôh=čîh=wîna ihkwêw-ahi êh=taši-manesê-niči nîšwi.
here=!=he woman-OBV.PL AOR=be.engaged.in–gather.firewood-3′/AOR two
"Suddenly here he (prox.) saw two women gathering firewood." (K-Wewi 22)

(The enclitic =čîhi in (27) is glossed as "!" for reasons of space, but it is more accurately rendered here and below as "it.was.suddenly.observed". The cliticized emphatic pronoun *wîna* 3S/EMPH ["he (prox.)"] here and in (39) below is an adjunct that establishes the point of view.)

5. Possessor and possessed

The order of possessor and possessed is also free. The possessor more often precedes the possessed, however, and this order is highly favored if the noun phrase is discontinuous. (28) illustrates a possessor preceding the possessed noun and (29) illustrates the opposite order:

(28) neniw-a   o-kwis-ahi   "a man's sons" (K-Kin 4)
      man-SG   3-son-OBV.PL

(29) ôs-ani   neniw-a   'the man's father' (K-FC 82; tr. HP)
      3.father-OBV man-SG

(30) and (31) exhibit discontinuous possessor–possessed constructions: in (30) the possessor is clause-initial while the possessed noun *okyêni* "his mother" follows the verb. (31) is an example of the rare ordering of the possessed head noun preceding the verb and the possessor following.

(30) îna   kwîyesêh-a   êh=pemi–nowî-niči   o-kyêni
      that.ANIM   boy-SG   AOR=along–exit-3'/AOR   3-mother.OBV
      'the boy's mother went out' (K-FC 224; tr. HP)

(31) înoki=čâhi   kîna=mekoho   o-nôkênaw-ani   ke-kîwâčihtaw-âwa
      now=so   you=EMPH   3-soul-OBV   2-make.O2.lonely.for-(2)>3/IND
      ke-tânes-a.
      2-daughter-SG
      'you have made your daughter's soul lonely by doing that' (K-FC 40; tr. HP)

6. Equational sentences

In equational sentences, both possible word orders are found for the two terms of the equation, Given and New. Given precedes New in (32) and New precedes Given in (33). A New term that is indefinite tends to precede the Given term (as in (33)), and Thomason (2003) points out that preverbal position is favored for certain other indefinites, but this preference is not completely consistent.

(32) manaha[7]   ne-tôtêm-enân-a   "this is our (excl.) brother" (K-FC 113)
      this.ANIM   1-sibling-1P-SG

(33) mesâpêw-aki mâhaki.   "These are giants."
      giant-PL   these.ANIM   (= "This is a story about giants.") (C-G 1)

7. Fixed word order in special cases

In certain contexts Meskwaki exhibits fixed word order. For example, if the possessor is itself possessed the possessor always precedes its possessed noun. (34) is an example of this order:

(34) o-mešôh-ani   o-tôtêm-ani   'his grandpa's brother'
     3-grandfather-OBV   3-sibling-OBV   (K-FC 332; tr. HP)

If a demonstrative and its associated head noun are discontinuous, the demonstrative always occurs earlier in the sentence than its noun. (35) illustrates this pattern with a discontinuous subject NP and (36) provides an example with an object NP:

(35) mâhaki   menwihčikê-waki   wâkošêh-aki
     these.ANIM   do.well-3P/IND   fox-PL
     'These Foxes have done very good' (K-FC 588; tr. HP)

(36) mani   manetôw-a[8]   anawit-amwa   ôtêwen-i.
     this.INAN   monster-SG   sneak.up.on-3>0/IND   town-INAN.SG
     "A monster is sneaking up on this town." (K-SGG 174)

8. Clauses with obviative subject and obviative object

In most Meskwaki clauses subject and object are unambiguously distinguished from each other by morphology. As stated above, nouns are marked for animate or inanimate gender; animate nouns are overtly marked for obviation (proximate or obviative). Verbs are inflected for the gender and obviation status of subjects and primary objects. The system of obviation does not permit both subject and object to be proximate. Thus the only cases in which word order might conceivably have any role in disambiguating which of two nouns is the subject and which the object would be sentences in which the subject and object are both obviative and it is thus clearly of interest to examine such sentences.[9]

For this purpose, we used several thousand pages of the Meskwaki texts in the NAA corpus edited by Goddard and Lucy Thomason. Although sentences with an obviative subject and obviative object are not common, fifty-four examples were found in which the subject and object are overt noun phrases (not merely inflectional) and both are obviative. These were found by searching for the verbal inflections that Meskwaki has for a first or nearer obviative acting on a second or further obviative, or the reverse. (Recall that if a first obviative is acting on a second obviative the direct inflection, with direct theme sign, is used, and if a second obviative is acting on a first obviative the inverse inflection, with inverse theme sign, is used.)

Below we report on the distribution of the various word order possibilities in clauses with both the subject and object in obviative status, with examples of each type. Of the fifty-four total examples, thirty-four exhibit verbs with direct inflection and the subject preceding the object. Three of these are VSO, twenty-five are SVO, and six are SOV. (37) illustrates VSO order:

(37) êh=anemi–pîtahôn-âniči   mešemôk-ani[10]   pešekisiw-ani.
     AOR=go.on–drag.in-3′>3″/AOR old.woman-OBV   deer-OBV
     "(He (prox.) watched as) the old lady (obv.) dragged the deer (obv.) off inside."
     (C-WH 14)

By far the largest group of examples of a nearer obviative subject acting on a further obviative object displays SVO order, presumably due to the nearer obviative subject occupying one of the preverbal positions associated with focus, as in (38):

(38) nenemehkiw-ahi   êh=pakam-âniči   înini   mači–manetôhêh-ani.
     thunder-OBV.PL   AOR=hit-3′>3″/AOR   that.OBV   evil–manitou-OBV
     'The Thunderers (obv.) had struck that evil manitou (obv.).'
     (In the presence of the man (prox.).) (K-WYB 48; tr. TB)

Six examples in our corpus exhibited SOV order with a nearer obviative subject and a further obviative object. In (39) the two preverbal NPs are presumably in the two preverbal focus positions; focus NPs are often found in expressions of surprise (cf. Dahlstrom 1995).

(39) ayôh=čih=wîna pašitôhêh-ahi   nesêmâw-ani   êh=tašihkaw-âniči.
     here=!=he   old.man-OBV.PL   tobacco-OBV   AOR=be.dealing.with-3′>3″/AOR
     "Suddenly here he (prox.) saw some old men (obv.) working on tobacco (obv.)."
     (K-EGC 31)

(37–9) all contain verbs inflected in the direct form with a nearer obviative subject preceding a further obviative object. The opposite order—further obviative object preceding a nearer obviative subject, with a direct verb—is found in ten examples in our corpus. Of those ten, five exhibit VOS order, as in (40) and (41):

(40) êh=anemi–nôm-âniči   înini   apenôhêh-ani   ow-îw-ani.
     AOR=go.on–carry.on.back-3′>3″/AOR that.OBV   baby-OBV   3-wife-OBV
     "His wife (obv.) went along with the baby (obv.) on her back." (K-Fish 127)

(41) êh=wêpi–=čihi='pi –nasâhkohw-âniči   înini
     konwâškêh-anî='nini.
     AOR=start.to–=!=HRSY –roast.on.a.stick-3′>3″/AOR   that.OBV
     frog-OBV= that.OBV
     "And to their surprise, they saw him (obv.) set about roasting that frog (obv.) on a stick." (JP-Apay 65)

In (41) the second înini "that (obv.)," cliticized to konwâškêhani "frog (obv.)" is the subject. Again, the enclitic= čihi is more accurately translated as "it was suddenly observed," conveyed in the translation by "to their surprise, they saw ..."

We have found four examples of direct verbs with a further obviative object preceding the verb and a nearer obviative subject following the verb, as in (42):

(42) čêwinâh=meko mešihkêhêh-ahi êh=nôšân-âniči
 at.the.same.time=EMPH baby.snapping.turtle-OBV.PL AOR=give.birth.to-3′>3″/AOR
 ow-îw-ahi.
 3-wife-OBV.PL
 "At exactly the same time his wives (obv.) gave birth to baby snapping turtles (obv.)."
 (K-MMD 27)

A single example in our corpus exhibits OSV order with a further obviative object preceding a nearer obviative subject, both in preverbal position:

(43) neniw-a ow-îw-ani ahpenêči kotak-ani neniw-ani
 man-SG 3-wife-OBV always another-OBV man-OBV
 mana~man-ânite,[11] ...
 REDUP~copulate.with-3′>3″/SUBJ
 "If another man (obv.) is always screwing a man (prox.)'s wife (obv.), ..." (K-Kin 63)

We turn now to inverse verb forms with a further obviative subject acting on a nearer obviative object. In this set, there are no examples in which the further obviative subject precedes the nearer obviative object; there are ten examples in which the nearer obviative object precedes the further obviative subject. There is one instance of VOS order, given below in (44):

(44) nâhkači êh=myâhkeškâkoniči[12] ihkwêw-ahi apenôh-ani, ...
 also AOR=injure.3″>3′/AOR woman-OBV.PL child-OBV
 "Also, when women (obv.) are injured by (giving birth to) a child (obv.), ..."
 'And when the women are being made ill by the birth of a child, ...' (tr. IP)
 (K-Auto 279)

There are five examples of OVS order in which the nearer obviative object appears in preverbal position and the further obviative subject follows the verb. (45) and (46) exemplify this pattern.

(45) kahôni='pi ow-îhkân-wâw-ani êh=mawinan-ekoniči nenosôni ...
 and.then=HRSY 3-friend-3P-OBV AOR=attack-3″>3′/AOR buffalo.OBV
 "And then one of their friends (obv.) was attacked by a buffalo (obv.), ..." (SP-SH 20)

(46) nâhka nekoti neniw-a, âkwi oškinawêh-a,
 also one man-SG not young.man-SG
 o-wîw-ani êh=mešen-ekoniči ašâh-ahi.
 3-wife-OBV AOR=capture-3″>3′/AOR Sioux-OBV.PL
 "And there was a certain man, no longer young, whose wife (obv.) was captured by the Siouxs (obv.)." (K-SD 1)

Four examples in our corpus exhibit OSV order with the nearer obviative preceding the further obviative, as in (47):

(47) o-mesôtân-ahi=kêhi='pi ašâh-ahi nes-ekoniwahi.
3-parent-OBV.PL=moreover=HRSY Sioux-OBV.PL kill-3″>3′/IND
"The thing was, they say his parents (obv.) had been killed by the Siouxs (obv.)."
(K-MFWB 1)

9. Discussion

The data in (37–47) show that in Meskwaki, syntactic role (as subject or object) does not determine word order. The first obviative usually precedes the second obviative (forty-four out of fifty-four times), regardless of syntactic role. It is, of course, entirely to be expected that the obviative of higher interest would precede the obviative of lesser interest. This is always the case if the verb is inverse (ten examples like 44–7). The rarity (absence in this sample) of the lower-ranked noun (the second obviative) coming first if the verb is inverse is also expected. Selecting inverse inflection means selecting the object as of current interest and it would clash with this to select the lower ranked subject for primary focus.

The ten sentences that have second obviative before the first obviative (40–3) but, despite this, a direct verb—the default inflection—all also have no possibility of ambiguity for semantic reasons. Despite the clash with the word order, the meaning is unambiguous.

It might be claimed that in (38) the syntactic roles are made clear by the order subject–object, but the sentence simply has the default interpretation that the first obviative is the subject of a direct verb. Where the roles might be reversed, as here, only this order is possible. Note that (45), with the order instead object–subject, has the default interpretation that the first obviative is the object of an inverse verb.

These patterns must be described by referring to obviation and meaning. Obviation is fundamentally discourse-generated and cannot be accounted for by a theory that examines nothing above or beyond the syntax of sentences.

10. Conclusion

Meskwaki evidence supports an analytical model in which there is an abstract mapping of syntactic roles and of the relations between words and grammatical elements, but Meskwaki appears to refute the claim that syntactic roles can be read off sentence structure as a universal property of language. The Meskwaki facts can be accommodated by a model in which syntactic roles are base-generated, and syntactic structures are generated in surface structure and labeled *in situ*, without movement, by the abstract map of relations. After all, if there is no basic word order, the notion of movement for purely syntactic reasons becomes otiose.

Notes

1. We are delighted to offer a contribution to this volume honoring our friend and colleague Lyle Campbell with whom we share an interest in the insights to be gained from close study of Native American languages in all their diversity. We are indebted to Lucy Thomason for the examples from the texts she has edited and for sharing her knowledge of Meskwaki discourse. And we acknowledge our great debt to our consultants in the Meskwaki community, especially Adeline Wanatee (1910–96) and Everett Kapayou (1933–2006).
2. Abbreviations in the examples for the manuscript sources, listed by author:
Charley H. Chuck
   C-G: Giants. NAA 2794.12.
   C-WH: Wampumhead: A Winter Story. NAA 2794.46(b).
Jim Peters
   JP-Apay: Apayashihaki. NAA 2674.2.
   JP-GTF: The Girl Who Had Ten Friends. NAA 2794.47(3)
Alfred Kiyana
   K-Auto: Autobiography. NAA 1834.
   K-CDWP: Ceremonial Dances, War Practices, and Traditions of the Whiteman. NAA 2656.2.
   K-EGC: The One Who Had an Elm Tree Growing Out of His Chest. NAA 2720.6.
   K-Fish: The Story of the Fish Clan. NAA 2667.
   K-IML: When Some Indians Moved Camp Long Ago. NAA 2730.6.
   K-Kin: Kinship Terminology and Archaic Vocabulary. NAA 2232 and 2277.
   K-MBES. A Man Who Was Blessed by an Evil Spirit Long Ago. NAA 2656.
   K-MFLA. A Man Who Fasted Long Ago. NAA 2664-2 (published as Dahlstrom 2015).
   K-MFWB. The One Who Made Four War Bundles. NAA 2779.
   K-MMD. The Man Who Married His Daughter. NAA 2664.3.
   K-O. The Owl Sacred Pack. NAA 2693 (published as Goddard 2007).
   K-SD: The Snail Dance. NAA 2606.
   K-SGG. Shooter, and His Grandmother and Grandfather. NAA 2794.66.
   K-Spot. The Spotted Cow Sacred Bundle. NAA 2007.
   K-W. Wisahkeha, His Father, His Mother, His Younger Brother, His Grandmother. NAA 2958a.
   K-Wewi. Wewipeha and His Wife. NAA 2794.88.
   K-WYB. Wapasaya's Younger Brother Meskwasona. NAA 2121.
Sam Peters
   SP-SH: Summer Hunters. NAA 2794.45(b):20–4.
Some of the examples contain English translations offered by bilingual consultants working with Michelson. These translations are enclosed in single quotes; the abbreviation for the text source is followed by the initials of the translator (tr.):
Translators:
HP: Horace Poweshiek (Meskwaki)

IP: Ida Poweshiek (Ida Snowball; Meskwaki)
TB: Thomas Brown (Sauk)
3. The examples are glossed following the Leipzig conventions (except when morphophonological processes obscure the morpheme boundary).
4. It is impossible for the possessum in a simple possessed noun construction as in (3) to be proximate if the possessor is third person. However, another strategy exists by which it is possible to refer to a proximate third person in terms of their kinship relation by forming a relative clause based on a verb of possession, giving a form something like, for example, "the one (proximate) who has her (obviative) as a wife," functionally equivalent to "her (obviative) husband (proximate)" (Goddard 1990a: 320, 1.3).
5. In LFG a separate component, functional structure, represents the relationship between predicates and the grammatical functions like subject, oblique, and so on, which the predicate requires. The component of functional structure exhibits relatively little cross-linguistic variation in comparison to constituent structure in LFG analyses, and many of the linguistic universals posited by LFG make reference to functional structure notions. See Bresnan et al. 2015 for more discussion.
6. The grammaticality of (17) holds even if *owiyêha* "anyone" appears to the right of the verb or to the right of the possessed noun. (Teasing of various kinds is culturally licensed between certain relatives, and proscribed between others, such as son-in-law and mother-in-law.)
7. *manaha* is the pre-pausal form of "this (anim.)."
8. *manetôwa* "god, snake, monster."
9. Another context in which word order might be predicted to play a role in disambiguating subject and object is that in which both subject and object are inanimate gender. The use of two full inanimate NPs, however, is apparently avoided with ordinary transitive verbs inflected for a first object. (There are also no inanimate possessors in Meskwaki.) In our corpus of several thousand pages of text we found only a single example of a two-place verb with the two arguments expressed by full inanimate NPs; it is given below in (i).

(i) mâhani=čâhi   nakamôn-ani   îni   nâtawinôn-i
    these.INAN=so   song-INAN.PL   that.INAN   medicine-INAN.SG
    êh=onakamônîmikahki.
    AOR=have.O2.as.song(s).0/AOR
    "And these songs are the songs of that medicine." (K-Spot 220)
    (lit. "And that medicine has these songs as its songs.")

The verb of (i) belongs to the class exemplified above in (9–10): two-place verbs which require a subject and second object. Here the second object precedes the subject but the meaning is clearly unambiguous. As is common with Meskwaki verbs of possession, the verb is inflected only for subject agreement and the item possessed is a second object. The verb in (i) bears an added suffix *-mikat* (with the final *-t* becoming *h* before the suffix *-ki*) that attaches to intransitive verb stems

that require animate subjects and derives an intransitive stem that requires an inanimate subject.
10. *mešemôkani* "old woman (obv.)" (with humorous deformation).
11. The subject of *man-* "copulate with" must be male.
12. The gloss of *myâhkeškaw-* is more specifically "injure by foot or body."

References

Bresnan, Joan, Ash Asudeh, Ida Toivonen, and Stephen Wechsler. 2015. *Lexical-functional syntax*. 2nd edn. Chichester: John Wiley & Sons.

Chomsky, Noam. 1995. *The minimalist program*. Cambridge, MA: MIT Press.

Dahlstrom, Amy. 1993. The syntax of discourse functions in Fox. In *Berkeley Linguistics Society 19. Special session on syntactic issues in Native American languages*, ed. by David A. Peterson, 11–21. Berkeley: Berkeley Linguistics Society.

Dahlstrom, Amy. 1995. *Topic, focus, and word order problems in Algonquian*. The Belcourt Lecture, delivered before the University of Manitoba on February 25, 1994. Winnipeg: Voices of Rupert's Land.

Dahlstrom, Amy. 2009. OBJ_θ without OBJ: A typology of Meskwaki objects. In *Proceedings of the LFG09 Conference*, ed. by Miriam Butt and Tracy Holloway King, 222–39. Stanford: CSLI Publications.

Dahlstrom, Amy. 2014. Multiple oblique arguments in Meskwaki. In *Papers of the Forty-Second Algonquian Conference 2010*, ed. by J. Randolph Valentine and Monica Macaulay, 56–68. Albany: SUNY Press.

Dahlstrom, Amy. 2015. Highlighting rhetorical structure through syntactic analysis: An illustrated Meskwaki text by Alfred Kiyana. In *New voices for old words: Algonquian oral literatures*, ed. by David J. Costa, 118–97. Lincoln: University of Nebraska Press.

Goddard, Ives. 1990a. Aspects of the topic structure of Fox narratives: Proximate shifts and the use of overt and inflectional NPs. *International Journal of American Linguistics*, 56(3).317–40.

Goddard, Ives. 1990b. Some literary devices in the writings of Alfred Kiyana. In *Papers of the Twenty-First Algonquian Conference*, ed. by William Cowan, 159–71. Ottawa: Carleton University.

Goddard, Ives. 1996. Writing and reading Mesquakie (Fox). In *Papers of the Twenty-Seventh Algonquian Conference*, ed. by David H. Pentland, 117–34. Winnipeg: University of Manitoba.

Goddard, Ives. 2007. *The owl sacred pack: A new edition and translation of the Meskwaki manuscript of Alfred Kiyana*. (Algonquian and Iroquoian Linguistics Memoir 19.) Winnipeg: Algonquian and Iroquoian Linguistics.

Greenberg, Joseph H. 1966. Some universals of grammar with particular reference to the order of meaningful elements. In *Universals of language*, ed. by Joseph H. Greenberg, 73–113. Cambridge, MA: MIT Press.

Halle, Morris, and Alec Marantz. 1993. Distributed morphology and pieces of inflection. In *The view from Building 20*, ed. by Kenneth Hale and Samuel Jay Keyser, 111–76. Cambridge, MA: MIT Press.

Mithun, Marianne. 1987. Is basic word order universal? In *Coherence and grounding in discourse*, ed. by Russell Tomlin, 281–328. Amsterdam: John Benjamins.

Reinholtz, Charlotte. 1999. On the characterization of discontinuous constituents: Evidence from Swampy Cree. *International Journal of American Linguistics* 65(2).201–27.

Thomason, Lucy G. 1995. The assignment of proximate and obviative in informal Fox narrative. In *Papers of the Twenty-Sixth Algonquian Conference*, ed. by David H. Pentland, 462–96. Winnipeg: University of Manitoba.

Thomason, Lucy G. 2003. *The proximate and obviative contrast in Meskwaki*. University of Texas dissertation.

Thomason, Lucy G. 2004. Two, three, and four noun phrases per clause in Meskwaki. In *Papers of the Thirty-Fifth Algonquian Conference*, ed. by H. C. Wolfart, 407–30. Winnipeg: University of Manitoba.

13

The Syntax of Alignment: An Emergentist Typology

William O'Grady

1. Introduction

Among the many advantages that speech confers on humans is the ability to convey thoughts by inflecting and arranging words in particular ways.[1] Explaining precisely how this is done has always been the first goal of language science. Progress has been uneven, of course, replete with false leads and dead ends, but various research priorities can be identified with some degree of confidence.

One such priority involves the phenomenon of alignment, which defines a fundamental divide in the morphosyntax of natural languages, as illustrated in Figure 13.1. Norman and Campbell (1978) describe the contrast as follows.

> In nominative/accusative languages, subjects of transitives and subjects of intransitives are handled in the same way, while transitive objects are handled differently. In absolutive/ergative languages, transitive objects are accorded the same treatment as intransitive subjects, transitive subjects being handled differently. (Norman and Campbell 1978: 141)

The study of alignment lies at the heart of the field of typology, an area to which Lyle Campbell has made many important contributions, including a remarkable overview of South America's 108 language families (Campbell 2012). Indeed, Campbell was among the first scholars to posit an ergative system of syntax for proto-Mayan

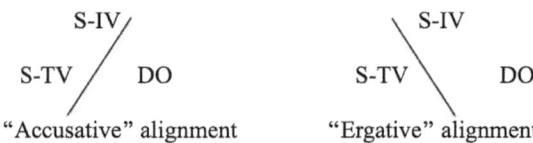

Figure 13.1 Two language types

Note: DO = direct object; IV = intransitive verb; TV = transitive verb.

(Norman and Campbell 1978; Campbell and Kaufman 1985; Campbell 2016, 2017)—a view that is now universally accepted.

There are essentially two approaches to the typology of alignment. One body of work considers the phenomenon from a functional perspective, with reference to the classic notions of subject and direct object (e.g., Norman and Campbell 1978; Comrie 1981; Campbell and Kaufman 1985; Dixon 1994; Payne 1997; among many others). Another line of inquiry seeks to characterize alignment and its consequences in more abstract terms, usually within the framework of generative grammar (e.g., Aldridge 2008; Deal 2015; Polinsky 2017, and the many references cited there).

I seek here to break a third path by outlining an approach to alignment that draws on an emergentist explanatory framework, whose key elements will be laid out in abbreviated form in the next section. Sections 3 through 6 consider a series of phenomena (case marking, word order, agreement, and relativization) that help shed light on the nature of alignment and on the profound consequences that it has for a language's morphosyntax. The chapter ends with some brief concluding remarks.

2. The basics of emergentism

A defining tenet of emergentism is that complex systems of all types—the universe, rush-hour traffic, the weather, cognition, language, to name but a few—are alike in at least one important way: their properties reflect the interaction of simpler and more basic forces. The challenge for linguistics is to identify those forces and to determine how their interaction contributes to the properties that define language.

A key component of the version of emergentism adopted here (dubbed "natural syntax" by O'Grady 2021) is that fundamental properties of language bear the mark of processing pressures.

> Processing determinism
> The properties of language are shaped by the need to minimize processing cost.

As we will see as we proceed, processing determinism favors representations and operations that are maximally efficient. Indeed, on the view that I put forward here, all syntax emerges from the maximally simple argument-structure template depicted below. The template consists only of a predicate position (PRED) and a position for a single argument, which I will call the "base argument' (represented as β).

> The semantic base
> PRED
> <β>

The base argument is thematically and topically unspecified. Depending on the choice of predicate, it could ultimately be an agent, a patient, or some other argument type. Moreover, depending on the context, the base argument can be overtly expressed or null (in certain languages); it can be used to convey new or old information; it can be definite or indefinite; and so on.

If I am right, this is where syntax starts, but not of course where it ends. The interaction between the demands of processing efficiency and the needs of communication force extensions to the semantic base that ultimately yield much of the syntax of natural language.

Alignment offers an excellent starting point for exploring this line of inquiry, both because it makes a fundamental contribution to the morphosyntax of language and because a number of its important properties are already well described, if not understood. I will focus here on two broad questions.

    i Why are there alignment contrasts?
    ii Why do these contrasts have the particular consequences that they do?

The first question raises the obvious existential issue: Why are there two major types of languages in the first place, one accusative and the other ergative? The second question focuses on three specific puzzles that arise in the study of alignment. (Here and elsewhere, I use the terms "subject" and "direct object" solely for descriptive convenience to refer to a verb's first and second arguments, respectively.)

    i Why do ergative and accusative languages differ with respect to which argument typically carries null case marking?
    ii Why do ergative languages typically manifest SOV or VSO order, while rejecting the SVO option that is so common among accusative languages?
    iii Why do processes such as agreement and relativization uniformly comply with the traditional accessibility hierarchy (subject > direct object > ...) in accusative languages, but not in ergative languages?

Let us begin by considering the question of case marking.

3. Case and alignment

There are two obvious ways to extend the semantic base in order to accommodate the encoding of events involving two participants—the hallmark of transitivity. One strategy is to add a second-argument position.[2]

    Addition of a second-argument position:
      PRED   PRED
      $<\beta>$ $\Rightarrow$ $<\beta\_>$
                    $\uparrow$
            added argument position

The other option is to extend the semantic base in the opposite direction by adding a first-argument position.

Addition of a first-argument position:
 PRED   PRED
 <β>   ⇒ <_ β>
            ↑
       added argument position

Both strategies for building out the semantic base yield the same dyadic argument structure that is essential to transitivity:

PRED
<1 2>

However, the manner in which this result is achieved turns out to be crucial, creating a contrast that underlies a good deal of the syntactic variation associated with alignment, including the morphosyntax of case.

As I see it, the role of case in signaling alignment is simply to track the base argument position, distinguishing it from whatever other position might be added to accommodate transitivity.

Case marking:
- The base argument carries the language's unmarked case (often zero).
- The added argument is marked by an overt case affix.

The use of null case for the ever-present base argument fits well with an established typological generalization: the most expected elements are expressed with a minimum of phonological complexity (e.g., Hawkins 2014:15–16).

Expectedness:
- The expected argument is minimally marked compared to other arguments.

Let us turn now to the two case systems most commonly found in the world's languages.

3.1 Accusativity

The first and most widely manifested option for extending the semantic base adds a second-argument position, thereby maintaining the association between the base-argument and first-argument positions.

Addition of a second-argument position:
 PRED   PRED
 <β>   ⇒   <β _>
  1   1 2

In accordance with the case marking principle outlined above, the item in the base-argument position should be minimally inflected (usually left bare, in fact), whereas the added argument in the second position should be associated with an overt case marker.

Turkish works this way (e.g., Kornfilt 1997), with a null suffix (the so-called "nominative") for its base argument in both intransitive and transitive sentences and an overt "accusative" suffix (-*ü* or one of its allomorphs) on its added second argument. (Ø = null case marking)

Turkish (Nominative = Ø; Accusative = -*ü*)
a. Intransitive verb: LEAVE
    Hasan   ayrıl-dı.   <β>   (β = *Hasan*)
    Hasan.NOM   leave-PST.3SG   ø
    "Hasan left."

b. Transitive verb: BUY
    Hasan   öküz-**ü**   al-dı.   <β_>   (β = *Hasan*; added arg. = *ox*)
    Hasan.NOM   ox-ACC   buy-PST.3SG   Ø -*ü*
    "Hasan bought the ox."

A case system of this type is usually called "accusative," reflecting the name of the case associated with the added argument position. See Table 13.1.

Table 13.1 Case marking in a classic accusative language

Argument	Case
Base argument	Nominative (usually Ø)
Added (second) argument	Accusative (overt; -*ü* in Turkish)

3.2 Ergativity

As noted above, the second option for building out the semantic base involves adding a first-argument position.

Addition of a first-argument position:
PRED   PRED
<β>   ⇒   <_ β>
 1   1 2

Here, the sole argument of an intransitive verb and the second argument of a transitive verb should be bare ("absolutive"), since both are associated with the base-argument position. In contrast, the first argument in a transitive clause should carry an overt case marker, reflecting its association with the added position.

West Greenlandic works this way, with the suffix -*p* on the first argument of a transitive verb, but no marking on either the sole argument of an intransitive verb or the second argument of a transitive verb.

West Greenlandic (data from Manning 1996:3)
  a. Intransitive verb: SLEEP
     Oli   sinippoq.   <β>   (β = *Oli*)
     Oli.ABS   sleep.3SG   Ø
     "Oli sleeps."

  b. Transitive verb: EAT
     Oli-p   neqi   neri-vaa.   <_ β>   (added arg. = *Oli*; β = *meat*)
     Oli-ERG   meat.ABS   eat-3SG.3SG -*p* Ø
     "Oli eats meat."

A case system of this type is usually called "ergative," reflecting the name of the case marker that appears on the added first argument (the subject of a transitive verb). See Table 13.2.

Table 13.2 Case marking in a classic ergative language

Argument	Case
Base argument	Absolutive (usually Ø)
Added (first) argument	Ergative (overt; -*p* in West Greenlandic)

3.3 The typology of case

There is nothing surprising about ergativity on the view I am outlining. Indeed, ergative systems of case marking are expected. That is because the addition of a first-argument position, which is signaled by the ergative case marker, is simply one of two logical options for extending the semantic base in order to accommodate transitivity.

An intriguing side effect of this approach to alignment is the revelation that the function of case is not to encode grammatical relations, contrary to the widely stated belief. By considering accusative languages only, it is easy to think that case serves as a marker of grammatical relations, with the nominative reserved for the subject and the accusative for the direct object. However, there is no such one-to-one mapping in ergative languages, where a single case form is used for the subject of an intransitive verb and the direct object of a transitive verb.

Recognizing that transitivity requires extension of the single-argument semantic base and that this can be achieved in either of two ways offers a new way to think about case. In particular, it is now plausible to propose that case marking has essentially the same primary function in all languages, regardless of their alignment type.

Case functions:
- Null case is reserved for the base argument.
- Overt case is used for the added argument.

On this view, accusative and ergative languages each work exactly the same way with respect to case marking, differing only in terms of which argument is taken to be basic and which one is added—a matter that can be reduced to the manner in which the semantic base is extended to accommodate transitivity.

4. Word order and alignment

An intriguing feature of the syntax of alignment is that SVO languages are typically not ergative (Nichols 1992;Mahajan 1994, 1997;Siewierska 1996; Lahne 2008), a puzzle for which there is now a natural explanation. The key generalization can be stated as follows:

Sidedness Harmony:
- Base arguments have a uniform sidedness in a language's canonical word order

The intuition here is that just as base arguments share a uniform case marking (usually null), so they tend to have a shared positioning preference on either the left side or the right side of the verb.

Sidedness Harmony has different consequences for the two major types of alignment. In accusative languages, the subject of an intransitive verb and the subject of a transitive verb (which are associated with the base argument position in this language type) should either both precede or both follow the verb. This state of affairs is compatible with the three most commonly manifested word order patterns attested in the world's languages (Table 13.3).

Table 13.3 Harmonic word order patterns in accusative languages

	SOV	VSO/VOS	SVO
Intransitive	**S**-V	V-**S**	**S**-V
Transitive	**S**-O-V	V-**S**-O/V-O-**S**	**S**-V-O

Note: The base argument is underlined and bold-faced.

Here, subjects of intransitive and transitive verbs uniformly occur on either the left side of the verb (SOV and SVO languages) or on the right side (VSO languages).[3]

In ergative languages, in contrast, the subject of an intransitive verb and the direct object of a transitive verb (the base arguments in that system of alignment) should both either precede or follow the verb. As illustrated in Table 13.4, this requirement is met in verb-final and verb-initial languages, but not in SVO languages.

Table 13.4 Harmonic word order patterns in ergative languages

	SOV	VSO/VOS	*SVO
Intransitive	**S**-V	V-**S**	**S**-V
Transitive	S-**O**-V	V-S-**O**/V-O-S	S-V-**O**

As the final column in Table 13.4 shows, sidedness harmony militates against SVO word order—the very result that has been reported in the typological literature.

A prediction now follows: ergativity should be permitted in SVO languages in which the basic order for intransitive patterns is VS, with the sole argument on the same side of the verb as the direct object in a transitive pattern.

> A sidedness pattern compatible with ergativity in an SVO language:
> Intransitive: V<u>S</u>
> Transitive: SV<u>O</u>

Interestingly, languages of this very type have been documented.

> For the vast majority of languages, the position of subjects is the same in intransitive clauses as in transitive clauses. However, there are a number of types of languages in which it is not. The first type are languages in which word order follows an ergative pattern. (Dryer 2011)

The example below is from Muna (a Malayo-Polynesian language spoken on two islands off the coast of Sulawesi in Indonesia).

> Transitive—subject to the left of the verb, direct object to right:
> S   V   O
> o katogha   ne-mbolaku   **kenta   topa**.
> ART crow   3SG.REALIS-steal   fish   dry
> "The crow stole the dry fish."
>
> Intransitive—subject to the right of the verb:
> V   S
> no-tende   tora   **dahu**.
> 3SG.REALIS-run   again   dog
> "The dog ran again.
> (van den Berg 2013:150, 163, cited by Dryer 2011)

Raina Heaton (personal communication) reports a similar pattern for Huastec, an ergative Mayan language of Mexico.

Another word order factor may be in play here too. Drawing on an observation by Beatrice Primus, Hawkins notes that the majority of object-initial languages (a highly unusual word order type) are ergative.

> the majority of languages classified hitherto as object before subject [have] ergative-absolutive morphology, including OSV languages (Dyirbal, Hurrian, Siuslaw, Kabardian, Fasu) and OVS languages (Apalai, Arecuna, Bacairi, Macushi, Hianacoto, Hishkaryana, Panare, Wayana, Asurini, Oiampi, Teribe, Pari, Jur, Luo, Mangaraya). (Hawkins 2014:189; see also Primus 1995, 1999)

The motivation for these particular word order patterns can be traced to a uniform sidedness preference for base arguments. As Dryer (2011) notes, ergative OSV and OVS languages tend to place the sole argument of an intransitive verb to the left, thereby creating a uniform position for the base argument.

<u>O</u>SV <u>O</u>VS
<u>S</u>V   <u>S</u>V

The end result is a system in which base arguments systematically appear sentence-initially, on the left side of the verb, consistent with the requirements of Sidedness Harmony.

5. Agreement and alignment

5.1 Agreement in accusative languages

Agreement in languages with an accusative system of alignment typically targets the sole argument of an intransitive verb and the first argument of a transitive verb (the "subject"), as in the following examples from English and Turkish.

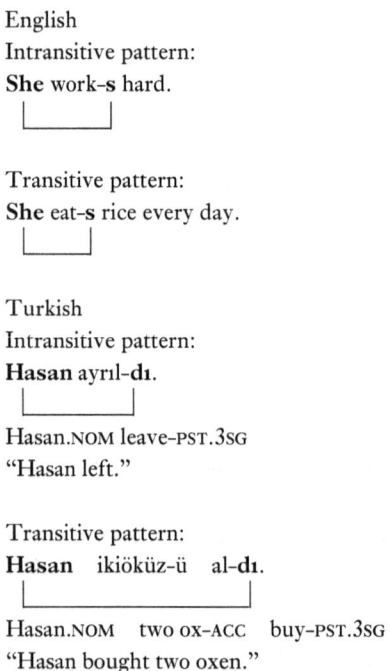

English
Intransitive pattern:
She work-**s** hard.

Transitive pattern:
She eat-**s** rice every day.

Turkish
Intransitive pattern:
Hasan ayrıl-**dı**.

Hasan.NOM leave-PST.3SG
"Hasan left."

Transitive pattern:
Hasan ikiöküz-ü al-**dı**.

Hasan.NOM two ox-ACC buy-PST.3SG
"Hasan bought two oxen."

The preferred pattern of agreement in accusative languages can therefore be summarized schematically as follows.

Agreement in accusative languages
Intransitive: Transitive:
  PRED   PRED
  <β>   <β _>
  1   1 2
Agr ⤴   Agr ⤴

Interestingly, there appear to be two ways of formulating an "accessibility hierarchy" for this type of system.

- The preferred agreement target is the first argument.
  First argument > ...

- The preferred agreement target is the base argument.
  Base argument > ...

There is a good and obvious reason for this overlap: the base argument in an accusative language corresponds to the first argument and vice versa. The two cannot be teased apart.

Accusative languages
PRED   PRED
<β>   <β _>
 1   1 2

As we will see next, the situation in ergative languages is quite different—with important consequences for our understanding of how agreement works.

5.2 Agreement in ergative languages

As noted in Section 3, the semantic base in an ergative language is expanded by the addition of a first-argument position, leaving the base argument in the second position.

Ergative languages
PRED   PRED
<β>   <_ β>
 1   1 2

As illustrated here, the first-argument and base-argument positions are dissociated in this type of argument structure. Not coincidentally, ergative languages manifest variation in agreement that is not seen in their accusative counterparts.

A first option, exemplified by Pashto, an Indo-Iranian language, targets the base argument—the sole argument of an intransitive verb and the second argument (the "direct object") of a transitive verb.

Intransitive pattern:
xəza   də-daftar-na   raɣ-a.
|_____|

woman   OBL-office-from   came-3FSG
"The woman came from the office."

Transitive pattern:
ma   **xəza**   wəlid-a.
      |_____|

I.ERG   woman   saw-3FSG
"I saw the woman."
(data from Babrakzai 1999:78, 103)

This pattern of agreement can be summarized schematically as follows.

Pashto: Agreement targets the base argument
   Intransitive: Transitive:
     PRED   PRED
     $<\beta>$ $<\_\ \beta>$
      1   1 2
   Agr ┘   └ *Agr*
    (-*a*)   (-*a*)

A second option is found in Enga, a language of Papua New Guinea, in which agreement systematically targets the first argument in both intransitive and transitive patterns.

Intransitive pattern—agreement with the sole argument:
nambá   p-e-ó.
|_____|

I   go-PST-1SG
"I went."

Transitive pattern—agreement with the first argument:
namba-mé   mená   dóko   p-í-ó.
|_____|

I-ERG   pig   DEF   hit-PST-1SG
"I hit (killed) the pig."
(data from Lang 1973 and Li and Lang 1979, cited in Van Valin 1981:367)

This agreement pattern can be represented schematically as follows.

Enga: Agreement targets the first argument

Intransitive:	Transitive:
PRED	PRED
<β>	<_ β>
1	1 2
Agr ⌐|	Agr ⌐|
(-ó)	(-ó)

5.3 The typology of agreement

In sum, we end up with the following typology of agreement for the two alignment options most frequently instantiated in language—accusative and ergative.

- In accusative languages (e.g., English, Turkish), where the base argument and the first argument are one and the same, there is no variation. Agreement favors the first/base argument.
    First/Base argument > ...
    In ergative languages, where the first argument and the base argument are dissociated in transitive patterns, there is the possibility of variation.
- In some languages (e.g., Pashto), agreement favors the base argument rather than the first argument.
    Base argument > ...
- In other languages (e.g., Enga), agreement favors the first argument rather than the base argument.
    First argument > ...

The three options share a fundamental property that helps shed light on why they exist in the first place. In all cases, the item most accessible to agreement is predictably and reliably present in essentially every sentence in the language. As depicted in the semantic representations below, all sentences—transitive or intransitive—have a base argument. Moreover, they all have a first argument, which may or may not also be the base argument (depending on whether the language is accusative or ergative).

The ubiquity of first and base arguments

Intransitive	Transitive (accusative lg.)	Transitive (ergative lg.)
PRED	PRED	PRED
<β>	<β _>	<_ β>
1	1 2	1 2

In sum, regardless of alignment type and regardless of the agreement option—first argument or base argument—the preferred target is consistently present and accessible. The end result is a maximally uniform and efficient implementation of agreement that fits well with the careful curation of processing cost, in accordance with the principle of processing determinism.

Indeed, the above observation opens the door to a new way of thinking about accessibility. Contrary to perspectives that associate the preferred argument with the subject, despite indications to the contrary in many ergative languages, an alternative now presents itself. The preferred target for an operation such as agreement need only meet one simple requirement: it should always be present and available, as illustrated in the tripartite schema above. In other words, the accessibility hierarchy can be reduced to just what its name implies—accessibility.

5.4 Uncommon forms of agreement

If the ideas that I have been outlining are correct, agreement systems target the sole argument in the semantic base and are built out from there, along the lines illustrated above. What is unexpected is a language in which a transitive verb agrees with just an added argument—the second argument in an accusative language or the first argument in an ergative language. Such patterns are aberrant, since the agreement operation fails to target the maximally accessible sole argument in intransitive patterns.[4]

Yet both types of pattern do seem to exist.

Agreement with just the second argument in Teiwa (Alor-Pantar) (data from Fedden et al. 2013:48, 35)
a. Intransitive pattern—no agreement:
 ha gi.
 you go

b. Transitive pattern—agreement with the added second argument:
 ha'an **n-oqai** g-unba'?
 |⎯⎯⎯⎯⎯⎯|
 you my-child 3SG-talk
 "Did you meet my child?"

Agreement with just the first argument of a transitive verb in the ergative language Halkomelem (Salish) (data from Wiltschko 2006)
a. Intransitive pattern—no agreement:
 í:mex te Strang.
 walking DET Strang
 "Strang is walking."

b. Transitive pattern—agreement with added first argument:
 q'ó:y-t-**es** **te Strang** te sqelá:w.
 |⎯⎯⎯⎯⎯⎯⎯⎯⎯|
 kill-TR-3SG.ERG DET Strang DET beaver
 "Strang killed the beaver."

However, these types of agreement patterns are rare, and special provisos seem to apply.

In the few languages that allow only second-argument agreement, the phenomenon appears to have developed "by accident," through the reduction of clitic direct object pronouns to phonologically similar affixes. This is evident in several Alor-Pantar languages within the Papuan family, including Teiwa (Fedden et al. 2013, 2014), as well as in the Austronesian languages Palauan (Levin 2019) and Roviana (Schuelke 2020).

Pronouns and direct object agreement in Palauan

	Singular		Plural (exclusive)	
	Pronoun	Agreement	Pronoun	Agreement
1st person	ngak	-ak	kemam	-emam
2nd person	kau	-au	kemiu	-emiu
3rd person	ngii	-ii	tir	-(e)terir

(Levin 2019: 173–4)

Languages in which agreement targets only the first argument of a transitive verb also seem to have a special property. In the absence of case marking, they use agreement to indicate the presence of an ergative system of alignment, with the overt agreement affix reserved for the added argument (the subject of a transitive verb). As illustrated in the Halkomelem example above, this strategy neatly parallels the use of overt marking for the added argument in languages with case systems.

6. Relative clauses and alignment

Despite its various unique properties, relativization manifests the very type of syntax observed for agreement, with a degree of uniformity in accusative languages that is not found itself in ergative languages.

6.1 Relativization in accusative languages

In accusative languages, relativization invariably favors the first argument. Indeed, in Classical Arabic, that is the only argument that can be relativized (Keenan and Comrie 1977). I use a gap (_) to informally indicate the canonical position of the relativized argument.

al rajul   [alaði saaʕada   _ al sayyida]
the man   who help.PST.3M.SG   the woman
"the man who helped the woman"

In many accusative languages, of course, it is possible to relativize more than just subjects, including direct objects, indirect objects, and even obliques—as happens in English. However, even in this situation, relativization of the first argument (the subject) seems to be favored: it manifests the least processing cost in adults (Hawkins 2004, chapter 7; Bornkessel-Schlesewsky and Schlesewsky 2009:22) and is acquired first by children (Kim and O'Grady 2016).

This pattern of preferred relativization can be characterized schematically as follows.

```
PRED      PRED
<β>       <β_>
 1         1 2
Rel ⌐J    Rel ⌐J
```

The next mostly likely target for relativization is the second argument.

The man [who the woman helped _]

Once again, there appear to be two ways of formulating an "accessibility hierarchy" for this type of system.

- The preferred agreement target is the first argument.
  First argument > Second argument ...

- The preferred agreement target is the base argument.
  Base argument > Second argument ...

As in the case of agreement, the existence of competing formulations stems from the fact that the base argument in an accusative language corresponds to the first argument, and vice versa. Moreover, regardless of how it is characterized, that argument has a special status for a very good reason: it is present in every sentence of every language, thereby enjoying a level of predictability and accessibility far beyond that of any other argument.

6.2 Relativization in ergative languages

Matters are different in ergative languages, where the base argument is associated with the second-argument position in transitive patterns.

```
Ergative languages
PRED      PRED
<β>       <_ β>
 1         1 2
```

As in the case of agreement, this opens the door to two possibilities. If relativization is fixed on the base argument, then the preferred target in transitive patterns will be the second argument. K'iche' works this way, as documented by Campbell (2000).

Relativization in the ergative language K'iche' (data from Campbell (2000: 253–4) and personal communication)
a. Relativization of the base argument of an intransitive verb:

ri	išoq	[ri	š-Ø-kam-ik _]	DIE
the	woman	REL	ASP-3SG.ABS-die-INTR	<β>

"the woman who died"   Rel ⌐J

b. Relativization of the base (second) argument of a transitive verb:

le išoq [le: š-Ø-u-kuna-x _ le: ačih] CURE
the woman REL ASP-3SG.ABS-3SG.ERG-cure-TR the man <_ β>
"the woman whom the man cured" ⌞ Rel

Relativization of the agent argument of a transitive verb in K'iche' is generally possible only if the verb is detransitivized, leaving the agent as the sole core argument—and hence the base argument. (AF.ANTI = a morpheme that signals an antipassive-like operation often called "agent focus" in the literature on Mayan.)

le išoq [le: š-Ø-u-kuna-n le: ačih _] CURE
the woman REL ASP-3SG.ABS-cure-AF.ANTI the man <β ...>
"the woman who cured the man" Rel ⌟

This pattern of relativization is exactly what one would expect, if the default relativizing operation is restricted to the base argument.

On the other hand, if the preferred target of relativization is the first argument, then subject relative clauses will be favored. The Mayan language Kaqchikel works this way.[5]

Relativization in the ergative language Kaqchikel (Mayan)
a. Relativization of the first argument of an intransitive verb:

ri achin [ri n-samäj _ ke la] WORK
DET man who ASP-work there <β>
"the man that works there" 1
Rel ⌟

b. Relativization of the first argument of a transitive verb:

ri ala '[ri ru-q'et-en ri xtän _] HUG
DET boy REL 3SG.ERG-hug-PERF DET girl <_ β>
"the boy who is hugging/has hugged the girl" 1 2
Rel ⌟

6.3 The typology of relativization

We end up with the following typology of relativization, which exactly parallels the syntax of agreement.

- In accusative languages such as English, where the base argument and the first argument are one and the same, there is no variation. The first/base argument is the preferred target for relativization.

    First/Base argument > ...

However, in ergative languages, where the first argument and the base argument in transitive patterns are dissociated, there is the possibility of variation.

- In some cases (e.g., K'iche'), the base argument rather than the first argument is the preferred target for relativization.
  Base argument > ...

- In other cases (e.g., Kaqchikel), the first argument is the target of choice.
  First argument > ...

In sum, a unifying logic underlies variation in the syntax of relativization in accusative and ergative languages, just as it does for the syntax of agreement. The preferred target—whether it is the first argument or the base argument—is predictably present in every single sentence (in every single language).

The ubiquity of first and base arguments
Intransitive	Transitive (accusative lg.)	Transitive (ergative lg.)
PRED	PRED	PRED
<β>	<β _>	<_ β>
1	1 2	1 2

As noted in Section 5.3, the accessibility hierarchy is therefore reduced to just what its name implies—accessibility. As the tripartite schema above illustrates, the preferred target for relativization, whether it is the first argument or the base argument, is uniformly and invariably present—hence accessible to the highest possible degree. This optimizes the efficiency of relativization, while at the same time aligning with the principle of processing determinism, a foundational tenet of emergentist typology. Put simply, key components of language are shaped by the need to minimize processing cost—a goal to which accessibility contributes in the way we have just seen.

The rationale underlying the typology of relativization departs quite fundamentally from the traditional logic of hierarchy-based generalizations, with their emphasis on standard grammatical relations. "Subject" and "direct object" are technical grammatical terms, not natural concepts, and therefore have no place in an explanatory theory of language that is constructed along emergentist lines. In contrast, notions such as "first argument" and "base argument" correspond to positions in semantic representations that exist independent of syntax. As such, they are a natural part of cognition and fit well with the larger picture that I have been sketching.

7. Conclusion

Alignment is one of the most fundamental mechanisms in all of language, with consequences that can be seen in many different phenomena within and across individual languages. For that reason, it has received a great deal of attention in the technical literature, although nothing resembling a consensus has yet emerged from the many efforts to understand its properties.

The particular idea that I have explored is that alignment phenomena emerge from the effect of processing pressures that favor the projection of a simple semantic base, consisting of a predicate and a single argument, as the minimum foundation for any sentence.

PRED
<β>

As we have seen, there are two logically possible ways to build out the semantic base in order to accommodate more complex constructions. One is to add a second-argument position; the other is to add a first-argument position.

Options for extending the semantic base in order to accommodate transitivity
a. Addition of a second-argument position:
    PRED   PRED
    <β>   ⇒   <β _>

b. Addition of a first-argument position:
    PRED   PRED
    <β>   ⇒   <_ β>

All languages appear to manifest a major asymmetry in their syntax: one of a verb's arguments is more accessible than the others (or perhaps even solely accessible) to a variety of syntactic operations, including case marking, agreement, and relativization. The technical literature offers a slew of terms for this privileged argument—"pivot," "focus," "primary argument," "topic," and "subject." I use a still different term—"base argument," but the choice of terminology is of no particular importance. The heart of my proposal lies in the search for answers to a series of questions about alignment and its syntactic consequences:

- Why are there two competing systems of alignment in the first place? (Section 3)
- Why do some arguments have null case while others have overt case? (Section 3)
- Why are the ergative case and the accusative case typically overt, while the nominative and the absolutive tend to be null? (Section 3)
- Why is ergativity rarely found in SVO languages? (Section 4)
- Why does the subject turn out to be the archetypal preferred target for agreement in accusative languages, but not in ergative languages? (Section 5)
- Why are certain types of agreement systems rare, if not impossible? (Section 5)
- Why does the subject turn out to be the archetypal preferred target for relativization in accusative languages, but not in ergative languages? (Section 6)

Further inquiry must now proceed in two directions. On the one hand, it is important to develop ever more detailed and comprehensive analyses of individual languages so as to better assess the account of alignment that I have put forward. Second, it is essential to examine the manner in which the semantic base is expanded to accommodate constructions other than transitive clauses, including ditransitives and other three-argument patterns. It is perhaps not too unrealistic to think that these lines of inquiry will shed further light on the nature of alignment in natural language.

Notes

1. I am grateful to Lyle Campbell, Raina Heaton, Miho Choo, and the editors of this volume for their helpful comments and advice.
2. I deliberately use representations that are as simple and spare as possible for reasons of practicality as well as for reasons of principle (emergentist approaches to syntax typically reject the need for "tree structures.")
3. However, Lyle Campbell (personal communication) reports that many rural dialects of Spanish in Latin America use VS order for intransitive clauses and SVO order for transitives, a nonharmonic pattern of word order given their accusative alignment.
4. Of course, nothing rules out the possibility of agreement with the added argument *in addition to* a first or base argument. There is therefore nothing aberrant about the accusative language Swahili, in which the verb agrees with both its first argument and the added second argument (Deen 2006), or the ergative language K'iche', in which the verb agrees with both the base argument and the added first argument (Campbell 2000:239).
5. The second argument of a transitive verb can also be relativized, although such patterns are significantly harder to elicit and more prone to errors; see Heaton et al. (2016). In this regard, Kaqchikel resembles many other languages with accusative systems of relativization, including English.

References

Aldridge, Edith. 2008. Generative approaches to ergativity. *Language and Linguistics Compass: Syntax and Morphology* 2, 966–95.
Babrakzai, Farooq. 1999. *Topics in Pashto syntax*. University of Hawai'i at Mānoa Ph.D. dissertation.
Bornkessel-Schlesewsky, Ina, and Matthias Schlesewsky. 2009. The role of prominence information in the real-time comprehension of transitive constructions: A cross-linguistic approach. *Language and Linguistics Compass* 3.19–58.
Campbell, Lyle. 2012. Typological characteristics of indigenous South American languages. In *The indigenous Languages of South America: A Comprehensive Guide*, ed. by Lyle Campbell and Verónica Grondona, 259–330. Berlin: de Gruyter.
Campbell, Lyle. 2016. Comparative linguistics of Mesoamerican languages today. *Veleia* 33.113–34.
Campbell, Lyle. 2017. Mayan history and comparison. In *The Mayan Languages*, ed. by Judith Aissen, Nora England, and Roberto Maldonado. 43–60. Abingdon: Routledge.

Campbell, Lyle. 2000. Valency-changing derivations in K'iche'. In *Changing valence: Case Studies in Transitivity*, ed. by R.M. W. Dixon and A. Aikhenvald, 236–81. New York: Cambridge University Press.
Campbell, Lyle, and Terrence Kaufman. 1985. Mayan linguistics: Where are we now? *Annual Review of Anthropology* 14.187–98.
Comrie, Bernard. 1981. *Language universals and linguistic typology*. Chicago: University of Chicago Press.
Deal, Amy Rose. 2015. Ergativity. In *Syntax – theory and analysis: An international handbook*. Vol.1, ed. by A. Alexiadou and T. Kiss, 654–707. Berlin: Mouton de Gruyter.
Deen, Kamil. 2006. Subject agreement in Nairobi Swahili. In *Selected proceedings of the 35th annual conference on African linguistics: African languages and linguistics in broad perspectives*, ed. by John Mugane, John Hutchison, and Dee Worman, 225–33. Somerville, MA: Cascadilla.
Dixon, R.M.W. 1994. *Ergativity*. Cambridge: Cambridge University Press.
Dryer, Matthew. 2011. Order of subject and verb. In *The World Atlas of Language Structures*, ed. by M. Dryer and M. Haspelmath. Munich: Max Planck Digital Library, chapter 82, <http://wals.info/> (last accessed August 16, 2021).
Fedden, Sebastian, Dunstan Brown, Greville Corbett, Gary Holton, Marian Klamer, Laura Robinson, and Antoinette Schappter. 2013. Conditions on pronominal marking in the Alor-Pantar languages. *Linguistics* 51, 33–74.
Fedden, Sebastian, Dunstan Brown, Frantisek Kartochvil, Laura Robinson, and Antoinette Schappter. 2014.Variation in pronominal indexing. *Studies in Language* 38.44–79.
Hawkins, John. 2004. *Efficiency and complexity in grammars*. Oxford: Oxford University Press.
Hawkins, John. 2014. *Cross-linguistic variation and efficiency*. Oxford: Oxford University Press.
Heaton, Raina, Kamil Deen, and William O'Grady. 2016. The status of syntactic ergativity in Kaqchikel. *Lingua* 170, 35–46.
Keenan, Edward, and Bernard Comrie. 1977. Noun phrase accessibility and universal grammar. *Linguistic Inquiry* 8.63–100.
Kim, Chae-Eun, and William O'Grady. 2016. Asymmetries in children's production of relative clauses: Data from English and Korean. *Journal of Child Language* 43.1038–71.
Kornfilt, Jaklin. 1997. *Turkish*. New York: Routledge.
Lahne, Antje. 2008. Excluding SVO in ergative languages: A new view of Mahajan's generalization. In *Varieties of competition*, ed. by Fabian Heck, Gereon Müller, and Jochen Trommer, 65–80 Liepzig: Institut für Linguistik Universität Leipzig.
Lang, Ranier. 1973. Grammatical sketch. In *Enga dictionary*, by A. Lang. Pacific Linguistics C-20, xviii–lvii. Canberra: Pacific Linguistics.
Levin, Theodore. 2019. On the nature of differential object marking: Insights from Palauan. *Natural Language and Linguistic Theory* 37.167–213.
Li, Charles, and Ranier Lang. 1979. Enga and other Papuan languages: The syntactic irrelevance of morphological ergativity. In *Ergativity: Towards a theory of grammatical relations*, ed. by Frans Plank, 307–24. London: Academic Press.

Mahajan, Anoop. 1994. The ergativity parameter: Have-be alternation, word order and split ergativity. In *Proceedings of NELS 24*, ed. by Merce Gonzàlez, 317–31. Amherst: GLSA.
Mahajan, Anoop. 1997. Universal grammar and the typology of ergative languages. In *Studies on Universal Grammar and Typological Variation*, ed. by Artemis Alexiadou, and T. Alan Hall, 35–57. Amsterdam: John Benjamins.
Manning, Christopher. 1996. *Ergativity: Argument structure and grammatical relations*. Stanford: CLSI.
Nichols, Johanna. 1992. *Linguistic diversity in space and time*. Chicago: University of Chicago Press.
Norman, William, and Lyle Campbell. 1978. Toward a proto-Mayan syntax: A comparative perspective on grammar. In *Papers in Mayan linguistics*, ed. by Nora England, 136–56. (Miscellaneous Publications in Anthropology, No. 6.) Columbia, MO: Department of Anthropology.
O'Grady, William. 2021. Natural syntax: An emergentist primer, <http://ling.hawaii.edu/william-ogrady/> (last accessed August 16, 2021).
Payne, Thomas. 1997. *Describing morphosyntax: A guide for field linguists*. Cambridge: Cambridge University Press.
Polinsky, Maia. 2017. Syntactic irgativity. In *Wiley Blackwell Companion to Syntax*, ed. by Martin Everaert, and Henk van Riemsdijk.Boston: Wiley-Blackwell.
Primus, Beatrice. 1995. Relational typology In *Syntax: An international handbook of contemporary research*, Vol. 2, ed. by Joachim Jacobs, Arnim von Stechow, Wolfgang Sternefeld, and Theo Vennemann, 1076–109. Berlin: de Gruyter.
Primus, Beatrice. 1999. *Cases and thematic roles: Ergative, accusative and active*. Tübingen: Max Niemeyer Verlag.
Schuelke, Peter. 2020. *Grammatical relations and syntactic ergativity in Roviana: A little-described language of Solomon Islands*. University of Hawai'i at Mānoa Ph.D. dissertation.
Siewierska, Anna. 1996. Word order type and alignment type. *Sprachtypologie und Universalienforschung* 49.149–76.
van den Berg, René. 2013. *A grammar of the Muna language*. Dordrecht: Foris.
Van Valin, Robert. 1981. Grammatical relations in ergative languages. *Studies in Language* 5.361–94.
Wiltschko, Martina. 2006. On "ergative" agreement and "anti-agreement" in Halkomelem Salish. In *Studies in Salishan*, ed. by Shannon Bischoff, Lyneika Butler, Peter Norquest, and Daniel Siddiqi, 241–73. Massachusetts Institute of Technology Working Papers on Endangered and Less Familiar Languages 7.

Subject and Scholar Index

absolutive antipassive, 49–61
action-denoting word, 235–7
Adena, 187, 191, 196, 199–200
age-grading, 65–6
agent focus, 49–67
agreement, 268–73
 accusative, 268–9
 ergative, 269–71
 gender–number agreement, 72–3
 person–number–case agreement, 74–5
 trigger of, 73, 74
 typology, 271–2
 uncommon, 272–3
alignment, 10, 13–14, 224, 230, 237–8, 260, 262, 276–7
 and agreement, 268–72
 and case, 262–6
 and relative clauses, 273–6
 and word order, 266–8
 hierarchical alignment, 211, 214–16
Amazonia
 Amazonian Fringe, 209–11, 214, 217, 218
 anaphoric-intensive, 112
 Bolivian Amazonian lowlands, 207
Andes
 Altiplano, 207
 Andean foothills, 207
animacy, 231–3
antipassive, 11
Araucanía, 167
archaeology, 187–91, 196
Areal Linguistics, 207
Argentina, 5, 13

argument index, 227, 231–5
associated motion, 218

beneficiary, 110, 120
Bolivia, 13
borrowing, 13, 19, 108, 112, 117, 126, 130–1, 134, 138–9, 141, 144, 145, 154–6, 172, 175, 177, 188–9, 194, 197, 200, 202
Brazil, 9, 14

Cahokia, 187–8, 190–2, 196, 198–201
Campbell, Lyle, 2–6, 130, 137, 144, 155, 157, 106, 115–17, 164, 167, 187–9, 191–2, 194, 202
canonical form, 115, 117–18, 121
canonical targets, 98–9
Capuchin missionaries, 167
Carr, Christopher, 191, 197
case, 14, 74, 262–6
 accusative, 263–4
 ergative-absolutive, 74, 230, 234, 264–5
 nominative-absolutive, 230
 typology of, 265–6
Caucasus, 11
Chaco, 5, 6, 207, 208, 210, 214, 217, 218
Chile, 13
Chiloé, 165, 168
Chiquitanía, 208
cognate, 48, 92, 94–7, 101–2, 106–12, 115, 117, 122, 139, 151, 158, 189
comparative method, 106–7, 115–17
comparative paradigms, 96–7, 100–2

Coña, Pascual, 168, 174
Cono Sur, 165
Croese, Robert A., 165, 170, 173–4

deixis
  deictic classifiers, 211, 212, 213, 214
  positional deictics, 211
  positional demonstratives, 212, 213
Delamarre, X., 107, 119
derivational operations, 227
diffusion, 132, 134, 136–8, 211, 212
diminutive, 114, 119, 124
direct verb form, 244–5, 249, 252–5
DNA, 196, 199, 200
  mitochondrial (mtDNA), 199
Drechsel, Emmanuel, 188, 190–2, 194–6, 200–1

emergentism, 261–2
etymology, 88, 94

farming/language dispersal, 4–5
Fields, Kent T. "Hutke", 199, 201
flat clause structure, 247–8
focus marker, 232
fortis/lenis variants, 109, 112–13
fragmentation, 210
Fryer, Brian J., 191, 196–8, 200, 202

genderlects, 211
Georgia, 11
glottalized consonants, 6, 11, 19, 20–1
  acoustic correlates of glottalized consonants, 28–31
  ejectives, 20–2
  glottalized resonants, 20–1
  laryngealized, 21, 38
  representations of Xinkan glottalized consonants, 23–7, 39–41
  voice quality measures, 34–5
  xinkan glottalized minimal pairs, 23
Goddard, Ives, 188, 191, 202
Gómez Moreno, M., 105
grammatical relations, 227–30, 231–3
grammaticalization, 3, 79, 112, 117–18, 120, 125, 212, 216
Gran Chaco región *see* Chaco
Grube, Nikolai, 140, 156
Guaporé-Mamoré región, 210

Hagenbach treasure, 109, 117
Harris 2013, 72, 75–8
Havestadt, Bernardus, 167, 174

Hervás, Lorenzo, 167
Hierarchy of person/animacy, 245
historical linguistics, 1–13, 15, 95–6, 131–2, 155
Holisky 1987, 74
Hopewell, 187, 188, 191, 194–202
Humboldt, Wilhelm von, 167
hypercorrection, 22, 41

Inca, 177, 179
inclusive–exclusive distinction, 211
incorporating construction, 49–67
interlingual literacy, 150, 154, 156
intransitivizing suffix –al, 72, 73, 82–4
inverse verb form, 245, 249, 252, 254–5

Jolkesky, Marcelo, 169–71

Kaufman, Terrence, 131, 132, 134–7, 141, 143, 145, 151, 154, 155, 157, 187–90, 202

Lakarra, J. A., 117–21
language change, 1–12, 15, 66
  change in progress, 60, 62, 65
  relative chronology, 130, 131, 134, 137, 138, 139
  semantic change, 117
language conservation, 3–4, 7, 8, 10
language contact, 4–8, 10, 12–13, 212
language description, 2–4, 7–8, 13, 14
language documentation, 1–11, 13, 15
language endangerment, 2–4, 9, 15
language policy, 208
language revitalization, 2, 4, 7, 10, 209
  Xinkan revitalization, 19, 20, 41–2
language universals 4, 6–7, 10, 246, 255, 257
LaPolla, R., 224
laryngealized consonants *see* glottalized consonants
Lenz, Rodolfo, 167, 170
Lévi-Strauss, C., 225
linguistic areas, 5–6, 19, 225
linguistic diversity, 1–10, 13, 15, 206, 208, 211, 218
linguistic typology, 1–4, 6–11, 13–15, 117, 265–6, 271–2, 275–6
loanword *see* borrowing
Luchon, 111

masdar, 72, 74
Mesoamerica, 4, 6, 11, 19–44, 47–67, 130–57, 178, 187–9

Michelena, L., 108, 119, 121
Middle Woodland, 188, 190–1, 194, 196–7, 199
Mills, Lisa, 191, 196, 199–200
Mississippian (complex, archaeological culture), 190, 195–7
Mithun, Marianne, 191, 197, 201–2
mounds, 188, 191, 195–6, 199–200
Moxos, 207, 208

negation, 218
nominal classification, 212
   classificatory verb, 212
   classifier, 50, 211–14
   gender, 114, 213–15, 243, 252, 257
   noun class, 212–14
nominal syntax, 234–7
nominal tense, 213, 216–18
   Extended Nominal Tense, 216, 217
   Independent Nominal Tense, 216, 217
   Propositional Nominal Tense, 216, 217
Norman, William, 131, 132, 134–7, 141, 143, 145, 151, 154, 155, 157
North America, 187, 188, 190–1, 200, 202
Northwestern Amazon, 210
noun composition, 115, 118
Noun Phrase (NP), 213, 216–17, 230, 232–4, 247, 250–2

object-denoting word, 235–7
oblique, 49–56, 59–65, 246–7, 257
obviation
   first obviative, 245, 252, 255; *see also* nearer obviative
   further obviative, 245, 252–5; *see also* second obviative
   nearer obviative, 245, 252–5; *see also* first obviative
   obviative, 14, 166, 215, 242–5, 248–9, 252–5
   proximate, 14, 243–5, 249–52
   second obviative, 245, 252, 255; *see also* further obviative
Olmec, 187–9, 191, 197
onomastics
   cognates, 106–10
   onomastic area, 108
   theonyms, 113–15
   women's names, 114
Oriente, 207

panpipes, 196–7, 199–200, 202
patronymic, 111

personal pronouns, 227
   bound, 227
   free, 227
   see also argument index
philology, 8–9, 12
phonological rules, 75
plesiomorphic features, 112
Plurinational Education System, 209
Polynesia, 169
possession, 14, 111–12, 120, 172, 212, 234–8, 243–4, 251–2
posture verbs, 212–13
prehistory, 4, 10, 12, 13, 169
processing determinism, 261
property-denoting word, 235–7
proximate *see* obviation

quipu, 174

reconstruction, 8, 10–12, 22–3, 47–9, 59–60, 97–8, 117–22, 132–9, 143–55
reduplication, 98–100, 119
reference tracking, 213–14
relational prefix, 227
relative clause, 273–6
   accusative, 273–4
   ergative, 274–5
   typology of, 275–6

Santa Cruz plains, 208
serial verbs, 118, 120
silver, 194–200, 202
sociolinguistics, 2, 4, 5, 8
   accommodation, 139, 142, 151, 154, 156
   attitudes, 131, 149, 152, 154–5, 202, 209
sound change
   assimilation, 93, 122
   expressive palatalization, 109, 112, 116, 126, 135
   haplology, 98–9
   merger, 47, 66
   metathesis, 11, 72, 75–8, 79–85
   metathesis in derived intransitive verbs, 82–5
   metathesis in derived transitive verbs, 75–8, 84–5
   *k(') > *ch(') shift, 130, 132, 140, 142, 144–5, 154
sound correspondences, 12, 88, 92–8
South America, 5, 13, 164–79, 206–19, 224–38
Spence, Michael W., 191, 196–8, 200, 202
switch reference, 211, 213–14

toponyms, 107, 123–4, 126
  toponymical suffixes, 112–13
Trask, R. L., 106, 113
Turff, Gina, 191, 197

Upper Rio Negro region, 210

Valdivia, Luis de, 167–8, 177–80
Van Valin, R., 224
verb phrase constituent tests, 248–9
verbal number, 211, 218
verbal syntax, 234–7
Vignec, 111
voice, 48, 58

Walworth, Mary, 201
Wanderwörter, 170, 177–80
weak crossover, 248–9
word class, 226–7
word order, 10, 13–14, 227, 231–3, 242, 246–55, 266–8
writing, 105, 130, 138–56, 189, 242
  epigraphy, 110
  hieroglyphic writing, 12
  systems, 208

Languages and Linguistic Families Index

Achi', 57
Achuar-Shiwiar, 172
Afro-Yungueño, 208
Aguaruna, 172–3, 178
Agutaynen, 93
Aikanã, 210
Akatek, 50, 52–3, 57
Akuntsú, 13–14, 225–6, 226–7
Algonquian languages, 13–14, 187–8, 191–2, 194–7, 200–2, 242–55
Allentiac, 167, 178
Amis, 93
Andean languages, 166, 170, 174, 180
Andoke, 210
Aquitanian, 12
Araona, 207
Araucanian languages, 165, 167–9, 171, 177–8, 180, 210, 214–16
Arawakan languages, 165–6, 172–5, 177, 179, 208–10, 216–17
Armenian, 87
Arosi, 93
Ashéninca, 173–4
Austronesian languages, 87–103, 107, 273
Awakatek, 51–2, 57
Aymara, 206, 208
Aymaran, 166, 172, 173–6, 179–80, 206–8, 210
Ayoreo, 208

Bali (Uneapa), 93
Barbacoan, 170
Basque, 10, 12, 105–29
Batsbi, 11, 72–85
Baure, 208

Bikol, 93–6, 100
Bororoan, 171
Bunun, 93

Cabécar, 178
Californian languages, 166
Callawaya *see* Kallawaya
Canichana, 207
Cariban, 178, 210, 216, 217
Cavineña, 207
Cayubaba, 207, 210
Cebuano, 89–90, 95, 101–2
Celtiberian, 105
Central Malayo-Polynesian, 95
Central Miwok, 178
Ch'ol, 53–5, 58, 66
Ch'olti', 53–4, 58
Ch'orti', 48, 53–5, 58–60
Chácobo, 207
Chamicuro, 174, 216
Chamorro, 93, 101
Chapacuran, 210, 216
Chholo, 207
Chicham languages, 172–3, 178–9
Chile dugu *see* Mapudungun
Chimane, 207
Chipaya, 207
Chiquimulilla, 19
Chiquitano, 171, 208
Chiriguano, 172, 179
Chocktaw, 191
Cholón, 170–1
Chonan, 167, 169
Chono, 169

Chontal, 53–4, 58, 66
Chorote, 216
Chuj, 52–3, 57, 60
Cree, 192–4

Delaware, 192, 194

English, 115–17
Enlhet-Enenlhet, 210, 216
Enlhet, 216
Epigraphic Mayan, 130–1, 136, 137, 139, 141, 143–4, 154, 157
Ese Ejja, 207
Etruscan, 110, 113–14

Fijian, 89, 92
Futunan, 92

Gascon, 122
Gaulish, 105, 108, 113
Gorontalo, 94
Gothic, 115–17
Greater Q'anjob'alan (GQ'), 131–2, 138, 141, 155–7
Greater Tzeltalan (GTz), 130–4, 138, 155–8
Guahiban, 210
Guaraní (Bolivian), 208, 216
Guaraní (Paraguayan), 166, 172
Guató, 180
Guaycuruan, 210, 212, 216, 217
Guazacapán, 19, 32
Günün-a Yajich, 167

Hanunóo, 93
Hawaiian, 89–91, 96–7
Hibito-Cholón, 170
Huambisa, 172–3, 178
Huarpean languages, 167
Huastec, 49, 56, 58–9
Huilliche, 165, 167–9, 171, 177–8, 180

Iban, 95, 101
Iberian, 105–8, 113, 115
Ifugaw (Batad), 95
Ignaciano, 173, 208
Ilokano, 89, 90
Indo-European languages, 12, 87, 105, 108–12, 113, 114, 115–17, 119, 122, 125, 126, 207–8
Isneg, 95
Isolate languages, 3, 10, 13, 105–8, 110, 113–15, 164, 169–70, 171, 178, 180, 207–8, 210, 212–17

Itbayaten, 93, 101
Itneg, 101
Itonama, 207, 210, 212–13, 214–15
Itzaj, 55–6, 58
Ixil, 49, 51–2, 57, 66

Jabutían languages, 171
Javanese, 91, 99, 101
Jê languages, 166, 171
Jivaroan *see* Chicham languages
Jumaytepeque, 19

K'iche', 57
Kadiweu, 216
Kaingáng, 166, 171, 178
Kallawaya, 207
Kambera, 95
Kamsá, 210
Kanoê, 210
Kaqchikel, 11, 47–67
Karajá, 171
Karirí, 171
Karitiana, 216
Karo, 216
Kavalan, 89
Kayardild, 216
Kelabit, 94
Kofán, 210
Krenák, 171
Kunza, 178
Kwazá, 210

Lacandón, 55–6, 58
Language Isolate *see* Isolate languages
Latin, 12, 87, 105, 108–12, 114, 117, 119, 125, 126
Leipon, 89
Leko, 207, 210
Leti, 103
Lokono, 174
Lule, 178

Macro-Gêan *see* Macro-Jêan
Macro-Jêan, 166, 171, 178–80, 208, 210
Maiduan languages, 178
Mak'á *see* Maká
Maká, 167, 216
Makuan, 210
Malagasy, 89, 92
Malay, 89–107, 100–3
Mam, 51–2, 57
Manobo, 94
Mansaka, 95

LANGUAGES AND LINGUISTIC FAMILIES INDEX

Mapuche *see* Mapudungun
Mapudungun, 10, 13, 164–80, 214, 215–16
Maropa *see* Reyesano
Matacoan famly, 3, 167, 178, 208, 216, 217
Maxakalí, 171
Mayan languages, 4, 11–12, 47–70, 130–62, 170, 178
Mekens, 216
Meskwaki, 14, 242–55
Miami-Illinois, 192–4
Millcayac, 167
Minangkabau, 95, 101
Misumalpan languages, 170, 178
Mixe-Zoquean languages, 170, 187–9, 197
Mobilian Jargon, 187–8, 190–2, 194–6, 199–202
Mochica, 165, 169–70
Mocho', 53, 57, 59, 66
Mocoví, 216
Moken, 93
Mokilese, 100
Mono-Alu, 93
Mopan, 55, 58
Mosetén, 207, 216
Movima, 207, 210, 212, 213, 216–17
Mundurukú, 170
Muskogee, 190, 191
Mussau, 89

Natchez, 187, 199, 201–2
Nambikwara, 216
Nambikwaran languages, 165, 210, 216
Nasa Yuwe, 178, 210
Ngaju Dayak, 92
Nias, 93
Nipissing, 194
Nisenan, 178
Niue, 90
Nivaclé, 167, 178, 216

Ofayé, 171
Ojibwa, 194–5, 197

Pacahuara, 207
Pacific coast languages, 169
Páez *see* Nasa Yuwe
Paiwan, 89
Palauan, 89–93, 96, 273
Pano-Tacanan languages, 207, 216
Panoan, 207
Paraguayan Guarani, 216
Parecís, 174
Pataxó, 7

Paunaca, 209
Peba-Yaguan, 210
Pehuenche, 168
Penobscot, 192–4
Pilagá, 216
Pipil, 6, 8
Piro, 173
Popti', 52–3, 57
Poqomam, 51, 57, 59
Poqomchi', 51, 57, 59
Proto-Arawakan, 165, 173–5, 177
Proto-Austronesian, 87–9, 90, 92–3, 101, 103
Proto-Aymaran, 175
Proto-Basque, 117–21
Proto-Cariban, 178
Proto-Central Eastern Polynesian (PCEP), 201
Proto-Central Pacific, 88
Proto-Ch'olan (pCh'), 130, 140, 157
Proto-Chibchan, 178
Proto-Jê, 166, 180
Proto-Macro-Jê, 171, 178
Proto-Malayo-Polynesian, 89–95, 97–9, 101
Proto-Mayan, 47, 60, 178
Proto-Mixe-Zoquean, 170, 188
Proto-Northern Jê, 178
Proto-Oceanic, 88, 90, 98, 100
Proto-Polynesian, 88, 90
Proto-Quechuan, 174
Proto-Southern Jê, 171
Proto-Tsouic, 87–8
Proto-Tupi-Guarani, 166, 172, 178
Proto-Tupian, 178
Proto-Xinkan, 20–1, 38
Puquina, 166, 180, 207, 216
Purépecha, 167, 178

Q'anjob'al, 48, 50, 52–4, 57, 59–60
Q'eqchi', 51, 57, 59
Qawasqar, 169
Quechuan, 166–7, 169, 172–80, 206, 207, 210, 216

Rennellese, 87, 88, 96
Reyesano, 207, 216
Rhaetian, 110, 113
Rikbáktsa, 171
Rondonia languages, 225
Rukai (Tona), 89

Sakapultek, 48–50, 57
Samoan, 89, 92, 98–9

Sanapaná, 214, 215
Shuar, 172
Sipakapense, 50, 57
Sirionó, 208, 216, 217
Southern Jê, 171, 179
Spanish (Bolivian), 207, 208
Sundanese, 93

Tacanan, 207
Tagalog, 91–4, 96, 99–102
Tagbanwa, 93
Tarascan, 167
Tariana, 216
Tektitek, 51–2, 57
Tetun, 95, 103
Thao, 101
Timucua, 178, 180
Tiruray, 99
Toba, 212, 216
Toba Batak, 91
Tojolabal, 52–3, 57, 60
Tok Pisin, 99–100
Tongan, 89–90, 92–3, 98
Trinitario, 173, 208
Trumai, 165
Tseltal, 55, 58
Tsotsil, 55, 58
Tsou, 87–8, 96
Tucanoan *see* Tukanoan
Tukanoan, 180, 210
Tupi, 170

Tupian, 10, 13–14, 166, 170, 172, 178–9, 208, 210, 216, 217, 225–7
Tz'utujil, 48, 57

Uchumataqu (Uru), 207
Ulwa, 170, 178
Uru-Chipayan, 180, 207
Uspantek, 51, 57

Vasconic, 113–15, 119, 120, 122

'Weenhayek, 208
Waorani, 210
Wari', 216
Wichí, 178
Witotoan, 210
Woleaian, 89
Wuvulu, 89

Xinkan languages, 19–38

Yaghan, 167, 169–70, 178
Yathê, 164, 180
Yucatec, 49, 55–6, 58, 60, 67
Yuki, 208, 216, 217
Yupiltepeque, 19
Yurakaré, 208, 210

Zamucoan, 208
Zaparoan, 210
Zuñi, 178

EU representative:
Easy Access System Europe
Mustamäe tee 50, 10621 Tallinn, Estonia
Gpsr.requests@easproject.com

www.ingramcontent.com/pod-product-compliance
Lightning Source LLC
Chambersburg PA
CBHW051110230426
43667CB00014B/2521